The Patterns Handbook:
Techniques, Strategies, and Applications

SIGS Reference Library

Donald G. Firesmith
Editor-in-Chief

Additional Volumes in Preparation

The Patterns Handbook:
Techniques, Strategies, and Applications

COLLECTED AND INTRODUCED BY
LINDA RISING

PUBLISHED BY THE PRESS SYNDICATE OF THE UNIVERSITY OF
CAMBRIDGE
The Pitt Building, Trumpington Street, Cambridge CB2 1RP, United Kingdom

CAMBRIDGE UNIVERSITY PRESS
The Edinburgh Building, Cambridge CB2 2RU, UK
http://www.cup.cam.ac.uk
40 West 20th Street, New York, NY 10011-4211, USA
http://www.cup.org
10 Stamford Road, Oakleigh, Melbourne 3166, Australia

Published in association with SIGS Books & Multimedia

First published in 1998

Design and composition by Barbara Crawford
Cover design by Mark Needleman

Printed in the United States of America

A catalog record for this book is available from the British Library

Library of Congress Cataloging-in-Publication Data is available.
ISBN 0-521-64818-1 paperback

For all the patterns fans at AG Communication Systems.
This is your story.

About the Editor

Linda Rising (risingl@agcs.com) is a member of the Technical Resource Center at AG Communication Systems. She has a Ph.D. from Arizona State University in the area of object-based design metrics. Her background includes university teaching experience as well as work in industry in the areas of telecommunications, avionics, and strategic weapons systems. She has been working with object technologies since 1983. Some of her publications including "A Training Experience with Patterns" in the October 1996 issue of Communications of the ACM, "Patterns: Spreading the Word" in the December 1996 issue of *Object Magazine,* and "The Road, Christopher Alexander, and Good Software Design" in the March 1997 issue of *Object Magazine.*

Linda and her husband, Karl Rehmer, are avid cyclists. They commute to work (a 20-mile round trip), even in temperatures of 100+ degrees. Linda is the director of the Utopia Road Recorder Consort, a group of software-developer Renaissance wannabes who gather to sing and play just for fun and to perform at AG Communication Systems a couple of times a year.

Foreword

A s someone prone to choosing cute titles (which my editors never allow), I would have called this book "The Patterns Storybook."

Everybody loves a story. Bob Hanmer notes that good patterns are like a story: they engage the reader's interest early or they develop intrigue and conflict through their forces and catharsis in their solution, and they echo the relaxed discussion of the postproduction coffeehouse discussion in their rationales and in the resulting context sections. Of course, not all stories are patterns, but that makes them no less powerful as sources of wisdom. And there are many stories to be told about the pattern community: stories about its history and even stories about its dark side. This is a book of those stories, stories that were in the form of conference papers, journal articles, essays, book chapters, patterns, and all the other forms that engineers and scientists use to disguise the stories they write. This collection weaves several story lines together. It is, at one level, the story of one organization's quest or, really, of its multiple quests, for patterns. The storyteller, Linda Rising, is a big-picture person in that organization. She tells how the organization—AGCS—both had to grow into the pattern community and then grow *with* the pattern community. The story has replayed itself in several companies and in several cultures, which all have wrestled with the pattern value system. If you've lived such a story, you'll find comfort and perhaps will learn something in this telling.

In his book *Haroun and the Sea of Stories*,[1] Salman Rushdie paints a beautiful image of stories that intertwine like multicolored streams of water from a common spring. The AGCS story in this book intertwines with many stories from outside AGCS, stories that influenced the work and direction inside the company. Some of these stories bear retelling; among these are the seeds of the folklore and the classics of a community or culture. Many of the chapters that follow are like that: they have appeared before, perhaps to a different audience, or perhaps in a different age, as judged by the time scales of rapidly evolving technology. Some among them are frequently cited today; others should be.

Just as these stories challenged, guided, and intrigued the AGCS folks on their journey, they remain good prods for introspection today. That, I think, is the major value of this volume. Read about others' perspectives and contrast them with your own. You won't agree with everything that appears on the pages that follow. The authors don't agree with each other on everything. But they share a dialogue, a thought process, and an evasive but discernible set of values and principles that define the pattern community. By reading their works, you will gain new insights into this dialogue, these processes, and these values, regardless of your level of experience with patterns. And the dissonance between the diverse views will resonate anew through you, the reader, in the forums you participate in.

There are fresh stories, too, many of them less than a year old at this writing. Some are hot-off-the-press pattern stories, some are new distillations and tutorials for readers who are pattern novices. And among both the old and the new stories are detailed accounts of pattern history and application. These stories offer practical food for thought for the practitioner or manager wondering how patterns would, could, or should play out in your own enterprise.

Of course, there are patterns here, too—groupings that form little stories in their own right. This is the stuff of patterns, the living literature of our disciplines. As living literature, I wish these pages were in a loose-leaf section. Polish your introspection again; think how you would contribute your experiences to the pattern, how you would have the authors improve the pattern, how you would adapt the pattern to your situation. You might even write the authors with your suggestions and become part of the community of colleagues supporting each other by sharing important design knowledge across our disciplines.

George Platts attends most of the PLoP conferences (the main pattern conference series) as a Lateral Thinking Coordinator. He muses that PLoP isn't really about patterns, it's about people. This book is, too. It reflects the thoughts of more contributors than I can easily count, and distills the expert knowledge of thousands more. It tells their stories. After you're done with this book, think what you're going to do with the results of your own introspection and where you fit into this large network of people. I'll be looking for your patterns and for your stories about how you found, refined, shared, and used them.

—JAMES COPLIEN

REFERENCE

1. Rushdie, Salman. *Haroun and the Sea of Stories*. New York: Viking Penguin, 1991.

Preface

You are about to read an extraordinary book. It is extraordinary because it is a collection of stories by a group of people who work for the same company and share not only their place of employment, but a focused interest in patterns. If you don't know much about patterns, this is a good place to begin. If you're an experienced patterns person, I hope you'll find some new information and insight that will increase your understanding and appreciation of this exciting new technology.

This is a book you will enjoy if you are a developer looking for a basic understanding of patterns and pointers to more detailed knowledge. This book will also be useful if you are in a managerial role. There is information on process and organizational patterns that you will find useful. Finally, there are suggestions for those of you who do technical training, to help you in your vital role in bringing patterns to an organization.

The book comprises three parts. The first two parts contain work by AG Communication Systems authors. Part One contains a collection of articles that provide an introduction to patterns. In Part Two, there are articles that describe our patterns experiences. Part Three is a collection of articles that function as resources. The appendixes consist of an annotated bibliography and a list of useful Web sites for more information.

This book combines resources not found anywhere else. It is not only an organizational success story, but it also provides you with the means to begin your own journey to patterns accomplishments! How can I be so sure that what worked for us will work for you? I guess my feeling is that success, like patterns themselves, is infectious. There's nothing more interesting to members in a corporate setting than stories of what others are doing to improve their business. I've found two interesting references that have helped me understand this. The first is *Tell Me a Story* by Roger Schank,[1] which describes how we learn from each other by sharing stories. I'll tell you more about this intriguing book in an article on writing patterns in Part Two. *Managing by Storying Around: A New Method of Leadership*[2] is a collection of stories by David Armstrong, the fourth generation of his family to lead Armstrong International. These two books don't talk about patterns—not directly—but they reinforce the underlying theme of this collection of stories; the effectiveness of shared experience.

Let me introduce you to our company. AG Communication Systems is based in Phoenix, Arizona, my home. The company is a joint venture of Lucent Technologies and GTE and is a leading developer and manufacturer of advanced telecommunications products and services, including switching, intelligent network, access, and wireless products. The company's core product, the GTD-5 digital central-office switching system, has an installed base of more than 17 million lines serving business, government, and industry, as well as residential subscribers serviced by the public telephone network. AG Communication Systems employs 2,000 people, about 700 of them in software development.

My role at this company is an unusual one. I'm the patterns "champion" or the self-proclaimed patterns "princess." I "do" patterns all day long! Sometimes I'll make a trip to another company to give a noontime presentation for a resident group of OO developers to help them answer the question, "What are patterns all about?" I see this book as something I would like to have had for all the trips I've made so far and will certainly use for all those I will make in the future. If I leave this book behind at another company, it will help "grow" the seeds I've planted and explain what we've been doing at AG Communication Systems. It's a handbook of our pattern adventures, complete with a collection of references.

REFERENCES

1. Schank, R. C. (1990). *Tell Me A Story.* New York: Charles Scribner"s Sons.
2. Armstrong, D. (1992). *Managing by Storying Around: A New Method of Leadership.* New York: Doubleday.

SYSTEM TESTERS
Back row, left to right:
Jim Kurth. Front row:
Ed Nuerenberg, Carl Gilmour

SYSTEM TESTERS
Counterclockwise from the
top: Ray Fu, Bob Nations,
Weldon Wong, Mike Sapcoe,
Bob Bianca.

SYSTEM TESTERS
Left to right: Jim Peterson,
Arvind Bhuskute, Neil Khemlani,
Ernie Englehart, Rich Lamarco

VP AND COACHES
Top to bottom: Bill Curtis;
Charles Schulz, Vice-President;
Tom Snelten.

WRITERS
Back row, left to right:
Norm Janoff. Middle row:
Ben Richards, Paul Bramble.
Front Row: Linda Rising,
Roger Tomas.

WRITERS
Back row, left to right:
Bill Haney, Don Olson.
Middle row: Patty Genualdi,
David DeLano. Front row:
Russell Corfman,
Mike Duell

Acknowledgments

This book has been one of the most exciting challenges of my long and mostly happy life. I want to thank Bill Curtis, my first "coach" at AG, who recognized something special about patterns and started this incredible happening. Thanks to my current coach, Tom Snelten, for his encouragement and support. Thanks to Alan Brown, Jodi Carr, and George Jester for releasing me from important quality duties so I could put the final touches on the writing. Thanks to Luci Crackau and Sue Bobbitt for their superb technical support. Special thanks to Charlie Schulz, our Vice President of Product Development. Charlie has been a believer in patterns from the start. It is his leadership that has enabled all this to become a reality. Finally, thanks to all my colleagues at AG Communication Systems. Some of them have contributed directly to this book but many more just provided encouragement, an essential ingredient for any undertaking. It is the open-hearted, open-minded approach that is the watchword of the people I work with every day that has made this the most successful, the most enjoyable work I have ever undertaken.

Thanks to all the good folks at SIGS, especially Don Jackson. Though he is no longer at SIGS, this book began as a gleam in his eye. He cheered me on every step of the way and held my hand, figuratively, when I wasn't sure where I was going. Special thanks to Peter Arnold. I know this book would never have been completed without him.

Finally, thanks to my husband, Karl—patient, understanding, loving, the best friend this writer ever had!

Contents

PART I
OVERVIEW

The notion of patterns originates in the work of a building architect named Christopher Alexander. In his book, *The Timeless Way of Building* (1979), Alexander describes something called "the quality without a name" (p. ix). The following excerpts from his writing explain Alexander's view of this unnamed quality and how it relates to patterns.

This quality is the most fundamental quality there is in anything. (p. 26)

In our lives, this quality without a name is the most precious thing we ever have. And I am free to the extent that I have this quality in me. (p. 47)

The search . . . for this quality, in our own lives, is the central search of any person, and the crux of any individual person's story. It is the search for those moments and situations when we are most alive. (p. 41)

That's it! The contributors to this book will tell you how being part of this company and the patterns community has made them more alive and happier in their work. What a wonderful, happy, productive message!

To define this quality . . . we must begin by understanding that every place is given its character by certain patterns of events that keep on happening there . . . each building and each town is ultimately made out of these patterns . . . and of nothing else. . . . To the extent they are alive, they let our inner forces loose, and set us free. . . . The more living patterns there are in a place . . . the more it comes to life as an entirety, the more it glows, the more it has that self-maintaining fire which is the quality without a name. (Alexander, 1979, p. x)

So patterns are tied to the unnamed quality and this has inspired this disparate collection of people to share their experiences with you, to answer the question, "What's all this I hear about patterns?" Their answers cover the multifaceted expressions of patterns and the distinct paths taken by these people to make this technology part of our everyday work.

> To reach the quality without a name we must then build a living pattern language as a gate. . . . This quality . . . cannot be made, but only generated, indirectly, by the ordinary actions of the people, just as a flower cannot be made, but only generated from the seed. (Alexander, 1979, p. xi)

The authors of the pieces in this collection were not managed or motivated to encourage their patterns activities. Their interest was generated by the nature of patterns themselves. The notion of patterns, the generativity of patterns has taken root, has planted seeds in the minds of these individuals. This phenomenon requires open minds and an open organization—open to new ideas, open to change, open to a completely different way of doing business.

These people came to patterns as part of a bottom-up activity. We are all software engineers. Our management kindly provided training and support but the willingness and energy were ours. We wholeheartedly follow in Alexander's footsteps because it makes sense and seems to make us more productive and happier in what we do.

Doug Lea has written an article about Christopher Alexander that appears in Part III of this book, "Christopher Alexander: An Introduction for Object-Oriented Designers." The title is a little misleading because the article, like patterns, is not strongly tied to object orientation. This article provides a valuable look at Alexander's work and is highly recommended for pattern beginners as well as old hands who want a better understanding of Alexander's pioneering work.

It is the fundamental character of patterns to capture the best of our collective experience in a form that enables sharing with other members of the community. Its simplicity is profound. We share our best with each other. As a result, we all improve and our collective best becomes better.

> It is a process which brings order out of nothing but ourselves . . . it will happen of its own accord, if we will only let it. (p. 3)

In today's business environment, letting this process happen requires extraordinary management insight. The process requires introspection, which means time, a scarce commodity when the rallying cry is "turn that around fast and move on to the next project." To make the best use of our experience requires an examination of our past and a sifting through of our common knowledge.

Valuable insight does not fall into our laps, it must be painstakingly excavated by sifting through mounds of data. One must carefully brush away superfluous dusty coverings here and chip at extraneous pieces there, restoring lost fragments, using the best tools—imagination and insight—to reach each precious nugget. These nuggets must be polished by use, with each user adding his or her turn at buffing and shaping. What emerges over time is a collection of best practices. Identifying this set of patterns, so they can be shared across an organization, can be an effective way to improve quality and productivity.

> We may then gradually improve these patterns which we share, by testing them against experience: we can determine, very simply, whether these patterns make our surroundings live, or not, by recognizing how they make us feel. (Alexander, 1979, p. 277)

How do I feel? Lucky to be a part of all this—in a company where patterns are received enthusiastically at all levels—part of a local community with a keen shared interest and, finally, a participant in a worldwide fellowship that constantly challenges me to move ahead. It's the grand intent of this book to share that sense of community with you and, ultimately, encourage you to join us!

> It is the people around us, and the most common ways we have of meeting them, of being with them, it is, in short, the ways of being which exist in our world, that make it possible for us to be alive. (Alexander, 1979, p. 65)

FAILURES AND SUCCESSES, WHAT PATTERNS WILL AND WILL NOT DO

OK, let's get it out up front. Patterns are not, repeat, *not* a silver bullet. They certainly won't single-handedly solve the software crisis! Patterns will not create expert designers from novices and suddenly, magically, make everyone in your organization a guru!

Please read Richard Gabriel's article in Part III, "The Failure of Pattern Languages." The patterns community prides itself on the avoidance of hype. One reason for this is that our industry is so plagued with hyperbole. Those who have been practitioners for any length of time have seen the latest buzzword come to the forefront and then die away a short time later without significantly affecting how we do our daily work.

We are also concerned about the ethical issues surrounding patterns. All we're doing is simply documenting what works. We want to ensure that proper credit is given to a mentor or a source of knowledge who first exposed us to the important idea that became a pattern. We're not creating new and astounding approaches. As Brian Foote has noted, we "practice an aggressive disregard for originality!" So, don't trot out the brass band or shout from the rooftops! Neil Harrison's article in Part III, "Potential Pattern Pitfalls or How to Jump on the Patterns Bandwagon Without the Wheels Coming Off," looks at several patterns problems: Pattern Madness, A Pattern Priesthood, The Law of Conservation of Complexity—this is worth reading!

Christopher Alexander is a creative genius. I am not. He had wonderful, lofty goals for architecture. I'd be happy just to see the smallest glimmer of hope on the horizon, a whisper of a happy prognosis that we're not doomed to repeat the same mistakes we made on the last project, the same mistakes that have been made on every project at every company since commercial software development began. The power of patterns is that documenting and sharing experience draws attention to the lessons to be learned. We're not reaching for greatness, just a better way of doing things.

As experienced professors, teachers, industrial trainers, mentors, and mothers all know, you can share your experience and knowledge with others and our protégés, students, and children can have the best intentions and work diligently to produce their best efforts, but still not create the expected result. This isn't a discouraging comment; it's a fact of life. I believe we will all perform on a higher plane after the education, training, or mentoring, even if we don't all reach the highest possible pinnacle.

I see software in crisis everywhere I look. You can pick up an article written 20 years ago on software development and then pick up one written yesterday and you'll find the same kind of introduction—the software is late, over budget, and there is concern about quality, reliability, maintainability—all those "ilities." Something as simple as documenting our best practices and ensuring that everyone knows the lessons the practices teach can go a long way toward improving things with surprisingly little effort and expense. The more of us there are in this activity, the better we will all become. Because my life is increasingly affected by the reliable performance of software, I'd like software development to be as quality conscious as possible. Patterns may help.

No business decision should ever be made without a careful analysis of benefits and costs. Only after such an analysis can good risk management take place. Given the frenzied pace at which business decisions are made today, it is doubtful that this analysis always occurs. What is more likely is that the current buzzword or most expensive consultant captures our attention and determines our future direction.

Members of the patterns community share a horror of being lumped into the buzzword category. The issues of overblown claims are of primary concern whenever groups of pattern enthusiasts gather, but we are also conscious of our own inner, almost childlike enthusiasm for patterns. Those of us who have fallen under the spell of Alexander and his work have rushed to cast our lot with this natural approach. As Gerald Weinberg (personal communication, May 12, 1995) has said, "None of us is as smart as all of us!" The mindful application of shared experience to repeated problems seems to cry out for recognition.

Design patterns, organizational patterns, management patterns, it seems that patterns are useful in any situation and rightly so. Every domain has a wealth of accumulated wisdom that can be shared with novices. Every situation has a handful of gurus whose ability to transfer insight is hampered by their limited numbers and the sometimes overwhelming demands to mentor. What better way to capture expertise and document it for new members of the circle?

Jim Coplien's article in Part III, "Software Development As Science, Art, and Engineering," is a beautifully written view of the intertwining roles of technology and the softer "ologies" and how they affect our work. Because this article celebrates the first anniversary of pattern material in the *C++ Report*, I thought we should also include the first article in the series, "Setting the Stage," for perspective and also because it does such a good job of introducing the concept of patterns.

The articles that comprise Part III wouldn't be complete without a contribution from Grady Booch. His treatment of "Patterns" is another elegantly crafted contribution to our collection. These articles should not only help introduce patterns, but also provide a strong sense that there are people issues here as well as technical ones, that this is feeling as well as doing, that we're cautious as well as enthusiastic.

Patterns will not bring peace to warring factions or food to starving children, but patterns provide such a hopeful, natural, simple approach that offers significant help for all those troubles that keep popping up over and over again.

Each one of us wants to be able to [build] . . . like this. It is a fundamental human instinct, as much a part of our desire as the desire for children. It is, quite simply, the desire . . . to complete a world . . . with something made by us. (Alexander, 1979, p. 9)

PAPER PREVIEWS

The articles in Part I of this book provide an introduction to patterns. Included in Part I are several articles that were previously published and that provide diverse explanations of what patterns are all about. The first is the text of my presentation on patterns, given in February 1996 at the Western Communication Forum in Dallas. This was previously published in the 1996 *Annual Review of Communications.*

This article is a good place to start our overview of patterns. It introduces the notion of patterns and their origin in Alexander's work, it provides a brief look at pattern form, and indicates some of the benefits of using patterns. The slides from my presentation are also included in the Appendix. These could be used as a brief introduction to patterns. That's how I began—with a presentation to our vice-president's staff. I think you'll see that it's straightforward, no hype, but gets the message out. Maybe it will work for you!

The next article, "An Overview of Patterns," was written by Russell Corfman. When I began talking about patterns, Russell was always on hand to request copies of papers I was distributing—and he read them! He was also the first in our company to study Alexander's works. Russell is a fellow bicycle enthusiast, who was chosen to help carry the Olympic torch across Arizona! He wrote this piece for a graduate course in software engineering. Russell does a particularly good job of explaining the pattern forces and the notion of generativity. Don't be discouraged after reading the article if you don't understand all these high-priced notions. I'm still puzzling over some of them myself!

After Russell's introduction, I'll tell you how we got things going in "Patterns: Spreading the Word," published in *Object* magazine in December 1996. This article might be helpful for those who are playing my role in other companies. You're interested in patterns and you want to infect others with your enthusiasm. I have no magic solutions but I'm happy to tell you what worked for me.

One of the things this article does not explain is that at the time I was starting to "spread the word," I was very unsure about the direction I was taking. Shortly before I made the initial presentation to our vice-president and his staff, I turned to the friendly folks on the patterns listserver[1] and asked for guidance. Unfortunately no one had gone down the lonely road I was about to choose. They were all anxious for me and lent support and encouragement. I love the folks on the listserver! They are like my extended family. The people in the patterns community have always been good friends and colleagues. I highly recommend them to you! It was at this time that I began some periodic reports to the listserver to keep everyone up to date on the happenings at AG Communication Systems. Somewhere along the line we got a lot of attention from the rest of the world—pretty impressive for a small company!

The third article in this section is one I wrote with Brandon Goldfedder. Its topic is training. I believe that this training is largely responsible for the successful adoption of the object-oriented patterns at AG Communication Systems. This article was previously published in the October 1996 issue of *Communications of the ACM*, which was devoted to patterns. The article outlines the training schedule and describes lessons learned from our experience.

The last article in Part I was written by Diane Saunders. Our approval process for external publications includes a sign-off by a member of marketing, and Diane was that person for my article on spreading the word. The article sparked her interest in patterns. She began talking to other pattern users across the company and ultimately conducted a phone interview with Christopher Alexander himself! According to Diane, Alexander is delighted with all the attention his work is receiving and especially happy that the software-patterns community is following the intent of his work, not just adopting a new buzzword. Her article was originally published in *Telephony*, probably the most respected and widely read trade magazine for the public network market.

The patterns used in our training were from the text entitled *Design Patterns* (1994), written by Erich Gamma, Richard Helm, Ralph Johnson, and John Vlissides, often called the Gang of Four, or GOF. If you haven't already purchased this book, do so. It is already a classic. We've included Steve Bilow's summary "Sorting Through the Plethora: The 'Unofficial' *JOOP* Book Awards," which sums up other major contributions to the object-oriented literature. Many of these are reviewed in Part III in our annotated bibliography.

---

[1] Information on all the patterns listservers may be found on the WWW Patterns Home Page, http://st-www.cs.uiuc.edu/users/patterns/patterns.html

Also in Part III, you'll find two articles by Ralph Johnson, "An Introduction to Patterns" and "How Patterns Work in Teams." These describe some of the GOF patterns and how they work together in a complete but simple example. Another interesting report from a member of the "gang," "Pattern Hatching—Perspectives from the 'Gang of Four'" by John Vlissides, also appears in Part III.

So, find a comfortable spot, perhaps one that follows Alexander et al.'s (1977) patterns: Light on Two Sides of Every Room (159), Garden Seat (176), or Low Sill (222). Fix a nice pot of tea and spend some time reading about patterns. This is how Alexander (1979) would describe it:

> Imagine yourself on a winter afternoon with a pot of tea, a book, a reading light, and two or three huge pillows to lean back against. Now make yourself comfortable. Not in some way which you can show to other people, and say how much you like it. I mean so that you really like it, for yourself.
>
> You put the tea where you can reach it: but in a place where you can't possibly knock it over. You pull the light down, to shine on the book, but not too brightly, and so that you can't see the naked bulb. You put the cushions behind you, and place them, carefully, one by one, just where you want them, to support your back, your neck, your arm: so that you are supported just comfortably, just as you want to sip your tea, and read, and dream.
>
> When you take the trouble to do all that, and you do it carefully, with much attention, then it may begin to have the quality which has no name. (pp. 32–33)

REFERENCES

Alexander, C.A., et al. (1977). *A pattern language.* New York: Oxford University Press.

Alexander, C.A. (1979). *The timeless way of building.* New York: Oxford University Press.

Gamma, E., Helm, R., Johnson R., & Vlissides, J. (1994). *Design patterns.* Reading, MA: Addison-Wesley.

Design Patterns: Elements of Reusable Architectures

Linda Rising

risingl@agcs.com

In the late 1970s, two books appeared that were written by Christopher Alexander and his colleagues, who are building architects. These books, *The Timeless Way of Building* (Alexander, 1979) and *A Pattern Language* (Alexander et al., 1977), presented the author's view of the recurring problems he saw in cities and towns, neighborhoods and buildings. Alexander describes these problems and their solutions using an expression he called a pattern:

> Each pattern describes a problem that occurs over and over again in our environment and then describes the core of the solution to that problem in such a way that you can use this solution a million times over without ever doing it the same way twice. (Alexander et al., 1977, p. x)

It's a sad commentary on the field of software engineering that articles written over 20 years ago and those written yesterday typically begin by lamenting the fact that software products are over budget, delivered late or not at all, with serious concerns about their quality and reliability. Unfortunately, software engineering gets little help from its underlying discipline, computer science. One common response to this dilemma is to look carefully at other, more mature engineering fields for guidance. We look at hardware engineering, manufacturing technologies, the list goes on.

After examining the field of building architecture and the work of Christopher Alexander, investigators have been observing similar recurring problems and solutions in software. There is clear evidence of patterns in all levels of software design, from high-level architecture down to detailed design.

Reprinted with permission of the International Engineering Consortium, Chicago, IL.

the 4ESS®, one of AT&T's large telecommunications switches. These patterns are certainly not object oriented. The same can be said for the patterns we are discovering on the GTD-5®, the large switch we develop for GTE and independent telephone companies.

There is a body of patterns literature (Coplien, 1995) concerned with organizational and process patterns also being crafted at AT&T. We are attempting to apply this knowledge in our move toward self-directed teams.

PATTERNS AND REUSE

Mature engineering disciplines have handbooks of solutions to recurring problems. For more on the use of a handbook, please read an interesting article on reuse comparing software engineering to chemical engineering (Kogut, 1995).

There is a contention in the software-engineering community that we are continually reinventing the wheel. This phenomenon can be clearly seen in any large company, where projects go their own way, with problems being solved that are similar or identical to problems being solved by other projects, sometimes down adjacent corridors in the same building. It's easy to point to a lack of communication and the classic "not-invented-here syndrome," but the fact is that there hasn't been an appropriate communication medium for transferring this knowledge. The widely applied code libraries did not even begin to tackle this problem.

Patterns form a more flexible foundation for reuse. A handbook filled with patterns documenting best practices would provide workable solutions for a given domain. A handbook like this would be particularly valuable for capturing domain expertise. What the patterns community is finding, however, is that the same patterns appear across projects and across domains. A group of developers at Siemens AG is writing a book of architectural patterns. Those of us who have been involved in reviewing these patterns can see that these are not specific to any particular domain, but would have wide application. Having a vocabulary of architectural patterns would be an excellent way to improve architectural design across the industry.

CONCLUSIONS

Among all the benefits of discovering and using patterns, the improvement in communication is the most powerful. The resulting improvement in productivity and quality should be immediate when teams can hold design discussions at a higher level, because the time spent in these discussions will be reduced and the product improved as a result of incorporating solutions with proven records of success.

This improvement in communication takes place not only within teams, but across teams as well. Moving from one team to another should not involve relearning design vocabulary. Everyone knows "binary search." Everyone knows "stacks and queues." Everyone should also know design patterns. Patterns enable implementors as well as designers to do their jobs better. The ideas of the best designers can be more easily communicated to implementors if patterns are used to facilitate that communication. Instead of having continual consultations with the architectural gurus, a well-defined vocabulary will enable novices to better understand the intent of the design.

Finally, the ultimate benefit of using patterns is that we all become better designers. As Weinberg (personal communication, May 12, 1995) has wisely noted, "None of us is as smart as all of us!" He was talking about the review process, but his observation is certainly appropriate here. When we all share our design knowledge, we can all build on that knowledge and thereby improve instead of reinventing solutions over and over again. What a wonderful prospect!

REFERENCES

Adams, M., Coplien, J., Gamoke, R., Hanmer, R., Keeve, F., & Nicodemus, K. (1996). Fault-tolerant telecommunication systems patterns. In J. Vlissides, J. Coplien, N. Kerth (Eds.), *Pattern Languages of Program Design 2*. Reading, MA: Addison-Wesley.

Christopher, A. (1979). *The timeless way of building*. New York: Oxford University Press.

Christopher, A., et al. (1977). *A pattern language*. New York: Oxford University Press.

Coplien, J. (1994, June). Generative pattern languages: An emerging direction of software design. In *Proceedings of the 5th Annual Borland International Conference*. Orlando, FL.

Gamma, E., Helm, R., Johnson, R., & Vlissides, J. (1995). *Design patterns: Elements of reusable object-oriented software*. Reading, MA: Addison-Wesley.

Kogut, P. (1995). Design reuse: Chemical engineering vs. software engineering. *Software Engineering Notes, 20*(5), 73–77.

Yourdon, E., & Constantine, L.L. (1978). *Structured design*. Englewood Cliffs, NJ: Prentice-Hall.

Presentation Slides: Western Communication Forum, February 1996

Origin

Christopher Alexander, a building architect:

The Timeless Way of Building
A Pattern Language

These capture recurring techniques and principles of architecture.

Each pattern describes a problem that occurs over and over again in our environment and then describes the core of the solution to that problem in such a way that you can use this solution a million times over without ever doing it the same way twice.

Software Analogy

Software engineers study other disciplines, looking for appropriate analogies.

After studying the work of Christopher Alexander, software developers are applying his methods to find patterns in software systems.

These patterns appear in high-level systems architectures and detailed design.

Pattern Description

A pattern has at least four elements:

Name: A word or simple phrase to describe the pattern.

Problem: A statement of the problem.

Context: When to apply the problem.

Solution: The components of the design, their relationships and responsibilities—but no implementation.

Are Patterns Object-Oriented?

The patterns community is primarily OO, so most patterns investigation is OO but patterns can be found in any development paradigm.

Patterns are not tied to any methodology or language.

Some pattern mining efforts are concentrating on non-OO systems, e.g., AT&T's 4ESS® and our GTD-5®.

Work is also in progress, capturing organizational and process patterns.

Patterns Handbook

Mature engineering disciplines have handbooks of solutions to recurring problems.

Software development also encounters similar problems over and over again.

The considerable interest in reuse recognizes these repetitive elements.

Use of large code libraries doesn't seem to be the answer.

A New Reuse Approach

Patterns provide a more flexible foundation for reuse.

A handbook of patterns would provide workable solutions for a given domain.

Since patterns are language-independent, no code libraries need to be maintained.

Benefits

Learning about existing patterns and searching for domain-specific patterns would:

Improve communication—among designers on a team, among designers on different teams, between a designer and herself.

Improve documentation—the use of pattern names in documentation carries a lot of information and produces a smaller, simpler, more maintainable document.

Reuse without creation and maintenance of code libraries, or being tied to a specific language.

Improve future designs as collective design experience is applied to new projects.

An Overview of Patterns

Russell Corfman
corfmanr@agcs.com

BACKGROUND

Over the past few decades, numerous software systems have been created. As computer technology has advanced, so has the complexity of these systems. More powerful computers, lower prices for hardware, and increasing demands from users have put increasing pressure on the software industry to produce more advanced systems that delight customers. As software systems have become larger and more complex, new methodologies and processes have been created to cope with the complexity.

New techniques and technologies have been appearing since the industry began. Better processes for system design, a new-and-improved testing method, a CASE (computer-aided software engineering) tool *extraordinaire*, the latest integrated development environment, yet another programming language, and so forth—all these things come and go. The literature keeps us informed of the latest techniques and technologies.

A wealth of knowledge, experience, stories, and folklore also has been generated over the years. Good, proven solutions to problems that recur over and over in various systems are being discovered. Unfortunately, the literature has not done as well in capturing and cataloguing these solutions (Coplien & Schmidt, 1995).

Much of this knowledge and experience is general but some is specific to the domains our industry encompasses. Accounting systems, business systems, defense systems, process control, operating systems, scientific computing, and telephony each have their own tricks of the trade—their own ways of effectively tackling the problems and complexities unique to their domain.

Many of the early pioneers of the software industry have retired or are reaching retirement age. Second-generation software designers are becoming more and more common.[1] We need an effective way of passing along the experiences, domain knowledge, and the patterns from these veterans to the designers who will maintain existing systems or craft new systems to replace the old (e.g., Adams et al., 1995).

Patterns supply a way to fill this void in the literature, to catalogue proven solutions, such as Gamma, Helm, Johnson, and Vlissides (1994) have, in order to give the expert's experience to novices. The Pattern Languages of Programming (PLoP) conference was founded to create a new body of literature composed of solutions to ordinary, yet by no means simple, problems found in software (Coplien & Schmidt, 1995).

DEFINING PATTERNS

Much of the work on software patterns is based on the work of the architect Christopher Alexander, and his pattern language for creating "towns and neighborhoods, houses, gardens and rooms" (Alexander, 1977, p. ix). Alexander defines a pattern as follows: "Each Pattern describes a problem which occurs over and over again in our environment, and then describes the core of the solution to that problem, in such a way that you can use this solution a million times over, without ever doing it the same way twice" (Alexander, 1977, p. x). As we shall see, Alexander's definition is not only appropriate for architecture, but also for software engineering.

Patterns are expressed in many forms and styles. A search for a clear and complete definition of a pattern may very well be an elusive endeavor. A room full of pattern experts may come to a consensus on which patterns are good, which patterns contain the "quality without a name" (Alexander, 1979, p. 17), or if they even are patterns. It is harder for these experts to consistently define what a pattern is and what makes it good. This may be because of the newness of patterns as a recognized technology or it may be because the concept of patterns must germinate and grow over time and blossom into understanding, something that "cannot be created from above directly; it can only be generated indirectly" (Alexander, 1979, p. 162).

---

[1] I have no references or empirical data for these statements. They are based on the assumption that the software industry was created in the 1960s and from personal observations at my place of employment.

In keeping with the generative spirit, first I will present two basic definitions of a pattern and then add detail to "grow" the reader's understanding. Coplien (1994) defines a pattern thusly: "A pattern is a solution to a problem in a context" (p. 19). Coplien and Schmidt (1995) describe patterns as follows: "Design patterns capture the static and dynamic structures of solutions that occur repeatedly when producing applications in a particular context" (p. xi).

These two definitions are similar. They both describe a pattern as a solution to a problem in a context. The latter adds the idea that the solution has been found more than once in various applications. This is important; it implies that a solution cannot be a pattern unless it has been found over and over again. This recurrence adds validity to the pattern. The more the application of a pattern can be found, the more one can be sure of the goodness of the pattern, the quality of the solution it presents.

Context is another interesting aspect of these two definitions that one must consider. A problem can have many different solutions. The solution that one chooses depends on the context of the problem. This implies that different patterns can be applied to a given problem. The appropriate pattern to use depends on the context of the situation. For example, suppose a person wants to travel from Seattle to Phoenix. The problem is what mode of transportation to take. Airplane, bicycle, bus, car, or train are all valid solutions to this problem. If the person is an avid cyclist, and has a month or 2 to kill, then bicycling may be the best choice. If the person has to get to Phoenix as soon as possible, then traveling by airplane would be most appropriate, unless that person fears flying or cannot afford a ticket, in which case the bus may be the best choice. If the person has always yearned to travel by train, this trip may present the opportunity to do so. These considerations define the context of the problem. These are the forces or trade-offs that are considered when determining which solution to use. For this example, the forces are

- Time available for traveling
- Cost of traveling
- Amount of luggage or cargo to transport
- Traveling conditions—the season and expected weather
- Comfort level of the different modes of transportation
- Desire to use the various modes of transportation

All the forces affect the different contexts, but the strengths of these forces vary and some may have no impact at all. The best solution is the one that most completely resolves these forces and the tension between them.

Here is another problem. Suppose a software development team is about to start a new software application and must decide which programming language to use. One context for this problem may be the task of developing a scientific visualization application that will run on a massively parallel super computer. Another context might be the task of developing a personal-information-manager (PIM) application that must run on various hardware platforms. Some of the forces in this example are:

- Programming languages the team members know
- Desire of the team members to use certain languages and the programming methods used to take advantage of language constructs (e.g., object oriented versus procedural)
- Availability of language and tool support
- Language portability between platforms
- Language support for concurrency
- Language support for efficient scientific calculations

Depending on the context, these forces will have different effects. For the scientific visualization application, the last two forces will have a large impact on the solution although they will have little, if any, impact in choosing a language for the PIM. The choice of language for the PIM will be affected greatly by the portability issue. The first three forces should have an effect on the solution for both applications.

When finding a solution to a problem, a designer must weigh the advantages and disadvantages of each alternative, and make trade-offs to decide which solution is the best. Coplien (1994, p. 20) states, "A pattern resolves the forces at play for a given design decision." The team choosing a language for implementing the PIM would not choose Microsoft Visual Basic® as that would not resolve the force of portability among platforms. If all team members are fluent in C, that would be a good choice because it resolves both the portability and knowledge forces. If most team members want to learn object-oriented techniques, then maybe C++ or Java™ would be a better choice. Finding the solution that best resolves all the forces at play is a matter of weighing the pros and cons of the various solutions to make the most beneficial decision.

GENERATIVE PATTERNS AND PATTERN LANGUAGES

In *A Pattern Language,* Alexander et al. (1977) present 253 patterns. These patterns compose what they call a pattern language. Alexander states,

An ordinary language like English is a system which allows us to create an infinite variety of one dimensional combinations of words, called sentences. . . . A pattern language is a system which allows its users to create an infinite variety of those three dimensional combinations of patterns which we call buildings, gardens, towns.

He goes on to say,

Thus, as in the case of natural languages, the pattern language is generative. It not only tells us the rules of arrangement, but shows us how to construct arrangements—as many as we want—which satisfy the rules. (Alexander, 1979, pp. 185–186)

What does this mean for software development? Can we develop a pattern language for generating "an infinite variety" of software systems? This is a very grand vision. Software pattern writers are creating pattern languages to help designers build software systems or parts of systems. For example, the CHECKS pattern language helps to generate the interface for accepting and validating user input (Cunningham, 1995), and the Caterpillar's Fate pattern language supports the transformation from system analysis to design (Kerth, 1995).

THE PATTERN AS LITERATURE

Some patterns may be known to just a few expert designers, whereas other patterns may be known to many. These patterns should be available to all designers who need them. The main goal of the patterns community is to identify the recurring solutions that occur in software systems and document them using the pattern form.

There are several pattern forms in the literature, the Alexandrian form (Alexander et al., 1977), the GOF (Gang of Four) form (Gamma et al., 1994), and the Coplien form (Coplien, 1995), among others. For more examples, see Coplien and Schmidt (1995). Some of these forms contain more elements than others; however, all contain the basic components: name, problem statement, context, description of forces, and solution.

It is important that a pattern be clear and complete, that it stands on its own, as the author will not be available to answer questions for most readers. The reader must get a clear understanding of the solution and the trade-offs it makes. The reader must understand when it is appropriate to apply the pattern and when it is not.

As with any literature, writing patterns is hard work. It has been found that an iterative approach to writing patterns is useful. The patterns presented in *Design Patterns: Elements of Reusable Object-Oriented Software* (Gamma et al., 1994) went through such a process with many people reviewing and offering suggestions and improvements to the authors on the Internet. The authors of *Pattern-Oriented Software Architecture—A Pattern System* (Buschman, Meunier, Rohnert, Sommerlad, & Stal, 1996) also took this approach, having set up an FTP site and an Internet discussion group for reviewing and improving the pattern system they proposed. See the Patterns Home Page (PHP) for more information.

A type of review called a writers workshop has also been found to be beneficial for writing patterns. This is the approach used for reviewing the papers submitted to the PLoP conference. Instead of the pattern authors lecturing to other conference attendees, these attendees, who are also authors, meet and review the pattern, offering suggestions for improving it.

CATEGORIZING PATTERNS

Patterns can be categorized by level or granularity. At the lowest level are language specific patterns, known as idioms. These include, for example, the C++ Orthodox Canonical Class Form idiom (Coplien, 1992, §3.1) and the Handle/Body Class idiom (Coplien, 1992, §3.5). Design patterns, such as those catalogued in Gamma et al. (1994), fall at the middle level. Design patterns are not language specific and can be implemented in a variety of languages. Patterns can, however, take advantage of certain language features that do not occur in all languages. For example, a design pattern that relies on inheritance cannot easily be implemented in C or Ada 83, but can be implemented in C++ or Smalltalk. At the highest level are architectural patterns such as the Model-View-Controller (MVC) or the pattern catalogue developed to help document the AT&T 4ESS™ telephone switching system (Adams et al., 1995).

There is no clear line between these levels of patterns. Each level blurs into the next. The C++ Handle/Body Class idiom is really just an implementation of the Bridge design pattern (Gamma et al., 1994). Design patterns can be integral parts of architectural patterns as is the case with Observer (Gamma et al., 1994), which is a part of MVC.

Design patterns have also been classified by purpose and scope (Gamma et al., 1994, §1.5). The purpose can be creational, structural, or behavioral. Creational patterns deal with the creation of objects. Structural patterns concern themselves with the composition of objects or classes. Behavioral patterns define how objects interact and how responsibility is distributed among them. The scope can be either class or object. Class patterns deal with the relationships between classes and their subclasses through inheritance. Object patterns deal with the relationships among objects. Object relations are dynamic and can be changed at run time, whereas class relations are static and fixed at compile time.

Design patterns have also been classified at a metalevel (Pree,1994, §3.6). Pree categorizes patterns in one of the following three classifications:

1. Patterns that rely on abstract coupling.
2. Patterns that are based on recursive structures.
3. Other patterns.

Classifying a pattern with this scheme involves decomposing a pattern into its elements (classes and objects) and evaluating the interactions and relationships between these elements. This classification scheme is concerned with the structure of the pattern and not with the problem the pattern solves. This scheme is most useful when attempting to identify patterns in an existing software system. First, the system structure is examined for occurrences of the classifications listed previously. Next, these occurrences are examined to identify known patterns. Finally, anything remaining is examined in order to identify possible new patterns.

Patterns can also be categorized by functionality or subject. Coplien and Schmidt (1995) organize the patterns into eight high-level units this way. There are units for systems and distributed processing, process and organization, events and event handlers, among others.

As a result of these classification schemes, designers are able to search the currently existing catalogues for patterns. As the number of published patterns increases, the search will become more difficult. More research is needed to classify effectively the growing body of patterns. A classification exercise took place one evening at the PLoP '95 conference. Pattern names were written on sheets of paper, then the sheets of paper were placed on the floor of a large room. Related patterns were grouped together and relationships were represented by connecting groups of patterns with string. The result was photographed. Admittedly, this exercise was more for fun than practical use; however, it demonstrates a growing concern among the patterns community—how to classify and catalogue patterns to make them available to designers.

CONCLUSIONS

The advantages of using patterns have not been quantified and it is questionable whether a good experiment can be designed and implemented to quantify them. Many of the following observations are gleaned from Schmidt (1995) and Helm (1995).

BENEFITS

• Patterns enable designers to communicate at a higher or more abstract level. Patterns introduce a new vocabulary. Each pattern name represents a word in this vocabulary, carrying with it all the details in the actual pattern description. Designers can discuss the design using this vocabulary without becoming bogged down with all the details. This enables designers to discuss design decisions more easily.

• Patterns ease communication of design issues across development teams. The pattern vocabulary allows design groups to share subsystem designs as well as interfaces. Different groups will have a better understanding of the subsystems they interface to.

• Patterns ease architectural design communication among developers, managers, marketing strategists, and others. The common vocabulary allows people in less technical roles to better understand the system architecture without becoming mired in the technical details.

• Patterns simplify documentation. The documentation will not need as much design detail because the pattern name will indirectly give it. This implies that the documentation should be shorter and should take less time to write, review, and maintain.

• Patterns enable reuse of architecture and design. Patterns should be platform independent. This means that an architecture and design using patterns should also be independent of the platform and remain stable even with major changes to the underlying platform. Only the implementation of the architecture and design should need porting.

• Patterns give expert knowledge to nonexperts. Designers with less experience will have access to expert solutions that are proven to be good. This is helpful to both newer software designers and to experienced software designers working in new domains.

LIABILITIES

• Everyone needs to know the pattern vocabulary. One of the benefits of using patterns is that of easing the communication of design. To derive this benefit, all players must be familiar with the patterns being employed. If some do not know the patterns, then communication breakdown occurs. This implies an investment in patterns training across the project or organization. New patterns will be written and existing ones may change. The issue of continuing education of new and changed patterns should be addressed.

• Patterns may cause confusion. Designers may confuse one pattern for another or confuse the contexts and trade-offs. This can cause communication breakdown to occur. Designers will unknowingly be discussing different things without realizing it. Worse yet, a poor design decision may inadvertently be made.

• Avoid pattern hype. Some designers will want to use a pattern just for the sake of using a pattern even if it is inappropriate to do so. Some may get carried away and use as many patterns as possible, without considering whether the pattern applies to the problem at hand. This can lead to a design that is more complex than it would have been if patterns were not used.

FURTHER READING

For the interested reader, there is a wealth of information on patterns. A good place to start would be with *Design Patterns: Elements of Reusable Object-Oriented Software* (Gamma et al., 1994) and proceedings from the PLoP conferences (Coplien & Schmidt, 1995; Vlissides,Coplien, & Kerth, 1996). The *C++ Report* has been running two columns with emphasis on patterns, one by John Vlissides and the other by James Coplien. Reading back issues of these columns would be beneficial.

For those with World Wide Web access, the Patterns Home Page (PHP), Portland Pattern Repository (PPR), and the Wiki Wiki Web are all worth visiting. There are also a number of electronic-mail discussion groups dedicated to various patterns topics. For information on them, see the Patterns Home Page.

To understand the basis for the patterns concept and to better understand the Alexandrian form, it is very beneficial to look at *The Timeless Way of Building* (Alexander, 1979) and *A Pattern Language* (Alexander et al.,1977). Though these books are about constructing towns, communities, and buildings, they offer insight into what a good pattern is and how it resolves the forces and tensions acting on it—something that software patterns should strive to emulate.

REFERENCES

Adams, M., Coplien, J., Gamoke, R., Keeve, F., Hanmer, R., & Nicodemus, K. (1995). Fault-tolerant telecommunication system patterns. In J. O. Coplien & D. C. Schmidt (Eds.), *Pattern languages of program design*. Reading, MA: Addison-Wesley.

Alexander, C. (1979). *The timeless way of building*. New York: Oxford University Press.

Alexander, C., Ishikawa, S., & Silverstein, M., with Jacobson, M., Fiksdahl-King, I., & Angel, S. (1977). *A pattern language*. New York: Oxford University Press.

Alexander, C., Silverstein, M., Angel, S., Ishikawa, S., & Abrams, D. (1975). *The Oregon experiment*. New York: Oxford University Press.

Buschman, F., Meunier, R., Rohnert, H., Sommerlad, P., & Stal, M. (1996). *Pattern-oriented software architecture—A system of patterns*. Chichester, England: John Wiley & Sons Ltd.

Coplien, J. O. (1992). *Advanced C++ programming styles and idioms*. Reading, MA: Addison-Wesley.

Coplien, J. O. (1994, July). Generative pattern languages: An emerging direction of software design. *C++ Report*, pp. 18–22, 66–67.

Coplien, J. O. (1995). A generative development process pattern language. In J. O. Coplien & D. C. Schmidt (Eds.), *Pattern languages of program design*. Reading, MA: Addison-Wesley.

Coplien, J. O., & Schmidt, D. C. (Eds.). (1995). *Pattern languages of program design*. Reading, MA: Addison-Wesley.

Cunningham, W. (1995). The CHECKS pattern language of information integrity. In J. O. Coplien & D. C. Schmidt (Eds.), *Pattern languages of program design*. Reading, MA: Addison-Wesley.

Gamma, E., Helm, R., Johnson, R., & Vlissides, J. (1994). *Design patterns: Elements of reusable object-oriented software*. Reading, MA: Addison-Wesley.

Helm, R., (1995). Patterns in practice. In *OOPSLA '95 Conference Proceedings*. Reading, MA: Addison-Wesley.

Kerth, N. L. (1995). Caterpillar's fate: A pattern language for the transformation from analysis to design. In J. O. Coplien & D. C. Schmidt (Eds.), *Pattern languages of program design*. Reading, MA: Addison-Wesley.

Patterns Home Page. http://st-www.cs.uiuc.edu/users/patterns/patterns.html

Portland Pattern Repository. http://c2.com/cgi-bin/ppr

Pree, W. (1994). *Design patterns for object-oriented software development.* Reading, MA: Addison-Wesley.

Schmidt, D. C. (1995). Using design patterns to develop reusable object-oriented communication software. *Communications of the ACM, 38*(10).

Vlissides, J. M., Coplien, J. O., & Kerth, N. L. (Eds.). (1996). *Pattern languages of program design 2.* Reading, MA: Addison-Wesley.

Wiki Wiki Web. http://c2.com/cgi-bin/wiki

Patterns: Spreading the Word

Linda Rising
risingl@agcs.com

Software engineers are always casting about, examining other engineering disciplines, looking for solutions to the decades-old problem called the software crisis. They have considered hardware, industrial engineering, manufacturing scenarios—the list goes on.

The latest investigation into a somewhat-related area is an especially provocative one. A group of respected individuals in the object-oriented community have been taking a hard look at the work of Christopher Alexander, an architect, a building architect. Alexander has some intriguing observations about an entity he calls a pattern, defined as follows:

> Each pattern describes a problem that occurs over and over again in our environment and then describes the core of the solution to that problem in such a way that you can use this solution a million times over without ever doing it the same way twice. (Alcxander et al., 1977, p. x)

I have been an active patterns advocate since I attended the OOPSLA '94 tutorial and purchased the GOF text (the Gang of Four: Gamma, Helm, Johnson, & Vlissides, 1995). This article recounts my subsequent spreading of the word about patterns at my company, AG Communication Systems (AGCS).

Acting on a suggestion from my manager, I scheduled a presentation for our vice-president and his staff (the Gang of Sixteen [GOS]) to get approval to buy copies of the GOF text and start training in the GOF patterns, with the long-term goal of collecting domain-specific patterns in a "Best Practices" handbook.

I also posted a report from the trenches to the patterns listserver. Thanks to the overwhelming response from pattern lovers everywhere, I felt I was not alone in struggling to introduce patterns to my company. I received several requests for the introductory materials I had created, so I posted an ASCII version of my presentation.

The GOS requested an evaluation phase. Members of the evaluation team included designated representatives of the GOS, some of our resident object-oriented (OO) gurus, and others who were just interested in patterns. There were about 20 team members in all.

We ordered copies of the GOF text for the team and others around AGCS. This next part is key: Put the book in the hands of knowledgeable designers and patterns will begin to take hold. It's not enough to derive a lot of benefit, but it is a powerful initial step. My advice to correspondents on the listserver was: Start spreading the word by ordering books. Get enough for an evaluation team and more because you'll find that others will want a copy. That's the biggest selling point for patterns—there is a book to follow and designers will start reading it!

The evaluation phase consisted of four 1-hour meetings over a 2-week period. We covered the five patterns and the example in Ralph Johnson's (1994) article. The evaluation meetings were open to anyone who was interested in patterns. That provided a larger audience for the information and more input for the discussions.

It was a thoroughly enjoyable experience—the chance to get together with other developers and talk about design problems and possible patterns solutions. This kind of self-examination doesn't often occur in today's pressured environment. Typically, we rush headlong into the next project without stopping to adequately reflect on what we should have learned from the last. As a result, we might make the same mistakes over and over.

Some members of the team expressed their concern over the lack of real-time, embedded-system considerations in the GOF text. These are not trivial enhancements and I anticipate that someone will provide them in the future. Until then, we're building on the GUI (graphical user interface) examples in the motivation. It's true that everyone can understand this context and that's a good beginning.

The evaluation phase was easy. The patterns sell themselves. I went back to the GOS with the results and the following suggestions:

1. Every interested designer should have a copy of the GOF text.
2. We should provide training for teams, to enhance communication and design knowledge.
3. Continue the noon-time brown-bag meetings, covering the rest of

the patterns, to keep the momentum and provide help for teams who really needed this information. The word was out and patterns were already appearing on some projects.

At this point, we were fortunate enough to find a training/consulting organization that would come in for a trial with our evaluation team (Goldfedder & Rising, 1996). The training was based on the GOF text and spanned an intensive 3 days. The evaluation team liked the course but found that 23 patterns in 3 days was too much. They also made some minor suggestions about format and the lab exercise(s).

Ralph Johnson (personal communication) has observed that "people can't learn patterns without trying them out. Also, people need to find them in their own problem domain." Ralph is absolutely right about the difficulty of learning patterns from lecture. The trial offering of the course uncovered that problem—even though all the members of that group had been through the GOF text with their brown bags.

Fortunately, the trainer spent time after class working with some of the students helping them to apply patterns to their design problems. This experience was so valuable that we wanted to incorporate this consulting opportunity in the training package and reduce the concentrated patterns presentations. The class schedule was changed from 3 full days to 1 full day followed by 4 half-days of training, allowing for 4 half-days of consulting. We tried to schedule each course offering for a specific team to provide the biggest leap in abstraction and communication.

Some of the questions raised during this part of the adventure included: What should we do next? Do we start patterns mining and how is that done? We also have another side of the house that is not object oriented. Managers of those developers were concerned that they were being left out of all the patterns activity. The GOF text was object oriented; the training was object oriented. How could the non-OO people be a part of this new technology?

The answers to these questions came in the guise of an exceptional fellow at Bell Labs, named Jim Coplien (Cope), and his colleague, Bob Hanmer, who introduced us to writers workshops. Cope showed us a new way to look at patterns. Cope and Bob are patterns "mining" the 4ESS®, one of AT&T's large telecommunications switches. The patterns they shared with us had no object diagrams or C++ code. Furthermore, some of our developers recognized some of the patterns as part of the object-oriented projects and the GTD-5®, the large switch we develop for GTE and independent telephone companies.

As a result of this experience, we have started patterns mining on the GTD-5® with the help of resident domain experts. We hope to share knowledge of patterns across the company and with the folks on the 4ESS®.

Ralph Johnson (personal communication) said, "You'll find that most people are not good at finding patterns. Fortunately, you don't need (or want) most people to be doing that. You want to make everybody feel included and wanted, but ultimately people will sort themselves out into those who will want to work on finding patterns and those who don't. . . . your organization's real job is to get a product finished, and patterns are a means to that end. Most people should just get on with their work."

We held writers workshops to look at some of the 4ESS® patterns. Thus far, most of the patterns have also been seen on the GTD-5®, so even if they weren't written here, they should be familiar to many of our developers. Some modification will be required for these patterns before they become ours.

Ralph Johnson comments on this activity (personal communication): "Working with people from AT&T who are working on similar problems is of course an outstanding idea. That is probably where you should put your energy for finding new patterns, because there will be a lot of synergy. Moreover, the best way to find patterns is to compare and contrast similar systems. So, you should take advantage of this opportunity."

We have a local patterns home page, which is currently behind a firewall. The patterns from the 4ESS®, from Cope's writers' workshop, and the patterns we have found on the GTD-5® are referenced here; each allows input from readers to enable the evolution and improvement of these patterns. This should allow us to create evolving, changing patterns that would eventually be part of a "Best Practices" handbook. There are also several links to other patterns locations (see the various on-line sources listed in the References).

We are also establishing a patterns-mining process. We are encouraging developers to write their own patterns, attempting to answer the questions, "What knowledge would be lost to the company if I were to leave tomorrow? What do I know that I have done a thousand times that I think everyone already knows?" Patterns then go through a writers workshop. After updates to the pattern have been made, the pattern is posted on our home page to evolve as others read the pattern and make comments. After a suitable interval, some of these patterns would become part of the "Best Practices" handbook and used for training newcomers to our projects and the company.

We are adopting Cope and Bob's approach of interviewing domain experts who don't have the time to write patterns. The interviews are taped and used for patterns creation by pattern crafters. After a pattern has been identified, it goes back to the domain expert, then through a writers workshop and onto the Web page.

We've also begun an experiment with our excellent System Test team. We conducted a patterns-mining workshop with 10 experienced system testers. In 2 hours we had "mined" 20 patterns. Then came the hard work of refining and reviewing. These patterns show the beginnings of a pattern language. My fellow pattern miner, David DeLano, and I took them to the patterns conference, PLoP (Pattern Languages of Programming), this year, where they were extensively "shepherded" and "workshopped" and have improved immensely.

The next step is to teach these patterns to the rest of the system testers and grow the language. When an established system test community has been created that speaks the pattern language, we will teach the language to others, such as management, designers, all those who interact with system tests. We hope this will bring about a shared world view based on the pattern language. The goal is to have a better understanding of recurring problems and their solutions. This will save us all time and make our organization more competitive.

I feel the time is right for patterns. People in the development community are looking for help and although patterns are not a silver bullet they offer considerable help with just a little investment.

REFERENCES

Alexander, C., Ishikawa, S., Silverstein, M., with Jacobson, M., Fiksdahl-King, I., & Angel, S. (1977). *A pattern language.* New York: Oxford University Press.

AGCS Patterns Home Page. http://www.agcs.com/patterns/index.html

Gamma, E., Helm, R., Johnson, R., & Vlissides, J. (1995). *Design patterns: Elements of reusable object-oriented software.* Reading, MA: Addison-Wesley.

Goldfedder, B., & Rising, L. (1996). A training experience with patterns. *Communications of the ACM, 39* (10), 60–64.

Johnson, R. E. (1994, September–October). How patterns work in teams. *ROAD,* pp. 52–54.

A Training Experience
with Patterns

Brandon Goldfedder

brandon@goldfedder.com

Linda Rising

risingl@agcs.com

A group of respected individuals in the object-oriented community has been taking a hard look at the work of Christopher Alexander, a building architect. Alexander has some intriguing observations about an entity he calls a pattern, defined as follows (Alexander et al., 1977, p. x):

> Each pattern describes a problem that occurs over and over again in our environment and then describes the core of the solution to that problem in such a way that you can use this solution a million times over without ever doing it the same way twice.

Software design patterns have been defined by other authors, including Jim Coplien and Doug Schmidt (1995, p. xi):

> Design patterns capture the static and dynamic structures of solutions that occur repeatedly when producing applications in a particular context.

Because members of the software-engineering community have been searching, unsuccessfully for the most part, for an answer to the problem of reinventing the wheel, the patterns investigation has been attracting considerable attention. Patterns were introduced to the object-oriented community at large at OOPSLA '94, where a tutorial entitled *Design Patterns: Elements of Reusable Architectures* was given and the *Design Patterns* text (Gamma, Helm, Johnson, & Vlissides, 1995) first became available. This article describes the initial steps taken to introduce patterns through training by the Dalmatian Group to AG Communication Systems. This training focuses on the patterns in the Design Patterns (Gamma et al., 1995) text since this early period. Training in patterns at AG Communication Systems and elsewhere has expanded to include patterns introduced at PLoP (Coplien & Schmidt, 1995; Vlissides, 1996) and "mined" from legacy systems.

INITIAL EFFORTS

The patterns initiative at AG Communication Systems began in April 1995 with an evaluation phase. Members of the evaluation team included functional area representatives, resident object-oriented gurus, and others who expressed an interest in understanding patterns. There were about 20 team members in all.

Copies of the *Design Patterns* (Gamma et al., 1995) text were ordered for the team and others. This was an important part of the process. We found that when the book is in the hands of designers, the patterns will begin to take hold. This is a big selling point for patterns—there is a book on patterns and designers will read it.

The evaluation meetings were open to anyone who was interested in learning about patterns. That provided a larger audience for the information and more input for the discussions. The evaluation phase was easy. The patterns sell themselves. The team had no trouble answering the following questions:

1. Is the notion of patterns a worthwhile technology for AG Communication Systems?
2. Are the patterns in the *Design Patterns* text worth a training investment?

The consensus on both these questions was an overwhelming yes.

At the end of the evaluation phase, the following recommendations were made:

1. Every interested designer should have a copy of the *Design Patterns* text.
2. Training in these patterns should be provided for teams in order to enhance communication and design knowledge. Some members of the team expressed their concern with the lack of real-time,

embedded-system considerations in the text. This was addressed in the training through the use of additional examples and implementation details lacking in the Gamma et al. (1995) text. During this first stage, patterns were already appearing on some projects.

BETA TRAINING

At this point, we began working with The Dalmatian Group. One of their trainers, Brandon Goldfedder, delivered a 3-day beta patterns course for the evaluation team in June 1995. After the course was presented, we considered feedback from the evaluation team members. Suggested improvements included: topic reordering, improvement of examples, additional motivational sections. It was also suggested that we reduce the amount of time spent reviewing object-oriented concepts to make room for more lab exercises.

The challenge for most students to absorb the material in just 3 days was an area of some concern. Ralph Johnson (personal communication) has observed that "people can't learn patterns without trying them out. Also, people need to find them in their own problem domain." This observation was confirmed by our experience with the beta course, even though the members of that group had been through most of the patterns in the evaluation phase.

During the evenings of the beta training, the trainer met with some of the students to suggest ways to apply patterns in their current projects. These students found this assistance valuable. As a result, we decided to incorporate consulting opportunities along with the training and change the course schedule from 3 full days to 1 full day followed by 4 half-days of training. This allowed 4 half-days of consulting. The opportunity for hands-on mentoring and consulting became an essential element for the success of patterns introduction.

We tried to target a specific team for each course offering to provide the biggest leap in abstraction and communication. Having a team go through training together also meant that examples meaningful for the team could be discussed and used in the consulting sessions. One team member who experienced the benefits of this mode of training wrote a pattern to describe the experience.

COURSE STRUCTURE

The course focused on applying the design patterns in the *Design Patterns* text (Gamma et al., 1995). Emphasis was placed on change management, specifically long-term maintainability and extensibility. In addition, integrating patterns into the development lifecycle through design reviews and documentation was a key focus. The class provided both an overview of important concepts as well as detailed discussion of the use of the patterns discussed in the *Design Patterns* text (Gamma et al., 1995). The format consisted of a lecture, discussion, and lab exercises. Labs and discussion material were designed to be extremely modular to allow reuse and modification for special versions of the course. This flexibility was necessary because of the diversity in both the language and the design skills of the students. Later incarnations of the course included an overview of patterns and advanced review sessions for each of the three categories of patterns: Creational, structural, behavioral, as defined in the *Design Patterns* text (Gamma et al., 1995). These presentations were built by reusing existing course modules and were modified as needed. New examples and additional slides were added for groups with special interests and backgrounds.

At the end of each class offering, both student and instructor critiques were reviewed and updates made to session plans, instructor notes, course slides, or supplemental slides. This ensured that the experiences of all the instructors of this class could be shared and the course improved in a controlled manner. The course went through several profound changes that helped to improve the class. The discovery of the best ways to teach certain patterns occurred naturally under this process.

COURSE IMPLEMENTATION

Lab exercises are essential in giving students the "aha" experience. After each category of patterns was covered with lecture and discussion, groups of three or four students were given a set of requirements and asked to present a design solution to the rest of the class for review. The class presentation and peer review addressed long-term maintainability, extensibility, and flexibility of the solutions. Exercises were done with pencil and paper or CASE (computer-aided software engineering) tools, depending on the students' work environment.

Covering all the patterns in a short period of time usually resulted in all the patterns blurring together or students spending more time understanding the details of many different examples than on the patterns themselves. To address this difficulty, a single example, an Alarm Monitoring System, was used for discussion and the lab exercises. The students could consider each exercise in the context of this running example without having to learn the details of a new problem setting. This also avoided considering any pattern as only useful for a single example and allowed the focus of the class to remain on the intent of each pattern.

We felt it was important to cover all the patterns in the book and to show how they complement each other. When students begin to use patterns and understand that any pattern is just one piece in the system, they begin to see design at a much higher level.

Some patterns were introduced through the discovery process. For example, students were given a traditional solution to the problem of designing an alarm system and asked which areas could not be modified without risking major upheaval to the system. We restructured the architecture to exploit this understanding. As each new requirement for change was presented, additional patterns were introduced as were additional examples common to the students' domain. As a result, students had a better, more complete understanding of the pattern and its appropriate use.

It was difficult to determine the amount of code to present in the examples. It is important for students to realize that patterns are applied in the design phase and not to be overly concerned with specific implementation issues. Without seeing some code, however, the discussion can become too academic. The challenge was to find an appropriate level of detail for the students to understand the implementation. We have observed that as the course progresses and in follow-up consulting sessions, the need to see code to understand the pattern decreases and the focus shifts to design issues.

A certification process seemed to be present. Some developers could not accept design guidance from someone without the details of C++ syntax and the behavior of compilers. Although design patterns are at a much higher level than code, students needed convincing that the code produced would be at least as good as their existing approaches. The exact mechanism used varied from class to class. In some classes, a quick code example sufficed. In other classes, a more detailed discussion of the code generation of the C++ compiler was required, often with explanations of virtual-table costs. This was especially true in introducing the state pattern. Often students solved the problem addressed by this pattern with complex conditional code or a complicated look-up table. The state pattern is conceptually simpler and implementation easier.

Brief discussion of implementation issues were conducted during class times as needed. Longer, more specialized discussions were postponed to breaks and follow-up consulting sessions. It is essential that the instructor be able to address these concerns. Once past this hurdle, developers were open to high-level concepts.

OBSERVATIONS

In contrast to our experiences teaching other software-engineering classes, there was little resistance to these new concepts. In many design classes considerable time is spent selling the concepts, but it is extremely difficult to show, in a convincing manner, implementation improvements to someone who is not open to new ideas or has become accustomed to solving problems one way. In this course, it is easy to provide justification for improvements to efficiency, maintainability, modifiability, and extensibility of the code as well as to show significant reduction of time spent in documentation through the use of patterns. The exact mechanism for showing these benefits varied significantly. In some classes it was sufficient to show the C++ implementation, in others it was necessary to discuss compiler output. By addressing these issues up front, rather than hand-waving them as insignificant, students could not easily dismiss this technology as not offering performance improvement.

When looking at students' ability to successfully apply this technology, the amount of C++ and object-oriented experience or years of experience in a single project were not significant. The exposure to a variety of systems was extremely important. There is an interesting lack of correlation between object-oriented project experience and acceptance of and ability to apply patterns. Some of the more experienced developers have been among the least able to understand what patterns are all about, whereas some of the developers from nonobject-oriented projects grasp the concepts readily. We believe that a lot of experience in only one language and/or project leads to a narrow focus and a belief in students' minds that they have a greater breadth of knowledge than may actually be present. Regardless of the language, methodology, or systems students have used, those who are exposed to more ideas remain in a learning mode and are more open to new ideas. Additionally, they have far more diverse experiences to call on. We have further found that this broadness provides benefit for system architects and good designers.

Frequently, students were unable to attend all the sessions in a week of training. To accommodate these students, we offered them a chance to make-up sessions in later courses. We observed that many would elect to take several days over again, in addition to the ones they had missed.

Going through the material again helped those who were struggling to sort out pattern details. Our response was to offer this option to anyone, whether he or she had missed scheduled training or not.

The use of patterns promotes a common vocabulary that allows a team to focus on problems rather than the details of implementation. It is exciting to see the change in the character of the reviews as higher levels of design can quickly be communicated. This also provides an interesting side effect: it is now possible to recognize and characterize the similar problems that projects share. We are in the process of documenting solutions to these common problems to allow cross-project knowledge transfer and reuse.

ONGOING EFFORTS

We recently introduced a 1-day overview of patterns to reach those who did not have the time to attend the full course. Most of the attendees felt that they could not afford *not* to attend the full course and signed up for the next full class.

Training of the object-oriented teams, over 100 people, was completed at the end of August 1995. This training period was followed by a few visits from the trainer to provide review sessions on each pattern category and to offer additional consulting opportunities. It was our experience that training alone, without the consulting and hands-on mentoring, would not have been as effective.

AG Communication Systems shares the same problem every organization has: new hires come in and others leave the company. Now that our developers have been trained by the Dalmatian Group, we need to introduce new employees to the patterns in the *Design Patterns* text (Gamma et al., 1995) and to the others in our growing collection. An internal training organization has taken over the task of "spreading the word" about patterns. This group offers courses in patterns using a project architecture as a running example; it also presents a users' course, a writers' course, and a brainstorming workshop to help experts mine patterns in a given area. The AG Communication Systems patterns model is one of capturing patterns from experts and creating courses to share these patterns with the rest of the company. In examining the behavior of other engineering disciplines, we find that students trained in the contents of an engineering handbook don't suddenly begin to leaf through this handbook whenever a new problem is presented. Instead, they simply use the handbook to reference details of a solution they already know. Therefore, training is an essential part of the use of patterns in any environment.

We feel the time is right for patterns. Patterns are not the long sought-after silver bullet, but they provide benefit with minimal investment. There's an interesting side effect in the patterns activities. Engineers at AG Communication Systems feel they're really on the cutting edge and they are! There's a sudden interest in reading the literature, buying books, attending conferences and classes, including the Pattern Language of Program Design (PLoP) conference. Several of us attended OOPSLA '95 to get all the new patterns information we could.

When asked about productivity benefits from patterns, we are quick to point out that people who are excited about their work and feel a part of something stimulating and challenging will be more productive, regardless of the technology that's involved. It's gratifying to be part of something that brings this kind of benefit to other software engineers. The use of metrics to show this productivity is under consideration. In the mean time, we rely heavily on subjective reports such as the one written by Michael Duell (1996).

ACKNOWLEDGMENTS

The authors would like to thank the reviewers of this article for their helpful comments and suggestions, which added greatly to the quality of the final version.

REFERENCES

Alexander, C., Ishikawa, S., & Silverstein, M., with Jacobson, M., Fiksdahl-King, I., & Angel, S. (1977). *A pattern language.* New York: Oxford University Press.

Coplien, J. O., & Schmidt, D. C. (Ed.). (1995). *Pattern languages of program design.* Reading, MA: Addison-Wesley.

Duell, M. (1996). *Experience in applying design patterns to decouple object interactions on the INgage™ prototype.*

Gamma, E., Helm, R., Johnson, R., & Vlissides, J. (1995). *Design patterns: Elements of reusable object-oriented software.* Reading, MA: Addison-Wesley.

Vlissides, J., Kerth, N., & Coplien, J. (Eds.). (1996). *Pattern languages of program design—2.* Reading, MA: Addison-Wesley.

Patterns: The New Building Blocks for Reusable Software Architectures

Diane Saunders

Twenty years ago, a building architect wrote two books detailing his design theory for constructing better buildings. Today, software designers are using those theories to design better software architecture.

The architect's theory revolves around patterns. Not the literal patterns, such as a series of squares and diamonds decorating a parquet floor, but the conceptual patterns inherent to successful design.

In his first book, *A Pattern Language,* the architect Christopher Alexander, says, "Each pattern describes a problem that occurs over and over again in our environment and then describes the core of the solution to that problem in such a way that you can use this solution a million times over without ever doing it the same way twice" (Alexander, 1979).

Alexander defines successful design as that which transcends the ages due to its usefulness and appeal to innate human aesthetics. So in a house built using Alexander's patterns, the parquet floor wouldn't be just a pretty decoration. Instead it's more likely to be there because the building pattern required a floor design signaling a transition from an informal room to a formal one.

Now let's make the leap from applying patterns to building architecture to applying them to software architecture, something even Alexander says he found "the biggest stretch and the most surprising." Although

---

intertwining human aesthetics with building designs seems a given, combining human aesthetics with software design sounds as likely a coupling as high art and polyester pants. Yet those in the forefront of software-design pattern use say aesthetics are also key to successful software architecture.

Jim Coplien, coeditor of the book *Pattern Languages of Program Design,* says, "By paying good attention to aesthetics, you reap untold benefits through human comfort and convenience, both for programmers and for end users. That ultimately improves the bottom line." To illustrate, Coplien applies the current metrics-driven software-design approach to building a public library. "Were we to take the metrics-driven approach that most management would have us follow," he says, "we'd view the library simply as a warehouse for books, and would build it as such."

Software design patterns were first used in 1987, but didn't enter the design vernacular until 1993, as word made its way through seminars and conferences. The touted bottom-line benefits of design patterns include better designs and quicker product-to-market schedules. But what exactly is a design pattern?

According to the book *Design Patterns: Elements of Reusable Object-Oriented Software,* "A design pattern names, abstracts and identifies the key aspects of a common design structure that makes it useful for creating reusable . . . design" (Gamma, Helm, Johnson, & Vlissides, 1994, p. 3).

So, if a designer finds him or herself trapped by design problems, a pattern says here's a solution.

A pattern isn't a block of code that is lifted and reused. "Design patterns provide a shorthand expression of rather complex ideas among team members very succinctly, freeing us up to concentrate on the ugly details of implementation," says Don Olson, an AG Communication Systems software engineer. AG Communication Systems, a telecommunications vendor in Phoenix, applies patterns to its new software designs. It creates software for intelligent networks, access, and central office switching.

Patterns occur in a hierarchy, starting with the most general and moving along to patterns that speak to the fine details embedded in a design. The more the pattern concepts overlap, the stronger the architecture.

Patterns are found through "patterns mining" of existing successful designs. Designers interview other designers to understand the philosophies and ideologies underlying the code. They record their findings, identify patterns, and test the patterns for broad use. If a pattern holds up under scrutiny, it's added to a "Best Practices" handbook.

A sampling of pattern names includes: Flyweight, Memento, Leaky Bucket, and Visitor. The catchier the name, the easier it is to remember and communicate.

Some companies consider their patterns proprietary and won't release their patterns to the general public. There are textbooks on the market that describe patterns, however. There are also pages on the Internet describing patterns, including a page dedicated to "antipatterns"—patterns that don't work.

"There are so many common design and implementation problems that every software engineer faces. The patterns document and code solutions to these problems so we don't have to keep re-inventing the wheel," says Patricia Genualdi, another AG Communication Systems software designer.

When applying patterns to new designs, a pattern is identified, then the code is written to suit the overall project. And although software patterns originated with object-oriented design, they can be and are being applied to any software language or architecture.

Pattern devotees acknowledge that patterns are still experimental and unproved quantitatively. Yet, they say, by finding and identifying patterns and applying those patterns during design, patterns offer a better and more natural way to write software programs.

"We're capturing telephony expertise that's slipping away," says Coplien. "We're starting to revisit the issues of design and system construction at the system level and at the very human level—two aspects of design that have been lost and sterilized in the past two decades" (Coplien & Schmidt, 1995).

REFERENCES

Alexander, C. (1979). *The timeless way of building.* New York: Oxford University Press.

Coplien, J. O., & Schmidt, D.C. (Eds.). (1995). *Pattern languages of program design.* Reading, MA: Addison-Wesley.

Gamma, E., Helm, R., Johnson, R., & Vlissides, J. (1994). *Design patterns: Elements of reusable object-oriented software.* Reading, MA: Addison-Wesley.

PART II

EXAMPLES AND

EXPERIENCE

Part I of this book introduced you to patterns. That should get things going for you, just as it did for us! You might have a lot of questions buzzing around in your brain at this point. Help is on the way—there's a FAQ (frequently asked questions) Web site,[1] archives of the patterns list-server,[2] and an article in Part III by Jim Coplien, "Software Design Patterns: Common Questions and Answers." After the buzzing settles down, you'll be ready for what happened next!

Let's set the stage. It's the fall of 1995. Nearly all our developers working on object-oriented projects have been trained in the patterns in the GOF (Gang of Four) text (Gamma, Helm, Johnson, & Vlissides, 1994). As a result of this training, we were beginning to see some successes. One of them was documented and presented at OOPSLA '96 by Mike Duell. This is the first article in Part II, "Experience in Applying Design Patterns to Decouple Object Interactions On the INgage™ IP Prototype."

Mike had gone through the design-patterns training and, in his own words, really "didn't get it!" When his team ran into the problem of object communication overload and used the *Mediator* pattern to solve it, he was sold. He is now one of our strongest patterns advocates and is working to find real-world, nonsoftware examples for all 23 patterns in the *Design Patterns* text (Gamma et al.,1994). Documenting real-world experiences is

---

[1] Patterns FAQs, http://gee.cs.oswego.edu/dl/pd-FAQ/pd-faq.html
[2] Patterns Listserver Archives, http://iamwww.unibe.ch/~fcglib/WWW/OnlineDoku/archive/DesignPattern

important. It dilutes the hype and provides a reality check for all us engineer types! There's also an experience report in Part III you'll enjoy reading; it's from a fellow at IBM, Russell Ramirez, and is entitled "A Design Patterns Experience Report."

Another real-world article has been included in Part III. This one, written by Doug Schmidt and Paul Stephenson, is entitled "Using Design Patterns to Evolve System Software from UNIX to Windows NT." This is an interesting article, not only because it describes actual project experience, but also because it introduces Doug Schmidt's patterns, *Reactor* and *Acceptor.* Doug's home page[3] is an exceptionally good source of pattern information, not only on his patterns for distributed systems, but also on the many patterns courses he teaches at Washington University. For those of you in academia or industry training, this is a site worth visiting!

Don't stop yet! There's yet another article you'll want to read. This one has seven authors sharing their experiences with patterns in companies all over the globe. "Industrial Experience with Design Patterns" has some engaging stories and some valuable "lessons learned."

COPE'S VISIT

Sorry for digressing, let's get back to our patterns history! In the midst of our successes, while we were feeling pretty good about what we were doing with patterns, something happened in our little community at AG Communication Systems that would forever change the way we looked at patterns—Jim Coplien (Cope) came to visit. Cope, who works in the Software Systems Research Center at Bell Labs in Naperville, Illinois, is a member of the Hillside Group and one of the "founding fathers" of the patterns movement. He had been experimenting with a patterns training course and wanted to try it out at our company. Cope has described this course as "wackier" and "more experiential" than most and we were definitely excited at the prospect! Cope is a famous C++ guru, whose book, *Advanced C++* (Coplien, 1994), was on everyone's recommended reading list. For more information see Steve Bilow's article and Bill Haney's review in Appendix A.

We got ready for Cope's visit! We gathered a dozen of our best developers (fresh from Design Patterns training) for a 2-day course with Cope and

---

[3] Doug Schmidt's home page, http://www.cs.wustl.edu/~schmidt

Bob Hanmer, a fellow with lots of experience on AT&T's 4ESS® switch. In the class, we learned that several veteran developers on the 4ESS® were due for retirement and folks at AT&T were uneasy about that loss. The project managers approached Cope with the idea of extracting that expertise and capturing it as patterns. At the time of our course, Cope and Bob had documented over 100 patterns, "mined" through a process of taping interviews with the experts and extracting patterns from the recorded conversations. A small subset of that collection was presented at the second Pattern Languages of Program (PLoP) Design Conference in 1995 and has been published in the Addison-Wesley patterns series. The patterns are included in Part III of this book; take a look at "Fault-Tolerant Telecommunication System Patterns."

As Cope and Bob presented some of the 4ESS® patterns, developers in the class commented that similar patterns had been seen on the GTD-5®. In fact, some of the patterns had been seen at other companies. We realized that they weren't just telecommunications patterns and certainly not unique to the 4ESS®.

Software development at AG Communication Systems falls into one of two arenas. In one is a large central-office telecommunications switch, the GTD-5®, developed for GTE and independent telephone companies. It contains over 3 million lines of Pascal and continues to perform well in terms of quality, reliability, and revenue. The other, non-GTD-5® projects are smaller and for the most part are written in C++. The focus of all the patterns activity up to this point had been almost exclusively directed toward the object-oriented projects. Cope and Bob expanded our patterns horizon to encompass our entire software-development community. Indeed, we began to think about nonsoftware patterns—patterns concerned with the organization of teams and with customer interaction.

PATTERNS COURSES

We were inspired! By the end of the first quarter of 1996, David DeLano and I were ready to pilot a Patterns Users course. David and I are part of the Technical Resource Center, with the assignment of helping make technology useful to development projects. We were leaning toward patterns to help us reach our goals. The Patterns Users course was a half-day introduction to what patterns are all about, based on what we had read and what we had learned from Cope and Bob. We continue to "grow" this course and offer it at least once every quarter. Each time we present it, we learn more about patterns! We like to keep the course size small, to allow lots of interaction. Alexander (1977) has a pattern that applies to this situation; it's called *Small Meeting Rooms* (151), which suggests that

> The larger meetings are, the less people get out of them. But institutions often put their money and attention into large meeting rooms and lecture halls. (p. 713)

Alexander (1977) further states that, "As size of group grows, more and more people hold back." He goes on to say,

> There is no particularly natural threshold for group size; but it is clear [from the graph in the pattern] that the number who never talk climbs very rapidly. In a group of 12, one person never talks. In a group of 24, there are six people who never talk. (p. 713)

Related to this is the location of the meeting rooms. As Alexander (1977) says, "The meeting rooms are not located where people work" (p. 715). The solution is to

> Make at least 70 per cent of all meeting rooms really small—for 12 people or less. Locate them in the most public parts of the building, evenly scattered among the workplaces. (p. 715)

We like to have classes of 12 but prefer smaller numbers.

We have also created a 2-day Patterns Writers course, much like Cope and Bob's. The first half-day is essentially the Patterns Users course. The attendees spend the second half of the first day writing a pattern. They can go back to their offices to do this or they can stay with us in the classroom and we will work with them. The next day we explain writers workshops and for the rest of the day we conduct writers workshops for each pattern written the previous day. We also keep this course size small, because the workshop effort takes time and is exhausting! Our target is to have classes with six writers. We have been teaching the Patterns Writers course since the second quarter of 1996.

I've presented some thoughts on pattern writing in my article, "Pattern Writing," which is included in Part II. I look at what other members of the patterns community have said about writing and then add some of my own views based on our experience in teaching the Patterns Writers course.

Writing is challenging under any set of circumstances, but writing patterns is especially difficult. Following a form helps. We've learned a lot about pattern documentation and have created our own pattern template. We began with Jim Coplien's and have added and changed components to meet our needs. The template is included in Part II of this book and can also be found on our external patterns home page.[4]

Going through the experience of writing a pattern helps in reading and understanding patterns written by others. Writing is a creative exercise and some are better at it than others. Some of our most experienced developers may not be good writers, but it's more important to capture the knowledge of our experts than to worry about writing talent, which is a secondary issue.

Richard Gabriel introduced writers workshops at the first PLoP Conference in 1994. The technique was borrowed from the writing community and offers a way for authors to gather and share comments on the writing of others in the group. We've included a couple of reports on this first patterns conference, Robert Martin's "Patterns: PLoP, PLoP, Fizz, Fizz," and Ralph Johnson's "A Report on PLoP '94." These articles help explain what goes on in this unusual conference!

There is some similarity between the writers workshop and the document review process, with the following exceptions. The emphasis in a writers workshop is on communication of ideas. Comments are made about clarity of expression, about whether the intent of the author's message is clear, and as much attention is paid to positive comments as to "suggestions for improvement." It is assumed that the author is an expert, writing about her or his experience, so no "defects" are counted or tracked. We have developed a short document that explains the process. It is included in Part II of this book and can be found on our Patterns Home Page.[4]

David DeLano has written an article on patterns mining that captures some of the thoughts we've had about the mining metaphor and our lessons learned in patterns mining at our company. For those of you who have performed similar experiments, our shared perspective may help. You can learn from what we have tried. I believe each organization has its own character and what works for us might not work for you. The best we can hope for in sharing our experiences is to give you ideas and food for thought.

SYSTEM TEST PATTERNS

The system test pattern language originates from a happy accident, one of many we've had in bringing patterns to life at our company! Mike Sapcoe,

---

[4] AGCS Patterns Home Page, http://www.agcs.com/patterns/index.html

one of our experienced system testers, took the Patterns Writers course and wrote a pattern about system testing. We had been looking for ways to capture and document patterns more effectively. With Mike's pattern as an incentive, we worked with Ray Fu, one of our system test leaders, and began mining with a workshop.

We sat in a room with a dozen of our best system testers and asked them to talk about recurring problems with known solutions. David and I typed furiously while the discussions raged around us. We were lucky to have the assistance of Greg Stymfal, a member of our patterns community with system test experience and effective facilitation skills. This role is critical in corralling a room full of old hands! The result of our first few workshops is an article that will be published in the Pattern series by Addison-Wesley. We've included the article in Part II so you can see the beginnings of our system test pattern language. Since this article was written, the patterns have grown considerably and continue to grow. Patterns are living things that change as we learn more about the problem, the context, the solution. Some may completely outlive their usefulness as procedures and other technologies change.

We grow these patterns by repeating the workshop experience, each time with a new set of testers. We present the existing patterns and ask for feedback, again typing energetically to keep up with the comments! We find that everyone agrees with the solutions in the patterns but can help us improve the pattern components with new stories. We have also split some patterns into two or more smaller patterns, spawning new patterns. During the workshops, the testers learn the existing patterns and we learn how to improve them.

Our goal is to have all our system testers go through the system test Patterns Workshop experience. We will then teach the patterns to our managers and the rest of the development community. This should provide a uniform view of the problems faced by system test and the solutions proposed by our experienced system testers.

The system test patterns and others we capture are valuable because they represent the way we do business. One of the challenges we face in publishing is that the best patterns contain stories of real projects. Unfortunately, these stories contain sensitive or proprietary information and can't be shared outside the company. Removing this information usually leaves a thumbnail sketch of a pattern, which may not have much credibility. We hope that our patterns are helpful even though you may find yourself asking, "Where's the beef?" This publishing restriction is shared across the industry. Because most members of the pattern community are not in academia, there is also little incentive to expend the effort to publish anything. We at AG Communication Systems are, again, lucky in that regard. We are rewarded for external publication. Nonetheless, the publishing dilemma is a problem we face as the patterns community grows and more patterns are uncovered.

Not everything should be documented as a pattern. We wrestled with this when documenting system test patterns. We finally convinced ourselves that if we wanted to capture the system test process, we would not use the pattern form but would write a process document for system testing. We were not telling our pattern readers how to do system testing, we were sharing what experienced system testers know, just as *Design Patterns* (Gamma et al., 1994) is not about the process of software design, but presents a collection of valuable design tips from experienced designers.

ORGANIZATION AND PROCESS

Teaching the patterns courses allows us to expand our user and writer base. We are also looking at nonsoftware patterns. Patty Genualdi, one of our software engineers, was enrolled in a graduate course and chose organizational and process patterns as a research topic for her class. Jim Coplien is actively involved in organizational patterns research and provided valuable sources and feedback for Patty's work. Her article provides an introduction to this different kind of pattern study. Patty's article, "Improving Software Development with Process and Organizational Patterns," can be found in Part II. Jim Coplien presented his collection of organizational patterns at PLoP '94 and it has been published in the Addison-Wesley Patterns series. We have included his article, "A Generative Development-Process Pattern Language," in Part III.

Norm Janoff is one of our process leaders. His article "Organizational Patterns at AG Communication Systems" appears in Part II and describes our experience in that arena. Norm relates the activities that took place during Jim Coplien's return visit. Cope brought a team of process experts from AT&T who helped us look at some of our organizational and process issues. We were interested in Cope's search for patterns that define hyperproductive teams. We were also curious about patterns that our own successful teams use. Share the best with all the rest was a watchword for this investigation.

DON OLSON'S WORK

Don Olson is our most famous patterns writer, who has an extensive collection of patterns[5] on the Wiki Wiki Web[6]. This fascinating Web site with the unusual name is a place where patterns folks gather to discuss a wide variety of patterns topics.

Don's first article, "Patterns on the Fly," combines the best of both worlds—design patterns and process patterns—and how they work together. He has some interesting tales to tell about patterns and how they affected not only his team organization, but also the software they developed. You'll be captivated by his style and the wonderful stories he tells!

Don was a participant in Cope and Bob's writing course in the autumn of 1995. In that class, we were all struggling to write a pattern. We were well aware that Jim Coplien was going to see all the patterns and each of us wanted to create something worthwhile. I remember when Don (struggling with project deadlines) arrived late the second day and shamefacedly held his hand-written contribution and apologized for not having time to produce anything noteworthy. He said all he could think of was a skiing pattern. We had been workshopping software patterns most of the day, so it seemed like comic relief to look at skiing!

As we read somewhat illegible xeroxed copies, Cope was obviously excited and finally called out, "This is a generative pattern!" We could see that Don had produced something special, but I don't think we fully grasped what Don had captured.

Generativity, in my humble opinion, is a difficult concept to grasp and even more difficult to implement in a pattern. Patterns at their best do not exist in isolation; they are part of a pattern language. This simply means that a collection of patterns can guide you through the process of creating an end product of some kind. Each pattern resolves the forces in the current context. As it does so, it changes the context and new forces arise. You will need other patterns to resolve these new forces, and, of course, the new patterns will change the context, and so on. The process is an unfolding—an organic, living encounter. We strive for this but there are very few examples of this kind of structure. The model we all strive to emulate is Alexander's (1977), *A Pattern Language*, which begins with patterns for cities and ends with patterns for rooms.

---

[5] Don Olson's patterns, http://c2.com/cgi/wiki? Regular Contributors
[6] Wiki Wiki Web, http://c2.com/cgi-bin/wiki

Don's pattern describes an indirect solution to a problem. Typically, we react to symptoms and do our best to address those symptoms without considering what the real cause of the problem might be. If Don Olson had written his pattern with that approach, he would have called it "Don't Lean Backward!" How many times have we tried to solve problems by simply recommending, "Don't Do That!" This method is almost never successful. The indirect approach attacks a root cause and brings about a real solution.

We use Don's pattern *HandsInView* in our patterns training classes as an example, not only of a generative pattern, but as a beautifully crafted piece of literature. The rationale in this pattern is towering. You can find it in Part II.

Don's second article, "A Pocket-Sized Broker," is included in Part II and recounts our experience with a variation of the *Broker* pattern presented in the collection of architecture patterns (Buschmann, Meunier, Rohnert, Sommerlad, & Stal, 1996) written by five software-patterns investigators at Siemens AG. Our *Broker* is slightly different from the classic version, but its impact on several of our projects has been considerable. It is certainly one of our patterns and product success stories! In Part III, we've included an extensive review of the Siemens architecture book, written by David DeLano for *C++ Report*. Most of the reviews in our annotated bibliography are short, a page or less, but David's is quite extensive—everything you always wanted to know about architecture patterns!

Don Olson is a master of the antipattern—this is not what you might think at first. An antipattern is not just a "bad" solution. An antipattern presents a solution that "sounds" good but doesn't work. Andrew Koenig's article in Part III, "Patterns and Antipatterns," claims that antipatterns may well be more valuable than "real" patterns, simply because knowing what doesn't work (and why) can be incredibly useful. There's an interesting Web site devoted to this topic, which includes presentations of antipatterns.[7] Many of Don Olson's antipatterns are there: *TrainTheTrainer, CargoCult, SacrificialLamb,* as well as some from Jim Coplien: *EgalitarianCompensation* and the associated "real" pattern, *Compensate Success.*

FRAMEWORKS AND PATTERNS

I keep referring to patterns and reuse, but the real reuse gains are to be made with frameworks. Frameworks are made of implementations of patterns.

---

[7] AntiPatterns, http://c2.com/cgi-bin/wiki?AntiPatterns

We include some good articles on this topic in Part III. One by Ralph Johnson, "Patterns and Frameworks," and a second from Hans Albrecht Schmid, "Design Patterns for Constructing the Hot Spots of a Manufacturing Framework," which clearly shows how patterns and frameworks work together.

Our own Ben Richards writes about a company project experience using the ACE framework. ACE is another of Doug Schmidt's creations; read more about ACE on Doug's home page (see footnote 3). Frameworks differ from the "old" view of reuse in what's commonly called the Hollywood principle—don't call us, we'll call you! The idea is that code reuse in the past meant components from code libraries were called from the user program. When a framework is used, the framework calls the code written by the user. Framework development is one of those concepts that sounds a lot easier than it actually is. I think you'll enjoy Ben's story.

REFERENCES

Alexander, C.A. (1977). *A pattern language.* New York: Oxford University Press.

Buschmann, F., Meunier, R., Rohnert, H., Sommerlad, P., & Stal, M. (1996). *Pattern-oriented software architecture, a system of patterns.* New York: Wiley.

Coplien, J.O. (1994). *Advanced C++ programming styles and idioms.* Reading, MA: Addison-Wesley.

Gamma, E., Helm, R., Johnson, R., & Vlissides, J. (1994). *Design patterns: Elements of reusable object oriented software.* Reading, MA: Addison-Wesley.

Experience in Applying Design Patterns to Decouple Object Interactions in the INgage™ IP Prototype

Michael Duell
duellm@agcs.com

In general, system requirements should specify the components of a system, as well as the interactions between components. Since system requirements rarely specify how these interactions should be encapsulated, a software design that tightly couples the components of a system will usually satisfy the initial requirements. The design flaws are usually not discovered until a later phase in the software life cycle, when changes in requirements lead to changes in software design. At this point, what should be a simple change propagates throughout the entire system due to the tight coupling of components.

Since some assumptions become invalid over time (Gause & Weinberg, 1989), the INgage IP Software Architecture Document stated that there was a possibility that the required interactions among communications objects would change as the prototype evolved to accommodate new technologies and support new telecommunications services. The anticipated change in the required interactions made it necessary to consider ways of decoupling communications objects in early designs in order to minimize the number of classes requiring modification.

This article describes the object interactions that caused the INgage IP team to explore patterns and the ways that the *Mediator* pattern was used so that changes in these interactions would not propagate throughout several classes. It also discusses some of the other benefits that were realized as a result of applying design patterns.

BACKGROUND

An IP (intelligent peripheral) is a network element that allows flexible information interactions between a user and the network. The specific information interactions depend on the services deployed on the IP. The basic hardware architecture of the INgage IP (Figure 1) consists of a control computer, one or more resource computers, and a Time Slot Interchange (switching matrix) all communicating over an Ethernet.

A layered software architecture, in which each layer is independently structured using object-oriented technology, is used for the control and resource computers. This article discusses objects in the Generic-Operating-Environment (GOE) layer of the control-computer software. The GOE layer sits between the Element Environment Operating layer and the Communication layer. The purpose of the GOE layer is to provide a common application programming interface (API), which decouples higher layer functions from the underlying operating system. Several communication-interface classes are required at the GOE layer. These communications-interface objects provide the interface between element objects in the Element Environment Operating layer and UNIX sockets (Feit, 1993) in the Communication layer, as shown in Figure 2.

The communication-interface classes differ in their data elements and some of their methods, but they all contain methods for managing connections with a process or device, as well as methods for sending data, and indicating when data is received. Depending on the particular class, the method for managing connections will either listen at a port and wait for

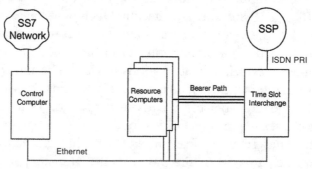

FIGURE 1   Basic IP architecture.

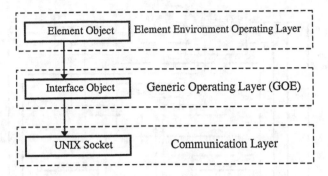

FIGURE 2   Control-computer software layers.

a process or device to connect, or connect to a process or device that is listening. Before attempting to establish connections, some objects are required to wait until other communication-interface objects have established at least one connection.

Figure 3 shows how complex the object interfaces would become if each object were to query the others to determine if it could attempt a connection. The *Mediator* and *Observer* behavioral patterns (Gamma, Helm, Johnson, & Vlissides, 1995) were determined to be candidates for simplifying the object interfaces by decoupling the object interactions.

OVERVIEW OF THE *MEDIATOR* AND *OBSERVER* PATTERNS

The intent of the *Mediator* pattern is to promote loose coupling by encapsulating object interactions. Once the interactions are encapsulated in the *Mediator,* colleague objects can refer to the *Mediator* rather than explicitly referring to each other. The structure of the *Mediator* is shown in Figure 4.

The *Observer* is a related pattern that encapsulates object interactions by using a subject object to store state information for the Observers. The subject automatically notifies the Observers of any changes. The structure of the *Observer* pattern is shown in Figure 5.

EVALUATION OF THE *MEDIATOR* AND *OBSERVER* PATTERNS

Although the *Mediator* and *Observer* are competing patterns, there are differences between them that made the *Mediator* a better candidate for decoupling

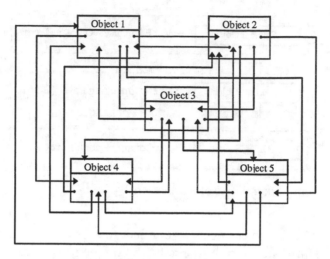

FIGURE 3   Tightly coupled objects.

the interactions of communications-interface objects. The *Observer* pattern uses the subject to encapsulate data and inform the observers of any change to that data. If there are any constraints, the subject and observers must cooperate to maintain them.

In the *Mediator* pattern, communication between colleague objects is centralized by requiring colleagues to refer to the *Mediator,* rather than to each other. Constraints on colleague objects are centralized in the *Mediator.*

The only data dependencies between communication-interface objects is the state of each object's connection (open or closed). Since these data dependencies are used only to constrain connection attempts by certain objects, and knowledge of other communication-interface objects is unnecessary, the object models for the communication interfaces can be simplified by encapsulating the constraints in a *Mediator.*

IMPLEMENTATION OF THE *MEDIATOR* PATTERN

The *Mediator* was implemented as a class using an in-house object-oriented language.[1] In its simplest form, the implementation of the *Mediator* employs two methods: CAN_I_CONNECT? and REPORT_CONNECTION.

---

[1] As this article is intended to relay experiences with the *Mediator* pattern and not a specific language, the implementation will be described in general terms.

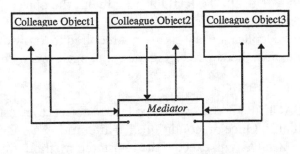

FIGURE 4   *Mediator* structure.

Before attempting to establish a connection, colleague objects must call the *Mediator's* CAN_I_CONNECT? method to determine if all interactions have been satisfied. When a connection is opened or closed, objects must call REPORT_CONNECTION to inform the *Mediator.* Additional methods were added to refine the *Mediator.* The GET_MEDIATOR_ID, CALL_BACK, and UPDATE_CONNECTION methods are described in the next three sections.

GET_MEDIATOR_ID METHOD

The GET_MEDIATOR_ID method accepts an object's name (in the form of a character string) and returns an integer that is associated with that object name. If an association has not yet been established for the object name, GET_MEDIATOR_ID will register the object name, create an association, and return the ID number. When the concrete *Mediator* is

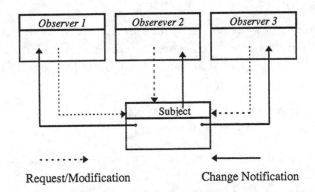

FIGURE 5   *Observer* structure.

initialized, GET_MEDIATOR_ID is called with the object names of the colleague objects to create the associations. By calling the GET_MEDIA-TOR_ID method, colleague objects are not required to know their ID numbers at compile time, thereby reducing the coupling between objects further.

CALL_BACK METHOD

The CALL_BACK method is used by colleague objects to register a method with the Mediator. Once preconditions for attempting a connection have been met, the *Mediator* will execute the registered method, thus providing the dispatch scheme. Use of the CALL_BACK method eliminates the need for the colleague object to loop and call the CAN_I_CONNECT? method until the *Mediator* returns YES. Unlike the Observer pattern, colleague objects must request each update explicitly by registering a method with the Mediator.

UPDATE_CONNECTION METHOD

UPDATE_CONNECTION is a private method within the *Mediator.* Whenever a colleague object uses REPORT_CONNECTION to report that a connection has been opened, UPDATE_CONNECTION is called to check if any other colleague objects are waiting for this connection. If a colleague object is waiting for the reported connection, the *Mediator* will call its own CAN_I_CONNECT? method with the waiting object's ID to determine if all of the required connections have been made. If the required connections have been made, UPDATE_CONNECTION will execute the method supplied by the waiting object via the CALL_BACK method. The *Mediator* then unregisters the callback method supplied by the waiting object.

A SAMPLE COLLEAGUE INTERACTION

Using the *Mediator* methods described in the previous three sections, a sample interaction is shown in Figure 6. In this example, Colleague 2 must establish a connection before Colleague 1 is allowed to attempt a connection.

INSIGHTS GAINED FROM USING THE *MEDIATOR* PATTERN

Since it is more difficult to change a component that is highly interrelated to other components (Stevens, Meyers, & Constantine, 1984), the original intent in decoupling interactions between communication-interface objects was to facilitate future maintenance of those classes. In addition to

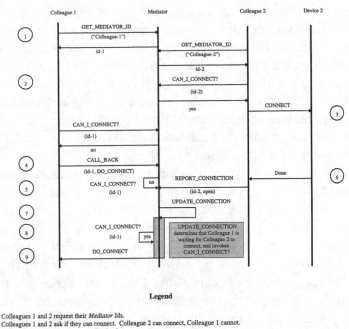

Legend

1. Colleagues 1 and 2 request their *Mediator* Ids.
2. Colleagues 1 and 2 ask if they can connect. Colleague 2 can connect, Colleague 1 cannot.
3. Colleague 2 attempts to connect to Device 2.
4. Colleague 1 supplies "DO_CONNECT" to the *Mediator* as a CALL_BACK method.
5. Upon receiving Colleague 1's CALL_BACK method, the *Mediator* checks to see if Colleague 1 can connect
6. The connection to Device 2 is complete. Colleague 2 reports this to the *Mediator*.
7. The *Mediator* invokes its UPDATE_CONNECTION and finds that Colleague 1 is constrained by Colleague 2.
8. The *Mediator* checks to see if Colleague 1 can connect, now that Colleague 2 has a connection. It can.
9. The *Mediator* invokes Colleague 1's DO_CONNECT Method

FIGURE 6   Sample object-interaction diagram.

achieving that goal, the *Mediator* also helped simplify the original design. Since a different designer had responsibility for each class, it was much simpler to provide a common set of *Mediator* methods to be used, rather than designing a complex interface to be shared by all five classes. By isolating the classes from their interactions, it became obvious that the interactions were not properties of the classes. Since the objects maintained their essential properties once their interactions were encapsulated in the *Mediator,* each resulting class model was a truer representation of its interface, and could be understood without knowledge of the other classes (Booch, 1994). For example, objects in the Element Operating layer that communicate with the Time Slot Interchange do so without knowing the state of the resource computer connection. Likewise, the Communication layer does not require the resource computer to connect to the control computer before it can connect to the Time Slot Interchange.

Testing the objects in isolation was also greatly simplified. The *Mediator* was unit tested without any of the colleague objects by invoking its methods from a driver. The colleague objects were tested without the need to write stubs for all of the other colleague objects. On the target hardware, connections were simulated by reporting them to the *Mediator,* and individual communication-interface objects were tested in isolation. Even when the implementation of one of the classes lagged the others by a few weeks, there was minimal impact to the schedule, since its interaction with other classes was encapsulated in the *Mediator.*

At one point the synchronous, blocking connect method of one interface class had to be changed to an asynchronous, nonblocking connect. This change was accomplished without impacting any other classes. Although changes to individual classes have been accomplished, there has not yet been cause to change any of the object interactions. When changes to an interaction (constraint) are made, they will be isolated to the one class where the interactions are encapsulated. One planned change is to make the *Mediator* data driven, so that changes in object interactions can be made by changing data rather than modifying the *Mediator* implementation. When a change in the *Mediator* is made, rigorous retest of the communication-interface objects will not be required, since none of their behaviors will change. Since the interaction between the communication-interface classes is separate from the classes themselves, rigorous unit testing of the *Mediator* will be sufficient to ensure confidence in the change.

CONCLUSIONS

For the INgage IP Team, the initial attraction to design patterns was the promise of minimizing the effects of imminent requirements changes. The team decided to expend effort up front in exchange for future maintainability. In the process of exploring behavioral patterns, it was discovered that they are beneficial much earlier in the software life cycle than during the maintenance phase. By encapsulating object interactions in a *Mediator,* classes were designed without excessive coordination between designers. Eliminating unnecessary dependencies allows parallel development of classes, which minimizes the impact that any one class may have on the development schedule. The loose coupling accomplished with behavioral patterns also makes iterative development more practical, since changes are localized. Replacing many-to-many interactions with one-to-many interactions also increases the testability of the individual classes and the system as a whole. Although improved maintainability and software reuse are often the justification for using design patterns, the benefits realized during initial design and testing are also significant reasons to consider their use.

REFERENCES

Booch, G. (1994). *Object-oriented analysis and design*. Redwood City, CA: Benjamin/Cummings.

Feit, S. (1993). *TCP/IP architecture, protocols, and implementation*. New York: McGraw-Hill.

Gamma, E., Helm, R., Johnson, R., & Vlissides, J. (1995). *Design patterns: Elements of reusable object-oriented software*. Reading, MA: Addison-Wesley.

Gause, D. C., & Weinberg, G. M. (1989). *Exploring requirements, quality before design*. New York: Dorset House.

Stevens, W. P., Myers, G .J., & Constantine, L. L. (1974). Structured design. In *Tutorial on software design techniques* (pp. 328–352). New York: IEEE Computer Society.

Pattern Writing

Linda Rising
risingl@agcs.com

There's a lot of discussion these days about pattern topics and among these certainly the pattern form is the most confusing. I think this confusion arises in part because when an expert knows something, she or he usually feels it is sufficient to simply say to the novice, "Remember to do this!" The trouble with this approach is beautifully expressed in a book that captures the essence of writing a good pattern—telling a good story (Schank, 1990):

> The . . . problem is simply that humans are not really set up to understand logic. People tell stories because they know that others like to hear stories. The reasons that people like to hear stories, however, is not transparent to them. People need a context to help them relate what they have heard to what they already know. We understand events in terms of events we have already understood. When a decision-making heuristic, or rule of thumb, is presented to us without a context, we cannot decide the validity of the rule we have heard, nor do we know where to store this rule in our memories. Thus, what we are presented is both difficult to evaluate and difficult to remember, making it virtually useless. People who fail to couch what they have to say in memorable stories will have their rules fall on deaf ears despite their best intentions and despite the best intentions of their listeners. A good teacher is not one who explains things correctly but one who couches explanations in a memorable (i.e., an interesting) format. . . . In the end all we have . . . are stories and methods of finding and using those stories (pp. 15–16).

ALEXANDRIAN FORM

Christopher Alexander (1977) created the pattern form.

> Each pattern has the same format. First, there is a picture, which shows an archetypal example of that pattern . . . after the picture . . . an intro-

ductory paragraph . . . sets the context . . . explaining how it helps to complete certain larger patterns. Then there are three diamonds. . . . After the diamonds . . . a headline, in bold type . . . gives the essence of the problem in one or two sentences. After the headline comes the body of the problem. This is the longest section. It describes the empirical background of the pattern, the evidence for its validity, the range of different ways the pattern can be manifested in a building, and so on. Then, again in bold type, like the headline, is the solution—the heart of the pattern . . . in the stated context. This solution is always stated in the form of an instruction—so that you know exactly what you need to do, to build the pattern. Then . . . a diagram . . . [of] the solution. . . .

After the diagram, another three diamonds. . . . And . . . a paragraph which ties the pattern to all those smaller patterns in the language, which are needed to complete this pattern. . . .

Each solution is stated in such a way that it gives the essential field of relationships needed to solve the problem, but in a very general and abstract way—so that you can solve the problem for yourself, in your own way . . . we have tried to write each solution in a way which imposes nothing on you. It contains only those essentials which cannot be avoided if you really want to solve the problem. In this sense, we have tried, in each solution, to capture the invariant property common to all [solutions of] the problem (pp. x–xiv).

GOF FORM

The form in the GOF (Gang of Four or Erich Gamma, Richard Helm, Ralph Johnson, and John Vlissides) text (1995) is described in the first chapter as comprising four essential elements:

1. The pattern name is a handle we can use to describe a design problem, its solutions, and consequences in a word or two. Naming a pattern immediately increases our design vocabulary. It lets us design at a higher level of abstraction. Having a vocabulary for patterns lets us talk about them with our colleagues, in our documentation, and even to ourselves. It makes it easier to think about designs and to communicate them and their trade-offs to others. Finding good names has been one of the hardest parts of developing our catalog.

2. The problem describes when to apply the pattern. It explains the problem and its context. It might describe specific design problems such as how to represent algorithms as objects. It might describe class or object structures that are symptomatic of an inflexible design.

Sometimes the problem will include a list of conditions that must be met before it makes sense to apply the pattern.

3. The solution describes the elements that make up the design, their relationships, responsibilities, and collaborations. The solution doesn't describe a particular concrete design or implementation, because a pattern is like a template that can be applied in many different situations. Instead, the pattern provides an abstract description of a design problem and how a general arrangement of elements (classes and objects in our case) solves it.

4. The consequences are the results and trade-offs of applying the pattern. Though consequences are often unvoiced when we describe design decisions, they are critical for evaluating design alternatives and for understanding the costs and benefits of applying the pattern.

The consequences for software often concern space and time trade-offs. They may address language and implementation issues as well. Since reuse is often a factor in object-oriented design, the consequences of a pattern include its impact on a system's flexibility, extensibility, or portability. Listing these consequences explicitly helps you understand and evaluate them (p. 3).

Each pattern in the GOF text is described following a consistent format:

Pattern Name and Classification
The pattern's name conveys the essence of the pattern succinctly. A good name is vital, because it will become part of your design vocabulary. The pattern's classification reflects the scheme we introduce [in a later section] (p. 6).

This article will not address the topic of pattern classification. Suffice it to say that no other publication has used the scheme developed by the GOF authors. This indicates more a lack of agreement on proper classification than a disagreement with the Behavioral/Creational/Structural approach in the GOF text.

Intent
A short statement that answers the following questions: What does the design pattern do? What is its rationale and intent? What particular design issue or problem does it address?

Also Known As
Other well-known names for the pattern, if any.

Motivation
A scenario that illustrates a design problem and how the class and

object structures in the pattern solve the problem. The scenario will help you understand the more abstract description of the pattern that follows.

Applicability
What are the situations in which the design pattern can be applied? What are examples of poor designs that the pattern can address? How can you recognize these situations?

Structure
A graphical representation of the classes in the pattern using a notation based on the OMT (Rumbaugh et al., 1991). We also use interaction diagrams (Booch, 1994) to illustrate sequences of requests and collaborations between objects.

Participants
The classes and/or objects participating in the design pattern and their responsibilities.

Collaborations
How the participants collaborate to carry out their responsibilities.

Consequences
How does the pattern support its objectives? What are the trade-offs and results of using the pattern? What aspect of system structure does it let you vary independently?

Implementation
What pitfalls, hints, or techniques should you be aware of when implementing the pattern? Are there language-specific issues?

Sample Code
Code fragments that illustrate how you might implement the pattern in C++ or Smalltalk.

Known Uses
Examples of the pattern found in real systems. We include at least two examples from different domains.

Related Patterns
What design patterns are closely related to this one? What are the important differences? With which other patterns should this one be used? (pp. 6–7)

The GOF text had a profound effect on the object-oriented community, but it provided little help for pattern writers. Surely the list of elements created by this thoughtful group of four must contain the essentials for good pattern writing. It's now our task to apply them.

PLOP AND MESZAROS

The First Annual Conference of Pattern Languages of Program Design (PLoP) was held near Monticello, Illinois in August 1994. Its focus was the work of the patterns writers of that time. The conference proceedings (Coplien & Schmidt, 1995) illustrates a variety of forms, approaches, writing styles, and pattern topics. Before the conference, authors worked with "patterns shepherds" to ensure that each pattern contained "a clear problem statement, a solution addressing the problem, and a clear statement of forces that motivate the solution" (pp. xi–xii).

Apparently the attendees of PLoP '94 experienced some confusion over the pattern form and the definition of its components. An article by Gerard Meszaros (personal communication, December, 1995) addresses these concerns and tackles the following questions: How to add new solutions for a problem with an existing pattern solution, a case study applying this pattern, and an analysis of the pattern components. In the case study, several solutions are presented for a problem. Meszaros clearly shows how the forces determine the appropriate solution(s) for the problem. Forces are attributes of solutions and a context is simply the situation in which the problem exists. It is the context that determines the best solution. Here is his analysis of the pattern elements:

Problem. The specific problem to be solved. Separate the problem from the constraints on the solution.

Solution. A solution to the problem. Many problems have more than one solution. The goodness of a solution is affected by the context or circumstances in which the problem exists.

Context. The constraints on the solution. These are often implied via a situation rather than stated explicitly.

Forces. The often contradictory considerations to be considered when choosing a solution to a problem. Each solution considers certain forces. It optimizes some and may totally ignore others. The relative importance of the forces is determined by the context.

The following relationships exist among pattern elements:

- A problem has a set of solutions.
- A solution solves a problem.
- A solution addresses or optimizes forces.

- Forces are attributes or consequences of a solution.
- A context indirectly determines the best solution since:
  — A context prioritizes forces that need to be optimized and
  — A solution optimizes a set of forces.

Following PLoP '95, Meszaros and Jim Doble in *Pattern Language of Program Design 3* (R. Martin, D. Riehle, F. Buschmann, eds. Reading, MA: Addison-Wesley, to be published in 1997), described a collection of Pattern Writing Patterns. Two that address pattern names are *Evocative Pattern Name* and *Noun Phrase Name.* The first pattern instructs the pattern writer to imagine how the name would be used by someone applying the pattern. The second describes the essence of a pattern as its transforming effect on a situation, resolving some set of forces. The result is a new situation or context for the application of the next pattern. He proposes a guideline for naming based on this transformation process. His recommendation is for a noun phrase that is easy to use in a conversation that focuses on the result of applying the pattern. The name shouldn't include verbs or prepositions since the name should improve communication and should be as simple as possible.

Another pattern in this collection is *Readable References to Patterns,* which I have followed in this article. The solution provides a form for patterns references: pattern-name [reference], in which the pattern-name is in italics and the reference is a well-known name, for example, GOF or a reference expanded at the end of the pattern or pattern language.

Two other interesting patterns are *Intent Catalog* and *External Pattern Thumbnail.* Both patterns require a thumbnail sketch of the pattern, similar to Coplien's abstract, described in a later section of this article. The *Intent Catalog* stores the thumbnail sketches for the patterns and provides a point of reference to another pattern. In *External Pattern Thumbnail,* the thumbnail sketch is used in a footnote in a pattern description.

PORTLAND FORM

The Portland Form, so named because its initial users were all from Portland, Oregon, is a narrative form, in contrast to the GOF Form, which captures a pattern in a series of sections. A pattern in this form contains statements like the following: This set of forces creates this problem, so here's the solution. The pattern takes its name from the solution. Each pattern is part of a set of related patterns. Higher level patterns resolve forces, which open up new problems with derived forces (Cunningham).

COPLIEN FORM

Jim Coplien's (1994) report on PLoP '94 included detailed considerations of the pattern form. He feels that the essence of the Alexandrian form should be present regardless of the style; that is, there should always be a clear definition of the problem, the forces, and the solution.

Coplien encourages the use of an abstract that helps a reader determine if the pattern is relevant for the problem at hand. The solution should be layered, with the most general interpretation at the highest level, following the style of a newspaper article, so that more details are uncovered as the reader progresses through the section.

He offers the following suggestions:

1. Patterns should be general but not abstract.
2. If considerable collaboration is involved, include a diagram of dynamic behavior, for example, an interaction diagram.

Coplien also focuses on good names. Names may suggest the problem, the solution, the resulting context or intent but the choice of name should be made carefully. Providing alternative names relevant to different domains can be helpful for readers. Abbreviations or nicknames can help solve the problem of different audiences for the pattern.

SANE'S CONTRIBUTION

In an article written by Aamod Sane (1995) summarizing the discussions within one group at PLoP '95, a pattern is described as telling the story of a design decision made in some context in which a problem requires a solution that must satisfy certain requirements or forces. The solution is only appropriate if the requirements are met. Even then, certain implementation issues must be considered. He suggests that different forms may be appropriate for different uses, although needless originality should be avoided. The pattern form should be standard. His suggestions for pattern components are essentially those of the GOF Form.

The Title of a pattern is a noun phrase describing the central design decision, for example, *Chain of Responsibility* (Gang of Four, 1995); the participants, for example, *Observer* (Gang of Four, 1995); or the function, for example, *Abstract Factory* (Gang of Four, 1995).

An abstract can be included for the casual reader. The abstract provides an overview of the problem.

The intent of the pattern explains at an abstract level what the pattern achieves. Sane gives the following description for intent: "If you take the primary patterns used in your application, 'instantiate' the Intent statements by replacing abstract pattern names with application-specific names, then all the intents together should form a good description of your application" (Sane, 1995).

In the motivation, a good example is essential for capturing the reader's attention, to convince the reader that the pattern solves an important problem. The author's motivation is not the reader's motivation. This can initiate a running example that can be followed through the pattern. This section should list the forces specific to the pattern. Different forces will pull your thoughts in different directions. The pattern must bring about an equilibrium.

The solution must show how the forces are resolved. This section may include a sketch. The solution usually has a set of preconditions that determine the applicability of the solution. Equally important are those circumstances in which the pattern is not appropriate.

Trade-offs are explained in the consequences section. Be sure to include all negative consequences of the pattern, all elements that can vary, and those that must not. Patterns typically restructure complexity. These must be made clear to the reader, who may stumble on these issues and discard the pattern if the trade-offs are not properly addressed.

Interestingly enough, Sane refers to a paper by David Parnas that I also feel has a message for pattern writers. This article is entitled "A Rational Design Process: How and Why to Fake It" (Parnas & Clements, 1986). The thesis of the article is that good designs, like good patterns (and as a former mathematician I can't help adding good proofs), are usually created by a rather disorderly process but are usually explained to others in a logical fashion. Creating the finished product does not always proceed in a clear, step-by-step manner as it might seem to the innocent reader.

BECK POSTING

Kent Beck posted some pattern writing exercises on the patterns listserver.[1] He describes pattern writing as story-telling. To motivate readers to remem-

---

[1] http://st-www.cs.uiuc.edu/users/patterns/lists.html

ber patterns, tell a story in which the pattern helped solve a real-life problem. Further, to encourage readers to avoid difficulties, relate a real-world episode in which the pattern was not used. This relates closely to another comment from Schank (1990):

> If a prior experience is understood only in terms of the generalization or principle behind the case, we don't have as many places to put the new case in memory. We can tell people abstract rules of thumb which we have derived from prior experiences, but it is very difficult for other people to learn from these. We have difficulty remembering such abstractions, but we can more easily remember a good story. Stories give life to past experience. Stories make the events in memory memorable to others and to ourselves. This is one of the reasons why people like to tell stories. (p. 10)
>
> We are more persuasive when we tell stories. For example, we can simply state our beliefs, or we can tell stories that illustrate them. If John explains to Bill that he is in a quandary about whether to court Mary or Jane, and if after listening to John's description, Bill responds "Mary," his reply would usually be seen as useless advice. We need justifications for the beliefs of others in order to begin to believe them ourselves. If Bill responds, "Mary, because Mary is Irish, and Irish women make good wives," he is being more helpful but not necessarily more believable. But if Bill responds with a story about a similar situation that he was in or that he heard about and how the choice was made in that case and how it worked out, John is likely to be quite interested and to take the advice offered by the story more to heart.
>
> Stories illustrate points better than simply stating the points themselves because, if the story is good enough, you usually don't have to state your point at all; the hearer thinks about what you have said and figures out the point independently. The more the hearer does, the more he or she will get out of your story. (p. 11)

Every pattern resolves conflicting forces. Beck suggests listing all forces, technical and human, that affect the solution to the problem. Order the list by importance for early development. Now, list alternative solutions, and for each solution, list pluses and minuses from the list of forces. This should help clarify the rationale.

Beck also prefers noun phrases for pattern names. He refers to Alexander's description (1979):

> The pattern is, in short, at the same time a thing, which happens in the world, and the rule which tells us how to create that thing, and when we

must create it. It is both a process and a thing; both a description of a thing which is alive, and a description of the process which will generate that thing. (p. 247)

BECK AND JOHNSON'S ARTICLE

Kent Beck and Ralph Johnson (1994) outline yet another pattern form. They indicate that the set of preconditions is similar to the context in other forms and the forces are described in several paragraphs as constraints:

Preconditions. The patterns that must be satisfied before this one is valid. The sequence in which patterns are considered is one of the most important skills possessed by experts.

Problem. A summary of the problem addressed by the pattern. The problem statement is used by the reader to decide if the pattern is applicable.

Constraints. The constraints describe the conflicting (sometimes mutually exclusive) forces acting on any solution to the problem. Typical examples are tradeoffs between execution time and execution space, or development time and program complexity. Clearly stating priorities between constraints makes patterns easy to debate.

Solution. A two or three sentence summary of the solution to the problem. The solution is often accompanied by a diagram illustrating the activity required to transform a system from one that doesn't satisfy the pattern to one that does.

AG COMMUNICATION SYSTEMS PATTERN FORM

The AG Communication Systems Pattern Form[2] began as the Coplien Form and has evolved as special needs have been identified. It contains the following components: Name, Aliases, Problem, Context, Forces, Solution, Resulting Context, Rationale, Known Uses, Related Patterns, Sketch, Authors, Date, References, Keywords, Example.

Finding a good name is a challenge. Alexander (1979) certainly agrees with this, "you must give [the pattern] a name. . . . [if] the pattern has a weak name, it means that it is not a clear concept, and you cannot clearly tell me to make 'one.'" (p. 267)

---

[2] The AG Communication Systems Pattern Template may be found at:http://www.agcs.com/patterns/template.html.

Most of our patterns have names reminiscent of procedures in a program, for example, *Validate Before Update*. These names were derived from the experts who provided the patterns and are meaningful for developers who need them, so we haven't tried to be too clever. Coplien has a talent for naming patterns. You can see this immediately in the names he chooses for Fault-Tolerant Communication Patterns: *People Know Best, Leaky Bucket Counters*. Don Olson also has a way with names: *CargoCult, SacrificialLamb, TrainHardFightEasy*.[3] We do our best but we've decided that names are not something we have time to worry about. If a good name leaps to mind, we grab it; otherwise, we try to find an appropriate name that will mean the same thing to everyone who uses it. The idea is to improve communication, not create catchy slogans for advertising jingles. Schank (1990) has the following interesting comment about names:

> Is "forty-two" a story? Of course it is, and it isn't. It doesn't sound like a story; it's more the name of a story, so to speak. In some sense, every story is simply the name of a longer story. No one tells all the details of any story, so each story is shortened. How much shortening has to take place until there is no story left? A story shortened so that it ceases to be understood is no longer a story, but what is understandable to one person may not be understandable to another, so it is clear that "story" is a relative term. In any case, as long as it is understood, it remains a story. For this reasons, there are some very short stories. (p. 39)

We feel the Problem, Forces, Context, and Solution should all be short and, ideally, fit on one page, for easier reading on-line. By scanning this information, the user can immediately determine whether or not the pattern is appropriate. Details, including interesting stories, should be included in the Resulting Context and Rationale. We encourage story-telling, naming names, and giving credit to mentors and other contributors. These make the patterns living literature with real impact on those who are trying to learn the lessons the patterns teach.

WRITERS WORKSHOP

The best way to learn to write patterns is to write one and then ask colleagues to help improve it in a writers workshop. This approach was introduced by Richard Gabriel at the first PLoP Conference in 1994 (Coplien

---

[3] For Don Olson's web site see: http://c2.com/cgi/wiki?search=olson

& Schmidt, 1995). The technique was borrowed from the writing community and offers a way for authors to gather and share comments on the writing of others in the group. For those of you who are familiar with the document-review process, there is some similarity, with the following exceptions. The emphasis in the writers' workshop is on communication of ideas. Comments are made about clarity of expression, about whether the intent of the author's message is clear, and as much attention is paid to positive comments as to "suggestions for improvement." It is assumed that the author is an expert, writing about her or his experience, so no "defects" are counted or tracked.

This helpful medium enables a writer of a pattern to hear feedback from colleagues in a nonthreatening setting. Everyone in a workshop should also be a pattern writer and, therefore, equally sensitive to comments. Writing patterns is difficult work, and those who have struggled to capture the essence of their experience in a pattern are in a good position to help others who have chosen the same path. The following is taken from Gabriel's (1996) text:

> A workshop is a group of people who periodically get together and read and critique manuscripts by fellow workshoppers. Usually the workshop group stays together a long time, although this isn't necessary. But, the longer a workshop's group is together, the better their comments will become, and the better each participant will become at knowing which comments to ignore and which to attend to.
>
> Participating in a workshop is better than giving your work to individual people, because a person tends to soften critical comments, particularly if he or she has a long-term relationship with the writer. In a workshop there can be a feeding frenzy when comments are harsh, and, although this might be tough on people with frail egos, it is crucial to producing accurate comments and feedback, and the writing (and the content) can rapidly improve.
>
> I recommend that we all start workshops, particularly around conference-paper submission time. Find people who are in your subfield and also in nearby subfields or even in unrelated ones. Hand out the material a few days in advance, but not too far in advance—real readers rarely take a long time to try to figure out your paper, so neither should the workshoppers. Start the comments by having someone summarize the paper. Then have people state what is new to them, what works about the paper. Finally, let people start saying what they didn't understand, what isn't clear. Talk not only about the contents of the paper but also about the writing. Make specific suggestions—for example, propose rewrites of specific passages. (pp. 142–143)

We have developed a short document that explains this process. It is included in this book in Part II and can be found on the AGCS Patterns Home Page.[4]

The expectation is, for any pattern, that it will evolve as users apply it, so that the set of known patterns becomes better over time, capturing an improved state of software design. As Alexander (1977) states:

> Patterns are very much alive and evolving. In fact, if you like, each pattern may be looked upon as a hypothesis like one of the hypotheses of science. In this sense, each pattern represents our current best guess as to what . . . will work to solve the problem presented. (p. xv)

REFERENCES

Alexander, C. (1979). *The timeless way of building*. New York: Oxford University Press.

Alexander, C., et al. (1977). *A pattern language*. New York: Oxford University Press.

Beck, K., & Johnson, R. (1994). Patterns generate architectures. *Proceedings of ECOOP '94*. M. Tokoro, R. Pareschi (Eds.), Springer-Verlag, Bologna, Italy, July 1994, pp. 139–149.

Booch, G. (1994). *Object-oriented analysis and design with applications* (2nd ed.). Redwood City, CA: Benjamin/Cummings.

Coplien, J. O. (1994, September). Progress on patterns: Highlights of PLoP '94. In *Proceedings of Object Expo Europe* [On-line]. Available: ftp://st.cs.uiuc.edu/pub/patterns/papers/ObjectExpoPLoP.ps

Coplien, J. O. , & Schmidt, D. C. (Eds.). (1995). *Pattern languages of program design*. Reading, MA: Addison-Wesley.

Cunningham, W. About the Portland form [On-line] . Available: http://www.c2.com:80/ppr/about/portland.html.

Gabriel, R.(1996). *Patterns of software*. New York: Oxford University Press.

Gamma, E., Helm, R., Johnson, R., & Vlissides, J. (1995). *Design patterns: Elements of reusable object-oriented software*. Reading, MA: Addison-Wesley.

---

[4] For the AGCS Writers Workshop see:http://www.agcs.com/patterns/writersworkshop.html

Meszaros, G., & Doble, J. (1997). In R. Martin, D. Riehle, F. Buschmann (Eds.), *Pattern Language of Program Design 3*. Reading, MA: Addison-Wesley.

Parnas, D. L., & Clements, P. C. (1986). A rational design process: How and why to fake it. *IEEE Transactions on Software Engineering, 15*, 251–257.

Rumbaugh, J., et al. (1991). *Object-oriented modeling and design*. Englewood Cliffs, NJ: Prentice-Hall.

Sane, A. *The elements of pattern style* [On-line]. Available: http://choices.cs.uiuc.edu/sane/home.html

Schank, R. C. (1990). *Tell me a story*. New York: Charles Scribner's Sons.

Writers Workshop Format

The workshop is a gathering of interested colleagues, led by a strong, neutral moderator. All participants should read the pattern before the workshop begins. The workshop provides the pattern author the opportunity to hear how the pattern is received by the group. The list that follows delineates the workshop process.

- *First the group reads the pattern.* Ideally, this should have been done prior to the workshop, but this is not always possible.
- *Next the author stands and reads selections from the pattern* that help explain the pattern to others. *The author becomes a "fly on the wall"* and does not participate in the discussion that follows.
- *A member of the group* (not the author or the moderator) *gives a summary of the pattern.*
- *The group gives positive comments.* These refer to elements of the pattern that the author should not change. During the discussion, style, content, and presentation are all fair game. The author is excluded. There is no eye contact with the author. The author's name is never mentioned; all references are to "the author."
- *The group offers suggestions for improvement.* The moderator constrains the discussion to the pattern at hand, usually with the comment, "point noted." Side issues can be captured for later consideration after all patterns in the workshop have been discussed.

  Those in the group who "know" the pattern should not try to clarify or speak for the author during the discussion. The pattern should "stand on its own."

  Trivial comments or extensive rewriting suggestions may be made by giving a marked-up copy to the author after the workshop. This kind of information can be very helpful and does not take time away from the workshop discussion.

- *The author rejoins the group.* The moderator still leads. The author thanks the group for their comments. The author then asks questions to clarify the suggestions. The author should never offer apologies. It can be good for the author to say what was "heard" from the group.

   The expectation is that the author is an expert and will act appropriately to suggestions. There is no need to check on whether the suggestions are taken to heart. The author can request a second workshop as a helpful next step.

- *The group thanks the author.* The moderator calls for the group to stand and applaud the author's contribution.

- If another pattern is to be considered in the workshop, *everyone moves to a different seat and someone tells an unrelated story.*

AGCS Pattern Template

Pattern Name
(Name of pattern goes here. Use italics for all references to pattern names per Meszaros' pattern writing patterns.)

Aliases
(Aliases, or None)

Problem
(Give a statement of the problem that this pattern resolves. The problem may be stated as a question.)

Context
(Describe the context of the problem.)

Forces
(Describe the forces influencing the problem and solution. This can be represented as a list for clarity.)

Solution
(Give a statement of the solution to the problem.)

Resulting Context
(Describe the context of the solution.)

Rationale
(Explain the rationale behind the solution.)

Known Uses
(List or describe places where the pattern is used.)

Related Patterns
(List or describe any related patterns.)

Sketch
(Describe the sketch, if needed.)

Author(s)
(Author's name here or "as told to" for pattern mining.)

Date
(Date string goes here, e.g., 3/1/96.)

References
(Give a list of references cited in the pattern.)

Keywords
(Give a comma delimited string of terms used for searching.)

Example
(Give an example implementation of the pattern. This can be code, pseudo code, etc. This section is optional.)

Patterns Mining

David E. DeLano
delanod@agcs.com

Several metaphors have been suggested and used to describe the process of discovering and documenting patterns. The concept of hunting or fishing for a pattern sounds enticing, but suggests too much randomness in the discovery process. Harvesting also seems to apply to the gathering of patterns, but patterns are not just there for the taking. It takes a great deal more effort to discover and document a pattern. To have a harvest, you must plant a crop. Patterns are not grown or created. They are present in the artifacts that already exist. These are some of the most common descriptions of pattern development that appear to describe the process, but fall short. This leads us to the two remaining metaphors that embody the essence of digging for patterns. These are paleontology or archeology and mining.

Using paleontology or archaeology as a metaphor is appealing. If we think of patterns as fossils or pots hidden away in the mass of earth that is our existing base of developed software, we can imagine the process of carefully sifting through rock and dirt, looking for skeletons or artifacts hidden in the rubble. Digging through the mass we sort through the bad and the good, separating the rocks from the bones, until at last we carefully brush the loose dirt away from our discovered relic. In the end, we carefully claim each piece from the earth and reassemble it for public viewing. This is an accurate portrayal of the patterns discovery process, but the vocabulary of the field becomes clumsy when used with patterns. Patterns paleontologist has a nice ring to it, but would be cumbersome over time. The primary objection to this metaphor is that the work of a paleontologist or archaeologist is usually put on display at a museum. Patterns are meant for everyday use.

We have settled on a mining metaphor to describe the patterns discovery process. The use of "pattern mining" or "patterns mining" is fairly pervasive in the patterns community. In the introduction to *Pattern Languages of Program Design 2,* Richard Gabriel writes, "Great pattern writers are miners, they create nothing except the wonderful explanation" (Gabriel, 1996, p. xii). *Pattern-Oriented Software Architecture: A System of Patterns* contains a short section entitled "Pattern Mining" (Buschmann, Meunier, Rohnert, Sommerlad, & Stal, 1996, pp. 420–422).

The mining metaphor embraces the same elegance found in the paleontology/archaeology metaphor without the baggage of cumbersome vocabulary. Miners dig into the earth in search of nuggets of treasure. The mined elements must be separated from the surrounding residue. There is, however, a certain predictability to mining. Mining engineers tend to know where to excavate for the minerals they seek. What they find is not always of high quality, just as patterns vary in usefulness. The excavation often uncovers a large quantity of matter in one location. "We don't find a single gold atom, we find veins and nuggets—accumulation. Patterns are discovered because they are well used; they form a vein that anyone can find" (Gabriel, 1996, p. xii). The mined elements need not be removed as gingerly as a fossil or artifact. The elements must be further processed before it become useful. After refinement—cutting, polishing, smelting, molding—we are left with a useful product. Often the result is one of lasting beauty or lasting resilience. So shall be the best of the patterns we discover. As for vocabulary, we are patterns miners participating in patterns mining.

We started mining patterns at AG Communication Systems in the spring of 1996. We have tried several techniques for mining patterns with varying degrees of success. All techniques have contributed to our pool of patterns. We have mined for patterns for two purposes: documentation of legacy systems and recurring use. The patterns mining activities can be broken into three categories: individual contributions, second-hand contributions, and patterns mining workshops. These approaches don't describe all types of patterns mining, but they do cover most of the patterns mining effort at AG Communication Systems.

INDIVIDUAL CONTRIBUTIONS

Our first experience with patterns mining was to write patterns of our own. During the training session with Jim Coplien (Cope) and Bob Hanmer (see Linda Rising's description of Cope's visit in the introduction to Part II), we were each asked to write a pattern from our own experience. We struggled through this creative process and learned by making our own mistakes. Most of us did not know that we would be writing a pattern when we signed up for the training session. We wanted to learn more about patterns. Halfway though the day, the trap was sprung and we spent the rest of the day working on our pattern. Our patterns weren't good, but some of them have grown into useful patterns over time. This was truly a baptism by fire. We learned more about patterns by trying to write one than any lecture or book could convey.

One important lesson we learned was that patterns don't apply to just object-oriented development. In fact, most of the work that Cope and Bob had done at that time concentrated on extracting patterns from a legacy system. These patterns weren't being mined for use on future projects. They were mined to capture valuable knowledge about how the system worked. Some of these patterns documented details about the architecture and design that had been lost from the existing documentation. Many had to do with the philosophy behind the development of the system, not the workings of the system. Eventually a few patterns were recognized and refined that could be used in the future, but the goal of the project was to document the system as it is. The patterns are now used to train new developers on the legacy system.

From this enlightenment we learned that the literary form of a pattern is far more powerful than the limited use of documenting a tried-and-true pattern. We used this newfound information to extend the patterns movement within AG Communication Systems to groups outside the realm of object-oriented development. This extension of purpose also led to the discovery of patterns in structured development, management, marketing, testing, and even sports. We also discovered that good patterns often crossed domains.

After the training with Cope and Bob, we had a handful of people who had at least attempted to write a pattern. This was our first group of individual contributors. We felt we had a mission to document all the patterns we knew. We thought this would be an easy task. After all, we just had to write what we knew. Time went by and very few patterns were written. (Except for the multitude of patterns that started appearing on the Wiki-WikiWeb authored by Don Olson.) We assumed that everyone had a number of patterns from his or her past experience that were just waiting to fly onto the paper. We weren't wrong; we just overestimated our capabilities. This activity does continue and patterns are written, from time to time, by designers from their own experience. We have expanded the pool of patterns writers through a training course developed by Linda Rising, based on the original training given by Cope and Bob. This experience led us to our first type of patterns mining: individual contributions based on expertise. It can be equated to digging for gold in your own backyard, with a slightly higher chance of discovering a treasure.

Eventually, individuals broadened their scope a bit and started searching for patterns in the design and code they had participated in creating over the years. This included the contributions of peers working in the same area. It opened up a lot of discussion about recurring problems in the design and how those problems were solved. These discussions brought back memories of the arguments that were experienced each time the problems were encountered. History repeated itself with the trying of different solutions that didn't quite solve the problem, until finally, the same solution was realized. This occurred because there was no documentation as to why the solution worked and why alternatives did not. The pattern form was a perfect media for documenting these problem–solution pairs. This led to the mining of a few more patterns that tended to be area or domain specific.

The effort for writing these patterns was still coming from individuals. There was no organization to the effort; contributions were made as time allowed. This was our second type of patterns mining: individual contributions based on experience. This is equivalent to expanding the search for treasure into our entire neighborhood, city, or state, and not limiting our search to gold. I think that this type of mining holds a lot of promise at AG Communication Systems, and is limited only by the time available for the search.

We have identified individual contributions as our first patterns mining category. Individual contributions can be based on the expertise of the individual writing the pattern or on the experiences of the individual and his or her associates.

SECOND-HAND CONTRIBUTIONS

A number of individuals have experienced and participated in the activities described up to this point. From here on the story gets much more personal. The main players are Linda Rising and me, as most of the second-hand contributions and patterns mining workshop contributions have emanated from our efforts.

After Cope and Bob's training, Linda decided that we should attempt to extract patterns from the AG Communication Systems legacy system, the GTD-5®, in the same manner as Cope and Bob. Having a few years of experience on the GTD-5® from somewhere in my past, I think I volunteered to head up this effort. Several experts were identified as pattern sources. We did not have even a slight expectation that these experts would write patterns on their own, so the candidates were interviewed. Each interview was scheduled for 1–2 hours depending on the availability of the expert. A tape recorder was used to capture the interview, as taking notes would have severely limited the amount of information derivable from one interview. This proved useful as it allowed interviews to proceed at a natural pace and minimized interruptions. Notes were only taken to capture sketches or things not evident from listening to the tape. The interview was kept to the allotted time, as each interview was limited to one tape. When the tape ran out, the interview was finished. The information contained on one tape was more than adequate for deriving patterns.

The first interview I conducted was quite successful. The interview candidate was already on tap to provide information on a particular area of the GTD-5® that lacked documentation for "the way things are." The patterns-mining interview provided both of us with an opportunity. From the interview, I wrote several patterns after listening to the tape two or three times. Linda listened to the tape and mined a couple more patterns. We gave the mined patterns and the tape to Brandon Goldfedder (see his article on Training in Part I) to review while on one of his training/consulting trips. Brandon further defined some of the patterns into a more generic form and added a few new ones. These last patterns may be of use in future work, but they did not document the system. The results of the mining are still under review. While we had the attention of the candidate during the interview, he has been too busy to review the generated patterns.

Other interviews have not been as successful at producing patterns. We have a lot of information on tape, but very few patterns have been written. Over time, more patterns may be mined from these tapes. This is our third type of patterns mining: second-hand mining from interviews with experts. For this type of mining, we have scanned the neighborhood and have found a yard that looks as if it contains a large mineral deposit. We have no idea of the size or quality of the deposit, but we are certain that a deposit is there and we know the neighbor is not digging for it. We excavate the neighbor's yard under his guidance to see if there is anything valuable in the mineral heap. This technique holds promise for the mining of patterns, especially for documenting the patterns contained in legacy systems.

I would recommend using an interview technique for patterns mining, especially if you are trying to extract patterns that exist in the heads of experts. Get a commitment from the interview candidate, not only for the interview time, but also to review the patterns produced from the interview. As a patterns miner, setting up the interview to benefit the expert as well as yourself will go a long way toward producing useful patterns. It is highly recommended that the interview be tape recorded. The benefit of listening to the interview multiple times is invaluable. It helps to have more than one patterns miner at the interview. Have several patterns miners listen to the tape to help mine for patterns.

After writing a few patterns and becoming absorbed into the pattern culture, you can start to see patterns in the work done by the people around you. Explanations of solutions to problems start to materialize as patterns. Even hallway conversations start to become sources for patterns. These sources for patterns come from the experience of the people around you. This becomes a valuable source for mining if you are able to recognize and document these patterns. The danger is that everything starts to look like a pattern.

This is the fourth type of patterns mining: second-hand mining from the experience of others. This type of mining is like looking over the fence into the neighbor's yard and seeing gold protruding from the surface. The neighbor has no inclination to extract the gold, so you do it for him.

As the local patterns culture evolves and patterns miners are identified, people with ideas for patterns seek out the pattern miners to document patterns or to edit patterns. This is an added burden for the pattern miner in that the pattern miner may not have intimate knowledge of the pattern. Though some experience in the area is an advantage, the miner is providing a value-added service by documenting or cleaning up the pattern.

This is the fifth type of patterns mining: second-hand mining as facilitator. This type of mining can be related to a neighbor knowing that there are valuable elements in his or her yard. He or she may have extracted some of the treasure but needs help in either mining the rest of the yard or refining the elements into something usable.

We have identified secondhand contributions as our second type of patterns mining category. Secondhand contributions can come from interviews with experts, from the experience of others, or from facilitating the effort of another pattern writer. In the AG Communication Systems' Pattern Template (see Pattern Template in Part II), we stipulated that the author of the pattern remains the originator of the pattern and the writer or editor is credited with an "as told to" or "edited by" tag.

What we have learned is that some people have patterns in their heads and some people are good at writing patterns. Occasionally there are people who have both these traits. Find people who are capable of writing good patterns and hook them up with the people who possess the patterns.

PATTERNS MINING WORKSHOPS

Last spring we had the privilege of having Jim McCarthy, the author of *Dynamics of Software Development,* visit AG Communication Systems. In preparation for his visit, Linda read his book and discovered that the guidelines in the book look like patterns for the software development process. She even rewrote one guideline, "Don't Flip the Bozo Bit," (McCarthy, 1995, pp. 23, 30–32) into AG Communication Systems form (see Pattern Template in Part II). She did this by moving text from the book into the appropriate section of the pattern template. Very little editing of the text was done.

Linda discussed the notion of his book containing patterns with Jim and uncovered a possible source of patterns. In a management meeting, an individual manager would start talking about a problem he or she was having. Another manager would recognize the problem and relate his or her experiences in resolving it. Other managers would chime in until someone would recognize that they all were talking about the same thing and would summarize the problem and the solution. Everyone would nod in agreement and write the problem–solution pair into their notes.

From this discussion, Linda proposed gathering a group of individuals with a common knowledge base into a session to discuss the patterns that were in their heads. After discussing the format for a while, the notion of a Patterns Mining Workshop was born. The workshop participants are the target group, a moderator, and one or more patterns miners. The more expertise in the target group, the more likely that a good set of patterns will be discovered. The moderator needs to keep the discussion on track, and it helps if the moderator has some experience in the target area as well as knowing what patterns are all about. The patterns miners need to be prepared to document as much of the workshop as possible.

Linda and I were the pattern miners for the first Patterns Mining Workshop. We sat off to the side of the group and used laptops to capture as much information as possible. We tried not to participate in the discussion unless we needed more information or needed the pace of the conversation slowed. It was the moderator's job to move the discussion along, staying on a topic long enough to get the information we needed, but not letting the discussion turn into a gripe session. We tried to tape the session, but found that taping a large group was nearly impossible. To clarify some of our notes, we contacted participants after the workshop.

The group that we chose for the first workshop was System Test. We had around 10 System Testers, a good number for a workshop. The participants had a wide range of experience and had worked on a variety of projects. The workshop was moderated by Greg Stymfal, who was a good facilitator and had some system testing experience. I, too, had some experience in system testing, which helped with the development of the patterns in the end. Greg kept the discussion moving, but the discussion tended to be a chain of one problem after another, without much in the way of solutions. In the end we were able to direct the discussion toward the resolution.

From this Patterns Mining Workshop, Linda and I wrote around 20 patterns. We put these patterns through several Writers Workshops (see Writers Workshop in Part II), which were attended by original Patterns Mining Workshop participants and others with system testing experience. We added a few more patterns and threw out a few. We completely rewrote some of the patterns, and others were fine-tuned. In the end we were left with 19 patterns that fit nicely into a pattern language. The pattern language was documented in an article that was submitted to the PLoP '96 conference and will be published in *Pattern Languages of Program Design 3* (DeLano & Rising, 1997). A copy of this pattern language can be found in Part II.

There are two copies of the patterns produced from the System Test Patterns Mining Workshop. The PLoP '96 submission contains versions that are edited for proprietary information and are essentially frozen at this time. The other copy exists on the AG Communication Systems intranet Web site. This version of each of the patterns is stand alone and continues to be updated from the experiences of the System Testers. New patterns have been added to the language. From this version of the patterns, an internal training class has been developed to train all System Testers in the nuances of the patterns. This follows the model of capturing patterns from experts and training others from them, as put forth in the article on Training found in Part I (see Goldfedder and Rising, this volume).

A note about pattern languages is warranted. Linda and I did not set out to develop a pattern language for system testing. Our only goal was to capture as many patterns about system test as we could. The resulting patterns just happened to fit nicely into a pattern language. However, this pattern language is incomplete and patterns are added as holes are found. The Patterns Mining Workshop format lends itself to the development of pattern languages, but I would warn against using it for this sole purpose. Writing a pattern language can be very slow and tedious. The probability of developing a cohesive pattern language is low. Be content to produce a group of patterns on a related topic. If a pattern language grows from this, it is best to let it occur naturally.

We have now identified our sixth and last type of patterns mining, and also our third patterns mining category: Patterns Mining Workshops. This type of mining can be compared to a couple of mining engineers meeting with everyone in the neighborhood to discuss the mineral content of their yards. The mining engineers can then go out and mine what appears to be the best of the deposits in the neighborhood. This may become the most useful type of patterns mining at AG Communication Systems. When coupled with training on the captured patterns, it provides a powerful device for developing the experience and expertise of the entire company.

This sums up the experience in patterns mining at AG Communication Systems. We have developed patterns using three categories of patterns mining: individual contributions, secondhand contributions, and Patterns Mining Workshops. Each of the categories has strengths and weaknesses. The individual situation, or context if you will, drives the appropriate application of each category. Use and experience them all. One hopes that our experiences can help make your patterns writing effort abundantly fruitful.

REFERENCES

Gabriel, R. (1996). Repetition, Generativity, and Patterns. In J. M. Vlissides, J. O. Coplien, & N. L. Kerth (Eds.), *Pattern Languages of Program Design 2*. Reading, MA: Addison-Wesley.

Buschmann, F., Meunier, R., Rohnert, H., Sommerlad, P., & Stal, M. (1996). *Pattern-Oriented Software Architecture: A System of Patterns*. West Sussex, England: John Wiley & Sons Ltd.

McCarthy, J. (1995). #4: Don't flip the bozo bit. In J. McCarthy, *Dynamics of Software Development*. Redmond, WA: Microsoft Press. Available: URL: http://www.agcs.com/patterns/Bozo Bit.html

DeLano, D., & Rising, L. (1997). System Test Pattern Language. In R. Martin, D. Riehle, & F. Buschmann (Eds.), *Pattern Languages of Program Design 3*. Reading, MA: Addison-Wesley.

System Test Pattern Language

David E. DeLano
delanod@agcs.com

Linda Rising
risingl@agcs.com

Testing of systems is presently more of an art than a science, even considering current procedures and methodologies that support a more rigorous approach to testing. This becomes even more apparent during the testing of large, embedded systems that have evolved over time. To deliver the best possible product, the role of a System Tester has become vital in the life cycle of product development. This pattern language has been derived from the experience of veteran System Testers to help System Testers evaluate the readiness of a product for shipping to the customer. Though these patterns have been derived from experience during the system test phase of the product life cycle, many of the patterns are orthogonal to all testing phases. In addition to System Testers, these patterns may be useful to Designers and Project Managers.

These patterns have been grouped according to their usefulness in the system testing process: The Test Organization, Testing Efficiency, Testing Strategy, and Problem Resolution. This is not a complete pattern language.

CONTEXT

As a pattern language, these patterns share a common context. Each of the patterns may add to this context or slightly modify it, but it is this common context that helps focus these patterns into a pattern language. The context for an individual pattern will only be given when it modifies the common context.

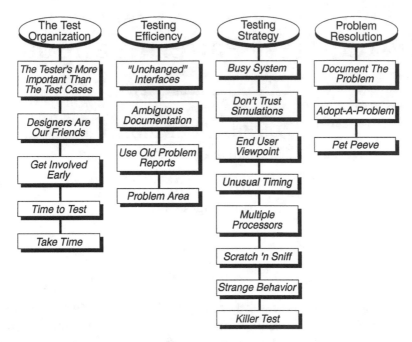

FIGURE 1   System Test Pattern Language.

A system is under development into which new features are being introduced. The system may consist of new development work or may be an existing, working system. There are a limited number of customers for the system and the features are being developed at the request of these customers. The customers then sell the features to the end users. New features integrate well into the system, but introducing new features runs the risk of breaking old features. These features are implemented in the system by Designers in a design group. The Designers are responsible for everything from analysis, design, and implementation, through unit testing and integration testing.

The features of the system are designed in parallel. As code becomes available, incremental loads of the system are released for testing. Each of these loads may include a combination of complete or partial features. This process compresses the development schedule, but it also results in the introduction of problem resolution and features in parallel. Problems resolved in one load need to be resolved in any feature development that is in progress.

The system, in this case, is a large embedded system. It consists of multiple processor units and each processor is controlled by a multi-processing operating system Events in the system are thus non-deterministic. Any feature of the system can have an interaction with any other feature in the system. Most of these patterns apply to the testing of any multi-processing, non-deterministic system. The set of all tests needed to completely verify such a system is infinitely large. The set of regression tests to reasonably test the system grows with every release, so that executing all of the tests would require more than the development schedule allows for a new feature release.

The features are being tested in parallel with the design effort by an independent group known as System Test, whose members are known as System Testers. The testing done by this group is largely "black box" in nature. There is a reliable process in place for testing the system, from unit testing to system testing. The System Test group is responsible for regression testing the system, the conformance of features to the specification, for certifying the equivalence of the system to prior releases, and the evaluation of the release of the system according to criteria set by the customer. These criteria are consistent with every release. System testing concentrates on the functionality of the system and ensures that the system continues to operate in a consistent manner. To accomplish this, the testing often takes the form of stressing or breaking the system.

These patterns do not represent the process of system testing any more than the Gang of Four book (Gamma, Helm, Johnson, & Vlissides, 1995) represents object-oriented design. The System Testers understand the system testing process. Instead, the patterns are a means of sharing some of the secrets of experienced System Testers. Following these patterns will help minimize stress and maximize the enjoyment of system testing.

FORCES

Just as these patterns share a common context, they also share common forces. The individual patterns may place more emphasis on specific forces, ignore some forces, or add forces that are not important to the pattern language as a whole. Forces for an individual pattern will only be given where they are emphasized, modified, or added.

Most of the forces for these patterns are elements of risk management. The patterns evaluate these risks to find an acceptable, intelligent balance among cost, time, content, and quality. The common forces are as follows:

- The scheduled interval for testing is short.
- Compressing the development schedule risks introducing problems.

- Compressing the test interval risks not finding all the critical problems.
- Not all problems can be found.
- A release with some non-critical problems is acceptable.
- Specifications are often unclear or ambiguous.
- Problems should be found and corrected as early as possible.
- Reporting problems is often negatively viewed.
- Testing resources, such as prototype systems or man hours, are at a premium.
- Software load stability is critical to progress.
- The content of a given software load is uncertain.
- Designers traditionally have a higher value within the organization.
- System Testers traditionally have a low status within the organization.
- Designers are preoccupied with new development.
- System Testers must have a global view of the system.
- Designers are primarily concerned with their own area of development.
- System testers represent the customer and end user point of view.
- End users don't always use features as specified by the customer.

THE TEST ORGANIZATION

The following patterns focus on the relationship of the System Testers to the rest of the organization. They are less technical in nature and are closely related to the patterns of James Coplien (1995), Neil Harrison (1996), Alistair Cockburn (1996), and Don Olson (1995).

PATTERN:
THE TESTER'S MORE IMPORTANT THAN THE TEST CASES

Problem
How should work be assigned to Testers to achieve maximum testing efficiency?

Forces
- Testers do not all have the same capabilities.
- Everybody needs to develop new capabilities.
- Creative testers are effective testers.
- Familiarity breeds contempt.

Solution

Assign tasks to System Testers based on their experience and talent. No matter how effective the test cases are, the testing results are highly dependent on the Tester. Davis (1995) states that "People are the key to success" in Principle 131 of *201 Principles of Software Development*.

Resulting Context

Testers will be more effective if their skills are used appropriately. The resulting test activity will be more efficient and the testers will be more productive.

Repeated applications of this pattern can result in burnout of the tester or the development of irreplaceable expertise. Testers who become too familiar with an area often overlook problems by making invalid assumptions. Career development gets overlooked when existing skills are always used and no new skills are acquired. It is sometimes better to give assignments a half step beyond a tester's capabilities.

Rationale

The Tester is the most important element in the testing equation. The same test case will not necessarily produce the same result in the hands of different Testers. Testers look at a list of errors differently. Some Testers know how to break the system vs. getting a correct result. Some Testers are good at finding problems. Some Testers are good at working with designers. Matching the skills of the Testers with the appropriate tasks will produce more effective testing.

DeMarco and Lister (1987) documented that there is a wide variance in performance between the worst and best performers for a given task. To be successful, the best performers should be assigned to the appropriate tasks and everyone should be given an assignment that best fits his or her skills.

PATTERN:
DESIGNERS ARE OUR FRIENDS

Problem

How can System Test work effectively with the Designers?

Solution

Build rapport with Designers. Approach Designers with the attitude that the system has a problem that both of you need to work on together to resolve. This gives the Designer and the System Tester a common goal. Always *Document the Problem*.

Resulting Context

The System Tester/Designer relationship becomes one of cooperation in an attempt to resolve a problem. Designers are less likely to become defensive and "run and hide" when a System Tester approaches.

Rationale

We are all employees of the same company and should work with each other to solve problems. Designers and System Testers are partners. Building good relationships with Designers gets things done faster. Personalizing problems makes Designers defensive. We can learn from each other and benefit both.

Related Patterns

All members of a team should remain open to the contributions of other members. "Don't Flip the Bozo Bit" (McCarthy, 1995; Rising, 1996) and close off the relationship, regardless of past history. *Design By Team* (Harrison, 1996) stresses the importance of working together to develop and design software. This notion can be extended to include the Designer/System Tester relationship.

PATTERN:
GET INVOLVED EARLY

Problem

How can System Test maximize the support from the Designers?

Forces

- During early development phases, System Testers have test plans to write.
- Impacts of social relationships aren't considered critical by the project.

Solution

Establish a good working relationship with the Designers early in the project. Don't wait until you need to interact with a Designer. By that time it is too late. Trust must be built over time. One way to accomplish this is to learn the system and the features at the same time the Designer is learning them. Attend reviews of the requirements and design documentation. Invite the Designer to test plan reviews.

Resulting Context

When a good working relationship is built over time, it is easier to resolve problems when they are discovered.

Be sure that the relationship with the Designer does not affect your judgment as an effective System Tester. There can be a tendency to avoid areas of conflict when friends are involved, to look the other way when problems are found in a certain area if the Designer is a close friend. It is also dangerous to have too much information about an area. This can lead to testing that depends on this knowledge instead of an objective black box view.

Rationale
We are all more willing to work with people we know. Waiting until the heat of battle to get to know the people who can help you resolve problems leads to delays in solutions. If a trusting relationship has already been established, the problem-solving process is smoother.

Related Patterns
Early involvement is important in establishing that *Designers Are Our Friends*.

PATTERN:
TIME TO TEST

Alias
Test When There's Something to Test

Problem
When is it appropriate to start testing?

Context
The system can be broken into areas, such as features or functional areas that are minimally dependent on each other. Once an area is released for system testing, it would not be impacted in future software loads. Remember that *Designers Are Our Friends*.

Forces
- Designers don't want testing to start until everything is "perfect."
- Testers want to start testing early.
- Testing an incomplete system may require retesting on later software loads.

Solution
Start testing when an area of functionality is available for testing, but not before. An agreement should be reached with the Designers that the area is ready for testing (see *Designers Are Our Friends)*. Track areas that aren't ready for testing so you don't waste time in those areas.

Resulting Context

More interval is available for testing if testing begins on early increments of the software loads. This also exposes the load to more testing, which will uncover more problems. More problems will be discovered earlier, when there is time to correct them.

By starting early, there is a risk that regression testing of the area will be required. Use an *End User Viewpoint* for this testing. Additionally, if testing is started too early, untested fixes start finding their way into the load.

Rationale

System testing should not start until all the software is finished. However, waiting until everything is complete leaves no time for doing all the system testing. System Test is often pushed to start testing as early as possible. However, starting to test the system too early is a waste of time. It is possible, however, to test parts of the system that are ready earlier than others.

Related Patterns

You must *Take Time* in determining whether an area is ready for testing.

PATTERN
TAKE TIME

Problem

How much time should Designers be given to finish work that is behind schedule?

Context

Testing for an area is scheduled to start, design is not complete. Remember that *Designers Are Our Friends*.

Forces

- Designers always want more time.
- More effort up front usually produces a better product in the end.

Solution

Give Designers the time they request, within reason. It is *Time to Test* other areas in the mean time.

Resulting Context

System testing will take less time if the design quality is better.

Rationale

Higher quality systems take less time to test than poorer quality systems. By giving Designers the time they truly need, there will be a significant pay-back in the end in avoiding the effort to test and fix all the problems in a poor quality system.

Increasing planned development time 15% cuts the number of defects in half (Remer, 1996).

All the forces of *Take Time* and *Time to Test* must be carefully weighed before deciding which pattern to follow.

TESTING EFFICIENCY

As stated in the context, it is not possible to completely test a system. The following patterns steer the tester toward areas that are more likely to contain errors. Test-plan development and testing can concentrate on these areas to find more problems earlier in the project.

PATTERN:
"UNCHANGED" INTERFACES

Problem

How should testing of third party interface functionality developed outside the company be scheduled?

Context

Interfaces developed outside the company are used in the system, in whole or in part, without changes to that interface. The interface could be a graphical user interface (GUI), a library, a hardware component or any other third-party product. The initial assumption is that if third party interface functionality is to be supported in the new system and if the same interface has been used in other systems and has not changed, then no testing or very limited testing is required.

Forces
- Time can be saved by not testing or performing limited testing of unchanged third party interface functionality.
- There is limited knowledge or training on third party software.
- The project feels that unchanged code will function as expected in the new product.

Solution

The System Tester must not fall into the trap of assuming that unchanged interfaces will function correctly in the new system. The System Tester must pay particular attention to any interface ported from outside the company that is not assigned for inclusion in the feature list of the new system. Since no one else is directly impacted by this change, the System Tester needs to be proactive in scheduling this testing.

Testing the correct operation of the interface on the new system should begin as soon as that interface is chosen for the new system. This will verify the functionality of that interface. Once the ported interface is operational in the new system, testing should begin immediately to ensure that the functionality is the same and that it does not affect the rest of the system. This can be done while the designers are working on the new features for the system.

Resulting Context

System test will find problems with ported interfaces early in the project's life cycle and limit the impact of any problems on the system release. This will allow focused effort on fixing the problems while there is still time to change how the system functions, what is included in the system, or when a system is ready to be released. Less overall effort and stress will be expended during system development, time will be saved, and the system will be released as planned.

Rationale

No matter how established a product is or how well written a chunk of code is, if it is not an in-house product there will always be problems with porting that functionality into a new system. If testing of the functionality is not begun immediately, problems will invariably be found at the worst possible time—right before release of the system.

Any product brought in from outside the company will not meet the quality, functionality, or customer expectations of the company. Thus, changes will be made.

PATTERN:
AMBIGUOUS DOCUMENTATION

Problem

How can possible problem areas of the system be pinpointed so that the most problems can be found in the least amount of time?

Context

Feature design documentation and/or user documentation is available. This documentation can be the requirement from which the feature is developed, documentation developed by the Designer, or documentation developed for the customer.

Forces

- Some areas of a system are more likely to have problems than others.

Solution

Study the documentation available on the system. Look for areas that seem ambiguous or ill-defined. Write test plans that cover these areas more thoroughly and concentrate testing in these areas (see *End User Viewpoint*). If Designers can tell you all about a feature, it probably works. It's what they can't tell you that needs attention during testing.

Call these areas to the attention of the Designers so that problems in these areas can be resolved prior to system testing. These areas should still be tested more thoroughly than areas that are well documented and well understood.

Resulting Context

Problems are likely to be found and corrected earlier.

Rationale

If there's more than one interpretation of the documentation, Designers will write more than one code interpretation. This must be uncovered during system test if it is not detected earlier. If you *Get Involved Early*, there is a better chance of getting documentation fixed early, and getting the implementation correct. If problems still exist, finding them early makes it more likely that they will be fixed. Good specs help everyone!

Related Patterns

Reviewing documentation reinforces the idea that *Designers Are Our Friends*.

PATTERN:
USE OLD PROBLEM REPORTS

Problem

What areas of the system should be targeted for testing so that the most problems can be found in the least amount of time?

Context

Testing of existing features is being considered. Problem reports from previous releases are available.

Solution

Examine problem reports from previous releases to help select test cases. Since it would be inefficient to retest for all old problems, look at problems reported after the last valid "snapshot" of the system. Categorize problem reports to see if a trend is determined that could be used for additional testing.

Resulting Context

Problems that still exist will be found and corrected.

Rationale

Because a problem report represents something that escaped in a previous release, this could be a good indicator of a problem in the current load. Problem reports tend to point to areas where problems always occur. Problem reports often represent a symptom that is difficult to connect with an underlying problem.

Additionally, fixes of a previous release are often done in parallel with new development on the current releases. These fixes don't always find their way into the current load.

PATTERN:
PROBLEM AREA

Problem

What areas of the system should receive concentrated testing, regardless of the features being implemented?

Context

Historical data is available for the system under test.

Solution

Keep a list of persistent problem areas and test cases used to verify them, not just for resolution of the current problems, but also for use in subsequent testing. Test these areas thoroughly, even if there are no new features going into them. Retest regularly using these test cases, even one last time before the release goes out the door.

These areas can be identified by considering the following: the experience of the System Testers; *Use Old Problem Reports*; *Ambiguous Documen-*

tation; and observing areas that designers tend to avoid from one release to the next.

Resulting Context
By testing problem areas early in the schedule, more time is available to correct any problems found.

Rationale
Areas of the system that historically have problems don't magically become error-free overnight. Some problems occur in every incremental release of the system. Some areas have problems in every release. These problems and problem areas should be tracked so that they can be systematically retested on every release of the system.

TESTING STRATEGY

Once a testing strategy has been set into place and testing has commenced, the following patterns help find problems that might not be found until it is too late to correct them. They also ensure that the delivered product will be acceptable to the customer.

PATTERN:
BUSY SYSTEM

Problem
Under what conditions should system tests be executed to find the most problems?

Context
Simulators exist that provide a reasonable amount of activity on the system.

Solution
Test in an environment that simulates a busy system. The level of activity need not stress the system, but should approach a level that the system regularly experiences.

Resulting Context
Tests that work fine under normal conditions often fail in an unacceptable manner when the system is busy.

Rationale
It is redundant to run a feature test case that has already passed during the system testing phase. However, these cases will often fail under a busy

system. A telephony system can be busied using a Traffic Load Simulator that simulates phone calls into the system. By running feature tests with a moderate amount of traffic on the system, problems are found that don't appear when the system is idle.

Related Patterns
Don't Trust Simulations.

PATTERN:
DON'T TRUST SIMULATIONS

Problem
How should the test environment be configured when using test simulations?

Context
Simulations of system use are available, including simulators of real uses of the system.

Forces
- Simulators are often a more accessible testing environment.
- Some testing cannot be accomplished without using simulations.
- It's impossible to have a real-world environment for all testing.

Solution
Test in an environment as close to the real world as possible.

Resulting Context
Systems that handle simulations, which tend to give predictable input to the system, often fail in the real world because of unpredictable behaviors. By supplementing the simulation with real world testing, such situations are minimized.

Rationale
There is a proper use for simulations, but they are not substitutes for real-world testing. Although a large portion of the testing can be done using simulations, testing of the system is not complete without providing real world scenarios in the testing process. A simulator can run a test case successfully 100 times, but the test case may fail when run by a human because of unpredictable behaviors that are introduced.

Related Patterns
Follow *End User Viewpoint* to accomplish real world testing.

PATTERN:
END USER VIEWPOINT

Problem
How do you test the new features in a system without repeating testing
that has already been completed?

Forces
- Duplicate testing takes more time in the schedule.
- There is a perception that code that has not changed since feature
  testing doesn't need system testing.
- Because of feature interactions, changes to one feature can break
  another.

Solution
Test outside the normal scope of the features. Take the *End User Viewpoint*.
Don't system test with the same tests used for feature testing. Use the cus-
tomer documentation. Test feature interactions.

Resulting Context
By testing from an *End User Viewpoint*, flaws in the system, as the end user
will use it, can be discovered and corrected before the system is shipped.
These tests expand the scope of previous testing and are not redundant.

Rationale
End users don't use systems as they are designed. Designers develop features,
but the system is sold to provide services to the end user. It is these services
that the end user sees, not the features that are developed by the Designers.

PATTERN:
UNUSUAL TIMING

Problem
What additional testing should be done that may not be covered by the
test plans for an area?

Solution
Test unusual timing. Run tests more quickly or slowly than expected. Abort
tests in the middle of execution. Real end users will have an *End User
Viewpoint*.

Resulting Context
Errors caused by unusual timings are detected and corrected.

Rationale
Things that work properly under normal timing conditions may break under unusual timing conditions.

Testing for unusual timing scenarios is often difficult to set up and run. Test cases that are difficult to run are the ones that probably need to be run the most.

PATTERN:
MULTIPLE PROCESSORS

Problem
What strategy should be followed when System Testing a system comprised of multiple processors?

Solution
Test across multiple processors.

Resulting Context
Problems that occur in one processor will probably occur in other processors. Tests that pass on one processor may fail on another.

Rationale
When a problem is found in one processor, that feature will usually have problems running on other processors. A dirty feature is a dirty feature.

A feature may be designed for a single processor, assuming that it will then work for all processors.

PATTERN:
SCRATCH 'N SNIFF

Alias
Problem Cluster

Problem
Once testing is started, what is a good strategy for determining what to test next?

Context
A problem has already been found in an area.

Solution
Test areas where problems have already been found.

Resulting Context
Problematic areas will be targeted sooner and problems resolved earlier.

Rationale
Problems tend to be found in clusters. A problem found in an area is a good indicator of other problems in the same area. *Scratch 'n Sniff*—if it smells bad, it probably is.

Bugs are like roaches: Find one and you'll find a lot of them. They also evolve quickly.

Testing can be organized so that a "first pass" is taken that tests the breadth of the system. Half of the problems found will be in 15% of the modules (Davis, 1995). Deeper testing of the areas with problems will likely find more problems.

Related Patterns
Use Old Problem Reports for areas that may need more testing.

PATTERN:
STRANGE BEHAVIOR

Problem
What should be done when a feature is working, but not as expected?

Context
The System Tester has participated in the system testing of previous releases of the product and is familiar with feature behavior.

Solution
Take any unusual behavior as an indication of a possible problem and follow up. This should be done even if the problem is not related to the test being executed. Look for features that behave differently. Be wary when familiar tests produce results that while acceptable, are not what was expected.

Resulting Context
A problem won't be missed because it doesn't produce feature behavior that is not significantly different from the expected outcome.

Rationale
Changes to the way a feature works, even though it may still work cor-

rectly, often indicate that the feature may have broken. If the change is deliberate, all System Testers should be notified.

PATTERN:
KILLER TEST

Problem
How can the quality of a system under development be determined?

Context
Development is drawing to a close. The system is stable. The features are stable and all parties involved, especially management, are interested in how close the system is to being ready for release.

Solution
Develop a favorite *Killer Test* (usually a set of test cases) that can be run at any time, a test that always seems to find problems. This test should provide good system coverage and should be expected to fail, in some manner, most of the time. You can borrow a *Killer Test*, but it is better if the test is based on your own experience, as the effectiveness of the test depends on the individual's skill and knowledge of the system.

Killer Test is only used toward the end of a releases and is above and beyond a common regression test. It tends to be free-wheeling in nature and typically hard to document. The success of this type of testing is directly related to the individual running the test, because *The Tester's More Important Than the Test Cases*. Don't wait until the very end of the release or there won't be time to correct the problems found.

Resulting Context
The results of the tests are a good gauge of the stability of the system. By finding and fixing the uncovered problems, the system becomes incrementally more stable.

Rationale
A test that usually fails and can be run in a reasonably short time gives a good measure of how the system is stabilizing. Additionally, since problems are likely to be found, this type of testing is highly efficient.

PROBLEM RESOLUTION

The following patterns aid in communication and resolution of problems.

PATTERN:
DOCUMENT THE PROBLEM

Problem
How should problems found in testing be communicated?

Context
A problem tracking system is available for problem documentation.

Forces
- Testers want to be sure that problems are fixed.
- Designers have good intentions but don't always get problems resolved.
- Problem tracking systems are often cumbersome.
- Problem tracking systems make problem areas very visible.
- People inherently avoid documentation.
- Problem reports are often used as indicators of a Designer's competence.
- Problem reports are often used as an indicator of project status.

Solution
Write a problem report. Don't argue with a Designer. Don't accept a well-intentioned promise that may or may not get results. Don't informally document the problem. The project should not keep a private list of problems.

Testers should not be penalized for documenting problems. Designers should not be punished when problems are documented against them.

Do your homework before reporting problems to Designers. Be sure you can explain what happened. Designers always want to see a system debug output.

Resulting Context
Problems documented in a problem tracking system are more likely to get resolved in a timely manner.

Rationale
Use all the tools that are available, even if they are cumbersome. By thoroughly and officially documenting a problem, information does not get lost and a timely resolution is more likely.

Documenting problems is always an area that a project wants to cut back. Cutting back causes many more problems than it seems to solve. In the end, it always takes longer to determine what the problems are than to resolve them.

Related Patterns

Remember, *Designers Are Our Friends* and System Testers should *Get Involved Early*.

PATTERN:
ADOPT-A-PROBLEM

Problem

How can nagging problems be resolved efficiently so that productive testing can continue?

Context

A problem has been uncovered in the system that has no clear cut solution. Resolving the problem will most likely take a great deal of effort, or worse, it might not get resolved. This pattern should be followed in the context of *Designers Are Our Friends*.

Forces

- Some problems are difficult to reproduce.
- Ambiguous problems result in ambiguous fixes.
- Designers don't have time to track down problems they may not be able to resolve.

Solution

Adopt a problem. Treat it as if it were your child. If you uncover a difficult problem, stick with it until it is resolved. *Document the Problem*. Retest the problem periodically to gather more data on it. Become the responsible Designer for the problem.

Resulting Context

Following the progress of the solution for a problem shows the Designer that you are concerned about getting the problem resolved. Taking an active role in resolving the problem can prevent the problem from bouncing among Designers. Periodically retesting the problem leads to a better understanding of the problem and more symptomatic data. As a result, the probability that the Designer can solve the problem and provide a solution in a timely manner is increased.

Once the problem is resolved, retest for it periodically to ensure that it stays fixed. If the problem reappears consistently, it may be a *Problem Area*.

Rationale

Designers have a multitude of things to do. They tend to work first on things that are known, concrete, and easy. Because of this, trying to resolve a difficult problem often gets pushed to a lower priority. By adopting the problem, there are in effect two people working on the problem. As the System Tester, you can continue to test and debug the problem to gain more information on it, be it information that the Designer requests or information that appears to be different from previously collected data. The attention you give to the problem also communicates to the Designer that you think it is important to get the problem resolved and are willing to help in facilitating the problem resolution. This second point is important, because you should not come across as a nagging irritant that won't go away, but as a willing participant in the resolution process. Be sure the problem doesn't become a *Pet Peeve*.

PATTERN:
PET PEEVE

Problem
The validity of a problem has been debated to the point of holding up progress. What should be done to resolve the debate?

Context
This problem should be applied in the context of *Adopt-A-Problem* and *Document the Problem*.

Solution
When a problem is adopted, be sure that the problem doesn't become an annoying thorn in the Designer's side. Don't carry concern for an unresolved problem to extremes, especially when you have no supporting documentation. Keep discussions at a professional level.

When the status of the problem becomes a detriment to progress, the System Tester should bring in a third party, such as a requirements group, to help resolve the impasse. At this point, stop following the status of the problem and start testing other areas. Don't involve the third party too early in the process.

Resulting Context
Problems are resolved and not forgotten, but no one goes overboard in focusing on one problem to the detriment of the rest of the system.

Rationale
When deciding to *Adopt-A-Problem*, a System Tester can become so focused

on a particular problem that it becomes a *Pet Peeve*. Carried to an extreme, this can destroy a good working relationship between the System Tester and the Designer. Problems in the system should not be taken personally by the System Tester (Davis, 1995).

KNOWN USES

The individuals involved in the mining of these patterns have many years of experience in System Testing on the GTD-5® and other projects at AG Communication Systems. The GTD-5® is a central office telephone switch that has gone through many major releases over the past 16 years. The other projects have benefited from this experience and validate the existence of these patterns. Some releases of the GTD-5® and other projects have suffered the consequences of not applying one or more of these patterns. In addition these patterns have been observed and used by some of these individuals while employed at other companies involved in the development of real-time embedded systems. More information on AG Communication Systems and its product line can be found at http://www.agcs.com.

ACKNOWLEDGMENTS

These system test patterns were mined in a patterns mining workshop held on May 10, 1996. The patterns were captured by David DeLano and Linda Rising with Greg Stymfal serving as facilitator for the group. The workshop was attended by the following AGCS System Testers: Dave Bassett, Arvind Bhuskute, Bob Bianca, Ray Fu, Hubert Fulkerson, Eric Johnstone, Rich Lamarco, Krishna Naidu, Ed Nuerenberg, and Lori Ryan. Many of these System Testers, as well as the following, have participated in reviews of the patterns: John Balzar, Terry Bartlett, Ernie Englehart, Carl Gilmore, Neil Khemlani, Jim Kurth, Bob Nations, John Ng, Jim Peterson, Mike Sapcoe, Bill Stapleton, Frank Villars, and Weldon Wong. Thanks to Dave Strand for suggesting the name *Scratch 'n Sniff.*

"Unchanged" Interfaces has been adapted from a pattern written by Mike Sapcoe during an earlier Patterns Writing course held by David and Linda.

We are grateful for the time and effort given by Ralph Johnson, Neil Harrison, and Brian Marick in shepherding these patterns. We would like to thank the participants of the PLoP '96 writers workshop for their many valuable comments.

REFERENCES

Cockburn, A. (1996). *A medical catalog of project management patterns* [On-line]. Unpublished manuscript. Available: URL: http://members.aol.com/acockburn/papers/plop96.htm.

Coplien, J. O. (1995). A generative development-process pattern language. In J. O. Coplien & D. C. Schmidt (Eds.), *Pattern languages of program design* (pp. 183–237). Reading, MA: Addison-Wesley. Available: URL: http://www.bell-labs.com/user/cope/Patterns/Process/index.html.

Davis, A. M. (1995). *201 principles of software development*. New York: McGraw-Hill.

DeMarco, T., & Lister, T. (1987). *Peopleware: Productive projects and teams* (pp. 45–47). New York: Dorset House.

Gamma, E., Helm, R., Johnson, R., & Vlissides, J. (1995). *Design patterns: Elements of reusable object-oriented software*. Reading, MA: Addison-Wesley.

Harrison, N. B. (1996). Organizational patterns for teams. In J. M. Vlissides, J. O. Coplien, & N. L. Kerth (Eds.), *Pattern languages of program design 2* (pp. 345–352). Reading, MA: Addison-Wesley.

McCarthy, J. (1995). #4: Don't flip the bozo bit. In J. McCarthy, *Dynamics of software development* (pp. 23, 30–32). Redmond, WA: Microsoft Press.

Olson, D. (1995). *Don Olson's patterns on the Wiki Wiki Web* [On-line]. Portland, OR: Portland Patterns Repository. Available: URL: http://c2.com/cgi/wiki?search=DonOlson

Remer, D. (1996). *Cost and schedule estimation for software development projects* (pp. SW 11–8, Guideline # 35). Los Angeles: UCLA.

Rising, L. (1996). *Don't flip the bozo bit* [On-line]. Phoenix, AZ: AG Communication Systems. Available: URL: http://www.agcs.com/patterns/BozoBit.html

Improving Software Development with Process and Organizational Patterns

Patricia Genualdi

genualdp@agcs.com

This article describes the Pasteur research program, which produced a process and organizational pattern language that can be used to improve productivity within software-development organizations. The researchers in the study included James Coplien, Brendan Cain, and Neil Harrison, of Bell Labs, now a part of Lucent Technologies.

The Pasteur research program focused on organizational role structure rather than more traditional artifacts and process steps. The researchers felt roles were more stable structures in modern software development. In addition, studying roles allowed them to gather data and observe the software-development process as it was practiced (Cain, Coplien, & Harrison, 1996).

After collecting and analyzing data from more than 40 organizations, the researchers found that successful organizations shared a number of attributes, values, and practices, despite the diversity of their products. Furthermore, these successful organizations did not have the same problems as unsuccessful organizations. The commonalties among successful organizations were found to be solutions to problems in unsuccessful organizations (Coplien, 1994). These practices were captured as patterns. A pattern is a solution to a problem in a context.[1] These patterns were solutions

---

[1] See the patterns-discussion FAQ: http://g.oswego.edu/dl/pd-FAQ/pd-FAQ.html

to organization or process problems, and collectively they form an organizational and process pattern language. Coplien claims this is a pattern language of good practice in established best-of-class organizations and that this pattern language provides a model of what makes great organizations great (Coplien, 1994). Incorporating these patterns into organizations should enable efficient and effective software development (Harrison & Coplien, 1996).

TRADITIONAL PROCESS METHODS

Current standards for process and organization, such as ISO 9000, focus on process reproducibility and reduction of performance variations. Organizations that follow these standards look to a process specification as the final word on development activities. In practice, there are several problems inherent in this approach (Cain et al., 1996).

The first problem is the lack of conformance between practice and specification. Many organizations do not build their process models with empirical models and data; instead they build "ideal" specifications and use these as a baseline for improvement, even though there is often a mismatch between the ideal specification and what is done in practice. For example, in one survey of developers in a large organization, 80% were working under officially granted process waivers. Clearly, the process standard didn't capture the essential, stable structure of the process (Cain et al., 1996). Coplien states that even in organizations with ISO process certification and healthy Capability Maturity Model (CMM) ratings, there is "only superficial correspondence between actual practice and the written process description" (Coplien, 1996).

The second problem involves incomplete and inconsistent process models. Most process models focus on tasks and events and fail to consider artifacts, roles, actors, and agents. Some processes like bug reporting can be understood from a task perspective. However, core processes of software development like architecture, design, implementation, and validation cannot be clearly understood from a task perspective (Cain et al., 1996).

Lastly, current process specifications do not capture long-term, stable process abstractions. Several dimensions of a process should be studied, including artifacts, organizational roles and structure, personal skill sets, and other factors. Due to resource constraints, however, this research has focused on organizational roles and structure, since these produce a more stable process abstraction and a better match for concurrent engineering organizations (Cain et al., 1996).

ORGANIZATION STUDIES

Instrumental organizations are defined in terms of coupling between actors or roles brought together by a common interest or objective. Role data was collected from more than 40 instrumental organizations, from engineers doing day-to-day design, coding, and fire-fighting problems. The organizations included large development organizations in AT&T and other telecommunication companies, as well as organizations producing software-development environment products, aerospace, and medical software (Cain et al., 1996).

CRC (classes, responsibilities, and collaborations) cards were used to gather data. The CRC cards supported highly participatory information-gathering techniques, which allowed the documentation of empirical behavior. In addition, the CRC cards allowed data to be collected in a group setting. Role play in a group setting is a powerful technique to help people recall past events and clarify corporate memory. Each card represents an organizational role, its responsibilities to the organization, and its collaborations with other roles (Cain et al., 1996).

There were drawbacks to using CRC cards, which included groupthink, consistency, and granularity. Groupthink is the tendency for a group to fall into a mode of social conformity. This was not a severe problem since most individuals in the study had strong personalities that avoided many of the problems of groupthink. The second drawback was consistency. Consistency is a problem when one organization has a name for a role and another organization uses the same name for a different role. The last drawback was granularity. The research group concentrated on roles but a complete understanding of process includes roles, actors, artifacts, and many other factors (Cain et al., 1996).

After collecting the CRC card data, the Pasteur environment was used to create graphical representations of the cards and analyze the data. The most common technique used was force-based relaxation rendering, in which the CRC cards are randomly displayed on a screen and allowed to move. Collaborations among the roles are an attraction force between the cards based on the strength of the collaboration. Cards with strong collaborations move toward each other, whereas cards with no or weak collaboration move away from each other. Eventually the cards end up in a stable state. Cards with many collaborations appear in the center of the display; these are usually key roles. Clusters are formed, indicating suborganizations. An interaction grid was also employed, a square matrix whose columns are roles that initiate collaborations and whose rows are the roles receiving the collaborations (Cain et al., 1996).

Using these visual techniques, the researchers were able to quickly gain insights into an organizational structure. The organizations themselves were also able to learn from these visualizations, because they provided portraits of the organizations that helped them understand structural problems. Usually the location of key roles confirmed expectations of team members, and helped explain exceptional or problematic behavior. One team noticed the remoteness of its architectural role in a social network diagram, which helped explain the lack of product focus in the organization (Cain et al., 1996).

In addition to studying visualizations, the researchers analyzed data based on roles, collaborations, and organization size (number of roles, not the number of people). In an organization with n roles, the possible number of collaborations is: $n(n+1)/2$. In most organizations, not all possible collaborations are exercised. The ratio of actual collaborations to possible collaborations is the communication saturation. As the number of roles increases, the number of collaborations increases as a linear function (not as the square of the number of roles as one might expect). This linear function is independent of the size of the organization. As a result, the communication saturation decreases. Smaller organizations usually have complete communication saturation, whereas larger organizations have communication saturations of 10% to 30%. Low saturation does not necessarily indicate a problem. Some roles may be independent and may not need collaborations with other roles. Large organizations probably have more role specialization to handle the complexity of the organization. Low saturation may increase the risk that critical information will not reach the right person or will not be received in a timely manner. None of the projects with large numbers of roles had high communication saturation; they were also not highly productive (Harrison & Coplien, 1996).

Good communication is important. The highly productive organizations that were studied had high communication saturation. There is, however, a cost associated with good communication, and it can be very high when organizations have a large number of roles. Organizations should simplify their structure by reducing the number of roles, making communication saturation easier and less costly (Cain et al., 1996).

Communication rates were also measured, using the communication-intensity ratio, the ratio of the busiest roles communication link count to the average communication link count of the organization. The intent was to measure to what extent communication is concentrated in a single role.

Ideally, an organization should have a low communication-intensity ratio; this indicates that communication is somewhat evenly distributed among the roles in the organization. Most productive projects had low communication-intensity ratios. A low communication-intensity ratio alone, however, does not ensure a highly productive organization. There were organizations with low communication-intensity ratios that had low productivity. As an organization grows, the busiest roles, usually producer roles, become even busier, instead of the communication being spread evenly among the roles. As a consequence, the busiest roles may end up devoting more effort to communication rather than producing the product (Harrison & Coplien, 1996).

PROCESS AND ORGANIZATIONAL PATTERNS

Organizations that were effective in productivity, quality, and short development intervals were an order of magnitude higher in productivity than other organizations studied. Highly productive organizations produced on the order of 10^3 lines of code per programmer month, whereas typical organizations produce 10^2 lines (Cain et al., 1996). By focusing on these organizations, the noise of programming language differences and other variables that are difficult to hold constant were ignored. These "hyper-productive" (Cain et al., 1996) or "hyperprogramming teams" (Harrison, 1996) displayed recurring themes. These recurring themes were captured as patterns that solve organizational and process problems. The following are examples from this collection.

Engage Customers is a pattern in which the customer role has significant communication links with the organization. The customer provides information to ensure not only that the product is built correctly, but also that the right product is built. Continuous engagement is key. Successful organizations engage the customer early and throughout product development. If a customer is not available, a surrogate customer can be designated (Harrison & Coplien, 1996).

Another pattern is the *Work Flows Inward* pattern. In this pattern, it is not enough for the developer to have a central role; the direction of communication to the central role also must be considered. When the central roles are consumers rather than producers of communication, the organization tends to be highly productive. These organizations are referred to as in-directed organizations (Cain et al., 1996; Harrison & Coplien, 1996).

An interaction grid of an in-directed organization shows that peripheral roles generate requests for work. These roles usually have external connections and are, therefore, in a position to convey external needs to the producer roles in the center of the organization. The producers then have the information they need to develop the product with just a few sources and have more time to produce (Harrison, 1996).

An interaction grid of an out-directed organization shows that the central roles create work for everyone else. If the producers are in central roles, they must get information from several sources and, therefore, have less time to produce. A common scenario in out-directed organizations is that the central roles are dominated by management roles. The collaborations in these organizations almost always flow from the manager in the center to other roles in the organization (Cain et al., 1996). Organizations such as these are dominated by the management of the project rather than the development of the product, and it is nearly impossible for these organizations to be very productive (Harrison & Coplien, 1996).

Another pattern of highly productive teams is *Distribute Work Evenly*. This pattern has not been officially documented; however, it is worth mentioning here. Most organizations focus on the developer role. In highly productive organizations, this focus does not become extreme. Communication is spread evenly throughout the organization, which gives an even balance of work. Members of highly productive teams work as a unit and divide the work evenly among themselves (Harrison, 1996). These teams have a small standard deviation in the distribution of work across roles (Cain et al., 1996).

These patterns, and indeed all the patterns in the collection, are meant to be used in a generative way, meaning they will indirectly help to generate the right process. The process can be defined as the "the patterns of activity within an organization." A parallel can be drawn between generating the right process and the right architecture (Coplien, 1995). The building architect Christopher Alexander stated that architectures "can't be made, but only generated, indirectly, by the ordinary actions of the people, just as a flower cannot be made, but only generated from a seed" (Alexander, 1979).

ORGANIZATIONS THAT CAN BENEFIT

The pattern language will most likely benefit young, emerging organizations in which there is a tight-knit group, the roles are defined, and eventually the organizational structure stabilizes. Established organizations, especially in the public service and utilities sectors, are usually bureaucracies. The aim of the pattern language is a changing, growing organization that is often not a traditional corporate structure. Although the patterns work better when building an organization from scratch, they can be applied to an organization in trouble to restore the ability of people to excel (Coplien, 1995).

Let's consider an example of how process and organization patterns helped an engineering organization in trouble. The engineering organization was at ParcPlace Systems. The organization had been through many changes in the last couple of years and was starting to see productivity losses. This organization, which had once performed well, was starting to show signs that the old ways were breaking down. Richard Gabriel, vice president of engineering, had attended PLoP (Pattern Languages of Programming Conference) in 1994 and had seen some organizational and process patterns. He invited Jim Coplien to visit ParcPlace. Before Coplien's arrival, copies of the process and organizational pattern language were distributed. When Coplien arrived, he spent time with the engineering staff doing organizational role-play, which captured the events in a recent project development. The project members tracked their responsibilities and role interactions using CRC cards. Coplien then gave the group some feedback and, later, a final report (Coplien, 1996).

Six months later, Gabriel claimed his organization had turned around. The organizational pattern names became part of the organization's day-to-day vocabulary. After seeing what was possible and knowing that the patterns came from "real" successful organizations, the engineering organization aspired to renewed success in their new business setting. At the time of Coplien's report, the organization had rounded the corner and was on the mend, morale was up, and the organization was becoming more productive (Coplien, 1996).

Organizational patterns are not a quick fix and are no more of a panacea than process reengineering programs designed around ISO 9000 or the CMM. The process and organizational pattern language helped the ParcPlace engineers overcome problems. The pattern names became part of their vocabulary, implying that patterns became part of their everyday mind-set (Coplien, 1996).

The patterns help an organization think of itself in terms of principles and values instead of concentrating on surface symptoms. In this sense, what happened at ParcPlace was truly generative; changes in values and principles led to lasting behavior changes. Changing behavior for its own sake often leaves principles and values untouched. Eventually, values and principles will win out even in organizations that give lip service to the changes dictated by a process program. This explains why so many organizations exhibit process behavior different from the formal process documents (Coplien, 1996).

PATTERN CHALLENGES

Introducing the process and organizational patterns into an organization does have challenges. Even though organizations exist that have these patterns, building new organizations using these patterns can be a very big task. In addition, the patterns describe practices that are different from those in most projects. Furthermore, cultural taboos and standards will leave many patterns out of reach for some organizations. Finally, some patterns, for example, *Domain Expertise in Roles*, presumes that experts are available, which may not be the case (Coplien, 1995).

CONCLUSIONS

Process and organizational patterns offer a new perspective on the software-development process and may prove to be effective in improving productivity within organizations. The patterns come from research based on real organizations and empirical studies. Instead of studying traditional process artifacts, the researchers studied social aspects of software development including roles and communication aspects. They found good communication paths are key in highly productive teams. In addition, the structure of the organization and how it affects the roles of the team was found to be important. These insights from the research have been codified into this collection of patterns. These patterns can augment existing processes and methodologies to provide positive directions for improving productivity in software-development organizations.

REFERENCES

Christopher, A. (1979). *The timeless way of building*. New York: Oxford University Press.

Cain, B. G., Coplien, J. O., & Harrison, N. B. (1996, November). Social patterns in productive software development organizations. *Annals of Software Engineering, 2*, 259–286.

Coplien, J. O. (1995). A generative development-process pattern language. In J. O. Coplien & D. C. Schmidt (Eds.), *Pattern languages of program design*. Reading, MA: Addison-Wesley.

Coplien, J. O. (1996, January). The human side of patterns. *C++ Report*, 8(1), 73–80.

Harrison, N. B., & Coplien, J. O. (1996, May/June). Patterns of productive software organizations. *Bell Labs Technical Journal*, 1(1), 138–145.

Organizational Patterns at AG Communication Systems

Norm Janoff
janoffn@agcs.com

A G Communication Systems (AGCS) became aware of organizational patterns in 1995 by way of design patterns. Linda Rising had introduced design patterns to AGCS earlier in the year. In response to a coach's question about other types of patterns, Linda distributed an article written by Jim Coplien, "A Generative Development—Process Pattern Language" (Coplien, 1995). The "paper introduces a family of patterns that can be used to shape a new organization and its development processes" (Coplien, 1994). Linda figured that would be the last she would hear about it. To her surprise, Charlie Schulz, V. P. of Product Development (PD), and the PD leadership team was very interested in organizational patterns. The leadership team realized that they could compare our organization to a "language [that as] a whole captures essential characteristics of high-productivity organizations" (Coplien, 1994). Linda was asked to coordinate a visit by Jim Coplien to AGCS in Phoenix to learn more.

Discussions between Linda and Jim settled on having Jim lead three teams through a CRC card exercise to determine the key roles and interactions among the roles for each team. CRC cards (which stands for classes, responsibilities, and collaborators) had been developed as a software-design tool by Beck and Cunningham to support their work on software architecture and implementation in the mid-1980s (Beck,1991; Coplien, 1996; Wilkinson,1995).

Concurrent with our introduction of organizational patterns, PD was in its first year of a major transition to self-directed work teams (SDWTs). The formation of these teams had dramatically increased a coach's span of control (up to 60:1) and allocated most administrative duties (budget, scheduling, quality processes) to designers as specialized roles, in addition to their regular design responsibilities. As expected with any major organizational change, there was a lot of grumbling in the halls about what wasn't working with the new teams. As it turned out, the generative pattern language (Coplien, 1994) provided objective criteria to evaluate the resulting organizational structure on a team or project basis against patterns that contained supporting design rationale. While the leadership team did not physically bring a copy of Jim Coplien's "A Generative Development—Process Pattern Language" article (Coplien, 1995) into their organizational-restructuring meetings, the resulting organization is consistent with a number of patterns presented in the article.

For example, Pattern 11, *Developer Controls Process* (Coplien, 1995), states "[P]lace the Developer role at a hub of the process for a given feature." The resulting context warns, "[T]hough Developer should be a key role, care must be taken not to overburden it." On the GTD-5 (a large real-time central office switching system), the developer was overburdened and the important administrative tasks distributed to "rolees" were being crowded out by schedule pressure and a general lack of skill and interest in performing these administrative tasks. The solution developed in PD was to create a new position to work with both the coach and designers in accomplishing these administrative tasks. While it is critical that developers be involved in budget, schedule, and quality issues, an engineer with skill and interest in these tasks can coordinate these activities, reflect developer concerns, and get the required information into the schedule or budget in a timely manner. This approach is consistent with Alistair Cockburn's *Sacrificial Lamb*, which is covered in his web site http://members.aol.com/acockburn/index.html.

Another issue facing SDWTs was the degree of the coach's interaction with team issues. SDWT training had emphasized that the team make its own decisions, and coaches tried to let the team grow in their decision-making capabilities. However, some teams on the GTD-5 appeared to be suffering from the lack of an ultimate decision maker. The project manager was too far removed and the coach was too distant for the teams or reluctant to make decisions for the teams, lest they be labeled as "unempowering." These issues match the forces in Pattern 12, *Patron* (Coplien, 1995), which says, "[G]ive the project access to a visible, high-level manager, who champions the project cause. The patron can be the final arbiter for project decisions, which provides a driving force for the organization to make decisions quickly." From this pattern the organization strengthened the project manager, who was once again charged with greater project responsibility and decision authority. The project manager asked coaches to be more involved in project issues and provide more active coaching.

Finally, *Conway's Law,* Pattern 14, (Coplien, 1995; alias, *Organization Follows Architecture,* or *Architecture Follows Organization*) proved its merit relative to the GTD-5 organizational structure. The mature GTD-5 had historically been functionally organized. With the need for rapid feature deployment, the organization moved to a feature organization with virtual functional areas to maintain the integrity of the source code. Difficulties arose between feature and function: Designers on features were sometimes too busy to review functional area code fixes, control over source changes across multiple features impacting the same modules was confusing, and source integrity was a concern.

The issue was whether the functional area teams would be responsive enough in the new world of rapid feature deployment. The functional areas claimed they could meet this challenge, and the organization changed back to functional teams with virtual feature teams to coordinate a specific feature across the functional areas.

These are three instances in which organizational problems were objectively compared to the generative pattern language. Changes were made to address the organizational problems.

Let's go back now to the work led by Jim Coplien with the three project teams at AGCS. The purpose of Coplien's visit was to enable the teams to "hold a mirror" to themselves to better understand their team dynamics.

The teams varied substantially with respect to the market served and team experience. The GPU (general processing unit) provides auxiliary processing within the telecommunication network. The team was experienced and had successfully developed a new platform and several update releases.

The IN (intelligent network) feature team had bonded during a previous project that did not receive market acceptance. The team examined was a subset of the former team; each remaining member shared a similar view of that experience. (See Don Olson's [1993] Pattern: *Train Hard, Fight Easy.*)

The third team, PDI/LDI, was a feature team on the GTD-5 charged with key changes to the software architecture that would enable future development to continue in an efficient manner.

In addition to Jim Coplien, the following AT&T representatives contributed to the meetings and the analysis of the discussion: Robert Brownlie, AT&T Quest; Lynette Parker, AT&T Operations Systems Architect (who does project management assessments and architecture reviews); and Pat Sciacca, AT&T Quest (who performs organizational intervention and is an expert on teams).

Overall the AT&T participants found the teams to be "at least a quartile above the other teams studied in the Pasteur project." This quote and what follows is a summary of AT&T's "Notes on AGCS Visit" (AT&T, 1995). For additional details on the Pasteur Project see Patricia Genualdi's article in Part II).

The observers saw "the intentional direction to move to SDWTs having interesting ramifications on software projects." In addition they commented that "the concentration on how to move the leader out of the SDWT may be causing some of the discomfort within the project teams." The observers also noted "the informal atmosphere and the sense of fun that seemed prevalent throughout the teams" and the fact that "the budgeting process . . . appears to be extremely simple and responsive."

What follows are the AT&T observers' and Jim Coplien's comments relative to each team. This information was used by each team in the spirit of continuous improvement.

Looking specifically at the PDI/LDI effort, comments reflected the following:

- The team defined roles using a top-down approach (i.e., by working from roles that existed previously, then paring them down to what they feel is necessary).
- Both the team and the observers felt that too many roles existed, or at least tasks within roles.
- Six months seems like too short a time for people to be in roles during a time when everyone is "learning" the roles. (As indicated previously, a new position was created to provide a champion for these roles.)

The organizational patterns make use of the Pasteur process research and tools. Jim Coplien analyzed the data via the Pasteur tools and provided the following observations:

- The coach and designer roles share the center of the network. Usually it is a bad sign to see the coach at the center (see Pattern 11: *Developer Controls Process* and Pattern 29: *Work Flows Inward* [Coplien,1995]). It is good to see the designer at the center, though they should be a work sink rather than source. Also, it looks as though the organization has fallen into one of the very patterns that self-directed teams try to avoid: management centrality. Most organizations we study have a much weaker management role than we find in this process.

- The Big Picture role is near the center: a wonderful role, well-placed in the network (see Pattern 13: *Architect Controls Product* [Coplien, 1995]).
- The tester role is tightly engaged and near the center; this correlates well to successful organizations (see Pattern 19: *Engage QA* [Coplien, 1995]).
- The capability leader has a strong role in the organization. Is this a crucial role? (Yes, the capability leader is the technical leader for a given feature, resolving technical problems and interface issues.)
- The architect is far too disengaged for my comfort; only five roles are more ignored. (Due to the role of the capability leader.)
- The function teams are more disengaged than I would like to see. (Yes, this was a problem. The organizational change back to functional teams on the GTD-5 is intended to resolve this issue.)
- The interaction grid suggests that the organization violates Pattern 29:*Work Flows Inward* (Coplien,1995). The feature coach, designer, and Big Picture roles initiate interactions with a wide cross-section of the organization, yet they're less frequently consulted by other roles.

Although the PDI/LDI team was developing one feature on the GTD-5 (other teams were also contributing to the project), the GPU team, while coordinating their release dates with the GTD-5, operated as an independent team. The AT&T observers provided the following comments:

- The project is 4 years old.
- They are working on the 4th or 5th release.
- They have release intervals of 6 to 18 months.
- The team is well versed in object language (C++).
- The team is smoothly functioning and mature, with well-understood roles and strong team sense.
- They operate according to a "chief programmer" paradigm.
- The chief programmer/team leader encapsulates the project history.
- The external customer interface is the architect—a really cool idea. They have evolved from using simulation to scenarios to use cases

to define requirements. They have expressed interest in getting the customer more involved in their use cases. Mainstream work progressed along several threads based on use cases. [E]xpect a lot of formal and informal coordination would be necessary to ensure that things are done when they need to be done.

- They have a very high quality product (very few defects detected by customer).
- An interesting inconsistency exists between apparent performance and formal expectation of performance: the most important customer expectation is on-time delivery, but this team admits that they have never managed an on-time delivery yet (but estimation is a priority and they are getting better).
- The projects are always under budget, even though this is apparently not as important as on-time delivery from the customer's perspective.
- We wonder whether there is a transition plan for when the team leader moves on. His role has been pivotal.
- Future success will depend on the team's ability to successfully transition the chief programmer role—either to another chief programmer or to a different team-operational paradigm.

Turning to the IN team, the following observations were recorded:

- This team is self-selected (Pattern 2: *Self-Selecting Team* [Coplien, 1995]) and self-directed (Pattern 11: *Developer Controls Process* [Coplien, 1995]).
- The project does not have a customer yet (Pattern 20: *Engage Customers* [Coplien, 1995]).
- The team believes in their product (doing a proof of concept).
- The team likes working with each other, is highly productive, and has good chemistry.
- The team has a high level of confidence in itself.
- The team is internally motivated. They look within the team for motivation, not outside.
- Team members are flexible and fill gaps as needed.
- Team members are willing (eager?) to learn new technical skills.
- The team has a very high truck number (the number of people hit by a truck that would severely damage a team—a higher number means the project is not as dependent on one or two team members).

- The team has strong social roles that are a result of these particular people in this combination.
- The team behaves hierarchically outside its comfort zone, but the team behaves participatively inside its comfort zone.
- It was impossible to differentiate among formal roles for this team. Instead the team was more energized by an exercise in which they identified their social or behavioral roles in the team (Pattern 6: *Domain Expertise in Roles* [Coplien, 1995]).
- Management has faith in the team (Pattern 12: *Patron* [Coplien, 1995]):
  — They believe in keeping together teams that work well.
  — They believe the potential for the team's product is high.
  — Management is willing to invest in the product without a customer.
- Frequent meetings are interspersed with individuals doing work.
- The team bonded as a result of sharing a negative experience (project canceled) and was formed from members who had a similar view of that experience.
- After that experience they got together to ask themselves what they could learn from the experience.
- The team trained together (Pattern: *TrainHardFightEasy* [Olson, 1993]).
- The team is adopting another emulous practice: When faced with idle time, they spend the time building general, application-independent reusable stuff: broker software, TCAP software, and the like. This (not!) keeps the team from being split up and staff reallocated at the end of design cycles (Pattern: *Casual Duty* [Olson, 1996]).

Organizational patterns have had a significant impact at AGCS at the team level as a result of management intervention. Coplien's (1995) "A Generative Development—Process Pattern Language" had a significant impact on how we organize to develop our software products.

REFERENCES

Beck, K. (1991). Think like an object. *UNIX Review, 9*(10), 39–43.
Coplien, J. O. (1995). A generative development—Process pattern language. In J. O. Coplien & D. C. Schmidt (Eds.), *Pattern languages of program design*. Reading, MA: Addison-Wesley.

Coplien, J. (1996, May/June). Patterns of productive software organizations. *AT&T Technical Journal, 75*(3), 52–63.

Olson, D. Patterns: http://c2.com/cgi/wiki? Regular Contributors.

Wilkinson, N. M. (1995). *Using CRC cards.* New York: SIGS Books.

HandsInView

Don Olson
olsond@agcs.com

Problem: The skier fails to commit downhill on steeps and bumps, resulting in slides, backward falls, and "yard sales."

Context: In order to explore the entire mountain environment, a skier must be comfortable and adaptable to any terrain and to rapid terrain change. To take advantage of this pattern the skier should be skiing at a level at which parallel turns can be linked consistently.

Forces:
- Fear of falling is the most basic of all responses.
- Reliance on equipment is essential.
- Continuous movement is essential.
- Fatigue can be a factor in long descents.
- Commitment downhill over skis is essential for skis to function as designed.

Solution: Concentrate on keeping the hands in view. Bring them into sight immediately after each pole plant and turn.

Resulting Context: Keeping the hands in view changes the alignment of the body from sitting timidly back and allowing the edges to skid out from under the skier. Thus, keeping the hands in view pulls the body forward and thus downhill, bringing the skier's weight over the downhill ski, forcing the edge to bite and turn.

Rationale: As steepness increases, the natural tendency of any sane person is to sit back against the hill and retain the perpendicularity the inner ear prefers. Unfortunately, skis must be weighted to perform as designed, the weight causing flex, which in turn pushes the edges into the snow in an arc, making a turn. Therefore it is essential to "throw" oneself down the mountain and over the skis, depending on them to "catch" the fall as they bite into the snow to turn underneath the perpetually falling skier. Intellectually this can be clearly understood but fear prevents execution. Concentrating on something as simple and indirect as "look at your hands" causes the desired behavior without directly confronting the fear. This is directly analogous to what occurs when an individual walks: The weight is thrown forward in a fall, with the consequent forward thrust of the leg to catch this fall, repeated for left and right sides in a continuous tension and release of yielding to gravity in order to defy it.

Originator: Anonymous ski instructor somewhere in Utah. Wherever you are, thanks for providing the breakthrough to better skiing for the author.

Patterns on the Fly

Don S. Olson
olsond@agcs.com

In real life, I'm a fly-fisherman. Oh sure, I spend 8, 10, 12 hours a day most weekdays and too many weekends cracking my skull over architecture and design issues, pounding out code, and having head-butting and bugling contests with other similarly hardheaded software types, but what constitutes unity and passion to me is lobbing a teeny bit of fur and feathers to cold-blooded stream-dwellers, trying to outsmart a creature with a brain the size of a pea.

Compared to the art and science of fly-fishing, software design resembles a primitive tribal contest. It is arbitrarily based on rules handed down by oral tradition and subject to interpretation by priests whose impartiality is betrayed by the amulets they wish to sell us to improve our game. Over the years, I've been continually struck by the fact that all of our paradigms, methodologies, process models, notations, CASE (computer-aided software engineering) tools, languages, operating systems, and other odds and ends of software creation always converged to the simplest, cheapest, and most error-prone part of the whole business: a line of code. Strange that so much sophistication and so many dissertations go into simply delivering each line of code as precisely and delicately as a correctly tied fly, and often with as little luck or success.

The fly-fisherman spends hundreds, even thousands of dollars on flyrods, reels, waders, vest, tools, fly line, leader, and tippet, just to deliver a dollar's worth of flotsam (or jetsam, if he's nymphing) to the nose of a trout. No matter how sophisticated the getup or how skilled the angler, if the fly isn't the correct one for the place and time, he goes home skunked. Just like a designer who has no legacy to draw on, if the angler can't read the signs on the water and in the air, doesn't read the literature of the sport, and correlate knowledge and experience to the correct fly choice, he's reduced to thrashing through his fly box, trying first one, then another, all to no avail. What the fisherman needs to know is how to select the right fly for this particular situation, and then present it so that it merges seamlessly with the environment. Sounds like a solution to a problem in a context, *n'est-ce pas?*

It rattled around in my head for a while, this odd parallel with software development. Expensive tools, training, big-buck consultants, whiz-bang programmers, all for naught if what we deliver is not exactly right for its time and place. Otherwise brilliant ideas in software design used out of context are stupid and pointless. How do we know when one solution is better than another? How can we pass on the lore we learn the hard way to guide others? When I'm standing midstream, scratching my head, staring into my fly box, and all around me I know there are trout, and I can even identify what they're feeding on, the question I'm asking is, "Which pattern will work here?"

> There are some persistent patterns that seem to be reinvented by a new expert every ten years or so, simply because truly good ideas never die, and other patterns appear because even bad ideas can take on a life of their own. Once thought of, they must be tried. Once tried, they must be fished. If they work, the ego kicks in. It's your baby and you caught a fish on it. Wow! We've got to tell the world about this! (Gierach, 1988, p. 95)

Right now, I guess, we're caught up in this "tell-the-world" phase in the patterns community. The incredible success of the Pattern Languages of Programming (PLoP) conferences, the need for members of the community to downplay the hysteria and fight the hype, the huge numbers of patterns and patterns literature being published on the World Wide Web, in software journals, and in books, all point to a wave swelling and soon to break over all of us in software development. Some of us will try to surf it, others will let it roll over them, and others will be caught in the wrong place and get smashed when it inevitably breaks, with the foamy hype obscuring the fresh ideas that flow toward the shore.

> Most new patterns have a brief moment in print, after which they retire to a few streams where they've caught on. There they live quiet but productive lives away from the hustle of fame, making their modest contribution to the rich regional nature of the sport. A few come into fashion and stay there for a while, and a precious few go on to become widely accepted, like the Adams or the Elk Hair Caddis. (Gierarch, 1988, p. 95)

If you've stuck with me so far, perhaps you've been waiting for the epigraph from Christopher Alexander to appear, and indeed, that was the original intent when I sat down to write about my team's experience with patterns. When the Hillside Group organized to promulgate Alexander's ideas to architecture in the world of software, it was a moment that I believe will enter the history of our occupation as one of the most important shifts in thought ever made. The fact that Alexander's work could translate so wonderfully to software was to many of us an epiphany that gave real hope for the future of our vocation, and struck a blow against those who still lobby that programming is but the work of automatons we surely will soon invent. In late 1994, the book *Design Patterns*, by Erich Gamma, Richard Helm, Ralph Johnson, and John Vlissides (1994), captured what amounts to the software equivalents of the Elk Hair Caddis, Royal Coachman, Adams, and Hare's Ear Nymph, those classic, immutable patterns that we can build and adapt with our own variations peculiar to our home waters. I think we're well on our way here.

But beyond the methods of building, Alexander understood that building was a human activity, from start to finish, from initial concept, through architecture, all the way to assembly and final trim. In 5000 years of building, have we ever mechanized it completely, or codified everything you needed in a few handbooks? If software design and development were even a hundredth as complex, how could we, in just 40 years, even begin to believe that it would someday become assembly-line work, or even the formulaic application of principles? If we could accept the fact that it would never be so simple as pushing a Big Red Button, then maybe the path we need to follow is more Alexandrian and less deterministically left-brained. Furthermore, because commercial software creation is less an individual activity than a group activity, we face a problem that goes beyond simply passing lore down through the ages, but also spreading it equally among members of teams. Beyond those patterns that preserve and transmit software lore, we need organizational patterns that tell us how to work as teams.

The team is made from relationships among its members, the patterns of interaction through subtle, implicit understandings and some explicit rules of communication, which together form the protocols. Each rule of these protocols is the atomic unit from which the team's behavior is constructed. These rules must work not to suppress but to unleash the power of each individual by making each feel safe, and yet also compel each to constrain those behaviors that are counterproductive.

In the best teams, we find Alexander's "Quality Without A Name" in the patterns of their relationships, where the individuals create a collective and singular design mind. Alexander called it "that self-maintaining fire," with the generative power to adapt and create, and to keep successful behaviors as they are discovered. Alexander continues, "In the same way, groups of people can conceive their larger buildings, on the ground, by following a common pattern language, almost as if they had a single mind" (Alexander, 1979, p. *xiv*).

What this suggests to me is that even with all the greatest software patterns in the world collected, bound, indexed, and cross-referenced, it won't be enough if we can't put teams together that function effectively enough to take advantage of this knowledge. And, equally, even the most well-integrated and managed teams cannot always succeed if they do not have a common design mind. As in any human endeavor that attracts intelligent people, it is the lack of any set of definitive answers that keeps us coming back. How do we generate a collective design mind?

> There were hundreds of people, each making his part within the whole, working, often for generations. At any given moment there was usually one master builder, who directed the overall layout . . . but each person in the whole had, in his mind, the same overall language. Each person executed each detail in the same general way, but with minor differences. The master builder did not need to force the design of details down the builders' throats, because the builders themselves knew enough of the shared pattern language to make the details correctly, with their own individual flair. (Alexander, 1979, p. 216)

This is all fine and good, once you have a team that knows this shared pattern language. But our projects don't span generations. In our Intelligent Networks group at AG Communication Systems, 6-month (or shorter) product cycles are common. We don't have years to cultivate a like mind, to create a culture. We need some short cuts. The trick is in getting teams together that are capable of learning and sharing this language, and convincing them to want to do so.

> Indeed this ageless character has nothing, in the end, to do with languages. The language, and the processes which stem from it, merely release the fundamental order which is native to us. They do not teach us, they only remind us of what we know already, and of what we shall discover time and time again, when we give up our ideas and opinions, and do exactly what emerges from ourselves. (Alexander, 1979, p. *xv*)

Introducing patterns into an organization is a recent experience of mine, and if there's any role that must be played in this endeavor, it's evangelist. Perhaps my zeal was a little excessive, at least judging by the wide-eyed backpedaling of some my fellow team members when I began talking, but in the end I think it was a benefit. Thanks to people like Linda Rising and David DeLano of AGCS, and Jim Coplien and Robert Hanmer of Lucent Technologies, I found allies and mentors who weren't shy about their enthusiasm for this new literary form. The skepticism that I encountered from my teammates in my early ranting may have been due more to the messenger than the message, but it at least got them looking, and when I suggested we become the guinea pigs for this stuff in our next project, they agreed. We started by taking, as a team, the Design Patterns course taught by Brandon Goldfedder of the Dalmatian Group. In the meantime, deeply inspired by Jim Coplien's organizational patterns, and the experiences we were having, patterns of our collective team experience began to emerge, among them, *Train Hard, Fight Easy*, and its antipattern, *Train the Trainer*.

PATTERN: *TRAIN HARD, FIGHT EASY*

Problem: Projects stumble, crumble, and bumble along as teams fail to organize themselves under pressure.

Context: Teams are thrown together and then presented with a project without first establishing team mentality or shared skills, knowledge, or vocabulary. Consequently, everyone learns "on the job" by trial and error, often guided by some resident guru whose biases and narrowness of view may prevent the team from examining a number of options, due both to the unevenness of experience and relative political power. The team, under schedule pressure, performs typically in one of two modes: *Guru Does All* or *Lets Play Team*.

Forces:
- Schedules determine everything.
- Good teams take time to form.
- It's not a perfect world, so make do with what you've got.
- Training flattens the knowledge distribution.
- Training sessions reduce formality and barriers.
- Common vocabularies are essential to teams.
- Training is expensive.
- Training costs stand out.

- Training is worthwhile.
- Good training is tough to get.

Solution: Train the team as a unit in relevant technologies. Give everyone the same tools and language.

Resulting Context: The individual differences among members diminish as learning is shared, particularly when relevant classes are given to the entire team at the same time. Additionally, team members become more familiar with one another's background, education, experience, and problem-solving approaches, as well as personal styles. The team is not using the project as the primary learning experience.

Rationale: The fact is that whatever training is required will be exacted, whether at the hidden expense of the project, or at the explicit expense of training costs. There is no escaping training of one sort or the other. In any project, without formal training, members tend to try to self-educate, resulting in a lack of common culture or vocabulary. Additionally, with schedule pressures, internal competition, egotism, and fear, members may degenerate into one-upmanship, hiding information from team members that makes them look especially good to management. Therefore, to give everyone an equal opportunity as well as iron out some of the initial team issues, sending the entire team through formal training sessions relevant to the project can consolidate expenditures and cut risks.

Training is only part of the answer, however. For newly formed teams without any experience working together, a trial project may be required, which is analogous to applied use of the newly acquired knowledge in a timely manner. For example, units in an army, though trained in the same basic skills, still perform mock battle exercises together to consolidate their team skills, as do baseball teams, etc. Software teams should be no different.

Experience: What was a generally acknowledged dysfunctional team at AGCS was permitted to stay together for the second phase of their project. At their members' insistence, they were all put through design patterns training, platform-specific training, and specific tools training as a group. Consequently, in the very early days of the second phase it was apparent that they had a common vocabulary, and had enough common shared knowledge of their new tools such that they could then pool all the specialized knowledge that each had developed on his or her own, rather than having specialists for each tool. Additionally, the classroom situations allowed members to relax and interact with one another as peers, because the material was new to practically everyone. The performance of the team in design activities was greatly improved, and morale improved to the point that all members decided to remain together, despite the events of the previous phase.

Related Patterns and Antipatterns:

- Jim Coplien's Organizational Patterns (A "MUST" READ!)
- *Guru Does All*
- *Let's Play Team*
- *Train the Trainer*
- *Trial Project*
- *Cult of Personality*
- *Sacrificial Lamb*

PATTERN: *TRAIN THE TRAINER*

(This is an antipattern.)

Problem: Training is expensive and time-consuming to give to entire teams.

Context: An entire team requires training in some technology.

Forces:

- Training can be very expensive.
- Training an entire team can eat up a lot of person-hours.
- Training teams as whole units helps positive team dynamics.
- On-the-job training is more expensive than classroom training.
- On-the-job training costs are buried rather than explicit as in classroom training.
- Time to become a qualified instructor greatly dwarfs time to take a single class; that is, people taking a class are not qualified to teach that class unless the content is so elementary that training isn't really needed.

Solution: Train just one, two, or a few individuals in formal classroom settings, then employ them to train other team members.

Resulting Context: Training costs are contained, and what is learned by the few is leveraged to train the many. Quality of instruction is liable to be uneven, however, depending on such factors as retention rates, teaching ability, materials preparation, subject complexity, and time in class. Also, the benefits of a shared team experience may be lost (see *Train Hard, Fight Easy*).

Rationale: Budget and/or schedule constraints may require a limit on team members' time in training. One must, however, be continually aware of the "pay-me-now-or-pay-me-later" syndrome. Training will occur, either in class or on the job. The determination as to which is more expensive in the long run is left as an exercise for the reader.

Related Patterns: *Train Hard, Fight Easy*

> Virtually all new patterns, however unique they look at first glance, draw heavily on the past. Some are what you'd have to call Frankenstein flies, made of parts stolen from the bodies of other patterns. (Gierach, 1988, p. 97)

The thrill of much of patterns discovery is the "Aha!" effect, but it manifests itself in different ways. Some software people are too sophisticated to actually jump up and shout like some of us less well-bred types, but their eyes glisten on at last seeing something they know encoded into a form that conveys the essence but doesn't dictate its manifestation as code. For others, patterns revealed whole vessels from the jumble of design ideas that had been mysteriously revealing parts of themselves over the years like clues in old mysteries or pot shards in ancient ruins. For a few, the light really went on, and, yes, they too became insufferable evangelists, so overjoyed that at last the code had been cracked. For some of these, it was the relief that flowed from knowing at last that here was the reason that software could never be mechanized completely. Whatever the character of that moment of recognition, an epiphany is essential. When a pattern, any pattern, reveals itself to a team member, the head nods knowingly in the sudden perception, and a design mind is awakened. In our team, the lights began to go on with increasing rapidity, and to fuse, and flash.

Now, having had the training, and with some time on our hands, we tackled what we had been discussing in the preceding weeks: an architecture for product development in our realm—Intelligent Networks. We had convinced management to keep us together during the hiatus between projects and used up all our credibility points in convincing them that their faith would pay off. What we were proposing was a broker-based framework, based on personal experience and all we had been reading in the literature. Now we just had to build one. To the wild-eyed zealots among us, the only way we were going to pull this off was to use patterns to aid in the discovery.

> This is usually how it works. You tie the first rough prototypes hurriedly, in a rush of anticipation and impatience, and fish them while the

lacquer on the heads is still a little tacky. If they work and you think you actually have something, you then figure out how to tie it. (Gierach, 1988, p. 98)

With the training fresh in our minds, and deep readings of the *Design Patterns* book (Gamma et al., 1994) taking root and growing organically into new forms, we plunged forward. We wrote a "Project Strategy and Plan," which borrowed heavily from Jim Coplien's organizational patterns, which helped us look organized and allowed us to manage the gaps in our organization. We began experimenting with implementations of some of the *Design Patterns* (Gamma et al.,1994) ideas, and then some of our own. Sooner than I think anyone really expected, we had a working prototype. Even more startling was that a process had also emerged that was supported by the architecture and vice versa. Coplien has said that software reflects the organization that builds it (*Conway's Law*), and now the reverse was also true. Some of the fish in our local waters were biting, asking about what we were doing, but of course, we'd been pitching our experiments at them all along. But we didn't yet have a customer. What was the good in what we had done?

PATTERN: *TRIAL PROJECT*

Problem: If an army platoon is issued weapons and put together after advanced infantry training, are they now a fighting unit? If nine experienced baseball players are handed gloves, bats, and a ball, are they capable of playing as a team right away? If an experienced software-development team is run through training in relevant technology, are they immediately capable of employing it effectively as a team ? Would you risk your company on it?

Context: A team of experienced software developers is formed and then put through training together in tools and technology that are relevant to an upcoming project or to prepare them for future development deemed essential by business research. *Train Hard, Fight Easy* has been taken to heart.

Forces:
- Training is only useful if it has been applied at least once.
- First mistakes are usually the largest.
- "What? You mean we spent $$$ on training and they're not ready yet?"
- The higher the stakes, the more preparation pays off.

Solution: Build a trial project together using the new learned technology. Make it a real project, but a small one of no profound consequence. Call it "preseason."

Resulting Context: The team learns to manage the dynamics of working together using the new tools and methods recently learned per the *Train Hard, Fight Easy* Pattern. The team is now battle-tested and motivated to tackle some real-world work.

Rationale: Training alone will not an effective team make, or even a single engineer create. Application of knowledge in a real setting is essential. A brief project of some weight and consequence, but not show-stopping value, should be given to the team to shake out their stiffness with the new lessons. It gives a team time to hit its stride, learn to turn that double play cleanly, set up an ambush, implement clean code meeting the agreed-on interfaces. And when things really work right, it builds trust, and lets each person's dominant strengths flow into those of others.

PATTERN: *CASUAL DUTY*

Problem: What should you do with a team with nothing specific (i.e., revenue generating activity) to do just now?

Context: A team is between projects, with uncertainty as to when the next assignment may arrive.

Forces:
- The team has been successful by some measure on a recent project.
- They're not generating any revenue right now.
- Other projects may need people.
- The team's cohesion is good.
- The team wants to stay together—nobody's trying to jump ship, or if anyone is, he or she does not substantially affect the team's balance.

Solution: Assign the team some fundamental work, on infrastructure, tools, process, whatever will benefit them in the future and perhaps some other teams as well.

Resulting Context: The team stays together, stays focused, improves their relationships, and produces work that is useful to them in taking on the next project and to the company as a whole.

Rationale: It's a pretty good bet that there are dozens of things you wish there was time to do or build in your organization. Some examples:

- Tools that could make life easier for developers
- Training and integration of third-party products
- Prototypes and theories to try
- Infrastructure and frameworks that you keep meaning to build
- Demo copies of tools to wring out
- Processes to document

If you have a team coming off a project that wants to stay together, and there's a fair chance that some money-making proposition will come in sooner or later, it makes sense to keep them together and focus them on a task that needs doing but always takes the back seat to profit-oriented development.

In our organization, management was wise enough to keep one of our teams together between projects, and in this time the team designed and built an architectural framework that has since become the basis for several new projects. This framework has already paid for itself with time savings and a timely and successful deployment of a commercial product built on it. Additionally, a couple of tools for project management and load building were produced as well, aiding current and future product development. Finally, the exercise really helped the team to unite technically, with a good definition of roles and working relationships.

The term "Casual Duty" comes from the military. When soldiers, airmen, or sailors are awaiting orders or clearances or are otherwise between jobs, they are assigned to casual teams which take care of a lot of necessary tasks that aren't covered by permanent teams. It makes a lot of sense because the teams can be used very flexibly, and it can often build morale and occasionally build new skills. It is true that sometimes casual duty may consist of picking up cigarette butts on the parade ground, or whacking weeds in a vacant lot, but often it can be meaningful work that benefits both the organization and the team.

We built a prototype, with Brandon's help, and found that by taking the *Visitor* pattern from the *Design Patterns* book, putting our own spin on it, and employing it in our particular broker, we had a simple, elegant, and very powerful core of an infrastructure (see *Transceiver-Parcel, Broker as Middleman, Broker as Matchmaker,* and *Broker as Divorce Attorney,* elsewhere in this volume). More patterns experimentation followed as we built components to connect to our broker. A *Builder* was used as the core of a command processor for provisioning. *Bridges* were used to insulate the system from database implementations. *Memento* worked its way into context management.

Proxies protected components in the system from the need to know the actual location of the services they requested. *Factory Method* combined with *Strategy* let us test any component without building dummy drivers. Out of these developed our own patterns, Frankenstein patterns: the previously mentioned *Transceiver-Parcel* and three flavors of *Broker*, plus *Trace Strategy* and *Menu*.

> Once the buildings are conceived like this, they can be built, directly, from a few simple marks made in the ground—again within a common language, but directly, and without the need of drawings. (Alexander, 1979, p. *xiv*)

A friend and former colleague, Bob Williams, liked to say that he was looking for engineers to whom you could say, "the component we need sounds like this. . . ." while giving a fairly sketchy description, and they would understand. *Design Patterns* almost enable this to take place, but in a regular and more precise way, though not so precise as to restrain creativity; rather, the patterns require that a human interpret them through the filter of experience and knowledge, to give a personal statement. In the best of worlds, each member of a team is empowered to express the best of themselves within a form, much as a poet uses the sonnet form, or a musician the twelve-bar blues form. But it isn't just some solipsistic expression that results, but a collaboration, an improvisational construction around a theme, jazz players riffing over an old standard. Here is where patterns really gave us an advantage—in bringing new personnel into the team, and passing our framework on to other teams.

After the initial architecture for our broker-based framework was understood, we began to take on new team members, and we found that since each had been through the same Design Patterns class as the team it was fairly easy to bring them into the fold regarding our broker, how it worked, and how they could build components that would integrate into the framework. As in a jazz jam session, if they knew the tune, and could play the changes, there was room to make it their own and still keep it harmonious, beautiful. It is possible that our architecture is simple and elegant enough to be understood quickly, but I am quite sure that without a pattern language to describe it, the learning curve would have been far steeper.

> Next, several acts of building, each one done to repair and magnify the product of the previous acts, will slowly generate a larger and more complex whole than any single act can generate. (Alexander, 1979, p. *xiv*)

New members to our team helped refine established ideas and found creative ways to use other patterns. Another project was kicked off using our framework, and this team adopted and then began to extend and improve on our work. Planners began to ask for our help in estimating jobs, and we discovered that this was less a black art than before because patterns helped us quantify complexity of design and even implementation. Underlying all this was an amazing phenomenon: although our team had some dominant personalities and widely varying levels of experience, somehow the playing field, while not leveled, was somehow big enough for everyone to contribute in a noticeable way. We were collectively more of a team with less conscious effort than any other team I'd been on in my 19 years in the field.

We've all worked in environments where a single guru pretty much designs everything, implements the hard parts, and doles out well-defined pieces to everyone else. Now this can work beautifully in getting the product out the door, but it also is a terrible thing to have happen in your organization. The guru effect can rob people of incentive, cramp their learning, and demoralize them from ever being creative, which in the competitive environments of today is a recipe for financial suicide. The benefits of the guru-centric organization are clear and on occasion it can be used beneficially, but there is always a price to pay in the end. What I was seeing in patterns-based development was a replacement for this time-honored method for success with one big difference. Rather than creating a guru-centric, radial organization, we had become something web-like, and this web provided strength in all aspects of team behavior, with no center to which the fate of the project was tethered. We were held together in our design mind, not in a structure of titles and power.

PATTERN: *GURU DOES ALL*

(Sometimes this is an antipattern.)

Also Known As: *Project Savior*

Problem: Schedule pressure overpowers a new team.

Context: A newly formed team is given a new project characterized by the following: tight schedule, changing requirements, uncertainty of design, uneven distribution of skills among developers, and new technologies.

Forces:
- Schedule is paramount.

- Only one or a few, at best, really has the domain knowledge and/or technical skill to immediately attack the project.
- Team dynamics are not yet formed
- Personalities clash.
- *Cult Of Personality* may develop.

Solution: Let the most skilled and knowledgeable individual drive the design and implement the critical pieces.

Resulting Context: Concentrating the critical responsibilities upon an individual eliminates much of the communication complexity and meeting time spent organizing the team. The Guru decides what must be done, chooses the choice parts for herself/himself, and dictates what else must be accomplished by the remainder of the team. Design knowledge does not necessarily need to be disseminated among developers, particularly if all interfaces are designed by the Guru. Negotiation is kept to a minimum.

Rationale: When expertise among team members is so extremely varied that training and team building cannot possibly bridge the gaps, the Guru can distribute work according to abilities and inclinations. The Guru can also present the unified face to management (see *Let's Play Team*).

We've all seen this occur, right?

PATTERN: *CULT OF PERSONALITY*

(This may be an antipattern in some instances.)

Problem: A team needs direction.

Context: A tight schedule, uncertainty of design, uneven distribution of skills among developers, and new technologies put a project into jeopardy. Perhaps drastic action applied to a *Sacrificial Lamb* has already occurred. There may even be a *Peacemaker* in place, or even a *Doormat*.

Forces:
- Powerful personalities can have profound effects.
- Powerful personalities can have huge, destructive egos.
- More than one Guru on a team may generate conflict or induce schism.
- Gurus are very often the only possible hope for a project.
- Reliance on Gurus rather than teams can lead to very low "truck numbers." (Thanks to Neil B. Harrison of Lucent for the metric!)

Solution: Bring in a legendary figure among the developers, or at least someone revered by management, to take over the lead.

Resulting Context: Guru-like figures who can inspire awe or at least intimidate team members can redirect a failing team through sheer force of personality. When the Guru's name is spoken in hushed tones, or is used as a seal of verification ("Well, Archibald says that . . .") then the goal has been reached and the team is now manageable. Those team members who are not awestruck may need removal or reeducation if the charisma of the Guru is insufficient. Such heretics can be unsettling elements in a reformed team.

Rationale: At times there is no remedy in the face of disaster other than to throw a compelling personality into the mix. But keep in mind the deleterious effects of this act. Gurus can cast a long shadow, and if you happen to have one who has a dictatorial bent, you will rapidly help build a team of developers who lack their own creative fire.

In our case, we had no single guru on the team, and it worked to our benefit since it forced each of us to bring everything we could into the design and development process. This is one of the benefits of collectively breaking new ground. We were, we found, not only using design patterns for the first time in a commercial venture, but we were also applying both Jim Coplien's organizational patterns along with some of our own to help find our way to success. By incorporating them into our contract with management, we publicly announced our intent to work in a new way not just technically, but organizationally. We found ourselves as a grand experiment in the Intelligent Networks group.

Did it reduce conflict? Not in the least. But our conflict was productive. Our disagreements focused on technical problems and design issues because we had this common language through which to express ourselves. There was a connection now between argot and application.

But though this method is precise, it cannot be used mechanically. (Alexander, 1979, p. 12)

I am convinced that good designers know good design in a way that goes beyond anything some process model or CASE tool can provide them. Still, we are confounded by those soulless robots who continue to clamor for the death of the programmer and the elimination of all steps but requirements specifications to create future generations of software. To me this view is just too confining. For one thing, writing requirements to that level of detail is not only not fun, but impossible. Let's face a fact: writing code is fun. To mark coding as the root of all evil and attempt to eliminate it totally is akin to the idea that the Puritans eliminated bear baiting not because it was cruel to the bear, but because it gave the spectators pleasure. We should capitalize on the fun part by finding a way to build the parts we understand as we understand them while continuing to explore those parts we don't have so well understood. In other words, fit the process to the people.

I used to tell this story when I was trying to explain my philosophy of designing Human-Computer Interfaces in my one try at project management a few years past. It's an old Vaudeville joke, but it fits just as well to any endeavor in which we face a trade-off between matching tasks to humans versus humans to tasks.

It seems a fellow needed a suit in a hurry, and he could only find one tailor who could agree to make him one on such short notice for a reasonable price. The tailor took his measurements, and told him to come back in a day.

The next day the fellow returned and the tailor gave him the suit to try on. When he did, he was horrified. One sleeve was too long, one was too short, the padding in one shoulder was way too much, and the buttons didn't line up with the button holes. The pant legs didn't match and the seat bagged out terribly.

"This is awful!" he told the tailor.

"Now, don't be so hasty," replied the tailor. "Look," he smiled, taking the man's sleeve. "If you hold your arm out like this, and put the other arm just so, and thrust out your rear a bit and walk on one tiptoe, and twist your chest this way and your neck like that, well there! It looks pretty good now, doesn't it?"

The man looked in the mirror again, and sure enough, the suit fit beautifully. He thanked the tailor and shuffled out of the store, walking so that he could preserve the proper fit of the suit.

As he was shuffling down the street, an old friend spotted him coming the other way, dragging one foot, the other on tiptoe, his torso twisted and his arms all askew.

"Bernie! Bernie, my god, what happened to you? You look terrible! Terrible!" his friend exclaimed in horror.

"Nice suit, though." (ba-da-dum!!)

I've seen plenty of things in everyday life just like this, as I'm sure you have, too. In software development, we are plagued by processes and methods, and worst of all, CASE tools, that are much like this suit, too. They look crazy when you start with them, they're uncomfortable as hell, but it's mandated by some process group and the gurus claim them the next wave, so you work at adapting. After all, we've got a schedule to meet! The process or tool output might even look good once you conform to it, but you move and look like hell, and your thinking isn't made any clearer, and in the end, when the crunch comes, you bang out the code the same old way, wearing your old, threadbare, but comfortable, suit.

This is one reason we decided to build our broker-based architecture, in order to decouple as much as possible all components in the system. This would allow our application and perhaps those that followed to develop more organically. Software doesn't consist of components that evolve in lock step with one another. Typically, we move ahead by starts and stutters, and the only way that success seems possible if not certain is by accepting the incremental approach to development, which allows us to build what we understand as we understand it within an architecture that the team as a whole and individually has bought into the process and understands. As patterns gave us a language in which to communicate the design in human terms, so this architecture mapped to our natural manner of actual development.

> The more we learn to use this method the more we find that what it
> does is not so much to teach us processes we did not know before,
> but rather opens up a process in us, which was part of us already.
> (Alexander, 1979, p. 13)

Purveyors of many CASE tools and methodologies think that with just the right tool or method of the moment, we can all become great software designers. But to paraphrase Dexter Gordon in the movie 'Round Midnight, design sense isn't something you put on like a suit; it's like a tree that grows inside of you.

Too much of software design is like torture—the designers try to forcibly extract the secrets of the right design by putting requirements on the rack, and then applying their processes and methodologies like instruments of pain. This is what I like to call the Medieval School. Rather we should observe past projects and designers and our own experience to learn how to recognize the secrets as they reveal themselves. Otherwise, like so many previous black-hooded methodologists and torturers alike, the information we extract is what we want or expect, rather than what is the truth for our design. This gentler, more enlightened path is what the patterns community is following.

We act as though design is a linear activity, squeezed like so much toothpaste from its tube, but it is not, at least in my view. Design is a web, and at the center of the web is the code itself, suspended by a thousand threads that trace from domain information, technology, recursive analysis, the people who do the work and the dynamics among them, the limits or benefits of platforms, operating systems, languages, compilers, debuggers, support tools, training, culture, experience, faith, and hope. Each thread's tension and weight shape the design, which in turn feeds back into the analysis, and it forever remains a dynamic, living thing, rather than the static model many believe it should be (more out of convenience to themselves than to the reality of the world we inhabit). These threads are verses of a poetry spun from the pattern languages we have discovered in webs we have woven before, some by accident, some by design, and some vicariously by reading the design poems of others.

> Yet architects themselves, have lost their intuitions too. Since they no longer have a widely shared language which roots them in the ordinary feelings people have, they are also prisoners of the absurd and special languages which they have made in private. (Alexander, 1979, p. 233)

Put on your asbestos shoes. It's time to turn the flame on.

Recently I had a running debate with someone on the Usenet regarding the automation of software development by the careful application of a certain model of analysis (to remain nameless). Now I grant that given specifications in sufficient detail, and a notation for modeling these specs, it would theoretically be possible to have an automaton actually write/generate the code perfectly from those specifications. But these specs would be so painful to write, particularly given that for any complex problem the analysis is practically continuous throughout the life cycle, that the level of effort would far exceed that gained back by the automation of the process. Isn't that why we have at last accepted the iterative approach to software development? Certainly we try to do as much up-front understanding as possible, creating requirements that allow us to at least determine an architecture. But it seems to me that when we try to do much more beyond that up front, beyond discovering what we stumble upon in the normal course of analysis (which will last as long as the software exists), then we are doing no more than throwing bones or interpreting entrails, and we lose what to me is the greatest joy in the creative act—continual discovery. Those who would turn this into the joyless tedium of endless hairsplitting based largely on supposition rather than building something and trying it out (within an architectural context, of course, and that is very important), think that programming is akin to assembly-line work. They consider programmers no more than lower caste "coders" who await the written instructions of their betters, like the cretin Renfield awaiting his marching orders from Dracula, meanwhile snacking on cockroaches and giggling nervously in the shadows. In fact, the very use of that term "coders" seems almost always a tip-off that the user is either completely unfamiliar with real-world software development, or has had the misfortune to work in an environment in which the divisions among analysts, architects, designers, and "coders" were so rigid that no one group had to concern itself with what consequences it bestowed upon its downstream partners, and could always attach blame for the inevitable project failure on those below them. "Shit runs downhill, and payday's Friday." In the wake of the many disasters in the short history of the discipline, there are still those who cling to this model of complete and utter omniscience of what may come. Don't believe it? Look at the job titles for software people in any number of companies in this country. There is still a caste system in place and it's worked in the past and how can you possibly argue with our success, blah, blah, blah. "FORTRAN got us to the *moon!*" God bless 'em.

An interesting tactic of this bunch is to point out that people used to code only in assembly languages and now work in higher level languages. From this they extrapolate that as we continue to evolve languages, eventually specification languages will result, which allow us to specify at a comfortably high level whatever it is we have to build. Unfortunately, this is pure crap. First, the step from assembled to compiled languages, while great in its time in the 1950s, is still no large bound. Aren't the mechanics of compiler design taught in every undergraduate computer-science curriculum? And tools like yacc and lex and bison are still finitely bounded; that is, what you can build with them can be mathematically described. Not so those organic systems that we typically build in the real world. I grant you that if you build something simple enough, or with no human interface (which really simplifies some systems), then it may be totally deterministic and modeled mathematically. But this "turn the crank" approach fails in any project of size or complexity because you can't grind into sausage what you can't even identify as meat. Well, maybe you can, but you sure as hell wouldn't want to buy or eat it.

Okay, flame off. Now that I've had my rant about process and tool fanatics, I'd better remember that we in the patterns community can be just as guilty of fanaticism or catholicism about our particular view of how to develop software. I continually have to remind myself to remain open, to keep reading, listening, and thinking. We have an incredibly rich pattern legacy already, and we're even building commercially successful software with them! But we're still at the very beginning.

> On the other hand, it's not really advisable to simplify your fly selection down to the elusive "few basic patterns" you sometimes hear about. Even if you could settle on the correct pattern for every bug you'll ever see on the water, there will still be those times when the correct fly doesn't work and you'll need something else to try. Something different. In other words, don't get too organized. (Gierach, 1988, p. 102)

We need humility. Especially me. Despite the evangelical fervor, despite taking the world by storm (if that ever happens), we still must remember that we know little and can learn much. I can't imagine that any career can be much fun at all unless what we are really doing is discovering in a world still largely unknown. With patterns, we not only have much ore to mine, but an almost limitless number of ways to refine and shape it for both utility and beauty.

> Professionals or amateurs, they cannot help but stamp their efforts with something of themselves. This is certainly most evident in the patterns we privately develop or the innovations we contrive (and it is a rare tyer [sic] who does not have many of these), but the personality of the tyer (sic) expresses itself in conventional and standard dressings as well. Ask a hundred fishermen to tie the perfect Adams, and no two of the flies will look precisely alike. The tilt of the wing, the wrap and density of the hackle, the angle of the tail, the thickness and taper of the body— all answer to something slightly different in each tyer's (sic) imagination. (Leeson, 1994, p. 50)

Transfer this sentiment to software design, and many will nod their heads, while a few will howl that this is the problem with software; it's not supposed to be that way! (Back in 1980, I had an engineer snarl at me at a party, "Wait 'til this Ada language is mandated. It'll make all you bastards program alike!") We compound the disagreement, of course, by talking about software as art, not cold science, or even warm science. Now art to me means, among other things, something displayed or appreciated outside its context, as in folk art, which may be everyday farm tools exhibited apart from the farm, or "found" art, which may be a urinal on display (signed R. Mutt, no doubt), or any painting which is shown not in the studio of its creation but in the distilled ambience of a museum. Now I doubt I will see, in my lifetime, code exhibited as art in a museum setting, or bought only for display upon someone's wall, no matter how gorgeous and original, or dense with social meaning. Between science and art, I think, lies craft, and if we really would be honest with ourselves, perhaps we should be looking at software design as craft. Part art, part science, sometimes inspired, it is made with specific materials and with some common form that distinguish it as software. Although distinct from other crafts, like all crafts software is made to serve a purpose, not simply for its own sake. Those of us who have had or continue to have pretensions of being great artists should perhaps think about being great artisans instead. After all, our labors have utility, we hope (and our customers insist!). I suppose that all the dead-on-arrival code and canceled projects could be salvaged in our collective consciousness by calling them programming art of a sort, but most of it was most likely not artistic in the least, but rather the product of drudgery, confusion, and boredom. That is not the source of great art, or great artifacts.

There is art in this, to be sure. For patterns to possess Alexander's quality without a name, they must be inspired, transcendent, and beautiful. Software, however, must be more than this, because on its own, software cannot exist as art, cannot bless our lives in its abstract form. Rather like spirit, which makes its presence felt in the works that array its essence, patterns give us a fuse with which to drive the heart of our work, the software we build, to a higher good. Is it not our obligation to do so?

Our team delivered a commercial product using our pattern-based framework, on time, and within budget. It was put into commercial production by the customer within 30 days, and we've had no problems beyond some initial quirks in the first week that were quickly resolved. The framework itself, before completion of this project, was already in use on another, and planned for three more. Were patterns useful?

They've sure helped my fishing.

The following patterns, definitions, and asides were all mentioned in the preceding article and are included here for completeness.

BIG RED BUTTON

Did you ever say something in jest that later came back to you as a statement of fact or belief? Well, then this tale should be familiar to you.

Years ago a company I worked for was spending money like crazy on tools to improve its software-development processes. Naturally, this was done not as the result of planning, nor early in the planning stages, but rather in panic in *media res,* as it were (I never get to insert Latin terms), in the middle of things after schedule slips but before budget tightening. A tool which was advertised to convert requirements into test procedures was purchased and training obtained. A suite of CASE tools which included code generation was bought and a whole new group to support them was created. You get the picture.

During a casual conversation with team members I joked, "Yep, by golly, we're gonna be able to feed in those requirements, push the Big Red Button on the wall that says 'Software' and the code will just pop out the other end, along with the test plans and procedures which will go into the automated validation facility, and presto! tested, documented, configured code and not a human in sight beyond requirements." Because we were a test tools development team building simulators and test language components and were acutely aware of the incredible complexity of integrating COTS products with in-house developed stuff, this seemed so ridiculous as to be funny for a minute or two. Okay, back to work.

A month or so later, against all odds, the Big Red Button surfaced again, in a management presentation. Here, in toner, on plastic, with a heading and a fancy border, was a proclamation of the seamless cradle-to-grave software environment that we would soon put into place, the sole interface to which would be a "Big Red Button."

Believe it, or not.

I'd like to say it got me a huge raise and promotion as a great visionary, but I just didn't understand how to market the concept. Damn! Do you think I can copyright the name?

PATTERN: *CARGO CULT*

(This is sometimes an antipattern, but sometimes it makes good sense.)

Problem: A project is in trouble and is far too visible.

Context: A project is about to melt down. Much criticism is directed at the project, its staff, and its leadership. People on the project are getting beaten up by rumor, management interference, and continual demands for replans, and their morale is suffering. The project is of some importance and cannot be scrapped.

Forces:
- Changes must be made, at least externally visible ones.
- For any hope of completing the project, the team must be kept intact.
- New leadership, organization, and context must be found, and fast!

Solution: Redraw the organization charts, showing the troubled project and leadership in a new, larger context, possibly demoting it in stature. If you must, toss out a *Sacrificial Lamb* or a *Culpable Goat*, but other than the charts, don't change anything else.

Resulting Context: Administratively, the project is now protected as well as being placed in a safer position within the bureaucracy. The illusion of a committed, forceful, and decisive leadership is preserved.

Rationale: Let's face it: reorganizations are difficult and seldom happen. Frequently, the only change is to the org chart, moving names around, redrawing boxes and arrows, as though the rearrangement of the symbols will actually reorganize the corporation, division, department, what-have-you.

The name *Cargo Cult* is drawn from the phenomenon of certain South Sea islanders who believed that by building mockups of airplanes and constructing runways that they could bring back the planes and all the wealth that accompanied them during World War II, when advance U.S. bases in the Pacific used the islands as staging areas. In other words, by reconstructing or simulating the artifacts of a situation, they could effect its occurrence. Such is the case with org chart cargo cultism.

The positive aspects of *Cargo Cult* emerge when you just want to get critics off your back. Perhaps you are rectifying the situation but just need to buy a little more time (you might enlist the help of a willing and understanding manager or colleague). Redraw the org chart, publish it, and let the confusion, anger, amazement, and political intrigue obscure the real outcome, i.e., no real change at all. Usually, those wannabe Machiavellis most enamored of org charts are the very people you need to tie up for a while as they try to determine how to scavenge the most benefit from the apparent shift of power. It's good for a few laughs, at least.

Known Uses: Anecdotally speaking, the most extreme case of this I have encountered was at a previous company where I was assured by an executive vice president that his division was a flat, team-based culture, with no hierarchy, because, "we don't have org charts. I forbid them!" Thus, with the simple elimination of the paper representation of the division, an entire 1,600-person entity was restructured. In fact, it was a *Cryptocracy*, in that there was certainly a deep hierarchy in existence, but no one was allowed to articulate its shape, or even understood how it might operate on any given day. Once the "troubles" came, however, changes had to be made. Subsequently, org charts were introduced as problems surfaced, apparently for the specific purpose of redrawing them and thus, *mirabile dictu!* rebuilding the organization. During the six reorganizations I witnessed (in 18 months!) although the charts changed, the powers did not, as either peoples' loyalties did not correspondingly shift, or displaced managers would find new avenues through which to wield their old power. Now and then some real change would occur in the organization, but it was fascinating to observe the changes in the org chart held as proof rather than any real change. Another name for this might be Voodoo Doll Management.

A historical example of this same phenomena may be the case of Earl Long, governor of Louisiana, who, when confronted by legislation that prevented him from serving a subsequent term as governor, ran and was elected as lieutenant governor instead, with a willing and subservient crony in the governor's slot. Earl still ran things, though bureaucratically he was the #2 man. In a sense, he just changed the org chart, for all the difference it made.

Moral: The chart is not the organization. The best you can hope for is that the chart reflects the de facto organization, but chances are, if you're relying on charts to navigate your realm, you're really hopelessly lost as to its true nature. It may be time to ask yourself, "Is this one of those *Cryptocracy* things that jerk Olson was crowing about?" If it is, perhaps you'll be desperate enough to try to *Map The Realm*.

Related Patterns: Jim Coplien's Organizational Patterns *Firewalls, Gatekeeper, Patron*, and *Developer Controls Process* are very useful at preventing situations where *Cargo Cult* may be needed, and may even be used along with it. You might also look at *Containment Building*, which is a particular flavor of *Cargo Cult*.

(Thanks to Linda Rising, David DeLano, Russ Corfman, Sherri Scott, Jeff Scott, Bipin Patel, and Karel Hull at AGCS for the workshop and review!)

PATTERN: *CONTAINMENT BUILDING*

Problem: A project is failing and is too visible.

Context: A project is about to melt down. People are leaving or are severely disgruntled due to the continuous external pressure and visibility. Much criticism is directed at the project, its staff, and its leadership.

Forces:
- The project is of some importance and cannot be scrapped.

- Changes must be made, at least externally visible ones.
- For any hope of completing the project, the team (or what's left of it) must be kept intact.
- New leadership, organization, and context must be found, and fast!

Solution: Add the failing project to another, larger project, changing its name, if required, and apparently altering its scope.

Resulting Context: This effectively contains the mess originating from the project, protected as it is inside the larger context. This move also appears as a reorganization, when in fact absolutely nothing but the org charts themselves have changed, just as in *Cargo Cult*. Sheltered from direct scrutiny and filtered through the layers of reporting that have been added and/or obfuscated, the still-intact team can find the breathing room it needs to rebuild morale, redirect, and recover. This pattern is frequently used in conjunction with others such as *Sacrificial Lamb*.

Rationale: Sometimes, you just gotta be sneaky, I suppose. Actually, this is a strategy I've seen in actual use and indeed it has worked. At first the name *Containment Building* seems inaccurate; containment buildings are built around nuclear reactors to contain disasters like leaks and meltdowns, preventing radiation from altering the gene pool of the cows that graze and the people that picnic nearby. But given the infectious destruction to morale that can spread if not contained through bureaucratic or other means, perhaps it is, after all, appropriate. The idea, of course, is to have the containment building in place before the meltdown occurs. If no meltdown occurs, cool. If it does, then your other projects, and your career, won't suffer any unwelcome mutations.

CRYPTOCRACY

A Cryptocracy (a term I hope I have coined) is an organization with a hierarchy that is generally acknowledged, but no one really knows what it is or how it works. It may have an amorphous, continuously shifting behavior as power moves through it depending on cosmic signs, recent bureaucratic victories, or injections of powerful personalities and their relationships to the population at large, and to each other as they build and betray alliances. It's fascinating to study.

A common panacea to such an organization is the organization chart, which more often than not fails to map the true structure but does provide a placebo effect manifested in *Cargo Cult* adjustments. It also tracks the movements of such entities as the *Sacrificial Lamb, Culpable Goat, Peacemaker,* and *Doormat,* and a collection of such charts over time makes an interesting historical artifact of the life of any organization.

PATTERN: *DOORMAT*

Used in the same context as *Peacemaker,* the *Doormat* is someone who enables outside powers to manage the team without a reorganization. The *Doormat* accedes to demands from leadership outside the team. A rehabilitated *Sacrificial Lamb* can make a good *Doormat* if he/she desires to ingratiate himself/herself back into the power structure.

PATTERN: *LET'S PLAY TEAM*

Problem: Schedule pressure overpowers a team.

Context: A tight schedule, uncertainty of design, uneven distribution of skills among developers, and new technologies put a project into jeopardy.

Forces:
- Schedule is paramount; the veins in management's forehead are pulsing.
- Tension and fear are high among team members.
- Project is impossibly behind or wrapped around the axle.
- Performance reviews are due prior to project completion.
- Milestones are primarily paper exercises.

Solution: Pretend to be a team. Present a unified face through a team lead or spokesperson, but otherwise do not collaborate. Ensure that every member has something to do, but that knowledge is vertical, with little communication among members. Assume everyone knows what's going on.

Resulting Context: To management, the team is progressing according to schedule. Members appear to be very busy, and milestones like requirements and design reviews are being met. Well, at least some mighty large documents have been produced!

Rationale: Management is not able to compromise on schedule, afford training, or resolve team conflict. The team is on the hot seat to meet the schedule and must preserve that illusion at all costs. Perhaps individual reviews will fall within the project life cycle and no one wants to be identified with failure or delay. Perhaps management's review or bonus is dependent on meeting milestones in a timely manner. The team members may not be on civil speaking terms and interaction is painful and nonproductive. There may be hope that either the project will get canceled in the nick of time, or that some other effort on which the project depends will be the first to admit delay or failure, thus permitting the team to avoid blame for delay (see *Schedule Chicken* and *Long Pole In The Tent*). Any and all of these may justify use of this pattern, and indeed have.

Related Patterns: *Guru Does All*

PATTERN: *LONG POLE IN THE TENT*

A person or a group is the *Long Pole In The Tent* if she/he, they, or it, is behind schedule or is suspected of being behind schedule, affecting other collaborating or dependent entities. The concept is of the longest pole supporting the tent being the most visible and therefore most culpable for the shape of the schedule.

MAP THE REALM

This can be a very interesting and even enlightening exercise. Go through your entire organization and ask the following questions:

- Who do you work for?
- Who do they report to?
- Who do you work with (name all interactions)?
- Who works for you?
- Who works for them?

Please draw the entire organization, from your view. Assemble and correlate the results.

If you can actually diagram more than four levels deep within your immediate organization, then the structure itself may be part of the problem. More than six levels and questions of value added by the middle layers surface. More than eight layers and the sclerosis of the organization will render correction or even diagnosis of the problem impossible.

Examine how the results appear vis-a-vis the "official" structure of the organization. This is particularly good to use in any culture that advertises itself as "team-based." By repeating this survey at irregular intervals, it can also be used to measure the progress from a hierarchical culture as it attempts to change itself into a flatter model.

PATTERN: *PEACEMAKER*

A *Peacemaker* is a place holder in an organization who tries to calm and hold things together until a leader can be found or a reorganization is complete. The *Peacemaker* should be someone who is well liked but who is not necessarily technically proficient. Usually, this individual has many years with the company, knows the political ropes, and can buy time for a team as well as the team's management.

Usually, the *Peacemaker* follows closely on the heels of the *Sacrificial Lamb* and precedes the guru who either evolves into the *Cult Of Personality* or *Guru Does All*. Based on availability, it may be necessary to use a *Doormat* instead. The tenure of a *Peacemaker* is rarely more than six months.

PATTERN: *SACRIFICIAL LAMB*

(This may be an antipattern.)

Problem: A project is visibly in trouble.

Context: The troubles, even failure, of the project are highly visible. People are angry and disgruntled and some are even leaving. The project is late or over budget or in serious technical difficulty. Action must be taken. The project shows up in every status meeting as a negative icon.

Forces:
- Management is pressuring to rectify or terminate the project.
- Solution must be swift, direct, and decisive.
- There will be no painless solution.
- Someone may need a "wake-up" call.
- Reputations need to be established for toughness.

Solution: Select someone to be punished, whether through demotion, rescoping or removal of responsibilities, or banishment to some area of no value or importance. Termination is the extreme measure and rarely used as the action is primarily symbolic. If the selected person really is responsible, then this pattern becomes *Culpable Goat*.

Resulting Context: Some critical managers may be temporarily mollified since action has been taken. Depending on the popularity of or respect for the individual chosen for sacrifice, teammates may be angry, fearful, or grateful. It will be immediately necessary to apply *Cult Of Personality, Guru Does All, Peacemaker*, or *Doormat* to complete the illusion of correction.

May be used in conjunction with *Containment Building*. All too frequently, this is used prior to, or along with, *Cargo Cult*, an antipattern.

Rationale: Failure has many causes in any environment. Unfortunately, too often it is necessary to concentrate the sins of all those involved into the persona of a single individual, as though this person, once corrected, will bear away all the ills that have befallen the project. It is primarily a ritual for the mollification of external concerns, and occasionally does remove a particularly troublesome individual; however, its usual application is the punishment of a symbol in place of the rectification of more fundamental organizational problems.

PATTERN: *SCHEDULE CHICKEN*

Everybody knows this scenario: a project of some size and many components, perhaps software and hardware, is under way. More than one team involved is slipping behind its schedule, but is loathe to report such delays, hoping instead that some other team will give in sooner and admit delay. Of course, it's best if the team that "loses" *Schedule Chicken* is one that other teams are depending on for inputs of software or hardware. Thus, schedule slips are contagious due to these dependencies, and the "losing" team takes the heat for slippages that really would have occurred anyway. It is not unusual for all teams to play *Schedule Chicken* to the bitter end, with delay finally revealed at some integration interval, or even at system integration. Then the fighting really begins!

In the interest of historical reference, the game of "Chicken" was popular in the 1950s, when fearless teens would drive cars at high speed at one another to see who would veer first to save his/her neck. Whoever did first was the "Chicken." (What Darwin would have thought of this ritual might have filled a few pages in his journal. One can only guess.) Another variation involved racing toward a cliff to see who would brake first, as in the movie *Rebel Without a Cause*. *Schedule Chicken*, though not played for thrills, does arise from the same motivation as regular Chicken, which is to save face in front of one's peers. That is, one strives to avoid becoming the *Long Pole In The Tent*.

THE TROUBLE WITH CONSENSUS

Imagine a method of governance that works as follows: Every citizen has a vote and every citizen has a veto (interesting that these are anagrams for each other). How much could be accomplished?

Not much, I'd guess, since in a population of any size there very, very rarely will be unanimity, or even consensus. Thus, it is necessary to resort to majority rule.

What has this to do with team-based cultures? Plenty! There is some size for an organization beyond which consensus politics just can't scale effectively, so we rely on majority rule with institutionalized protection for minority interests. In the name of consensus, however, some organizations find themselves paralyzed as any management person can cast what is a virtual veto by refusing to buy in to a group consensus.

Such was the fate of an outfit I used to work for, which required that any effort be either initiated secretly ("it's easier to beg forgiveness than to ask for permission") or lobbied to the point of exhaustion. So many managers and directors and vice presidents were involved in even low-level matters that the disagreement of any one of them could effectively scuttle any decision on which consensus was required. Engineers spent little time actually in design and a great deal of time working up business cases to justify design activity. It wasn't until months after I left this job that it occurred to me that in their zeal to become a consensus-based organization, there was no distinction made as to when consensus should apply. And yet, ironically enough, in this very same place, some decisions were made by fiat, decreed by some vice president and implemented, despite the fact that there was nearly universal disagreement regarding the policy.

In our small teams, consensus works beautifully, allowing a range of disagreement but enabling us to bring in all participants to a solution. Enlarge the scope by even one or two people, that changes.

REFERENCES

Alexander, C. (1979). *The timeless way of building*. New York: Oxford University Press.

Gamma, E., Helm, R., Johnson, R., & Vlissides, J. (1994). *Design patterns: Elements of reusable object oriented software*. Reading, MA: Addison-Wesley.

Gierach, J. (1988). *The View From Rat Lake*. New York: Fireride.

Leeson, T. (1994). *The Habit of Rivers*. New York: Penguin Books.

Coplien, J. O., & Schmidt, D. C. (Eds.). (1995). *Pattern languages of program design*. Reading, MA: Addison-Wesley.

A Pocket-Sized Broker

Don S. Olson
olsond@agcs.com

Sometimes you don't need the Victorinox Champion. Sure, every blade and screwdriver, the awl, punch, can opener, reamer, corkscrew, magnifying glass, pen, scissors, pliers, fish scaler, ruler, toothpick, tweezers, hook disgorger, saw, and nail file has its use, and does indeed get used once in a while. But it's an awfully huge knife to lug around when one blade and the toothpick are all you ever use. It's good to be prepared for all possibilities—don't get me wrong—but sometimes you not only can do with less, you can get away with it, too. You might even be better off for it.

What follows are four patterns: *Transceiver-Parcel, Broker as Intermediary, Broker as Divorce Attorney, Broker as Matchmaker*. However whimsical the titles, these are the same real parts of an overall architecture that we have found to be very useful, lightweight, and easy to build. Moreover, it was a lot of fun.

Our object in building our particular broker was to remove everything we didn't need, and probably wouldn't need, so that we could immediately do something useful with it. Amazingly, it worked very well. We not only built a product using these pieces, but we also sold it for real money, and it worked fantastically well once deployed. Even more amazingly, before we were finished with the framework on its first project outing, another team decided it looked useful to them, too. All of a sudden, it was being passed around like the only canteen on a desert hike. Everybody wanted a taste.

Broker-based architectures certainly aren't novel; in fact that's an understatement. One could almost say that we've a plague of them, or something to that effect. They're mostly pretty powerful and very grand, suitable for all occasions. They are the Victorinox Champions. If we'd had the time and money, we might have latched on to any one of them and learned how to use it. Necessity being the mother of invention, however, our poverty of time and money turned into a benefit, and although we won't claim our little pocket-sized broker to be the global solution, it's a pretty good enough solution for a large class of problems.

As an old Russian once said, "Better is the enemy of good enough."

PATTERN: *TRANSCEIVER-PARCEL*

Problem: You desire to decouple components of an application using one of the *Broker* patterns. Components will be developed by many people, and they need to spend their time designing the guts of the components, not worrying about their integration. Additionally, it is completely a peer-to-peer system, rather than a client-server model.

Context: You don't care about efficiency, but you want an *elastic* architecture which you can extend by adding components or reduce by removing them, because every customer, market, or situation has different needs which you want to be able to meet without taking a meat-axe to some monolithic application. All your components should use the same method of communication, but you don't want them to have to know what the actual method of communication is for the environment, hence the commitment to the *Broker* idea.

Forces:
- Each component must be able to both send and receive messages.
- Components may be distributed or exist in the same process.
- You want the dumbest broker imaginable, that is, all it knows are parcels.
- As far as communication goes, you want the dumbest components possible.

Solution: Each transceiver can send and receive parcels, which contain a visit method [see *Visitor* pattern; Gamma, Helm, Johnson, & Vlissides, 1995]. The broker, when routing a parcel, invokes an *execute* method on the receiving transceiver, passing the address of the parcel as an argument. The transceiver in turn invokes the *visit* method on this parcel, which contains whatever method calls the parcel needs to make to cause the transceiver to do the bidding of its originator (another transceiver). See Figure 1.

In the most generic version, the *visit* method of all parcels would invoke the same method in any transceiver, which in turn could encapsulate whatever mysterious machinations occur to perform the service. In our implementation, however, many of the method calls from parcel *visit* methods

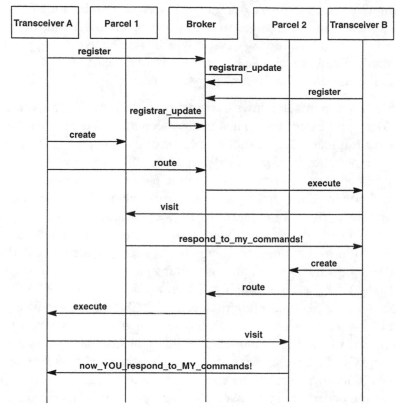

FIGURE 1   Interaction diagram for broker pattern.

were negotiated between developers of the transceivers. This could have added unwanted coupling, but was managed and controlled sufficiently such that anyone on the team, desiring to use any transceiver, could simply examine the .h file for that transceiver's public interface. Additionally, one of our development rules was that the developer responsible for a given transceiver was also responsible for developing the parcels which would visit it. So the developer of the requesting transceiver only had to create the parcel(s) for which the receiving transceiver subscribes. The parcel to be sent, having been developed specifically for communicating with that transceiver, contained the correct type for which the transceiver subscribed to induce the broker to route it, and voila! communication between components. The transceivers could vary with absolutely no effect on either the parcels or the transceivers sending them.

Resulting Context: New services, i.e., transceivers can be added to the existing system with no changes to the broker or the other transceivers. Transceivers can add additional services which respond to existing parcels visit method, or new parcels can be created to extend existing transceivers, or provide communication for new transceivers.

Rationale: This approach allows the creation of the simplest broker that still could support extensions to it such as a secondary registrar (for managing failed transceivers), broadcasting, and other capabilities. The broker and all types of transceivers are derived from the transceiver base class and all types of parcels are derived from the parcel base class so that the communication interfaces among all pieces are easily understood by developers working on them. Integration issues were reduced considerably; in fact, system integration became the least of our concerns. Another benefit was found in training new members to the team, particularly if they had received the same Design Patterns training (see *Train Hard, Fight Easy*; Olson, 1995). With the understanding of *Visitor* (Gamma et al., 1995), *Proxy* (Gamma et al., 1995), *Builder* (Gamma et al., 1995), *Bridge* (Gamma et al., 1995), and *State* (Gamma et al., 1995), the newcomer could easily grasp the architecture as well as the fundamental building blocks for any existing or future piece of it. *Broker* (GoV96) was not yet published and so we were proceeding with our own peculiar version of that concept adapted to our specific needs and understanding; however, the design was robust, efficient, and general enough to permit immediate reuse in the Local Number Portability, along with nearly all the other components.

Originator: The designers and developers of the #800 product team at AG Communication Systems.

PATTERN: *GOING POSTAL, OR BROKER AS INTERMEDIARY*

Problem: You desire to decouple components of an application.

Context: You don't care about efficiency, but you want an elastic architecture which you can extend by adding components or reduce by removing them, because every customer, market, or situation has different needs which you want to be able to meet without taking a meat-axe to some monolithic application or client-server model. Besides, since your team consists of more than one developer, you don't want to practice the "Big Bang" type of integration at the end of development but would rather be able to dry-run the inevitable at the beginning. You need an architecture that specifies the interfaces in sufficient detail to enable this, but leave enough wiggle room to add capabilities without perturbations throughout the system.

Forces:
- Efficiency is no big thing, but it couldn't hurt (if it is, see *Broker as Matchmaker;* Olson, 1996).
- Decoupling, flexibility, and extensibility are essential, since you're never quite sure what components will be needed.
- Components may be distributed or exist in the same process (if distributed across processes, or processors, see *Broker as Divorce Attorney;* Olson, 1996).
- Components shouldn't care where they are; they should be distributable with absolutely no changes.
- You want the dumbest broker imaginable.

Solution: Create a broker component which understands how to do only two things: register a component called a transceiver, for the messages, or parcel it is willing to receive; and route parcels to the transceivers based on the types of parcels for which they have registered. Thus, the broker contains a *registrar* object, which maintains the list of transceivers and what parcel they desire to receive, and a special transceiver object, which knows how to effectively route the incoming parcel to their destinations based as directed by the *registrar*.

Resulting Context: Here's the interesting thing: the transceiver from which the broker inherits happens to also be the base class for all components for which the broker routes parcels (see *Transceiver-Parcel;* Olson, 1996). This means that all the pieces of the application, including the broker, communicate through the same mechanism. A transceiver registers with the broker by sending it the only parcel for which the broker itself really subscribes, which the broker handles exactly the same way as any transceiver. The broker too invokes the visit method on the parcel, which in turn invokes the register method on the broker, which hands the sending transceiver's subscription to the registrar. All nonregistration parcels are handed to the *registrar*, which tells the broker where to route them. The broker invokes the execute method on the transceiver(s), which subscribe(s) for each parcel type, which in turn invoke(s) the visit method on the parcel, which in turn invokes whatever methods it cares to on the visited transceiver.

As in many human bureaucracies, the broker, though the most visible to the transceivers in the system, is hardly the brains of the operation. The *registrar* is like the secretary who maintains the files and writes the executive's speeches and controls the itinerary; the broker does as told by its *registrar*.

Rationale: One of the joys of this model was in explaining it to other people. First it was necessary to describe the *Visitor* pattern (Gamma et al., 1995), then our own use of it in the *Transceiver-Parcel* patterns. After that, all that remained was to show how the broker was a special kind of transceiver, pass on a few sample transceiver-parcel pairs, and turn them loose building new components. It really was that simple, and that was one of the primary objectives. The remaining objectives of easy distribution, redistribution, and improved efficiency are covered through the variations described in the accompanying patterns *Broker as Divorce Attorney* (in a really ugly divorce) and *Broker as Matchmaker*.

Real-life Analog: This is familiar to anyone who invests in the stock market, and, I assume, is the model referred to most generally when the term "broker" is used in computing. You, the investor, want to do something smart with your money, and since stocks are touted for their superior long-range return on investment, you decide to put some of your money into the market. Of course, most of us have no idea how the stock market really works. In order for the market to work effectively, it has to be made easy for us to move our money in and out and around. If, in order to invest, we had to fly to New York, take a cab to the New York Stock Exchange, master the arcane hand signals, learn who's who, etc., etc., I can't imagine that the flood of money that has flowed into the market recently from small investors would have amounted to more than a few drips (no reflection on small investors, really). In reality, we deal with brokers. We give our money cheerfully to the broker with instructions as to where we want it to go. The broker then does whatever it is he or she does to execute our instructions, making the telephone calls, sending faxes, e-mail, messengers, whatever it takes to buy our selected stocks. We, as clients, don't care or need to know precisely how this all happens so long as we receive acknowledgement that it has been accomplished. The broker insulates us from the arcane protocols of the stock market, geographic and time differences, even cultural and linguistic shifts. When we want information on our investments, we can contact the broker who will send us a nice report (and, analogous to the *Visitor*, will invoke our "read" method on the report). The broker may even arrange for periodic reporting of the progress of our investments (a version of direct brokering—see below) so we don't have to continually interrupt his or her busy day. Unless we're particularly compulsive about daily fluctuations, we can work entirely through our broker, from initial investment to ultimate redemption, after we've made our mountain of money. Or, as one friend describes the client-broker relationship, "turn your money and my experience into my money and your experience."

We *indirectly* communicate with the market through the broker. Everything is done through the broker, and he/she serves as our only interface to the complexities that comprise the market. It's easy for us, as clients, and makes greater efficiency possible. The drawbacks arise when we are unable to contact our broker. If the broker is out, whether for lunch or embezzlement, we are utterly and completely without recourse, at least for the near future. So for simplifying our lives we accept dependency on the broker. Oh, and we also must accept the *mordida* ("little bite") that the broker places on us in the form of commissions. In the computing world, we might equate this to the time penalty of routing all communications through the broker. You don't get something for nothing, after all.

See Also: *Broker* (GoV96), *Visitor* (Gamma et al., 1995)

Originator: The designers and developers of the #800 product team at AG Communication Systems.

PATTERN: *GOING TO COURT, OR BROKER AS DIVORCE ATTORNEY* (IN A REALLY UGLY DIVORCE)

Problem: Your broker-based application will be distributed across processes and/or processors, but *how* it might be distributed may vary.

Context: Perhaps an entire family of products is to be based on this architecture, to be delivered on a variety of platforms, scaled to all sizes of systems, from small, single processor, to multiprocessor, distributed installations. As use of these products increases, such as traffic demands in the telecommunications business, redistribution may be necessary. In other words, how the components will be grouped or scattered will be different from delivery to delivery and product to product.

Forces:
- All components might exist in the same process.
- Components might as easily be distributed.
- The day may come when components need to be redistributed.
- New components may be added.
- Components may be removed.
- All of this change, addition, and removal, may have to be dynamic, i.e., while the existing system is running.

Solution: Use one broker per process (or more, if you are so inclined). Each broker should have a proxy for each type of transceiver it appears to have in its own address space. The proxy fields the parcels routed to it by stripping out their essential information, packing this data into the necessary messaging package for that implementation, and sends it off to some *gateway*, which each broker also possesses. The *gateway* performs the inverse process of the proxy, by extracting the information, repackaging it into the parcel it was originally, and routing this to the local broker for delivery. The gateways in our implementation were parcel *factories* (Gamma et al., 1995), and all shared a single input queue per process. See Figure 2.

Resulting Context: No transceiver really knows where another transceiver exists, nor does the broker, to whom proxies look just like the transceivers they represent. The broker remains as dumb as ever, and the transceivers can live in blissful ignorance of how their parcels actually get to their destinations.

Rationale: This is another case all too common in real life, and unfortunately, despite its benefits in computing, it can be quite unpleasant for humans experiencing it. Consider an ugly divorce case. Let's not dwell on details or circumstances, but suppose that one or both parties are so angry that they care only to deal through their attorneys or have been instructed to do so by their attorneys. (Soon-to-be-ex-) wife speaks to her attorney, who in turn speaks to the attorney of (soon-to-be-ex-) husband, who then relays the message to his client. Buried in this transaction are the filters and protocols the two attorneys must apply to effectively stay within their legal and ethical bounds. The benefits of this model are that the estranged spouses deal with someone familiar to them and in whom they believe they can confide, and their respective attorneys worry about how to effect the desired communication, although it typically occurs over an expensive lunch put on account and added to the $400 per hour fee for acting as brokers of bile and bad news. But to return from that digression, the individual litigants don't have to know the law, or how what they're communicating gets to where it's going, or even where their (soon-to-be-ex) spouse actually is. I'd prefer not to go too deeply into the negative aspects of this means of communication, since rarely in computing do we see an analog of acrimonious divorce proceedings (or the avarice of divorce attorneys), but one penalty is the compounding of the aforementioned mordida. When the two clients are fighting over the contents of a single household pot, it seems not at all unusual for the brokering parties to be the true beneficiary of the convenience of this setup. This might serve as a subtle warning about

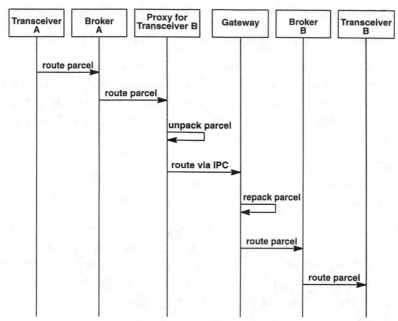

FIGURE 2   Interaction diagram for broker with proxy.

watching the complexity of your broker-to-broker protocols, or the extent of the network through which they communicate.

In computing, this model allows clients (parties of the first part) of a process to behave as though everything they need (parties of the second part) is in their own address space, or at least within the immediate grasp of the broker with which they are registered. The broker handles tracking down the other client(s) with which the party of the first part wishes to deal, whether that party of the second part resides locally in another process or across the network in some obscure corner of cyberspace. Implicit in this is the possibility that more than two brokers could be involved, a situation which, thankfully, is not typically reflected in divorce proceedings, and for which, again thankfully, future divorcees mustn't pay. In computing, of course, there may be performance penalties if the number of broker-to-broker connections becomes great, but this is less a consideration when stacked up against the perceived benefits of hiding from clients the protocols necessary for communicating across the network.

Originator: The designers and developers of the #800 product team at AG Communication Systems.

PATTERN: *GOING TO THE CHAPEL, OR BROKER AS MATCHMAKER*

Problem: The basic broker architecture is too inefficient for the application.

Context: In many applications, real-time considerations are paramount, as customers may have contractually specified performance. This is not uncommon in the telecommunications area, and for all the simplicity that the basic indirect broker provides, it can get expensive to pass every parcel through it.

Forces:
- The basic broker is so nice and clean.
- The basic broker costs too much in processing overhead.

Solution: Allow the broker to perform the first parcel routing as an introduction between the sending and receiving transceivers, supplying the address of the latter to the former (and vice versa, if necessary). After that, the two transceivers can correspond directly with one another. At completion of their communication, the broker will be notified.

Resulting Context: The communication between the two transceivers is much more efficient, having removed the broker from the loop. Of course, if the two transceivers are in different processes, then they must handle the interprocess communication themselves, which requires the equivalence of a proxy for the other transceiver and thus increases coupling. Typically, however, this direct mode of brokering is used when coupling is a minor concern and efficiency the highest priority, so the trade-offs usually favor its adoption.

Rationale: Although marriage brokers are not as common as they once were, we still have dating services. In fact, due to the increased working hours needed to earn the cash to fund investments through our stock brokers (the "indirect" model, remember?), some of our number are unable to find the time to seek companionship on our own and have resorted to elite dating services which claim to find us our perfect match, saving us valuable time in weeding through potential candidates, and also insulating us from a great deal of uncertainty, and hence, fun. In any case, the model in real life is copied in our computing model.

In the hope of meeting that special someone, you register with a marriage broker or dating service. The broker in turn checks your profile and sees if a suitable match exists in her/his network of clients. If there is someone who is "subscribing" for your particular type, the broker arranges for an introduction. This is the point at which your connection becomes direct in that you and the entity with which you want to ultimately interact are directly connected to one another. At this point the broker steps out of the picture. It's between you and your paramour to establish the protocols. In both the real-world model and the computing model, as long as interactions between you and your paramour continue, the broker remains out of the loop. In the event of a break off in communications, digital or romantic, the broker will want to know so that she/he can serve the client's interest yet again when a suitable match reveals itself.

Originator: The designers and developers of the #800 product team at AG Communication Systems.

REFERENCES

Gamma, E., Helm, R., Johnson, R., & Vlissides, J. (1995). *Design patterns: Elements of reusable architecture.* Reading, MA: Addison-Wesley.

Buschmann, F., Meunier, R., Rohnert, H., Sommerlad, P., & Stal, M. (1996). *Pattern-oriented software architecture: A system of Patterns.* New York: John Wiley & Sons.

Olson, D. Patterns: http://c2.com/cgi-bin/wiki? Regular Contributors.

Frameworks and Design Patterns[1]

Ben H. Richards
richardb@agcs.com

A framework is a high-level design construct expressed in reusable code. A pattern is a solution to a problem in a context, but design patterns can be considered low-level design constructs that cannot be directly expressed in reusable code. Frameworks are conceptually larger than design patterns, since usually frameworks will contain many design patterns. These two concepts are closely related.

There are two general classes of frameworks: black box and white box. The more common is the white-box framework, which requires that the user understand how various pieces of the framework interact in order to build a system with it. Users create classes that inherit from the framework and overload methods of the provided base classes. This requires specific knowledge of how the framework behaves, so there is a steep learning curve.

Black-box frameworks are used compositionally to construct a system. Objects from the framework are plugged together without deriving new classes. Black-box frameworks are more like higher level object systems where the user plugs together domain objects to build the particular model she has in mind. Most of the time when using a black-box framework, no new code is written at the same level as the framework. A mature black-box framework can then reduce the number of expert programmers needed, since users can build their own custom systems with the framework.

---

[1] Product and corporate names may be trademarks or registered trademarks of other companies and are used only for explanation and to the owner's benefit, without the intent to infringe.

However, if functionality is needed in the system that is not supported by the framework it is more difficult to add to the framework than it would have been for a system programmed "from the ground up." The new code would have to be general enough to cover all of the applications that the framework does, not just the specific application under development. An example of a black-box framework is the Accounts framework by Ralph Johnson et al.[2] The following examples are white-box frameworks.

A framework is much more than a reusable class library, though that is how it is packaged and delivered. All frameworks are class libraries, but not all class libraries are frameworks. One rule of thumb to help determine whether you have a framework or a class library is to consider whether the business objects contain and invoke elements of the library, or whether your objects will be invoked by the library. The latter is probably a framework. Typical frameworks provide an infrastructure within which the new system is built. They force a certain paradigm of program control, for example, an event-driven system is provided with Doug Schmidt's ACE framework[3] using the Reactor or the MicroSoft Foundation Classes or other Windows (and X/Motif) frameworks. In these examples, stimuli applied to the system are handled by the framework, which then dispatches business objects to do the work. The business objects can then make use of the framework to help complete the task, or to talk to other parts of the business model.

Given that distinction between a framework and a class library, I would like to discourage your writing a framework. Frameworks are expensive and difficult to build. If you have the option (read luxury) of buying one, do it. Consider please what it takes to write a good pattern. The problem that the pattern addresses must have occurred many times and have been solved with the same approach, that is, using the solution the pattern describes. If the solution does not work in some occurrences of the problem, the reasons must be known (or discovered) and documented. If the solution was not used this must also be explored. Through research, introspection, peer

---

[2] Information on Accounts can be found at: http://st-www.cs.uiuc.edu/users/johnson/Accounts.html

I would also like to acknowledge that much of the content of this essay has been distilled from presentations by Professor Johnson of the University of Illinois given in seminars at Champaign/Urbana over NTU, and at OOPSLA '95 and '96.

[3] ACE can also be used as "just" C++ wrapper classes on, for example, IP sockets, in which case it would be used as a class library. Information on ACE can be obtained from: http://www.cs.wustl.edu/~schmidt/ACE.html.

review, and communication these experiences are forged into a pattern. This pattern can be deemed "good" only by those who have shared in solving the same problem over and over again.

Similarly, frameworks are refined by fire. The framework will never be completed on the first or second try, by definition. A framework is reusable code. It can not have been exercised in all its dimensions after being used that few times. Nobody is smart enough to design a good framework without multiple systems having made use of it. In the same way a pattern is a creation of experience and is not valuable in and of itself, a framework is not created for its own sake; alone it is worthless. It must be used and reused to be valuable. The systems created with the framework are the measure of the framework, as the problems solved with the pattern are the measure of the pattern. It's difficult to write a good framework because you have to do so much more than code up a class library. It has to be used in several systems before it begins to solidify. New systems will exercise the framework in new ways never anticipated by the framework designers.

In writing frameworks, many iterations will be required where complete systems are written using the framework. When the framework breaks down, or starts to get in the way instead of facilitating good design of the system, it should be reworked. To solve problems encountered by the users (system developers), design patterns are often beneficial. They are applied to the framework to provide the right abstractions to allow for clean business objects and algorithms. As systems are built, these problems arise in the framework and it changes to accommodate them.

Frameworks and patterns are both difficult to create. Each can also be difficult to learn to use properly. Once in place, however, each offers significant gains in efficiency of development of new systems. They both offer tried and accepted solutions to reoccurring problems in software development. In addition, each can help to normalize vocabulary for communication of ideas and concepts relating to the system in question. In our latest project two team members new to distributed systems were able to quickly get their programs talking by using ACE. Instead of worrying about details of how to connect and how to wait for connections they were able to immediately talk about what they wanted to communicate. The implementation was taken care of by ACE components; the names of these components became part of their day-to-day vocabulary. Instead of talking about protocol details and system calls, they just said *Acceptor* and *Connector,* and each knew exactly what the other was talking about. These are patterns whose implementation is included the ACE framework.

In another facet of our project, we were able to add a new subsystem to a product by deriving a few new classes from our framework. All of the control and communication infrastructure came for free, and we could concentrate on the responsibilities of the new subsystem. I would like to think we have a framework there, but we just have a start. Although the current control and communication infrastructure supports extending the same system, reusing it for new systems would no doubt cause problems. Generalizing and abstracting out application-specific assumptions is very difficult. Without a brand-new application, we don't know which abstractions and assumptions in the infrastructure are application specific.

If the time had been spent at the beginning of the project to actually create a functional framework, that considerable effort might still have been an academic exercise. It would have been no easier to extend the system. Since the time was spent up front by the original designers to make the system flexible, later development on the subsequent releases of the same product was easier than it might have been. Currently, we have not planned the time to refine the general solutions we do have in the system into a framework, and other projects will discover the same things we have and the same things that people discovered before us. Spending the considerable effort to extract the reusable code and make it a framework does not guarantee a good return on the time investment.

Another common characteristic of patterns and frameworks: they both lurk just outside of our grasp, lying in legacy systems like diamonds in the rough. To leverage this experience, we must steal. We must take the time to study the systems that have gone before and learn from others' mistakes and successes. When posed with a problem in system design, a developer will not immediately try to imagine all possible permutations of the problem, only the problem defined by the current context. In other words, the solution for the specific problem at hand is discovered, not a pattern for solving all instances of the problem. If there is a system to get out the door, do carefully consider the design for flexibility and extensibility and look elsewhere for direction and solutions. Do not immediately concern yourself with writing an infinitely reusable framework—the system the framework is to support will not get done, and the framework will not get reused unless there is considerable organizational support for it and a genuine business case for it. If you really want to write a framework (or a pattern), you must have a body of work to start from.

PART III
RESOURCES AND
MORE INFORMATION

The following collection of articles provide the view of major pattern contributors—Jim Coplien, Robert Martin, Richard Gabriel, Kent Beck, the GOF (Gang of Four)—the list is impressive. When I began "spreading the word" about patterns, I tried to keep a list of pointers to these important articles, to help others travel the path I had cleared. I spent countless hours answering requests for this information. I have also covered the material in noontime presentations and at our monthly Tech Forums. It's all here in one place for your enjoyment and edification! The collection is not complete, of course, and it grows continually, as does our knowledge of patterns.

Fault-Tolerant Telecommunication System Patterns

Michael Adams, James Coplien,
Robert Gamoke, Robert Hanmer,
Fred Keeve, and Keith Nicodemus*

The patterns presented here form a small, partial pattern language within the larger collection of patterns in use at AT&T. We chose them because of their interconnectedness and the diversity of their authorship, and because they are probably well known to the telecommunications programming community. Many of these patterns work in other domains, but for this article we expect telecommunications designers to be our primary audience.

Two of the unique characteristics of telecommunications software are its reliability and human factors. Many switching systems, including the ones referred to in these patterns, are designed to be in virtually continuous operation—they may be out of service no more than two hours in forty years. In many cases this requirement limits design choices.

The systems must also be designed so that maintenance personnel efforts are optimized. This can lead to largely automated systems or systems in which remote computers monitor and control the switching equipment.

* The authors can be reached at James Coplien cope@lucent.com, Robert Hanmer hanmer@lucent.com, Robert Gamoke r.j.gamoke@att.com.

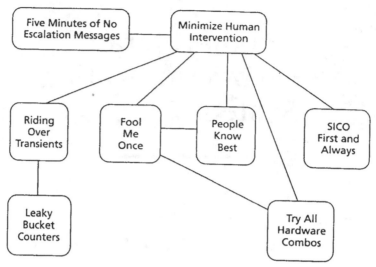

Figure 1   Pattern map.

GLOSSARY

1A: A central processor for telecommunications systems.

1B: A second-generation central processor based on the 1A architecture.

4ESS Switch, 5ESS Switch: Members of the AT&T Electronic Switching System product line.

Application: The portion of systems software that relates to its call processing function.

Call Store: The system's memory store, used for static or dynamic data.

CC: Central control (the central processor complex), either a 1A or a 1B processor.

FIT: Failures in a Trillion, a measurement of the failure rate of hardware components (one FIT equals one component failure in 109 hours).

PC: Processor Configuration, the initialization and recovery mechanisms (independent of the application) that deal with the common underlying hardware/software platform. PC is also used as a verb, to indicate a certain level of system reboot.

Phase: A level of system recovery escalation.

Program Store: The memory stores used for program text.

SICO: System Integrity Control.

Stored Program Control: A term used to differentiate between central control-based switching and the older relay- and crossbar- based systems.

Transient: A condition that is transitory in nature. It appears and disappears. Lightning might produce transient errors.

PATTERN: *MINIMIZE HUMAN INTERVENTION*

Problem: History has shown that people cause the majority of problems in continuously running systems (wrong actions, wrong systems, wrong button).

Context: Highly reliable continuously running digital systems, for which downtime, human-induced or otherwise, must be minimized.

Forces:
- Humans are truly intelligent; machines aren't. Humans are better at detecting patterns of system behavior, especially among seemingly random occurrences separated by time. (See the pattern *People Know Best.*)
- Machines are good at orchestrating a well thought out, global strategy; humans aren't.
- Humans are fallible; computers are often less fallible.
- Humans feel a need to intervene if they can't see that the system is making serious attempts at restoration: A quiet system is a dead system. Human reaction and decision times are very slow (by orders of magnitude) compared to computer processors.
- Human operators get bored with ongoing surveillance and may ignore or miss critical events.
- Normal processing (and failure) events happen so quickly that it is infeasible to include the human operator.

Solution: Let the machine try to do everything itself, deferring to the human only as an act of desperation and a last resort.

Resulting Context: The result is a system less susceptible to human error. This will make the system's customers happier. In many organizations, the system operator's compensation is based on system availability, so this strategy actually improves the operator's lot.

Application of this pattern leads to a system in which patterns such as *Riding Over Transients, SICO First and Always,* and *Try All Hardware Combos* apply as well, providing a system with the ability to proceed automatically.

Rationale: A disproportionate number of failures in high-availability systems are due to operator errors, not primary system errors. By minimizing human intervention, overall system availability can be improved. Human intervention can be reduced by building in strategies that counter human tendencies to act rashly; see patterns like *Fool Me Once, Leaky Bucket Counters,* and *Five Minutes of No Escalation Messages.*

Notice the tension between this pattern and *People Know Best.*

Authors: Robert Hanmer and Mike Adams.

PATTERN: *PEOPLE KNOW BEST*

Problem: How do you balance automation with human authority and responsibility?

Context: A highly reliable, continuously operating system that tries to recover from all error conditions on its own.

Forces:
- People have a good subjective sense of the passage of time, how it relates to the probability of a serious failure, and how outages will be perceived by the customer.
- The system is set up to recover from failure cases. (See the pattern *Minimize Human Intervention.*)
- People feel a need to intervene.
- Most system errors can be traced to human error.

Solution: Assume that people know best, particularly the maintenance folks. Design the system to allow knowledgeable users to override automatic controls.

Example: As you escalate through the 64 states of processor configuration (see *Try All Hardware Combos*), a human who understands what's going on can intervene and stop it, if necessary.

Resulting Context: People feel empowered; however, they are also held accountable for their actions.

This is an absolute rule: people feel a need to intervene. There is no perfect solution to this problem, and the pattern cannot resolve all the forces well. *Fool Me Once* provides a partial solution in that it doesn't give humans a chance to intervene.

Rationale: Consider the input command to unconditionally restore a unit. What does "unconditional" mean? Let's say the system thinks the unit is powered down; what should happen when the operator asks for the unit to be restored unconditionally? Answer: try to restore it anyhow, no excuses allowed; the fault detection hardware can always detect the powered-down condition and generate an interrupt for the unit out of service. Why might the operator want to do this? Because the problem may be not with the power but with the sensor that wrongly reports that the power is off.

Notice the tension between this pattern and *Minimize Human Intervention*.

Author: Robert Gamoke.

PATTERN: *FIVE MINUTES OF NO ESCALATION MESSAGES*

Problem: Rolling in console messages: the human-machine interface is saturated with error reports rolling off the screen, or the system is consuming extreme computational resources just to display error messages.

Context: Any continuously operating, fault-tolerant system with escalation and where transient conditions may be present.

Forces:
- There is no sense in wasting time or reducing the level of service trying to solve a problem that will go away by itself.
- Many problems work themselves out, given time.
- You don't want the switch to use all of its resources displaying messages.
- You don't want to panic users by making them think the switch is out of control (see *Minimize Human Intervention*).
- The only user action related to the escalation messages may be inappropriate to the goal of preserving system sanity.
- There are other computer systems monitoring the actions taken. These systems can deal with a great volume of messages.

Solution: When taking the first action in a series that could lead to an excess number of messages, display a message. Periodically display an update message. If the abnormal condition ends, display a message that everything is back to normal. Do not display a message for every change in state (see *Riding Over Transients*).

Continue to communicate trouble status and actions taken to the downstream monitoring computer system throughout this period.

For example, when the 4ESS switch enters the first level of system overload, post a user message. Post no more messages for 5 minutes, even if there is additional escalation. At the end of 5 minutes, display a status message indicating the current status. When the condition clears, display an appropriate message.

Resulting Context: The system operator won't panic from seeing too many messages. Machine-to-machine messages and measurement provide a record for later evaluation and make the system's actions visible to people who can deal with them. In the 4ESS overload example, measurement counters continue to track overload dynamics; some downstream support systems track these counters.

Other messages, not related to the escalating situation that is producing too many messages, will be displayed as though the system were normal. Thus the normal functioning of the system is not adversely affected by the volume of escalation messages.

Note the conflict with *People Know Best*.

Rationale: Don't freak out the user. The only solution to 4ESS switch overload for an on-site user is to resort to the command "Cancel Overload Controls," which tells the system to ignore its overload indicators and behave as though there were no overload.

This is a special case of *Aggressive versus Tentative*.

Authors: Robert Hanmer and Mike Adams.

PATTERN: *RIDING OVER TRANSIENTS*

Alias: Make Sure Problem Really Exists

Problem: How do you know whether or not a problem will work itself out?

Context: You are working with a fault-tolerant application in which some errors, overload conditions, and so on may be transient. The system can escalate through recovery strategies, taking more drastic action at each step. A typical example is a fault-tolerant telecommunication system using static traffic engineering, for which you want to check for overload or transient faults.

Forces:
- You want to catch faults and problems.
- There is no sense in wasting time or reducing level of service while trying to solve a problem that will go away by itself.
- Many problems work themselves out, given time.

Solution: Don't react immediately to detected conditions. Make sure a condition really exists by checking it several times, or use *Leaky Bucket Counters* to detect a critical number of occurrences in a specific time interval. For example, by averaging over time or just waiting a while, you can give transient faults a chance to pass.

Resulting Context: Errors can be resolved with truly minimal effort, because the effort is expended then only if the problem really exists. This pattern allows the system to roll through problems without its users noticing them and without bothering the machine operator to intervene (like *Minimize Human Interaction*).

Rationale: This pattern detects "temporally dense" events. Think of such events as spikes on a time line. If a small number of spikes (specified by a threshold) occur together (where "together" is specified by the interval), then the error is a transient. This is used by *Leaky Bucket Counters, Five Minutes of No Escalation Messages,* and many others.

Author: James O. Coplien.

PATTERN: *LEAKY BUCKET COUNTERS*

Problem: How do you deal with transient faults?

Context: You are working with fault-tolerant system software that must deal with failure events. Failures are tied to episode counts and frequencies.

For example, in 1A/1B processor systems used in AT&T telecommunication products, as memory words (dynamic RAM) get weak, the memory module generates a parity error trap. Examples include both 1A processor dynamic RAM and 1B processor static RAM.

Forces:
- You want a hardware module to exhibit hard failures before taking

drastic action. Some failures come from the environment and thus should not be blamed on the device.

Solution: A failure group has a counter that is initialized to a predetermined value when the group is initialized. The counter is decremented for each fault or event (usually faults) and incremented on a periodic basis; however, the count is never incremented beyond its initial value. There are different initial values and different leak rates for different subsystems (for example, the leak interval is a half-hour for the 1A memory [store] subsystem). The strategy for 1A dynamic RAM specifies that for the first failure in a store (within the timing window) you must take the store out of service, diagnose it, and then automatically restore it to service. On the second, third, and fourth failures (within the window), you just leave it in service. On the fifth failure (again, within the window), you must take the unit out of service, diagnose it, and leave it out.

If the episode transcends the interval, it's not transient: the leak rate is faster than the refill rate, and the pattern indicates an error condition. If the burst is more intense than expected (i.e., it exceeds the error threshold), then it represents unusual behavior not associated with a transient burst, and the pattern indicates an error condition.

Resulting Context: A system in which errors are isolated and handled (by taking devices out of service), but transient errors (e.g., errors caused by excessive humidity) don't cause unnecessary loss of service.

Rationale: The history is instructive: in old call stores (1A memories that contained dynamic data), why did we collect data? For old call stores, the field replaceable unit (FRU) was a circuit pack, while the failure group was a store composed of 12 or 13 packs. We needed to determine which pack was bad. Memory may have been spread across seven circuit packs; the transient bit was only one bit, not enough to isolate the failure. By recording data from four events, we were better able to pinpoint (with 90 percent accuracy) which pack was bad, so the machine operator didn't have to change seven packs.

Why go five failures before taking a unit out of service? By collecting data on the second, third, and fourth failures, you can make absolutely sure you know the characteristics of the error; thus you reduce your uncertainty about the FRU. By the fifth time, you know it's sick and you need to take it out of service.

Periodically increasing the count on the store creates a sliding time window. The resource is considered sane when the counter (re)attains its initialized value. Humidity, heat, and other environmental problems cause transient errors, which should be treated differently (i.e., pulling the card does no good).

See, for example, *Fool Me Once,* which uses simple leaky bucket counters. This is a special case of the pattern *Riding Over Transients.* The strategy is alluded to by Downing, Nowack, and Tuomenoska (1964).

Author: Robert Gamoke.

PATTERN: *SICO First and Always*

Problem: You are tying to make a system highly available and resilient in the face of hardware and software faults and transient errors.

Context: You are working with a system in which the ability to do meaningful work is of the utmost importance, but rare periods of partial application functionality can be tolerated (for example, the 1A/1B processor-based 4ESS switch from AT&T).

Forces:
- Bootstrapping is initialization.
- A high-availability system might require (re)initialization at any time to ensure system sanity.
- The System Integrity Control Program (SICO) coordinates system integrity.
- The System Integrity Program must be in control during bootstrapping.
- The focus of operational control changes from bootstrapping to executive control during normal call processing.
- Application functioning is very important.
- The System Integrity Program takes processor time, but that is acceptable in this context.
- The system is composed of proprietary elements, for which design criteria may be imposed on all the software in the system.
- Hardware designed to be fault tolerant reduces hardware errors.

Solution: Give the System Integrity Program the ability and power to reinitialize the system whenever system sanity is threatened by error conditions. The same System Integrity Program should oversee both the initialization process and the normal application functions so that initialization can be restarted if it runs into errors.

Resulting Context: In short, System Integrity Control plays a major role during bootstrapping, after which it hands control over to the executive scheduler, which in turn lets System Integrity Control regain control for short periods of time on a scheduled basis.

See also *Audit Derivable Constants After Recovery.*

Rationale: During a recovery event (phase or bootstrap), SICO calls processor initialization software first, peripheral initialization software second, then application initialization software, and finally it transfers to executive control. Unlike a classic computer program in which initialization takes place first and "normal execution" second, the SICO architecture does not make software initialization the highest-level function. System integrity is at an even higher level than system initialization.

The architecture is based on a base level cycle in the executive control. After bootstrapping, the first item in the base cycle is SICO (though this is different code than that run during bootstrapping). So, after the SICO part of bootstrapping is done, the base level part of SICO is entered into each base level cycle to monitor the system on a periodic basis.

The System Integrity Control Program must be alert to watch for failures during both bootstrapping and normal base-level operation. There is a system integrity monitor in the base level that watches timers. Overload control and audit control check in with SICO to report software and hardware failures and (potentially) request initialization, while watching for errors within their own realms.

During bootstrapping and initialization, system integrity employs a number of similar mechanisms to monitor the system (for example, Analog Timers, Boot Timers, *Try All Hardware Combos,* and others).

Much of the rationale comes from AUTOVON, Safeguard, missile guidance systems, and other high-reliability real-time projects from early AT&T stored program control experience. See Meyers, Routt, and Yoder (1977).

Author: Robert Hanmer.

PATTERN: *TRY ALL HARDWARE COMBOS*

Problem: The central controller (CC) has several configurations. There are many possible paths through CC subsystems, depending on the configuration. How do you select a workable configuration when there is a faulty subsystem?

Context: You are working with highly fault-tolerant computing complexes, such as the 1B processor.

The processing complex has a number of duplicated subsystems. Each one consists of a CC, a set of call stores, a call store bus, a set of program stores, a program store bus, and an interface bus. Major subsystems are duplicated with standby units to increase system reliability rather than to provide distributed processing capabilities. There are 64 possible configurations of these subsystems, given fully duplicated sparing. Each configuration is said to represent a configuration state.

The system is brought up in stages. First, you need to have the memory units working. Second, you need to talk to the disk, so you can pump stuff into memory (which allows you to run programs to pump the rest of the stores, so code can recover other units). Third, after the base system is configured and refreshed from disk, you can bring up the application.

Forces:
- You want to catch and remedy single, isolated errors.
- You also want to catch errors that aren't easily detected in isolation but which result from interaction between modules.
- You sometimes must catch multiple concurrent errors.
- The CC can't sequence subsystems through configurations, since it may be faulty itself.
- The machine should recover by itself without human intervention (see *Minimize Human Intervention*).

Solution:
Maintain a 64-state counter in hardware. We call this the configuration counter. There is a table that maps from that counter onto a configuration state: in the 1A, it's in the hardware; in the 1B, it's in the boot ROM. Every time the system fails to get through a PC to a predetermined level of stability, it restarts the system with a successive value of the configuration counter.

In the 5ESS switch there is a similar 16-state counter. It first tries all side zero units (a complete failure group), then all side one units (the other failure group), hoping to find a single failure. The subsequent counting states look for more insidious problems, such as those that come from interactions between members of these coarse failure groups.

Resulting Context: The system can deal with any number of concurrent faults, provided there is at most one fault per subsystem.

The state will increment when a reboot (PC) fails.

Sometimes the fault won't be detected right after the reboot sequence (i.e., not until more than 30 seconds after the resumption of normal activities). This problem is addressed in *Fool Me Once*.

Sometimes, going through all 64 states isn't enough; see *Don't Trust Anyone* and *Analog Timer*.

Rationale: This design is based on the FIT rates of the original hardware—and on the extreme caution of first-generation stored program control switching systems.

Note that the pattern *Blind Search* apparently violates this pattern, because it uses a store to hold the identity of the out-of-service module; this is addressed in the pattern *Multiple Copies of Base Store*.

Author: Robert Gamoke; 5ESS information, Fred Keeve. See Downing, Nowak, and Tuomenoska (1964, pp. 2005–2009].

PATTERN: *FOOL ME ONCE*

Problem: Sometimes the fault causing a processor configuration (PC) is intermittent (usually triggered by software, such as diagnostics). After a PC is complete, users expect the configuration state display to disappear from the system's human control interface and the system to be sane. If the configuration display state continues to be displayed for more than 30 seconds, users may become concerned that the system may still have a problem. But if the system in fact trips on another fault, it may reboot itself (take a phase) and reinitiate the initialization sequence using the same configuration as before (or, worse, start the configuration sequence at the beginning), which raises the probability that the system will loop in reboots ("roll in recovery") and never attempt different configurations.

TABLE 1. Configurations Established by Emergency Action Switching (Status of Units after a Switch Performed by the Indicated State)[*]

PC State	CC0	CC1	PS0	PS1	Bus0	Bus1	Other Stores
X000	U	U	U	U	U	U	U
X001	C	C	U	U	U	U	U
X010	U	U	U	U	C	C	U
X011	U	U	A	S	A	S	T
X100	U	U	A	S	S	A	T
X101	U	U	S	A	S	A	T
X110	U	U	S	A	A	S	T
X111	U	U	S	A	A	S	T

[*] (Downing, Nowak, & Tuomenoska, 1964, p. 2006)
X: Don't care; A: Active; S: Standby; U: Unchanged; C: Complemented; T: Marked as having trouble.

Context: You are working with a highly available systems using redundancy, and you are employing the pattern *Try All Hardware Combos*.

You're going through *Try All Hardware Combos*. The system finds an ostensibly sane state and progresses 30 seconds into initialization, beyond boot and into the application. The application "knows" that the hardware is sane if it can go for 30 seconds (using *Leaky Bucket Counters*). When the system reaches this state, it resets the configuration counter. However, a latent error can cause a system fault after the configuration counter has been reset. The system no longer "knows" that it is in PC escalation, and retries the same configuration that has already failed.

Forces:
It's hard to set a universally correct interval for a Leaky Bucket Counter; sometimes, 30 seconds is too short. The application (and customer) would be upset if the Leaky Bucket Counter were set too long (for example, a customer doesn't want to wait a half-hour for a highly reliable system to clear its fault status). Some errors take a long time to appear, even though they are fundamental hardware errors (e.g., an error in program store that isn't accessed until very late in the initialization cycle, or until a hardware fault is triggered by a diagnostic run out of the scheduler). People's expectations are among the most important forces at work here. In spite of the

potential for some classes of faults to be latent, the application and user feel assured that the system must be sane if it's been exercised for 30 seconds.

Solution: The first time the application tells PC that "all is well," believe it and reset the configuration counter. The second and subsequent times, within a longer time window, ignore the request.

The first request to reset the configuration counter indicates that the application's 30-second Leaky Bucket Counter says that everything is fine. Set up a half-hour Leaky Bucket Counter to avoid being fooled. If the application tries to reset the 64-state configuration counter twice in a half-hour, ignore it. This indicates recurring failures that would result in reboots.

Resulting Context: Any subsequent failures will cause the configuration counter to advance, guaranteeing that the next PC will use a fresh configuration. For a single subsystem error that is taking the system down, this strategy will eventually reach a workable configuration. Once the system is up, schedule diagnostics to isolate the faulty unit (see *People Know Best*). The system will be able to handle repetitive failures outside the shorter window, thereby reinforcing *Minimize Human Intervention.*

Rationale: See the forces. It's better to escalate to exceptionally extravagant strategies like this, no matter how late, if it eventually brings the system back on line. The pattern has been found to be empirically sound.

Author: Robert Gamoke.

ACKNOWLEDGMENTS

Many thanks to Gerard Meszaros of BNR, who served as the PLoP '95 shepherd for these patterns, and to all those who reviewed these patterns in the writers' workshops at PLoP.

REFERENCES

R. W. Downing, J. S. Nowak, & L. S. Tuomenoska (September, 1964). "No. 1 Electronic Switching System," *Bell System Technical Journal, 43,* 1961–2019.

M. N. Meyers, W. A. Routt, & K. W. Yoder (September, 1977). *Bell System Technical Journal, 56,* 2 1139–1167.

Industrial Experience with Design Patterns

Kent Beck[*], James O. Coplien[†], Ron Crocker[‡],
Lutz Dominick[§], Gerard Meszaros[¶],
Frances Paulisch[**], and John Vlissides[***]

INTRODUCTION

Software developers have a strong tendency to reuse designs that have worked well for them in the past and, as they gain more experience, their repertoire of design experience grows and they become more proficient. Unfortunately, this design reuse is usually restricted to personal experience and there is usually little sharing of design knowledge among developers. A design pattern is a particular form of recording design information such that designs which have worked well in particular situations can be applied again in similar situations in the future by others. The availability of a catalog of design patterns can help both the experienced and the novice designer recognize situations in which design reuse could or should occur. Such a collection is time-consuming to create, but it is our experience that the invested effort pays off.

[*] 70761.1216@compuserve.com
[†] cope@lucent.com
[‡] crocker@cig.mot.com
[§] Lutz.Dominick@mchp.siemens.de
[¶] gerard@osgcanada.com
[**] frances.paulisch@mchp.siemens.de
[***] vlis@watson.ibm.com

©1996 IEEE. Reprinted, with permission, from Proceedings of ICSE, Berlin, Germany, March 1996, pp. 103–114.

A pattern is said to be a "solution to a problem in a context." The basic structure consists of a name for the pattern, a problem statement, a context in which the problem occurs, and a description of the solution together with additional information such as the associated tradeoffs, a list of where this pattern has been applied, etc. The form consists of structured prose and sketches (such as OMT diagrams and interaction diagrams). There is general agreement that the pattern identifies a set of "forces" or constraints which are subsequently resolved in the solution.

Design patterns have received a lot of attention lately, especially in the object-oriented community. The reason for the recent interest in design patterns is not the novelty of the designs themselves, but rather the vision that a diverse community of experienced software practitioners, communicating mostly via the Internet, can share and collectively grow a set of design repertoires in the form of patterns. The patterns community is sufficiently enthused about the prospective advantages to be gained by making this design knowledge explicit in the form of patterns that hundreds of patterns have been written, discussed, and distributed.

A BRIEF HISTORY OF DESIGN PATTERNS

Software design patterns had their origin in the late 1980s when Ward Cunningham and Kent Beck developed a set of patterns for developing elegant user interfaces in Smalltalk.[5] At around the same time, Jim Coplien was developing a catalog of language-specific C++ patterns called idioms.[9] Meanwhile, Erich Gamma recognized the value of explicitly recording recurring design structures while working on his doctoral dissertation on object-oriented software development.[16] These people and others met and intensified their discussions on patterns at a series of OOPSLA workshops starting in 1991 organized by Bruce Anderson[3,4] and by 1993 the first version of a catalog of patterns was in draft form (summarized in an article by Erich Gamma, Richard Helm, Ralph Johnson, and John Vlissides[17]) which eventually formed the basis for the first book on design patterns.[18] All of these activities were influenced by the works of Christopher Alexander, a building architect and urban planner[1,2] who coined the term "pattern" to refer to recurring designs in (building) architecture. In the summer of 1993, a small group of pattern enthusiasts formed the "Hillside Generative Patterns Group" and subsequently organized the first conference on patterns called the "Pattern Languages of Programming" (PLoP) in 1994.[11]

THE PATTERNS COMMUNITY

The success of the PLoP conference in August '94 and the unveiling of the so-called "Gang-of-Four"[18] book at October '94 OOPSLA created a surge of interest in the topic of design patterns. Due to their basically simple nature, patterns are subject to "overhype," particularly by those who do not fully understand what the real capabilities are or how hard it is to write good patterns. Several mailing lists have been set up by Ralph Johnson at the University of Illinois, and this has led to the development of an internet-based community of software developers interested in patterns. A World-Wide-Web site* is also maintained at the University of Illinois which serves as a central location for information on patterns. Most of the active members of this online patterns community are practically oriented experienced software developers and, as such, they are quick to correct any overly high expectations placed on patterns by newcomers.

The practical nature of patterns themselves and the people writing and using patterns should not be underestimated. As Ralph Johnson once wrote:[20] "One of the distinguishing characteristics of computer people is the tendency to go 'meta' at the slightest provocation. Instead of writing programs, we want to invent programming languages. Instead of inventing programming languages, we want to create systems for specifying programming languages. There are many good reasons for this tendency, since a good theory makes it a lot easier to solve particular instances of the problem. But if you try to build a theory without having enough experience in the problem, you are unlikely to find a good solution. Moreover, much of the information in a design is not derived from first principles, but obtained by experience."

Presumably due to the nature of patterns being used to record and reuse existing design knowledge, the patterns community has been said to have an "aggressive disregard for originality."[15] As a concrete example of this, all design patterns in the Gang-of-Four book[18] are based on designs which occur in two or more existing, real applications. Perhaps because no one feels like they "own" a particular design, there is a distinct feeling that the members of the patterns community are working toward a common goal in developing a broad collection of patterns as opposed to the competitive nature common to other disciplines (e.g., which person publishes a certain theorem first).

---

*http://st-www.cs.uiuc.edu/users/patterns/patterns.html

Since the patterns community is one that shares information in an open forum and builds on the experiences of others, it seemed natural to us to submit a joint paper on our experiences with patterns. We focus, in particular, on the lessons learned in our respective industrial settings as a first step toward answering the questions "Patterns sound very promising, but how are they actually used in the industry? and What benefits, if any, do they bring in practice?"

INDUSTRIAL EXPERIENCE WITH PATTERNS

SMALLTALK BEST PRACTICE PATTERNS—KENT BECK (FIRST CLASS SOFTWARE)

I have been writing what I intend to grow into a comprehensive system of patterns for Smalltalk programming, called the Smalltalk Best Practice Patterns (SBPP). I'll report here on the status of these patterns and my experience teaching them to and watching them used by two clients developing commercial software in Smalltalk.

The SBPP are intended to accelerate the pace at which teams of Smalltalk developers begin realizing the benefits of objects and Smalltalk by communicating the techniques used by expert Smalltalkers. Although many patterns are still under development, a core set of patterns are finished that cover most of the important design and coding problems.

The best developed section contains 90 patterns for coding. It presents successful tactics for Smalltalk-naming conventions, reuse of the collection classes, common control flow patterns, and code formatting. The emphasis throughout is on communicating through code. The patterns are intended to generate code that meets the simple style rule "say everything once and only once." The section on design has 15 patterns, most of which exist only in outline form. When finished, they are intended to cover similar material to *Design Patterns.*[18] I teach these patterns using presentations similar to "Patterns Generate Architectures."[6] The section on user interface design has 25 patterns for designing user interfaces and 15 patterns for implementing them in Smalltalk. These patterns are not yet ready to be taught. The final section covers project management. These 30 patterns focus on the non-programming tasks of programmers—testing, documentation, and scheduling.

Hewitt Associates
Hewitt Associates has a group of five Smalltalk programmers working on the next generation of a system implemented originally on large, main-

frame computers. They have extensive experience with objects, although the team members have varying levels of familiarity with objects and all are new to Smalltalk.

Initially, the team met once a week for several months. As the coding patterns became available, they discussed a few patterns a week. Now that production coding has begun, discussing and learning about programming style is done primarily as part of group code reviews. I spent two days with the team when they started coding seriously. We alternated working on projects with presentation and discussion of the most important patterns.

The resulting code is remarkably good. The most experienced members are making excellent design decisions that I only appreciate after having them explained carefully to me. Even the junior members of the team, new to Smalltalk and objects, are writing idiomatic Smalltalk code. I have noticed the pattern titles becoming part of the spoken vocabulary of the team—"Oh, that's a Parameters Object," "We need a Guard Clause here."

Orient Overseas Container Limited (OOCL)

OOCL has a much more ambitious effort, with 25–30 developers working to replace centralized applications with a worldwide distributed architecture. The project grew very quickly, which resulted in some chaos as the team tried to find a common identity and culture.

David Ornstein and I introduced patterns two ways. First, we held two "Smalltalk Bootcamps," where teams of 10–12 develop a simple application from requirements to tested, documented, shipping code in three days. We interspersed discussion of important patterns and software engineering issues with frantic development. The lessons learned here seem to stick very well. In contrast, patterns presented in lecture style were not learned as readily.

An activity we held with some success was a Pattern Bowl. We chose a piece of code to review. We divided the audience (25 developers) into two teams. Each team got points for recognizing the presence or absence of patterns in the review code in a limited amount of time. The winners received guardianship of a token trophy until the next Pattern Bowl. We were happy with the results for two reasons. First, the code in question got a very thorough review. Everyone in the room had a pretty good grasp of what it did and how it did it. You could use a Pattern Bowl to communicate critical shared code. Second, the teams were forced to discuss the meaning of patterns, because there were penalties for mis-identifying a pattern.

Overall, patterns have had a big impact mostly on the early members of the team, five or six bright new Smalltalkers we spent a lot of individual time with. Their designs are sophisticated, their code idiomatic. Later additions, including some experienced Smalltalk programmers, showed reluctance to simply follow the dictates of the patterns, preferring their own style. The unfinished state of the patterns has definitely made teaching them to experienced programmers more difficult.

I have always tried to write my patterns with a substantial section in the middle that presented the motivation for the pattern, why possible alternatives don't work, and led up to the conclusion. OOCL asked me early on to strip all that out, leaving patterns with a name, a problem statement, and a solution. I put together such an abridged version. It has been widely used as a reference and development guide, often being posted on cubicle walls within sight of the workstation.

Conclusion

I have seen the SBPP, even in their half-finished state, have dramatic effects on the quality and quantity of code produced by teams. I am pleased at how the patterns often encourage good code not by admonishing against mistakes, but by presenting a positive set of habits. The effects on communication of adding the names of patterns to the team's shared vocabulary is emerging as a powerful positive force.

Experienced programmers often resist adopting patterns. I suspect the best way to engage developers with strong notions of how things ought to be done is to encourage them to modify and extend the patterns with their own favorite tricks.

Patterns make good projects better. They do not resurrect bad projects. Most of the many things that can go wrong with a project can still go wrong, whether or not patterns are used. Patterns solve a limited (but critically important) set of communication problems with team development, and make individuals more productive. They cannot substitute for effective project management.

PATTERNS IN AT&T—JAMES COPLIEN

AT&T Patterns Programs

There are many independent patterns efforts afoot across AT&T; we touch on just a few of them here.

Fault-Tolerant Architectures. Patterns capture proven, mature practices in a domain such as building architecture or software design. AT&T has several core competencies that are fundamental to our history of quality customer service. High-availability system design and fault-tolerant software are among these core competencies. Many of these core competencies can be captured as patterns, since they solve a wide variety of reliability and availability problems that arise during architecture and design.

We approached two development communities and asked management to point us to their experts on operations, administration, maintenance, and provisioning. This program of "pattern mining" collected dozens of patterns from a handful of experts. We refined these patterns and captured them on-line in HTML* where they were made available to the general AT&T research and development community.

Process Patterns. We have used patterns in the domain of process and organization, as well as in the domain of software architecture. Patterns are a literary form that conveys a solution to a problem in a context: though most practitioners are exploring architectural patterns, there is no reason to limit them to software design. We have found the recurring patterns of outstanding software development organizations through an extensive research program.[10] We can use those patterns to solve organizational and process problems.

Object Patterns. Little of our patterns work relates to the object paradigm. Objects are just one way of partitioning systems, and they are not always the best way to organize high-availability or fault-tolerant architectures. Besides, there are many more proven, mature patterns in the architectures of legacy systems than there are in the young, rapidly changing object-oriented systems.

Early work in AT&T to gather proven C++ programming idioms has culminated in a collection of widely used programming techniques.[9] One can think of these as proto-patterns; they were in fact one of the foundations from which contemporary patterns practice grew. The seminal *Design Patterns* book[18] built on these and other patterns to provide a general, language-independent collection of patterns by which object-oriented programming competency might be judged. These patterns are seeing wide use in mature AT&T projects. We have steered some young object-oriented projects away from patterns, however. Most new object-oriented projects must learn a design method and a new programming language, in addition

---

* HyperText Markup Language, the publishing language of the World Wide Web.

to building a new architecture. We have noticed that incorporating more than three significantly new practices in a project increases risk, so patterns are put off until the project masters the initial changes.

How Patterns have Helped Us

Training. We have just started to use the fault-tolerance and high-availability patterns in architectural training. There are two aspects to this training: pattern training per se, and pattern supplements to architectural training. Pattern training is largely for organizations that are "pattern consumers." These organizations are building new projects, using patterns as audits and drivers for design. We have found this training to be effective on many levels. Not only do attendees deepen their understanding of patterns in general and of specific core competency patterns, but they also deepen their appreciation for architecture and telecommunications foundations. Most of these courses are conducted as workshops that are highly participatory, with design exercises and pattern-writing exercises. We believe that it is difficult for designers to appreciate patterns fully unless they have written one.

Some architecture courses are slowly adopting patterns as an adjunct to materials presented in a traditional format. So far, we haven't found this use of patterns to be a significant aid to the learning process. Patterns are probably perceived as a distraction to the traditional educational structures, and we conjecture that pattern-based architecture education might work better if the whole course were pattern-based. We plan further work in this area.

Architecture Documentation. In our pattern mining exercise, a new development project was the client for patterns extracted from contemporary projects. When architects from the contemporary project saw the patterns, they saw a solution to a problem that had been plaguing them for some time. Earlier attempts to capture the project architecture had failed to resolve the tradeoffs between a good description of the vertical architecture and architectural layering; patterns provided a way to unify those two perspectives. The original "source" organization is now one of the most active pattern organizations in AT&T, mining its own patterns as architecture documentation.

Shaping New Architectures. By "mining" the fault-tolerant patterns of contemporary AT&T software systems, we can lay the groundwork for emerging and future project architectures. Much support for the emerging patterns work in AT&T came from a new project for which high availability is of paramount importance. The new project is evaluating the fault-tolerance and high-availability patterns gleaned from contemporary systems to see which ones are well-suited to the new system's market and technology.

Requirements Acclimation. Requirements documents draw on market foresight and experience. Most analysts focus on the market foresight of the sales and marketing force, but draw on their personal anecdotes or on review input for the experience component. Patterns provide a written experience base that can feed the requirements process in the following way. As formative projects acquire patterns from their peers and predecessors, they go through them to select those that address problems in the project requirements. Once in a while, a pattern will solve a problem that seems like it should be in requirements, but the requirement is found to be missing. Such requirements are added to subsequent editions of the requirements document. We did not foresee this benefit of patterns at the outset, but it has proven to be a valuable use of patterns in new projects.

Process Assessment. We use the process patterns to assess the health of development organizations. Our process research effort receives many requests for process improvement assistance; we use the process patterns as one set of tools to identify and remedy problems. These patterns, which have been published,[10] are being similarly used in many companies outside AT&T.

Yet to be Done

Designers find individual patterns illuminating and inspirational. We have patterns at all levels, from architectural frameworks down to design patterns and idioms.[7] The number of total patterns numbers in the hundreds. Scale is a major obstacle to systematic and effective patterns usage.

We are currently evaluating pattern organizing schemes, indexing schemes, and other attacks on the scale of the pattern knowledge base. Bob Hanmer has instituted an indexing scheme where the Intent appears as part of the index entry, but not as part of the pattern itself. We are also planning to work with knowledge engineers to help organize patterns according to expected search criteria.

DESIGN PATTERNS AT MOTOROLA—RON CROCKER

Much like AT&T, Motorola has several independent efforts investigating the use of design patterns for system development. Unfortunately, I can only discuss with any substance the effort that I'm involved with.[*]

---

[*] Another effort is documented elsewhere.[24]

Design Patterns vs. Software Architectures
At Motorola Cellular Infrastructure Group (CIG), recent efforts in applying design patterns to the development process have centered on the relationship between software architecture and design patterns. For some time now, the focus of the systematic improvement efforts at CIG have centered around finding an approach for system development that allows for "large-grained" reuse.[13] Initially, this program focused on the use of object-oriented approaches early in the life cycle, primarily to provide a foundation for this reuse. These attempts were not totally successful. Analyzing these projects indicated some common characteristics that effectively limited any large-grain reuse, including:

- Strong coupling of OO artifacts within a single product
- Short-term needs superseded longer-term needs, even when the benefits were clear.

These findings are not particularly surprising given the strong product-oriented culture of Motorola. However, reaching corporate goals of a factor of 10 improvement in time-to-market requires substantially less work in development—you simply can't do the same amount of work in 1/10th the time.

Enter the centralized software architecture organization, led by the Strategic Software Technologies organization within CIG.[12, 14] As an organization, CIG has accumulated considerable domain expertise and has some very seasoned software architects. In evaluating several purported software architectures, again we found some common symptoms:

- A lack of preciseness in the specification made them ambiguous.
- The architects developed their own terminology to talk about concepts that we would have immediately recognized had they used "our" vocabulary.
- We did not have direct/immediate access to the architects.

Each of these problems led directly to communication problems, which lessens the effectiveness of the architecture. Because the architectures are ambiguous, they can be interpreted in ways other than intended. Because the language was "foreign," the ambiguities tend to be amplified and the architectures become product-centric. Finally, questions about the architecture have nowhere to be directed and are hence left unanswered.

Our search for technology solutions turned to design patterns. From previous readings, we knew that design patterns offered an approach for describing architectural entities independent from their implementation. We were concerned about the roots of design patterns coming from the object-oriented community, since our organization has little OO experience. Our approach was to simply not use design patterns in an OO form. We would use design patterns to capture problem-domain-specific entities in an implementation-independent way for sharing across projects (and products).

Current Status
So far, we have a small catalog of design patterns focused on (in telephony terms) fault management. There is already an implicit design pattern being used in many of our products for handling faults in the equipment. It's robust and understood by the senior technical staff. The problem with this pattern is that it's only implicit. It exists in the heads of the senior people and in the code. In the cases where we reuse this pattern, the pattern is "rediscovered" from the code and re-implemented, often with minor improvements. None of these improvements, however, affect the basic "higher-order" pattern. These are the sort of patterns that we will be cataloging. Based on some near-term results using the fault management pattern, other problem areas are being identified for "patternification." Our expectation is that these patterns will interact to form a fabric of patterns for telephony.

Pattern Applicability Spaces
We have a model of the world depicted roughly in Figure 1. We separate the development process into three large "buckets": Products, Problem-Space (entities), and Solution-Space (entities). The Products are implementations of solutions for specific customer use. CIG examples of products would include base stations, cellular telephone switches, and customer database products. Each of these products is rooted in its problem-space entities. Base stations require mobility management capabilities and radio management capabilities. These capabilities tend to be largely independent of both the product itself and implementations of the product. The issues identified above (product-specific nature of OO artifacts and specialized architectural language) have the effect of masking the inherent problem-space nature of these capabilities. The solution-space is where we implement both problem-independent capabilities and product-specific instances of the problem-space capabilities. For example, for the majority

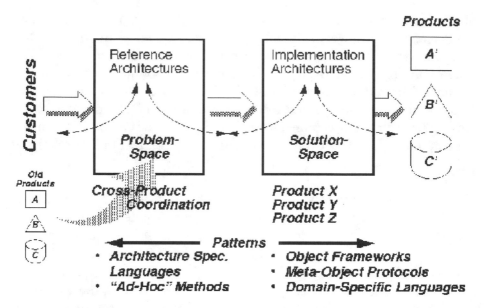

FIGURE 1.   Architectural spaces.

of the patterns described in *Design Patterns*[18] we would consider solely solution-space architectures ("Implementation Architectures") that are problem-space independent; other problem-spaces may see those as both problem-space and solution-space patterns.

Each of the spaces has an architectural basis. The Problem-Space architecture we call "Reference Architecture" to indicate that it is not a concrete implementation but rather a guide to developing products incorporating these problem-space entities. We view the critical aspects of these architectures being the definition of the (behavioral aspects of the) entities and their interactions, and therefore focus less on the particular implementation issues. The Solution-Space architectures we call "Implementation Architectures" since their primary focus is on particular instances of products.

This brings us to consider technologies that can aid in describing the architectures in the given spaces. We consider design patterns a technology that spans the spaces, and believe that design patterns represent a technology that can be used to smooth the transition between spaces and final products. Other technologies we have investigated (object frameworks, meta-object protocols, and application-specific languages) tend to reside in the solution-space, as they apply more directly to the issues relating to implementing designs.

Summary
There are two thrusts in our use of design patterns. The first is in using the technology to encapsulate problem-space entities for larger-grained reuse across product families as described above. The other is in using object frameworks and application-specific languages to implement these patterns for easier implementation. Those investigations are ongoing and not at a point to report progress. Nevertheless, we have seen some effects of using design patterns in our efforts so far:

- Design patterns have little to do with object-oriented technology. This technology is independent of object-oriented technology. The software systems from which we are extracting design patterns are not object-oriented, and the resulting design patterns are not object-oriented. These design patterns can be implemented using object-oriented designs, but it is not required to be this way.
- Design patterns represent a mechanism for easily sharing design information among groups of architects. We have found that with the design patterns we have written, they have been quickly understood by both the senior architects and the product developers. Other approaches have been less successful in bridging this gap.
- Writing good design patterns is difficult and time-consuming. In our efforts so far, we have spent much time on understanding how to write good design patterns so that they provide enough information to the reader to be useful. Our initial design patterns have gone through many iterations to ensure quality. This implies that only high-value problems should be captured using design patterns, and therefore choosing the appropriate problems becomes an issue.
- It is hard to quantify the impact of design patterns on our development effort. Currently, there are no metrics capable of distinguishing the impact of design patterns from other changes in our development process. Without further efforts on such metrics, we will never know the true benefit of this technology.

EXPERIENCES USING PATTERNS AT BNR— GERARD MESZAROS

At BNR, the research and development subsidiary of NorTel (formerly known as Northern Telecom), we first became aware of the term "patterns" at OOPSLA 1993. We instantly recognized that we had been doing something very similar for quite some time as part of a major re-engineering effort of our DMS-100 family of telephone switches.[23] We have used the "pattern" and similar forms to capture project knowledge in a number of areas. While many of these patterns are specific to our problem domain and form the basis of our competitive advantage, we freely publish the more generic ones in the recognition that we get far more in return for a relatively small investment. The patterns we write and use can be roughly categorized as process/method patterns and technical patterns.

Process/Method Patterns
Capturing a Design Methodology as Patterns. As part of developing a new architecture to allow rapid development and delivery of telecommunications services (a.k.a. "Features"), we realized that service developers would require guidance in using the architecture. We began to develop a "service design" methodology. As the "pattern form" was as yet undeveloped, we captured the methodology as a series of "semantic models" starting with requirements and domain model, leading to the architecture model, the design model, and finally the implementation model. Specific aspects of each model were identified and the heuristics for transforming them to the related aspect of the next model were captured.

Many of these patterns were "prescriptive" in that they described how to get from one model to another. As an example, a number of the patterns describe how to find and identify similar concepts in different requirements documents and capture the common concepts in the domain model of a service. These patterns effectively are a "recipe" for doing abstraction for people to whom this does not come naturally.

Architecting Method. In the process of re-architecting our call processing system, we have come to recognize a number of key patterns of behavior of architects that lead to good architecture. Many of these patterns are technical in nature. We have captured a number of these for review and publication at PLoP-95.[19]

The non-technical patterns include ones such as "Just say NO to Politics" (let the project managers solve the question of how the work is divided; architects should concentrate on ensuring that the design decisions are made for technical reasons.)

Technical Patterns
We had discovered a number of recurring patterns in the design of telephone services. We had coined terms for many of these, such as *modifier service* (a

service which observes another service and adds additional behavior at appropriate points).

The patterns mailing list on the internet gave us early access to the patterns that were to be published in *Design Patterns*.[18] We also invited Richard Helm to come teach an introductory course on these patterns. We recognized many of the patterns in our system, often to the point of being able to list our own specializations of the general patterns being described.

We quickly found ourselves expressing our designs in terms of these patterns. They gave us a precise yet concise way of synchronizing our thoughts which saved a lot of effort. No longer did we have to describe a key portion of the design, since we had a common understanding of what was meant by "this object is using the *Observer Pattern* to monitor this other object."

Patterns in Software Architecture. We have found patterns to be particularly useful for defining and describing software architectures. Many patterns (*Observer, Strategy, Composite, Half-Object Plus Protocol,* to name a few) are particularly useful when defining the the architecture of a system because they encapsulate potential changes to the system. The actual mechanisms used to implement these patterns can vary widely based on cost-space tradeoffs but can be hidden from the core objects (business objects) involved.

Reflections on the BNR Experience

Personality Types. Using patterns written by others only takes an open mind; writing patterns takes a special mind! Most people whom we have exposed to the concept of patterns can quickly become proficient at using the common ones. But we have found that only a small percentage of people can write patterns. With respect to patterns, there are three kinds of people: those who see patterns everywhere and can describe them, those who can recognize patterns but can not describe them easily, and those who are oblivious to the pattern surrounding them. This difference seems to stem from a basic orientation of people to focus on similarities as opposed to differences between things.

Impact of Patterns. We have not attempted to measure the impact of patterns on productivity, but we have noticed that communication between people with a "shared space" of patterns is quicker, more complete, and less likely to be misunderstood. At the programming level, we have had people design what might be rather complex designs much more quickly than expected by using one or more design patterns.

PATTERNS IN INDUSTRIAL AUTOMATION AT SIEMENS—
FRANCES PAULISCH/LUTZ DOMINICK

Various operating divisions at Siemens are investigating the effectiveness of using patterns to improve their software production and these activities are coordinated through our department. Many of the software design patterns that are not subject to non-disclosure are being published by our colleagues in the book *Pattern-Oriented Software Architecture*.[8] In this section, we focus on our particular project where we are investigating the effectiveness of applying patterns to technologically oriented applications like the process control of steel mills.

Identifying an Initial Set of Patterns

Our project team, the "pattern mentors," consists of two (software) pattern specialists and two (industrial automation) domain specialists. The first step was to identify potential patterns in interviews with domain experts and then to iteratively refine them (again in consultation with domain experts). In each round we focused on a specific knowledge area. We invited the experts to give a short introductory talk about the solutions they used in their projects and we introduced the notion of patterns. Then we had a discussion to discover the patterns that the projects teams had been using intuitively. Roughly three interviews were required to finish a set of patterns. In their final form, the domain experts agreed that the pattern met our two major criteria of:

- correctly representing the problem-/solution-pair and
- being a useful representation of knowledge demanded by
  their projects.

In one case two experts initially claimed that their solutions to a similar problem were incompatible with each other, but after seeing the problem-solution-pair posed as a pattern, agreed that their solutions were indeed very similar.

As an additional "sanity check" we also presented several patterns to experts of a different but related area who had not taken part in the discussion. The level of detail used in the pattern-form was found to be appropriate for providing an understanding of the related areas.

The current state of our project is such that the final proof, the evaluation of the effectiveness of these patterns in concrete steel mill projects, has not yet been achieved, but we are working toward this goal. Our work demonstrates that a small team of people with knowledge of both patterns and of the domain can build up a set of domain-specific patterns which serve as a basis for demonstrating the effectiveness of patterns to the domain experts. Once such a set of essential patterns has been identified and the domain experts have agreed to the effectiveness of their representation in pattern-form, how should one go about extending the set of patterns?

Identifying Additional Patterns
Ideally, domain experts should be the pattern authors because they have the best knowledge of the domain, but there are several hindrances which must be overcome to accomplish this. The domain experts:

- need time to learn what patterns are and how to identify and use them,
- need practice at abstracting away detail and writing patterns, and
- are so tied up in their daily projects that they find it hard to take the first hurdle and actually write patterns.

Although necessary during the introduction of patterns into an organization, it is exceedingly difficult to write patterns, as we did, based on second-hand experience. Doug Lea of SUNY Oswego, who was in a similar situation consulting with avionics engineers developing a set of online design patterns for avionics control systems as part of the Adage project,[21] reports that he wrote many of the patterns himself after consultation with domain experts for reasons similar to what we experienced.[22]

Making Patterns Available Online
To make the patterns more accessible and attractive to the domain experts, we recorded all of our patterns in HTML in a platform-independent online catalog of patterns. This catalog was organized as a set of three axes which relate to the application domain (in our case the level of automation, the physical structure of the milling machine, and the product-quality features of the milled steel).

The online catalog allows the use of multiple entry points, navigation among the patterns, and a hierarchical structure. The navigation aspect is especially important when the pattern collection grows larger than about 50 patterns, which can no longer be linearly organized in book-form. We used links to hide information which is not immediately relevant to the user so that they can see that the information is there if they want it, but are not distracted by it. Furthermore, many terms are connected to an online glossary, which resulted from a partial domain analysis of the application area. It is too early to tell how useful this online collection of patterns is to the domain experts, but initial indications are positive.

Initial Experience in Using Patterns
Our initial experience in using patterns indicates that patterns are more likely to be accepted and applied if a significant portion of the design is covered by either a group of low-level patterns or a single higher-level "architectural" pattern. Our users expect some kind of tool support, especially when they are faced with ca. 30 or more patterns. In cases where no appropriate technological design pattern is judged to be ideally suited, the users tend to choose structure-oriented patterns such as "pipe-and-filter" or "layered architecture" over process-oriented patterns.

Future Directions
Many of the realizations made within the software reuse community, such as:

- the importance of high-level management commitment, and
- the effectiveness of making a strict distinction between the teams responsible for developing components and those responsible for identifying and maintaining them

apply equally well to the industrial use of patterns.

   We have noticed a strong relationship between the technological design patterns and software design patterns. The technological design patterns we have discovered thus far are planned to serve as the basis for a software application framework for the process-automation of steel mills. Here, we are particularly interested in investigating the interplay between the technological and the software design patterns (e.g., representing the process-control of a conveyor belt as a pipe-and-filter architecture).

DESIGN PATTERNS IN DESIGN REVIEWS—JOHN VLISSIDES

Having served as a consultant to a half-dozen companies, I'm struck by the similarities in what they all try to do. Each project has its unique aspects, certainly, but they are mere variables in a recurring formula. Every project has included a user interface component communicating with some sort of computation component, usually backed by a database. Every project sought to decouple these components to one degree or another. Everyone wanted to use object technology, though not everyone understood why. And while the average experience level varied, every development team struggled with the design process: false starts, iteration, and delays were the norm. These recurrences are mostly beneficial; they let one know what to expect and how to impart the most benefit. But two recurring problems proved troublesome. The following sections describe these problems and how design patterns have helped me deal with them.

Unearthing the Design and its Rationale

The first of these irritants was the quasi-courtroom tactics I had to adopt to get to the truth of a design. Developers usually had trouble explaining the gist of what they had done, either because they had no means to express it or because they honestly didn't know. I was confronted with one spaghetti class diagram after another. The unstated hope was that I would come to understand the design by sheer osmosis. In reality, there was never time for that.

My only recourse was relentless interrogation. I would ask question after question until I had built up a consistent mental model of the system. Inevitably that would involve backtracking—someone would contradict what was said earlier, causing a partial collapse of my mental model. Sometimes the collapse would come only after we had gone down a series of blind alleys. The more successful attempts along these lines tended to raise more questions than they answered: Why did you design it that way? Is what seems to be gratuitous complexity really worthwhile? What are your assumptions, and why are they realistic? What happens six months from now when I need new capability *X*?

Which leads me to the second irritant: shallow design rationale. Often the developers simply didn't know why a design was the way it was. No one bothered writing down the reasons for each major change to the design, let alone the incremental ones. As a result, we had to reverse-engineer the design choices time and again—an uncomfortable process for all concerned.

Enter Design Patterns

After four years of this, things finally began to change when in early 1993 I started incorporating early drafts of material that eventually became *Design Patterns*[18] into my consulting engagements. Rough as that material was, it gave me something concrete to offer in the way of exemplary designs. It also focused my thinking so that I could more readily identify designs based on what the developers were trying to do. No longer did I have to assume that they had developed something entirely new for me to fathom. Instead, I considered the flexibility they were pursuing as a way to isolate a design pattern. Then I could concentrate on mapping the classes they had defined to those in the pattern. If there was some semblance of correspondence, I could feel good about their design and offer constructive criticism immediately. If I could see no correspondence, then I would introduce the pattern to them. Sometimes the flexibility they sought was ill-defined or spurious; the pattern would elude me in those cases. Thus the catalog of design patterns became a kind of sounding board, a test suite for valid design. Of course, this experience helped us refine the patterns themselves.

Sharing Design Patterns

For all these benefits, though, the burden of pattern application fell largely on my shoulders. The patterns weren't complete or polished enough to give to the development teams ahead of time. I trotted them out as needed, but because they were hard to share with others, they tended to stay confined to my head. Their consummate benefits didn't emerge until the team members could internalize them as well.

That couldn't happen until *Design Patterns* appeared on bookshelves in late 1994. For my first major engagement thereafter, I insisted that each developer read and understand the book prior to our meeting. I had no delusions about this request; I thought few would read it all, let alone understand it. But that was their responsibility, and I expected most people to have at least looked at it.

As it turned out, not only had everyone read it, but a core group (5 out of 12) had a remarkably good grasp of the patterns we discussed. There was also enthusiasm, not just for design patterns, but also for the developers' own design as well, because they found that they had used some design patterns unwittingly. Seeing the design patterns was a vindication of sorts—it legitimized approaches they had been unsure of.

The Biggest Payoff: Communication

But the best part of the encounter was the high level of communication we achieved. We discussed designs not in terms of classes and objects and methods but to a great extent in terms of design pattern concepts: participants, applicability, consequences, trade-offs. Discussion remained at the design pattern level unless and until there was a controversy, at which point we might drop down to the nuts and bolts. But that was infrequent. I'm happy to report that pattern concepts dominated our discussions.

In fact, I came away from this engagement feeling a satisfaction I hadn't felt after any other, and I attribute it unreservedly to the use of design patterns by all concerned, not just myself. Another engagement along these lines has been scheduled for this fall. The project under review will be a different one, with another, somewhat larger development team at its helm. As a further twist, several of the team members from the earlier engagement will participate. They will act as I did, but to small subgroups of the overall team. That will help spread the burden and hopefully permit even more incisive discussions.

LESSONS LEARNED

Despite our diverse backgrounds and experiences, several common lessons can be drawn from our own experiences with patterns as well as from our colleagues in the patterns community. Table 1 shows the sources of the summary observations listed below. Although in some cases it is difficult to give a binary answer, checkmarks indicate that this company has made this experience. Unfortunately, we do not have any measurable data on the impact of patterns available yet, at least not in a form we could currently publish. But the consistency among our experiences with patterns leads us to believe in the value of lessons listed here.

TABLE 1.   Sources for Summary Observations

Patterns . . .	FCS	AT&T	Motorola	BNR	Siemens	IBM
Are a good communications medium	✓	✓	✓	✓	✓	✓
Are extracted from working designs	✓	✓	✓	✓	✓	✓
Capture design essentials	✓	✓	✓	✓	✓	✓
Enable sharing of "best practices"	✓		✓	✓	✓	✓
Are not necessarily object-oriented		✓	✓	✓	✓	
Should be introduced through mentoring	✓				✓	✓
Are difficult/time-consuming to write			✓	✓	✓	
Require practice to write					✓	✓

Patterns serve as a good team communications medium. Typically, when several pattern-aware software developers are discussing various potential solutions to a problem, they use the pattern names as a precise and concise way to communicate complex concepts effectively.

Patterns are extracted from working designs. Each design pattern discussed above was extracted from existing, working designs (and in the case of the organizational patterns of AT&T, from existing organization) and not created without experience. The design patterns capture the essence of working designs in a form that makes them usable in future work, including specifics about the context that makes the patterns applicable or not.

Patterns capture the essential parts of a design in a compact form. This compact representation helps developers and maintainers understand and therefore not contort the architecture of a system. Making this often only implicitly understood knowledge explicit allows for more effective software development.

Patterns can be used to record and encourage the reuse of "best practices." This is especially important for helping less-experienced developers produce good designs faster. A collection of design patterns in handbook-form is useful for teaching software engineering. However, note that, in partial contrast to handbooks from other engineering disciplines, a design pattern is not a rule to be followed blindly, but rather should serve as a guide to the designer and/or provide alternatives when being applied to a particular situation.

Patterns are not necessarily object-oriented. Although the design patterns as we describe them come from the object-oriented community, there is nothing inherent in design patterns that makes them object-oriented. Not coincidentally, there is nothing inherent in object-oriented programs that make them candidate sources for design patterns. Our experiences have shown that design patterns can be found in a variety of software systems, independent of the methods used in developing those systems.

The use of pattern mentors in an organization can speed the acceptance of patterns. Pattern mentors can help provide a balance between encouraging good design practices based on patterns and discouraging overly high expectations of designs based on patterns. Initially, pattern mentors can help developers recognize the patterns that they already use in their application domain and show how they could be reused in subsequent projects. Pattern mentors should also watch that the wrong patterns are not applied to a problem (i.e., people tend to reuse things that they know and the same temptation will apply to patterns, regardless of whether the pattern actually fits the problem).[4]

Good patterns are difficult and time-consuming to write. Writing good patterns is a skill that does not come easy. Furthermore, the writing of a pattern typically involves an iterative process in which the pattern is presented to others and/or applied in projects, relevant comments are incorporated, and the process repeated until the result is adequate. However, we have found that, as one gains experience at writing patterns, the effort for recognizing and writing them is reduced.

Pattern practice is of utmost importance. After the initial phase of learning about patterns by seeing many good examples, one comes to appreciate the true value of patterns best from recognizing and writing them oneself.

CONCLUSIONS

In our joint experience, we have seen that the use of patterns can have a dramatic impact on the way a team develops software. The improved communication through patterns alone is a valuable asset. Giving novices the opportunity to learn from positive examples which already form the basis of a shared team vocabulary can help speed their contribution to the team. On the other hand, good patterns are hard to write, especially for those developers to whom abstraction does not come naturally. It is difficult to find a balance between the advantages and disadvantages, especially when measurable results are not yet available. It is clear that many people in the software engineering community recognize the emergence of patterns, but only few have had any opportunity, until now, to learn about their benefits and drawbacks in practice.

REFERENCES

1. Christopher Alexander. *The Timeless Way of Building.* Oxford University Press, New York, 1979.
2. Christopher Alexander et al. *A Pattern Language: Towns, Buildings, Construction.* Oxford University Press, New York, 1977.
3. B. Anderson and P. Coad. Patterns workshop. In *OOPSLA'93*

Addendum to the Proceedings, Washington, D.C., January 1994. ACM Press.

4. Bruce Anderson. Towards an architecture handbook. In *OOPSLA Addendum to the Proceedings.* ACM Press.

5. Kent Beck. Using a pattern language for programming. In *Addendum to the Proceedings of OOPSLA'87,* volume 23,5 of *ACM SIGPLAN Notices,* page 16, May 1988.

6. Kent Beck and Ralph Johnson. Patterns generate architecture. In *European Conference on Object-Oriented Programming (ECOOP),* 1994.

7. Frank Buschmann and Regine Meunier. A system of patterns. In James O. Coplien and Douglas C. Schmidt, editors, *Pattern Languages of Program Design.* Addison-Wesley, 1995.

8. Frank Buschmann, Regine Meunier, Hans Rohnert, Peter Sommerlad, and Michael Stal. *Pattern-Oriented Software Architecture: A System of Patterns.* John Wiley and Sons, 1996. (in preparation).

9. James O. Coplien. *Advanced C++: Programming Styles and Idioms.* Addison-Wesley, 1992.

10. James O. Coplien. A generative development-process pattern language. In James O. Coplien and Douglas C. Schmidt, editors, *Pattern Languages of Program Design.* Addison-Wesley, 1995.

11. James O. Coplien and Douglas C. Schmidt, editors. *Pattern Languages of Program Design.* Addison-Wesley, 1995.

12. R. Crocker and J. Engelsma. Continuing investigations into an organizational-wide software architecture. In *ICSE-17 Workshop on Software Architecture,* April 1995.

13. R. T. Crocker. Reaching for '10X' improvements—why OO isn't the answer! In *Proc. of 10th International Conference on Advanced Science and Technology,* pages 91-96, March 1994.

14. J. Engelsma and G. P. Saxena. Building competence in software architecture at Motorola's Cellular Infrastructure Group. In *OOPSLA '94 Workshop on Software Architectures,* Oct. 1994.

15. Brian Foote. quoted during the PLoP '94 conference (see [CS95]), 1994.

16. Erich Gamma. *Object-Oriented Software Development based on ET++.* PhD thesis, University of Zurich, Institut für Informatik, 1991. (in German). Also available through Springer-Verlag, Berlin, 1992.

17. Erich Gamma, Richard Helm, Ralph Johnson, and John Vlissides. Design patterns: Abstraction and reuse of object-oriented design. In O. Nierstrasz, editor, *European Conf. on Object-Oriented*

Programming (ECOOP), Kaiserslautern, Germany, July 1993. Springer Verlag, LNCS 707.

18. Erich Gamma, Richard Helm, Ralph Johnson, and John Vlissides. *Design Patterns—Elements of Reusable Object-Oriented Software.* Addison-Wesley, 1995.

19. Allen Hopley. Levels of abstraction. In *Pattern Languages of Programming Conference,* 1995.

20. Ralph E. Johnson. Why a conference on pattern languages? *Software Engineering Notes,* 19(1):50-52, January 1994.

21. Doug Lea. Design patterns for avionics control systems. Available through WWW site http://st-www.cs.uiuc.edu/users/patterns/patterns.html, 1994.

22. Doug Lea. Personal communication, 1995.

23. Gerard Meszaros. Software architecture in BNR. In David Garlan, editor, *Proc. of 1st Intl. Workshop on Architectures for Software Systems,* 1995. held in cooperation with ICSE-17.

24. D. Schmidt. Experience using design patterns to develop reuseable object-oriented communication software. *Communications of the ACM,* October 1995.

Sorting Through the Plethora: The "Unofficial" JOOP Book Awards

Steven Bilow

stevebil@msgate.tek.com

After four years of writing this introduction to the annual JOOP book issue you have probably figured out that I like books. Well, okay, I admit it . . . I like some books. Come to think of it, that may actually be a bit too general so, while we're at it, I'll admit this too: I also dislike a lot of books. In fact, when I first began writing book reviews for *The C++ Report,* in 1991, I would take everything I wrote, give it to my wife Patt, and ask her to soften up each negative statement I made. That was my way of making certain that no one tried to run me over in the parking lot at OOPSLA and Object World. More than five years later, I'm pleased to inform you that, as yet, no one has tried such a thing (at least I assume the runaway bookmobile was just an easily explained aberration!).

Of course, in all honesty, my policy that I will not review a book that I've not read from cover to cover prohibits me from reviewing a lot of books. There are simply too many books out there. So if I begin reading one and I dislike it, I just stop. You know what that means, right? No review.

Now, this problem I have with finding books I like enough to read from end to end gives me a tremendous amount of compassion toward those of you who don't automatically get these books in the mail. I receive a plentiful quantity of books as standing reviewer orders. I open the packages, begin to read, form some initial impressions, and decide whether or not to carry on. You don't customarily have such a luxury. You must stand in the aisles of book stores, talk to your friends, read reviews, read newsgroup discussions, and so on. Using these techniques exclusively, it is surely an arduous task to locate a book that fulfills your needs.

For these reasons, over the past four years I have enthusiastically embraced the opportunity to introduce this special JOOP issue on books. I relish the notion that I might actually have the capacity to assist readers in overcoming the obstacles that hinder their ability to sort through the plethora of object-oriented books.

So, here I am again. Back for round four! Before I begin, though, I am bound by my own convictions and sense of ethics to explain to you, as always, my fundamental philosophy of reviewing. (1) These are my opinions, not JOOP's opinions, not SIGS' opinions, so hold me and not them accountable. (2) Opinions are just that . . . opinions. Take them for what they are worth, which I believe is a fair amount. But, if you disagree, your friends disagree, or your pet hamsters disagree, that is quite fine. Reviews are blatantly subjective. With that said, I'd like to share with you my recent perspectives on the world of object-oriented books. Have some fun; I will!

ON SELECTING A BOOK

In a certain sense, selecting a book is not as difficult as you might imagine. For example, if you need to find an object-oriented design book you can probably eliminate *Madame Bovary* and *The Fountainhead*. Of course, since Grady Booch cites Ayn Rand, the latter may not be quite true. But, I am relatively certain that *Madam Bovary* may be safely eliminated! In any case, kidding aside, there are some simple methods for narrowing the scope of a search.

First we need to consider subject. C++ books are not OOD books. They may discuss aspects of both topics but they do not have the same fundamental motivations. It is important to consider the specific information you require. If you need to learn syntax and semantics, read a language book. If you wish to learn design, read a design book.

For the record, I do know that you are all quite intelligent people and I realize that everything I've said up until now is not very profound. But, I think it does serve the purpose of introducing a few more subtle criteria. So, let's take a quick look at some of the more engaging aspects of book selection.

In my view of the world, a good computer science book has several essential qualities. These include creativity, value added, well-articulated discussions, clear and concise examples, consistent and fully supported arguments, practical application, theoretical support, high quality writing, grammatical correctness, and balance. I'd like to discuss a few of these points and, in the course of doing so, give you some examples of books I think effectively implement them.

This year, I plan to do things a bit differently. This year I have developed some "unofficial JOOP book awards" and I'd like to announce them in this column. I was going to send each winner to Hawaii for a week but was unable to obtain the funding. So, instead, all they win is the publicity they get from being mentioned in this esteemed publication. Of course, they are free to go to Hawaii anytime they wish; it just won't be on me, Richard, or Rick!

THE "UNOFFICIAL JOOP BOOK AWARDS"

The first point I'd like to consider is creativity. As an example, let's look at the subject of C++.

THE MOST CREATIVE LANGUAGE BOOK

The fact of the matter is that, like it or not, there are currently hundreds of books on the market on the many and diverse aspects of C++. Three authors have written books that are now C++ legacies: Stroustrup, Lippman, and Coplien. Stroustrup and Lippman describe, in very complete terms, the foundation of the C++ language. Coplien covers every element of the language ignored in other books. In fact, Coplien covers things that are not covered in any other text. In other words, Jim has one very distinguished quality. For his benefit I was going to paraphrase Chris Alexander and call it a "Quality Without a Name." But in all honesty, the quality does have a name and that name is "Creativity." Coplien's book is good because it is unique. It has a creative approach to the language and it distinguishes itself from all other books in the field. Its creativity is one of the primary reasons that I recommend it above other books on C++. So, the award for "Most Creative Language Book" goes to Jim Coplien's *Advanced C++: Programming Styles and Idioms.*

THE HIGHEST VALUE ADDED BY AN O-O BOOK

Of course, just writing a creative book says nothing about whether you are able to write one that is useful. (Jim's is, by the way!) There are many books with creative but impractical, or worse, creative but pointless examples. To be useful to a person in need of information a book must add value. A wonderfully refined book that contributes nothing new to its specialization is worthless. There are certain books on object technology that I believe fall, quite effectively, into this "high value" or "super-content rich" category. These include *Design Patterns* by Gamma, Helm, Johnson, and Vlissides; *Object-Oriented Software Engineering* by Ivar Jacobson; Bertrand Meyer's *Object-Oriented Software Construction;* Gregor Kiczales's *The Art of the Metaobject Protocol;* and Grady Booch's *Object-Oriented Design with Applications.* Each of these books has the potential for a prolonged existence because, rather than simply giving a new slant to current ideas, each has advanced the state of object technology. This award was a close call for me but, when I think about the needs of software engineering professionals, my choice for "Highest Value Added by an O-O Book" is *Design Patterns* by Gamma, Helm, Johnson, and Vlissides.

THE BEST USE OF EXAMPLES IN SUPPORT OF A BOOK'S ARGUMENTS

When you choose to devote your precious time to studying a book, you need to be certain you are being given valid information. It is extremely important that the books you read effectively employ theory, pragmatics, and examples to support the information the author wishes to impart. One book that makes good use of diagrams in support of its points is *Object Lifecycles* by Steve Mellor and Sally Shlaer. In contrast, *Design Patterns* by Gamma, Helm, Johnson, and Vlissides uses a formal template to explain each example. Both of these are effective methods for articulating wisdom, and both are excellent books. However, being partial to graphical representation, my choice for "Best Use of Examples in Support of a Book's Arguments" is *Object Lifecycles* by Steve Mellor and Sally Shlaer.

THE MOST IMMEDIATELY USEFUL BOOK

When I evaluate a book that I am considering reading, I give maximal weighting to the book's level of practicality. I personally am a language theory fan; however, the vast majority of readers want to acquire information and directly, immediately apply it. *Designing Object-Oriented Software* by Rebecca Wirfs-Brock, B. Wilkerson, and L. Wiener is a superlative example. Their technique is supported by the simplest possible design tools (index cards). You don't need Rational/ROSE, or Objectory, or another computer-based tool to apply the techniques, with great success, in complex projects. In past years, I would have given Rebecca this award (and frankly she deserves it in many ways). Nonetheless, I really do have to say that *Design Patterns* is the most useful book I have ever seen in the realm of computer science texts, and thus the award for "The Most Immediately Useful O-O Book" goes to *Design Patterns* by Gamma, Helm, Johnson, and Vlissides.

Some Special Awards For Those Who Should Be Writing Books

This, of course brings me to the first of my "special achievement" awards. Since Rebecca didn't win the previous award, I have a special one for her! To Rebecca Wirfs-Brock, I give the special award for "Best Author Who Should Take the Time to Write a New Book." She is such a wealth of practical knowledge that I think a new book is well overdue. Perhaps because her intellect is in such hot demand, she simply does not have time. But I for one am anxiously waiting!

Two other "special achievement" awards go to Mr. Kent Beck. Kent gets the award for "Best Introduction to an O-O Book" for his funny, insightful introduction to the book *Pattern Languages of Program Design 2*. The book is worth the price just to read Kent's 2 pages! He also gets a very special award as "Potential Author Most Likely to Be an Overwhelming Smash Hit if He Ever Decides to Put What's in His Head Onto Paper." Bravo Kent; but where the heck is the book?

The Best Book for Managers

If you are not a manager then most likely you work for one. Now if I'm working with objects, I'd sure as heck like my boss to understand them. There is one book that goes a very long way toward making that happen, authored by Adele Goldberg and Kenny Rubin. So, "Best Management Book" goes to Adele and Kenny for *Succeeding with Objects*.

The Best Design Book

If Goldberg and Rubin should sit on the desk of every manager, then there is a book I think should be on the desk of every software engineer. To me, it is the best object design book ever written. That book is called *Object-Oriented Software Engineering* by Ivar Jacobson. I will not dwell on it because I've mentioned it for the past three years, but *Object-Oriented Software Engineering* gets the hands-down prize for "Best Design Book." After all this time, I still refer to it more than any other book on my shelf.

The Most Accessible Book on Object Theory

I mentioned earlier that an important feature of a good software book is its "theoretical soundness." Most books cover a minimal amount of theory, but very few are theoretically rich. Those that are frequently deserve awards for being obscure, conceited, dull, or any number of things other than exciting. I must tell you, however, that I have finally found a theory book that is actually both well balanced and intelligible. In fact, it's *very* good and manages to keep a reader's attention fairly well. It was edited by Carl Gunter and John Mitchell and is a collection of essays on objects, types, coherence, record calculi, and inheritance called *Theoretical Aspects of Object-Oriented Programming*. To this book I give the award for "Most Accessible Book on Object Theory."

THE BEST RESEARCH-ORIENTED BOOK

When it comes to theory, there is one topic that has rarely been addressed in the literature with any coherence: object-specific software metrics. There are a couple of books on the topic. One is called *Object-Oriented Software Metrics* by Mark Lorenz and Jeff Kidd. It has quite a lot of pragmatic value but does not dwell on either formalism or rigor. The other is by Brian Henderson-Sellers and is called *Object-Oriented Metrics: Measures of Complexity*. This book is the first to discuss software metrics for object-oriented software with any sense of mathematical rigor and without sounding like a doctoral dissertation. It does not attempt to be the definitive treatise on metrics (which is good because it isn't). But it does attempt to take a very academic approach to the subject while making it comprehensible to the computer science masses. It is an outstanding contribution to the literature, and so *Object-Oriented Metrics* by Henderson-Sellers gets my vote for "Best Research-Oriented Book on Object Technology." Congratulations Brian!

THE BEST METHODOLOGY COMPARISON

There are an awful lot of design and analysis techniques out there today. So many, in fact, that it is difficult to know which one to use when. Recently, several attempts have been made to clarify this confusion, either by comparing techniques directly or compiling essays by various methodologists. One of these books seems to be quite effective—a text recently published by SIGS Books, compiled by Andy Carmichael, called *Object Development Methods*. If you want to understand the various methodologies, then this is a very good book. Good enough, in fact, that I give it the award for "Best Methodology Comparison."

THE BEST PROCEEDINGS

Collections of essays frequently come in the form of conference proceedings. Commonly these are among the driest, most stoic forms of communication.

Needless to say, I frequently do not care for them. Of course, I recently edited the *OOPSLA '95 Addendum to the Proceedings* and now have a new respect for the poor people who have to compile such things. But I'm still not a proceedings fan. There is, however, one exception, which exists in the form of two books: the proceedings from the conference called "Pattern Languages of Program Design." These volumes comprise a fine collection of state of the art essays on pattern technology. Therefore, I'd like to give the award for "Best Proceedings" jointly to the books *Pattern Languages of Program Design* and *Pattern Languages of Program Design 2.*

THE BEST CLARIFICATION OF AN OVER-HYPED TECHNOLOGY

Early on, I presented an award for being pragmatic. Along those lines there is one more "pragmatism" prize that needs to be handed out. There are things that happen in the world which we may or may not like, but which become pervasive. Two of those things, in the world of objects, are the programming language Java and the Common Object Request Broker, or CORBA. Some people are fans of one or both of these; and others dislike them for various reasons. Nonetheless, they are both very popular topics.

Two books are worthy of mention that have nothing in common save the fact that they clarify technologies that have been hyped enough to be both pervasive and confusing. These are *Understanding CORBA* by Randy Otte, Paul Patrick, and Mark Roy and *Java as an Object-Oriented Language* by Mark Lorenz. A year ago, the second of these books did not exist and the first was tremendously timely and important. At that time, the CORBA book would have received this award. But I have to tell you, my cousin the playwright, my wife the human resources specialist, and the news guys on CNBC have all been talking about Java. They are not even computer people and they've heard the hype, which means it's pretty widespread. To me "widespread hype" indicates a strong need for rational discourse. Mark Lorenz accomplishes that discourse by comparing Java with other object-oriented languages in his Management Briefing. He does it in such a timely manner that I've chosen to give *Java as an Object-Oriented Language* the prize for "Best Clarification of an Over-Hyped Technology." Nice job, Mark.

THE BEST PERSONAL EXPERIENCE AND BEST BOOK OF 1996

There is one more "Management Briefing" that I need to talk about. I've been holding off until the end because I am very excited about it. It is published as part of the SIGS Management Briefing Series and is called *Software Patterns* by Jim Coplien. Jim is absolutely, blatantly articulate. He will probably be embarrassed about this, but that is just too bad. Jim Coplien is surely among the brightest practicing software technologists. His *Software Patterns* is a manifesto in the direct lineage of the cognoscenti throughout the 20th century. He is writing from pure passion for the discipline of patterns. He does not want us to agree with him, just to clearly understand his position. No junk, no hype, just clarity. After reading his book, which you can do in one to two evenings, you will understand his position. You may not agree with all of it, but you will understand it. He'd be quite happy if you'd adopt his position as your own and, who knows, you may just do that. If not, at least you will have a firm, consistent foundation for discussion. Coplien's book will go a long way toward directing the future of patterns development and, because of that, he gets two awards: "Best Personal Experience with Object Technology" and "Best New Book of 1996." Sorry if I embarrassed you, Jim, but you deserve it. The only bad news is that now I have to update my Top 10. Darn.

CONCLUSION

As you can see, there are books that remain on my list year after year. There are also new additions each year. This year, the list did not change very much but, at the same time, I've tried to give you some perspectives on many of the recently released publications. As always, I'll be interested in your feedback. In fact, if this issue is well received, who knows, maybe someday there will be a real contest and real prizes. But, for now, the winners must be content with the mere fact of winning. Congratulations to all of them! As for you, the folks who have to sort through the many hundreds of books each year, I sincerely hope that I have followed my own rule and added both some humor and a lot of value to your book selection process.

Patterns

Grady Booch
egb@Rational.com

I'm generally not an excitable person. My idea of a great summer after-noon is reading a book along side some crisp Colorado mountain stream, miles away from anything containing a transistor. Not quite the excitement of bungee jumping or, perhaps even more intense, subclassing from a deep class lattice while mixing in a couple of other abstract base classes to achieve some desired polymorphic behavior—neither activity is for the faint of heart. However, there is one emerging development in the world of objects that does genuinely excite me: the methodical identification of patterns.

First, let me introduce some of the key players. There are at least two centers of gravity in this great search: one in the U.S. and another in the UK. In the U.S., one group involved in this endeavor includes the diverse talents of Ralph Johnson (University of Illinois), Erich Gamma and John Vlissides (Taligent), and Richard Helm (IBM). Independently, Mary Shaw, Rebecca Wirfs-Brock, and Peter Coad have both contributed to the study of patterns. In the UK, Bruce Anderson (University of Essex) has catalyzed significant study into the codification of patterns. At the last two OOPSLA conferences, he established workshops focused on the creation of an architecture handbook the purpose of which is ultimately to serve as a catalog of patterns.

The notion of patterns is significant, especially to all things object-oriented, because it represents a higher-leverage form of reuse. The search for patterns encompasses far more than finding the One Perfect Class; rather, it focuses upon identifying the common behavior and interactions that transcend individual objects.

The study of patterns is not unique to software; indeed, the importance of patterns has long been recognized in other technical disciplines such as biology, chemistry, physics, and architecture. In a manner of speaking, the field of software engineering is just beginning to awaken to the importance of patterns. For example, Herbert Simon, in his study of complexity, observed that "hierarchic systems are usually composed of only a few different kinds of subsystems in various combinations and arrangements." In other words, complex systems have common patterns. These patterns may involve the reuse of small components, such as the cells found in both plants and animals, or of larger structures, such as vascular systems, also found in both plants and animals. In his classic work *The Sciences of the Artificial,* Simon went on to illustrate how these patterns manifest themselves in social and biological systems, and how the existence of such patterns helps to simplify the inherent complexity of systems.

The oft-referenced Christopher Alexander has made similar observations in the domain of architecture, and his work has instigated a minor revolution in that field. He notes that, for the architect, "his act of design, whether humble, or gigantically complex, is governed entirely by the patterns he has in his mind at that moment, and his ability to combine these patterns to form a new design." Perhaps a bit dramatically, he goes on to suggest that "the more living patterns there are in a place—a room, a building, or a town— the more it comes to life as an entirety, the more it glows, the more it has that self-maintaining fire which is the quality without a name."

I have found the same to be true in well-structured object-oriented systems. Using the terms suggested by Rob Murray, I distinguish between *strategic* and *tactical* design decisions. A strategic decision is one that has sweeping architectural implications, e.g., the decision to use a particular client/server architecture, ODBMS, or GUI model. A tactical decision is one that has more local implications, such as the protocol of a specific class or the signature of a member function. Both kinds of decisions are important to the success of a software system, no matter how one measures "success." However, our strategic decisions have the greatest impact on our ability to craft simple, elegant architectures.

In object-oriented systems, strategic decisions manifest themselves in the form of class lattices (which capture our decisions about the static relationships among abstractions) and collaborations of objects (which capture our decisions about the common interactions among our abstractions). Several years ago, I suggested the term *mechanism* to describe any such structure whereby objects collaborate to provide some behavior that satisfies a requirement of the problem. While the design of a class embodies the knowledge of how individual objects behave, a mechanism is a design decision about how collections of objects cooperate. Mechanisms thus represent patterns of behavior.

Whereas abstractions reflect the vocabulary of the problem domain, mechanisms are the soul of the design. During the design process, the developer must consider not only the design of individual classes, but also how instances of these classes work together. Lately, I have been influenced by the work of Kenny Rubin and Adele Goldberg (on object behavior analysis) and Ivar Jacobson (on use-case analysis), whose ideas suggest the use of scenarios to discover these collaborations. In a sense, the use of scenarios drives the whole analysis and design process. Once a developer decides upon a particular pattern of collaboration, the work is distributed among many objects by defining suitable methods in the appropriate classes. Ultimately, the protocol of an individual class encompasses all the operations required to implement all the behavior and all the mechanisms associated with each of its instances.

One contribution Linnaeus made to the field of botany was the suggestion that patterns may be found in the very patterns of animal and plant structure and behavior. I am no Linnaeus, but let me suggest a similar classification of patterns in object-oriented systems.

As it turns out, mechanisms are actually in the middle of a spectrum of patterns we find in well-structured software systems. At the low end of the food chain, we have idioms. An *idiom* is an expression peculiar to a certain programming language or application culture, representing a generally accepted convention for use of the language. Richard Gabriel, one of the architects of CLOS, helped me understand that one defining characteristic of an idiom is that ignoring or violating the idiom has immediate social consequences: you are branded as a yahoo or, worse, an outsider. For example, no programmer would use underscores in function or variable names in CLOS, although this is common practice in Ada. In C++, there are many such idioms inherited from the C culture such as idioms for indexing and error handling. Part of the effort in learning a programming language is learning its idioms, which are usually passed down as folklore from programmer to programmer. However, as Jim Coplien has pointed out, idioms play an important role in codifying low-level patterns. He notes that "many common programming tasks [are] idiomatic," and thus identifying such idioms allows "using C++ constructs to express functionality outside the language proper, while giving the illusion of being part of the language."

At the high end of the food chain, we have frameworks. A framework is a collection of classes providing a set of services for a particular domain;

a framework thus exports a number of individual classes and mechanisms that clients can use or adapt. Frameworks represent patterns and, hence, reuse in the large.

Whereas idioms are part of a programming culture, frameworks are often the product of commercial ventures. For example, Apple's MacApp (and its successor, the Apple/Symantec Bedrock project) are both application frameworks, written in C++, for building applications that conform to Macintosh user interface standards. Similarly, the Microsoft Foundation Library and Borland's ObjectWindows library are frameworks for building applications that conform to the Windows user interface standards. In each case, we find more than a bag of independent classes. Rather, the most mature architectures consist of a set of classes plus a modest number of well-articulated mechanisms that serve to animate these classes. For example, in MacApp there are clear mechanisms for drawing in a window, saving data in a document, and cutting/copying/pasting across applications using the clipboard.

I have an unsubstantiated hypothesis that most interesting patterns within frameworks are domain-dependent. Recently, I have encountered commercial efforts to build frameworks in such diverse domains as patient health care, securities trading, and telephone switching systems. Across these domains, these products are architecturally very different. However, within each vertical application domain there are clear patterns of idioms and mechanisms that serve to simplify the problem at hand.

In the domain of GUI-centric systems, for example, there are a number of such patterns. Consider the mechanism for drawing things in a window. Several objects must collaborate to present an image to a user: a window, a view, the model being viewed, and some client that knows when (but not how) to display this model. The client first tells the window to draw itself. Since it may encompass several subviews, the window next tells each of its subviews to draw themselves. Each subview in turn tells its model to draw itself, ultimately resulting in an image shown to the user. In this mechanism, the model is entirely decoupled from the window and view in which it is presented: views can send messages to models, but models cannot send messages to views. Smalltalk uses a variation of this mechanism called the model-view-controller (MVC) architecture. A similar mechanism is employed in almost every object-oriented graphical user interface framework.

In Smalltalk, the MVC architecture in turn builds on another mechanism, the dependency mechanism, which is embodied in the behavior of the

Smalltalk base class (the class Object) and thus pervades the entire Smalltalk class library.

Johnson and Anderson, together with their respective colleagues, have begun to enumerate and codify the patterns they have found in object-oriented systems. At the low end of the food chain, for example, we have patterns for double dispatching (faking the semantics of multiple polymorphism in a mono-polymorphic language such as C++ or Smalltalk) and delegation (a common pattern for distributing behavior within whole/part structures). In the middle of the food chain, the domain of mechanisms, we have patterns such as MVC, as well as patterns for message passing, command interpretation, and error handling. At the high end of the food chain, we have patterns for whole applications, e.g., blackboard architectures (a central architecture for many systems embodying opportunistic control) and subsumption architectures (an architectural pattern suggested by Rodney Brooks at MIT for structuring processes in autonomous robots).

Identifying patterns in software systems is difficult, but ultimately pays off in the form of simpler, more resilient architectures. My observation is that this identification involves both discovery and invention. Through discovery, we come to recognize the key abstractions and mechanisms that form the vocabulary of our problem domain. Through invention, we devise generalized abstractions as well as new mechanisms that specify how objects collaborate. Ultimately, discovery and invention are both problems of classification, and classification is fundamentally a problem of finding *sameness*. When we classify, we seek to group things that have a common structure or exhibit a common behavior.

Crafting object-oriented systems is thus far more than what the naive object-oriented zealot will tell you; namely, to focus on inheritance lattices. Inheritance is not the only important thing. Rather, for all the kinds of patterns we have described here, patterns of behavior represent an intelligent distribution of responsibilities among a collection of classes; inheritance allows us to express these patterns with elegance and simplicity, but it is the very distribution of behavior that is central to the meaning of each pattern. It is therefore the task of the developer to distribute such behaviors so that they may be combined in interesting ways, giving rise to the "self-maintaining fire" that is the mark of a profound object-oriented architecture.

A Generative Development— Process Pattern Language

James O. Coplien
cope@lucent.com

INTRODUCTION

This paper introduces a family of patterns that can be used to shape a new organization and its development processes. Patterns support emerging techniques in the software design community, where they are finding a new home as a way of understanding and creating computer programs. There is an increasing awareness that new program structuring techniques must be supported by suitable management techniques, and by appropriate organization structures; organizational patterns are one powerful way to capture these.

We believe that patterns are particularly suitable to organizational construction and evolution. Patterns form the basis of much of modern cultural anthropology: a culture is defined by its patterns of relationships. Also, while the works of Christopher Alexander [Alexander] deal with town planning and building architecture to support human enterprise and interaction, it can be said that organization is the modern analogue to architecture in contemporary professional organizations. Organizational patterns have a first-order effect on the ability of people to carry on. We believe that the physical architecture of the buildings supporting such work are the dual of the organizational patterns; these two worlds cross in the work of Thomas Allen at MIT [Allen].

There is nothing new in taking a pattern perspective to organizational analysis. What is novel about the work here is its attempt to use patterns in a generative way. All architecture fundamentally concerns itself with control [Carlin]; here we use architecture to supplant process as the (indirect) means to controlling people in an organization. Not only should patterns help us understand existing organizations, but they should help us build new ones. A good set of organizational patterns helps to (indirectly) generate the right process: this indirectness is the essence of Alexandrine generativity. In fact, organizational patterns might be the most generative approach to software architecture patterns. Alexander notes that architectures "can't be made, but only generated, indirectly, by the ordinary actions of the people, just as a flower cannot be made, but only generated from the seed." [Alexander]; A set of simple patterns together cause complex emergent behavior. As with many of the principles in Timeless Way, this is curiously reminiscent of the Way of Non-Action (Yin) of the Tao Teh Ching; we also find it in the triple-loop thinking of Swieringa and Wierdsma's organizational learning model [Swieringa and Wierdsma].

At this writing, the work is speculative: only limited use has been made of these patterns in formulating new organizations. The "goodness" or "badness" of such patterns is difficult to test by experiment. First, any metric of organizational goodness is necessarily multidimensional and complex. Second, it is difficult to do large-scale social experiments with tight enough control variables that the effectiveness of a pattern could be verified. Third, such an experiment would take a long-term commitment (months or years), more than most software organizations are willing to expend in light of fragile and evolving markets.

For these reasons, the patterns fall back on case studies and on common sense. We look at recurring patterns of interaction in organizations, note recurring patterns between those patterns and some measures of "goodness," and then do analysis to explain the correlation. The patterns presented here all combine empirical observations with a rationale that explains them. The claim that the language as a whole captures essential characteristics of high-productivity organizations has been validated by the CEOs of many small, highly productive organizations who have read these patterns. [Gabriel].

The patterns meet other "standard" criteria emerging in the patterns movement. Each is stated as a problem or opportunity. Each is analyzed for the forces at play within it. Each instructs us to do something explicit. This form follows the pattern work of Alexander, whose books on architecture serve as a model for the modern software patterns movement. Some of these organizational patterns hark back to Alexander; where appropriate, a distinctive reference appears in the text of the form [§*pattern-number*] to refer the reader to a pattern in Alexander's *A Pattern Language* [Alexander].

Though there are organizations that exhibit these patterns, combining them into a new organization, built from scratch, is a daunting task. The ideal organization envisioned by these patterns differs greatly from the state of the art in software development. These patterns are drawn from peculiar organizations with peculiarly high productivity. The patterns describe practices much different from those found in most project management texts.

Language Context

This paper presents generative patterns that can be used to build an organization and to guide its development process in the domain of software development. By "organization," I mean not so much an institutional organization as one of the communities of mutual interest that form naturally in any culture. These are sometimes called *instructive organizations*. An organization is usually responsible for some deliverable. The endeavor of building that product within that organization is called a *project*. The patterns of activity within an organization (and hence within its project) are called a *process*. Organization, project, and process can be viewed as partial facets of each other. We might find hierarchies or networks of organizations; if so, the patterns here apply in particular to the innermost ones, and in lesser degrees to the more encompassing organization structure (see Divide and Conquer).

I am not so much interested in small (read "simple") projects as in ambitious, complex commercial endeavors that may comprise hundreds of thousands or millions of lines of code. Such projects are common in telecommunications development, and their processes and organizations are a challenge to design. These organizations range in size from a handful of people to a few dozen people. Larger organizations (of hundreds or thousands of people) are beyond the scope of most of the patterns in this language. If such large organizations can be broken into smaller, *decoupled* organizations, the patterns apply to each of the parts.

This pattern language probably applies more to young and emerging organizations than to legacy organizations. Legacy organizations, particularly in the sectors of public service and utilities, are almost always destined to be bureaucracies. Young organizations proceed through several stable stages of growth, starting with a visionary and a tightly-knit group. Roles emerge and become more refined as these organizations grow. The organization may grow to the point where it exhibits an internal structure of sub-organizations, each one of which can be the subject of the patterns here. The organization atrophies as it goes into maintenance mode, taking on a stable structure. The patterns here aim at changing, growing organizations, which don't often lend themselves to traditional corporate structures.

All development organizations serve a purpose. This paper does not explore patterns for chartering a development organization, but presumes that an organization is formed within the industry, or within a company, to meet a business need economically. Questions of business practicality are beyond what can be dealt with in depth here. One might look at "Web of Shopping" [§19], "Household Mix" [§35] in Alexander as analogies to how such groups should be formed. Even grosser patterns such as "Site Repair" [§104] provide analogies for finding corporate contexts suitable to highproductivity organizations.

There are "common sense" considerations that don't appear in the contexts or solutions of these patterns. Cultural taboos and standards will leave many of these patterns outside the reach of some organizations. For example, Domain Expertise in Roles presumes that experts are available in the job market. If the domain is breaking brand new ground, experts may not yet be available. Even in familiar territory, experts are scarce, and the culture may not allow the extravagant measures necessary to procure them. As another example, the pattern language makes every attempt to avoid working back project benchmarks from an end date (Size the Schedule). Customers often want to see intermediate benchmarks at agreed intervals, and intermediate benchmarks drive some cultures too deeply for an individual development group to fix. These problems do not invalidate the language, but they may require that some patterns be skipped for a given organization. It is likely that some of these patterns are foundation patterns, and have a larger impact than others if they are skipped: Domain Expertise in Roles, Organization Follows Location, Architect Also Implements, and others are likely foundation patterns.

The success of this pattern language is almost certainly sensitive to contexts that demand future research and exploration. How well-defined is the product at the outset? How much external tool support is available? How short should the edit-compile-go turnaround cycle be? How sensitive is the organization to the fault density or fault tolerance of the product system? We also need to study in more depth the degree to which these are, or are not, drivers for successful organizations.

LANGUAGE FORCES

While the language encodes well-known and reasonable folklore and practice about organizations, it also draws on unconventional insights gained through empirical studies of outstanding organizations. This pattern language builds on three years of research in development process and organizational analyses carried out by AT&T Bell Laboratories. The data come both from within AT&T and from other companies in computer-related fields. During this research, we used a largely visual representation of the organizations we studied, and built a catalogue of "Gamma patterns" of organizations, their structures, and their processes. These Gamma pattern visualizations are the source of many of the recurring generative patterns that we encode here. For example, the pattern Engage QA appears as a tight coupling between the QA role and the process as a whole in many highly productive organizations we studied. The original visualizations for these organizations are shown along with the pattern Developer Controls Process and with the pattern Engage QA.

This language builds a system which is part of a larger system: a development culture in a corporate environment. Executing this language perfectly is no guarantee of success. While the language attempts to deal with interfaces to marketing and to the corporate control structure (e.g., through Firewalls), the remainder of the organization must be competent. Other patterns are needed to shape the remainder of the organization. We find hints of these patterns in the pattern languages of Kerth [Kerth] and Whitenack [Whitenack].

This language certainly works best when the raw materials are available to build an enthusiastic organization. While the patterns work better when building an organization from scratch, they may be applied to an anemic organization to restore the ability to excel that people may once have had, before the culture drained that ability away. Some "Site Repair" [Alexander 104] would likely be necessary before these patterns could be applied to a legacy organization. Some patterns are best-suited to the problems of mature organizations that experience difficulties (Work Flows Inward; Divide and Conquer; Hub-Spoke-and-Rim; Prototype).

THE QUALITY WITHOUT A NAME

Some organizations have the "quality without a name:" they are true to their purpose because they profit their stockholders, serve their customers well, and provide a sustaining, fulfilling, and supporting workplace for their employees. Organizations that reach this level of maturity are likely to excel in all other measures. Do the patterns presented here make it possible to construct such an organization? While these patterns define a culture that helps sustain morale and business success, they don't address quality of work life and morale directly. These patterns touch only lightly on key factors such as the mutual trust between worker and peer, employee and employer, and company and customer. Other factors, such as cultural diversity, the corporation's community involvement, and extracurricular activities at work are beyond the scope of this language. I don't omit these factors here because I feel they are unimportant, but defer these issues to experts in organizational psychology and sociology. Though many of the patterns here have sociological overtones, and likely have a generative effect on morale and other social indicators, other pattern languages must be woven with this one to round out the sociological picture. This perspective leads to the obvious conclusion that these patterns alone do not guarantee success, but it also provides a guiding light for further research.

LANGUAGE RATIONALE

This language takes inspiration as much from Alexander's architectural language as from his pattern language principles. The opening phrases of the language evoke the same sizing and context perspectives as we find in Alexander. Many of the organization patterns are refinements of Alexander's Circulation patterns [§98]. The philosophy of establishing stable communication paths across the industry has strong analogies with the Alexandrian patterns that establish transportation webs in a city [§16]. Here, we are concerned with "transportation" of information between individuals and development groups. We capture the communication between roles, which are a higher-order abstraction than individual actors.

NOTATIONS

This work draws on data gathered as part of the Pasteur process research program at AT&T Bell Laboratories. In the Pasteur program, we studied software development organizations in many companies worldwide, covering a wide spectrum of development cultures. The Pasteur analysis techniques are based in part on organizational visualization. Many of the patterns in this pattern language have visual analogues in the Pasteur analyses. I sometimes use visualizations to illustrate a pattern.

There are two kinds of pictures used in the Pasteur studies. The first is a social network diagram, also called an adjacency diagram. Each diagram is a network of roles and the communication paths between them. The roles are placed according to their coupling relationships: closely coupling roles are close together, and de-coupled roles are far apart. Roles at the center of these pictures tend to be the most active roles in these organizations, while those nearer the edges have a more distant relationship with the organization as a whole.

The second kind of picture is an *interaction grid*. The axes of the interaction grid span the roles in the organization, ordered according to their coupling to the organization as a whole. If a role at ordinate position p initiates an interaction with a role at coordinate position q, we put a point at the position (p,q). The point is shaded according to the strength of the interaction.

The pattern texts, and particularly the design rationales, often make reference to documents or projects that typify the pattern. "QPW" refers to Borland's QuattroPro for Windows development, and on process research conducted there by AT&T Bell Labs in 1993. The research is further discussed in the proceedings of BIC/94 [Coplien], in a column by Richard Gabriel [Gabriel], and in an article in *Dr. Dobb's Journal* [Coplien 1994b].

The notation "ATT1" refers to a high productivity project inside AT&T, characterized by concurrent engineering in a small team environment. Findings from research on that project have not yet been published.

The analyses occasionally make reference to the work of Thomas Allen, whose relevant perspectives can be found in his book on technology information flow [Allen].

I often draw from a whimsical book on architecture called *The Most Beautiful House in the World,* by Witold Rybczynski (1989).

Acknowledgments

Brendan Cain supported much of the early process research underlying these patterns. The research of Peter Bürgi who spent time as a cultural anthropologist in our Research organization, has strongly influenced the pattern language. The pattern language took shape and had its first applications in the formative months of the Global Configurator project at Indian Hill, whose many members I thank for the opportunity to work with them. Joint work with Neil Harrison of AT&T's Global Business Communications Systems helped refine, validate, and prove in many of the patterns. Many thanks to Richard Gabriel, Ward Cunningham, Desmond DeSouza, Richard Helm and Ralph Johnson, for participating in a structured review of these patterns; Gabriel also facilitated the review at PLoP. Many thanks to the many people at PLoP who also reviewed these patterns, and especially to Larry Podmolik, Mary Shaw, Dennis DeBruler, Norm Kerth, Bill Opdyke, Brian Foote, Bruce Whitenack, Steve Berczuk, Frank Buschmann, and Robert Martin. Kent Beck was the PLoP shepherd for this document. Mary Zajac and Joe Maranzano in AT&T provided much useful feedback from a management perspective. Mary proposed the patterns "Phasing it In" and "Apprentice". Many comments and pattern ideas, most noteworthy of which is Mercenary Analyst, came from Paul Chisholm at AT&T.

THE PATTERN LANGUAGE

PATTERN 1: SIZE THE ORGANIZATION

Problem: How big should the organization be?

Context: You are building a software development organization to meet competitive cost and schedule benchmarks. The first release of the end product will probably be more than 25,000 lines of code. The development organization is embedded in the context of a larger organization, usually that of the sponsoring enterprise or company (see the Rationale). This applies specifically to organizations that create software, and may not as directly apply to organizations whose job is integrating existing software, for example.

Forces:
- Too large, and you reach a point of greatly diminishing returns. Large organizations are ships that are hard to steer. Too small, and you don't have critical mass. Overly small organizations have inadequate inertia and can become unstable.
- Size affects the deliverable non-linearly. Communication overhead goes up as the square of the size, which means that the organization becomes less cohesive as the square of the size while the "horsepower" of the organization goes up only linearly.
- New people interact much more strongly with others in the organization, and interact more broadly across the organization, than mature members of the society who have assimilated its context.

Solution: By default, choose 10 people; experience has shown that suitably selected and nurtured small team can develop a 1,500 KSLOC project in 31 months, and a 200 KSLOC project in 15 months, or a 60KSLOC project in 8 months. Do not add people late in development, or try to meet deadlines worked backward from a completion date.

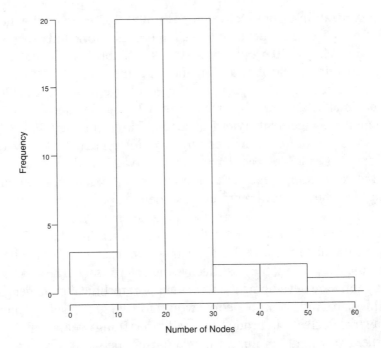

FIGURE 1   Pattern 1: Size the Organization. Most organizations we have studies have a remarkably similar number of roles. This graph is a histogram of the
distribution of roles (nodes) per process. While this is not the same as the staff
level (which is the number of actors, not the number of roles), it provides guidance in sizing an organization.

Resulting Context: An organization where nearly everyone can have
"global knowledge." We have found empirically that most roles in a project can handle interactions with about six or seven other roles; with 10
people, you can almost manage total global communications (and a fully
connected network may not be necessary). On the other hand, 10 people
is a suitable "critical mass."

This pattern is closely coupled to the patterns that support organizational growth below, Phasing it In and Apprentice. This pattern also interacts with Prototype.

Rationale: Keeping an organization small makes it possible for everybody
to know how the project works. Projects that do well have processes that
adapt, and processes adapt well only if there is widespread buy-in and
benefit. The dialogue necessary to buy-in and benefit can accrue only to

small organizations. Tom DeMarco has noted that everybody who is to benefit from process should be involved in process work and process decision-making. Having 10 people at the start is probably overkill, but it avoids the expense and overhead of adding more people later.

This pattern is for large projects. Projects larger than 25KSLOC can rarely be done by an individual (see Pattern 3, Solo Virtuoso).

Different management styles (leadership-based, manager-based) lead to the success or failures of different organization types (democracy, republic, oligarchy). Leadership-based management styles help these organizations work; the compelling need for a democracy is less felt, because project members feel they are well-represented under an appropriate management style. [This may be a new pattern about management style.]

A single team is better than a collection of sub-teams. The faster a team breaks up into sub-teams worrying about their own responsibilities rather than those of the larger team, the less effective the enterprise will be as a whole.

Many software development cultures support technical manager groups up to this size. Adding more people would force a group split, which can cause a large decrease in productivity, all other things being equal.

Further study might evaluate the relationship between this pattern and Alexander's "The Distribution of Towns" [§2] and related patterns. Here, we stipulate that the social organization must be small; it reflects a "Subculture Boundary" [§13] and "Identifiable Neighborhood" [§14]. Alexander emphasizes the grander architectural context that balances support for the ecology with the economies of scale that large towns can provide, while supporting the xenophobic tendencies of human nature. Small organizations like that being built here rarely exist in isolation, but in the context of a broader supporting organization. This relationship to the larger organization invokes Patron.

As to adding people late in development, staff-month myths abound. One manager writes: "On [one] project, I grew from 10 to 20 people to meet a customer contract. With [the] new people, [I] wound up three months late because of 'absorption' of new folks into the organization."

PATTERN 2: SELF-SELECTING TEAM

Problem: There are no perfect criteria for screening team members.

Context: You are building a software development organization to meet competitive cost and schedule benchmarks. You are staffing up to meet a schedule in a given market.

Forces:
- Empowerment depends on competency and the distribution of knowledge and power. The worst team dynamics can be found in appointed teams. The best team dynamics can be found in self-selecting teams.
- Broad interests (music and poetry) seem to align with successful team players.

Solution: Build self-selecting teams, doing limited screening on the basis of track record and broad interests.

Resulting Context: An empowered, enthusiastic team willing to take extraordinary measures to meet project goals.

PATTERN 3: SOLO VIRTUOSO

Problem: How big should the organization be?

Context: You are building a software development organization to meet competitive cost and schedule benchmarks. The first release of the end product will probably be less than 25 KSLOC. Rapid growth is not anticipated after the first release

Forces:
- Some select individuals are able to build entire projects by themselves.
- Organization size affects the deliverable non-linearly. Communication overhead goes up as the square of the size, which means that the organization becomes less cohesive as the square of the size while the "horsepower" of the organization goes up only linearly.

Solution: Do the entire design and implementation with one or two people.

Resulting Context: An organization limited to small developments. Though there is a singleton development role, other roles may be necessary to support marketing, toolsmithing, and other functions. The productivity of a suitably chosen singleton developer is enough to handle sizable projects; here, we establish 25KSLOC as a limit, but see the rationale below for further parameters.

The pattern is not "License to Hack". Don't give up technical review, validation, and verification at appropriate times in development (Review the Architecture, Engage Customers).

This approach is rarely applicable, as it doesn't resolve some of the forces (many of them applicable) mentioned in Size the Organization. Where those forces don't apply, this pattern is a big win.

Rationale: There are numerous examples of successful single-person developments. The dynamics of this development are different from those for a small team. The productivity of a single individual can be higher than a collection of several productive individuals. We have seen single-person developments generate 25KSLOC of deliverable code in 4 months (a craft interface for a telecommunication system); two-person developments do 135 KSLOC in 30 months. Many of these adhered faithfully to all stipulated reviews and verification steps.

Success, of course, depends on choosing the right person. Boehm notes a 20-fold spread between the least and most effective developers. A telecommunications developer recently told me that "having the right expertise means the difference between being able to solve a problem in a half hour, and never being able to solve the problem at all." This pattern reduces the "truck number" of the organization (the number of people whose absence would threaten the organization were any one of them hit by a truck).

PATTERN 4: SIZE THE SCHEDULE

Problem: How long should the project take?

Context: The product is understood and the project size has been estimated.

Forces:
- If you make the schedule too generous, developers become complacent, and you miss market windows. If the schedule is too ambitious, developers become burned out, and you miss market windows. If the schedule is too ambitious, product quality suffers, and compromised architectural principles establish a poor foundation for future maintenance.
- Projects without schedule motivation tend to go on forever, or spend too much time polishing details that are either irrelevant or don't serve customer needs.

Solution: Reward developers for meeting the schedule, with financial bonuses (or at-risk compensation; see Compensate Success), or with extra time off. Keep two sets of schedules: one for the market, and one for the developers. The external schedule is negotiated with the customer; the internal schedule, with development staff. The internal schedule should be shorter than the external schedule by two or three weeks for a moderate project (this figure comes from a senior staff member at a well-known software consulting firm). If the two schedules can't be reconciled, customer needs or the organization's resources—or the schedule itself—must be re-negotiated.

Rationale: MIT project management simulation; QPW. Another manager suggested that the skew between the internal and external schedules be closer to two months than two weeks because, if you slip, it usually reflects a major oversight that costs two or three months.

PATTERN 5: FORM FOLLOWS FUNCTION

Alias: Aggregate Activities into Roles

Problem: A project lacks well-defined roles.

Context: You know the key atomic process activities.

Forces: Activities are too small, and their relationship too dynamic, to be useful process building blocks. Activities often cluster together by related artifacts or other domain relationships.

Solution: Group closely related activities (that is, those mutually coupled in their implementation, or which manipulate the same artifacts, or that are semantically related to the same domain). Name the abstractions resulting from the grouped activities, making them into roles. The associated activities become the responsibilities (job description) of the roles.

Resulting Context: A partial definition of roles for a project. Some roles (mercenary analyst, developer) are canonical, rather than deriving from this pattern.

Rationale: The quality of this pattern needs to be reviewed. The idea came from the approach taken in a large project re-engineering effort I worked with in March of 1994.

Louis Sullivan is the architect credited with the primordial architectural pattern of this name [Rybczynski 1989, p. 162].

This pattern interacts with other structural patterns such as Organization Follows Location, Organization Follows Market, and Architect Also Implements. Also see Engage Customers.

One manager notes: "In my experience from Project Management Audits . . . projects both leave out roles (e.g., no named architect) and define several people with the same role. The second is most problematic, since it causes staff confusion. But the missing role also occurs because projects have inexperienced managers. This is a big problem . . . around System Engineering roles, or lack thereof."

PATTERN 6: DOMAIN EXPERTISE IN ROLES

Problem: Matching staff (actors, people) to roles.

Context: You know the key atomic process roles, including a characterization of the Developer role.

Forces:
- All roles must be staffed (with qualified individuals). Spreading expertise across roles complicates communication patterns. Successful projects tend to be staffed with people who have already worked on successful projects.

Solution: Hire domain experts with proven track records. Any given actor may fill several roles. In many cases, multiple actors can fill a given role. Domain training is more important than process training. Local gurus are good, in all areas from application expertise to expertise in methods and language.

Resulting Context: This is a tool that helps assure that roles can be successfully carried out. It also helps make roles autonomous.

Other roles (Architect, Mercenary Analyst, and others) are prescribed by subsequent patterns.

Rationale: Highly productive projects (e.g., QPW) hire deeply specialized experts.

Alexander's Old People Everywhere [§40] talks about the need of the young to interact with the old. The same deep rationale and many of the same forces of Alexander's pattern also apply here.

The pattern Apprentice helps maintain this pattern in the long term.

A seasoned manager writes, "The most poorly staffed roles are System Engineering and System Test. We hire rookies and make them System Engineers. (In Japan, only the most experienced person interacts with customers.) We staff System Test with 'leftovers'; after we have staffed the important jobs of architecture, design, and developer."

PATTERN 7: PHASING IT IN[1]

Problem: Hiring long-term staff beyond the initial experts.

Context: Key project players have been hired and cover the necessary expertise, but the project needs more staff.

Forces:
- You need enough people for critical mass. Staff are not plug compatible and interchangeable.
- The right set of initial people sets the tone for the project, and it's important to hire the key people first. Too many people too early create a burden for the core team.

Solution: Phase the hiring program. Start by hiring experts, and gradually bring on new people as the project needs to grow.

Resulting Context: The organization can staff up to meet development load. This pattern is closely related to Apprentice.

Rationale: This is a well-known management technique that allows the project to establish an identity early on, and to grow graciously.

PATTERN 8: APPRENTICE[2]

Problem: You can't always hire the experts you need.

---

[1] Proposed as a pattern by Mary Zajac at AT&T.
[2] Proposed as a pattern by Mary Zajac at AT&T.

Context: The project is incrementally staffing up after the first round of experts have been brought on board.

Forces:
- You need enough people for critical mass. Staff are not plug compatible and interchangeable.

Solution: Turn new hires into experts (see Domain Expertise in Roles) through an apprenticeship program. Every new employee should work as an apprentice (not just a mentee) to an established expert. Most apprenticeship programs will last six months to a year—the amount of time it takes to make a paradigm shift.

Resulting Context: It will be possible to maintain expertise in the organization. This pattern also reduces the organization's "truck number" (the smallest number of people such that, if any one of them were hit by a truck, the organization will have lost a critical resource) by spreading knowledge around. The "masters" feel valued and the apprentices are given a good environment to learn.

Rationale: It is better to apprentice people than to put people through a "trial by fire" that may damage the project. This approach makes it possible to form domain-specific teams.

PATTERN 9: ORGANIZATION FOLLOWS LOCATION

Problem: Assigning tasks and roles across a geographically distributed work force.

Context: A product must be developed in several different hallways, on different floors of a building, in different buildings or at different locations.

Forces:
- Communication patterns between project members follows geographic distribution. Coupling between pieces of software must be sustained by analogous coupling between the people maintaining that software. People avoid communicating with people who work in other buildings, other towns, or overseas (see the Rationale).

People in an organization usually work on related tasks, which suggests that they communicate frequently with each other.

Solution: The architectural partitioning should reflect the geographic partitioning, and vice versa. Architectural responsibilities should be assigned so decisions can be made (geographically) locally.

Resulting Context: Sub-organizations that can be further split or organized by market or other criteria (see Organization Follows Market, Work Flows Inward, and others). You still need someone to break logjams when consensus can't be reached, perhaps using Architect Also Implements or Patron.

If the organization is modularized along geographic boundaries, and the architecture is not, then it will be impossible to apply Architect Also Implements.

Rationale: Thomas Allen [Allen] has found that social distance goes up rapidly with physical separation (see also "House Cluster" [Alexander §37] of Alexander). Our empirical experience with co-development projects overseas reveals that failure to follow this pattern can lead to complete project failure. This is a crucial pattern that is often overlooked or dismissed out of consideration for political alliances. Peter Bürgi's studies of geographically distributed organizations in AT&T underscore the importance of this pattern.

We have seen few geographically distributed organizations that exhibit positive team dynamics. There arc exceptions, and there are rare occasions when this pattern does not apply. Steve Berczuk at MIT notes: ". . . communications need not be poor between remote sites if the following itcms are true: 1) the number of developers on a project, including all sites is small; 2) most of the communication is done via something like email (wide distribution and asynchronous communication—in [one case of his experience] . . . more people were in the loop than if the primary means of communication had been hallway chats); 3) The people involved have been together for SOME time so that they feel like they know each other; 4) Folks aren't so burned out by 'unnecessary' travel that they are willing and happy to travel when it is needed. In some situations pattern 7 is not possible because of the nature of the project, so we need a way to address the issue of remoteness." (Personal communication with Steve Berczuk, August, 1994.)

There are times when the market demands geographic distribution; see Organization Follows Market.

PATTERN 10: ORGANIZATION FOLLOWS MARKET

Alias: Framework Team

Problem: There is no clear role or organizational accountability to individual market segments.

Context: The market comprises several customers with similar but conflicting needs. The project has adopted sound architectural principles, and can organize its software according to market needs.

Forces:
- The development organization should track and meet the needs of each customer. Customer needs are similar, and much of what they all need can be done in common. Different customers expect results on different schedules.

Solution: In an organization designed to serve several distinct markets, it is important to reflect the market structure in the development organization. One frequently overlooked opportunity for a powerful pattern is the conscious design of a "core" organization that supports only what is common across all market segments. Ralph Johnson calls this a *framework team*. It is important to put this organization in place up front.

Resulting Context: An organization that can support a good architecture. The success of this pattern is necessary to the success of Architect Also Implements. Architect Also Implements should be seen as an audit, refinement, or fine-tuning of this pattern.

Rationale: Most of the rationale is in the forces. Two of the major forces relate to individual customer schedules, and to posture the organization to respond quickly to customer requests. Two important aspects of domain analysis are broadening the architecture (e.g., by working at the base class level), and ensuring that architectural evolution tracks the vendor understanding of customer needs. A single organization can't faithfully track multiple customer needs, and this organization allows different arms of the organization to track different markets independently.

PATTERN 11: DEVELOPER CONTROLS PROCESS

Problem: What role should be the focal point of project communication?

Context: An imperfectly understood design domain, where iteration is key to development.

Forces:
- Totalitarian control is viewed by most development teams as a draconian measure.
- The right information must flow through the right roles. You need to support information flow across analysis, design, and implementation.
- Managers have some accountability. Developers should have ultimate accountability, and have the authority and control of the product; these are often process issues.

Solution: Place the Developer role at a hub of the process for a given feature. A feature is a unit of system functionality (implemented largely in software) that can be separately marketed, and for which customers are willing to pay. The Developer is the process information clearinghouse. Responsibilities of Developers include understanding requirements, reviewing the solution structure and algorithm with peers, building the implementation, and unit testing.

Note that other hubs may exist as well.

Resulting Context: An organization that supports its prime information consumer.

The Developer can be moved toward the center of the process using patterns Work Flows Inward, and Move Responsibilities.

Though Developer should be a key role, care must be taken not to overburden it. This pattern should be balanced with Mercenary Analyst, Firewalls, Gatekeeper, and more general load-balancing patterns like Buffalo Mountain.

Rationale: We have no role called Designer because design is really the whole task. Managers fill a supporting role; empirically, they are rarely

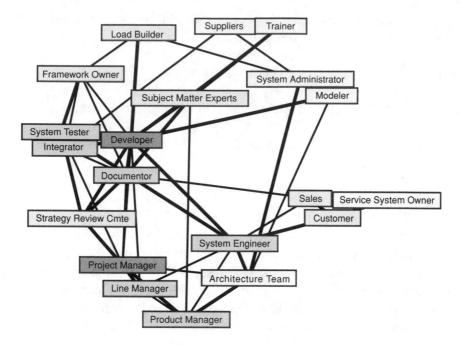

FIGURE 2   A developer-centric design and implementation process (Pattern 11).

seen to control a process except during crises. While the Developer controls
the process, the Architect controls the product. (In the figure, the Architect
role is split across Framework Owner and Architecture Team.) This communication is particularly important in domains that are not well understood, so that iteration can take place to explore the domain with the customer.

PATTERN 12: PATRON

Problem: Giving a project continuity.

Context: A development organization where roles are being defined.
Patron works only if Developer Controls Process is in place.

Forces:
- Centralized control can be a drag. Anarchy can be a worse drag.
  Most societies need a king/parent figure. An organization needs a
  single, ultimate decision-maker. The time to make a decision
  should be less than the time it takes to implement it.

Solution: Give the project access to a visible, high-level manager, who champions the cause of the project. The patron can be the final arbiter for project decisions, which provides a driving force for the organization to make decisions quickly. The patron is accountable to remove project-level barriers that hinder progress, and is responsible for the organization's "morale" (sense of well-being).

Resulting Context: Having a patron gives the organization a sense of being, and a focus for later process and organizational changes. Other roles can be defined in terms of the patron's role.

The manager role is not to be a totally centralized control, but rather a champion. That is, the scope of the manager's influence is largely outside those developing the product itself, but includes those whose cooperation is necessary for the success of the product (support organizations, funders, test organizations, etc.). This role also serves as a patron or sponsor; the person is often a corporate visionary.

Rationale: We have observed this in Phillippe Kahn in QPW; Sethi et al. in C++ efforts in AT&T; for a manager in a high-productivity Network Systems project; and in another multi-location AT&T project .

This relates to the pattern Firewalls which in turn relates to the pattern Gatekeeper.

Block talks about the importance of influencing forces over which the project has no direct control [Block]. The etymology of the term patron is instructive.

PATTERN 13: ARCHITECT CONTROLS PRODUCT

Problem: A product designed by many individuals lacks elegance and cohesiveness.

Context: An organization of Developers that needs strategic technical direction.

Forces:
Totalitarian control is viewed by most development teams as a draconian measure. The right information must flow through the right roles.

Solution: Create an Architect role. The Architect role should advise and control Developer roles, and should communicate closely with them. The Architect should also be in close touch with Customer.

Resulting Context: This does for the architecture what the Patron pattern does for the organization: it provides technical focus, and a rallying point for technical work as well as market-related work.

There is a rich relationship between this pattern and Patron that should be explored.

Resentment can build against a totalitarian Architect; use patterns like Review the Architecture to temper this one.

Rationale: We have no role called Designer because design is really the whole task. Managers fill a supporting role; empirically, they are rarely seen to control a process except during crises. While the Developer controls the process, the Architect controls the product. The Architect is a "chief Developer" (see pattern Architect Also Implements). Their responsibilities include understanding requirements, framing the major system structure, and controlling the long-term evolution of that structure.

The Architect controls the product in the visualization accompanying the pattern Engage QA.

> *Les oeuvres d'un seul architect sont plus belles . . . que ceux d'ont plusiers ont taché de faire. [The works of a lone architect are more elegant than those attempted by several together.]*
>
> Pascal, *Pensées*

PATTERN 14: CONWAY'S LAW

Problem: Aligning organization and architecture

Context: An Architect and development team are in place. The architecture is fairly well-established.

Forces:
Architecture shapes the communication paths in an organization. De facto organization structure shapes formal organization structure. Formal organization structure shapes architecture. Early architectural formulations are only approximations and are unstable.

Solution: Make sure the organization is compatible with the product architecture. At this point in the language, it is more likely that the architecture should drive the organization than vice versa.

Resulting Context: The organization and product architecture will be aligned.

Rationale: Historical. Gerard Meszaros (BNR) notes that you want to bind the organization to the architecture only after the architecture has stabilized. If your bind the organization to the architecture too early, architectural drift will lead to interference between individuals' domains of control.

PATTERN 15: ARCHITECT ALSO IMPLEMENTS

Problem: Preserving the architectural vision through to implementation

Context: An organization of Developers that needs strategic technical direction.

Forces:
Totalitarian control is viewed by most development teams as a draconian measure. The right information must flow through the right roles.

Solution: Beyond advising and communicating with Developers, Architects should also participate in implementation.

Resulting Context: A development organization that perceives buy-in from the guiding architects, and that can directly avail itself of architectural expertise.

Rationale: The importance of making this pattern explicit arose recently in a project I work with. The architecture team was being assembled across wide geographic boundaries with narrow communication bandwidth between them. Though general architectural responsibilities were identified and the roles were staffed, one group had expectations that architects would also implement code; the other did not.

One manager suggests that, on some projects, architects should focus only on the implementation of a common infrastructure, and that the implementation of non-core code should be left solely to the Developer role.

It would be convenient if architecture could be defined as any building designed by an architect. But who is an architect? Although the Academie Royale d'Architecture in Paris was founded in 1671, formal architectural schooling did not appear until the nineteenth century. The famous Ecole des Beaux-Arts was founded in 1816; the first English-language school, in London, in 1847; and the first North American university program, at MIT, was established in 1868. Despite the existence of professional schools, for a long time the relationship between schooling and practice remained ambiguous. It is still possible to become an architect without a university degree, and in some countries, such as Switzerland, trained architects have no legal monopoly over construction. This is hardly surprising. For centuries, the difference between master masons, journeymen builders, joiners, dilettantes, gifted amateurs, and architects has been ill defined. The great Renaissance buildings, for example, were designed by a variety of non-architects. Brunelleschi was trained as a goldsmith; Michelango as a sculptor, Leonardo da Vinci as a painter, and Alberti as a lawyer; only Bramante, who was also a painter, had formally studied building. These men are termed architects because, among other things, they created architecture—a tautology that explains nothing (Rybczynski 1989, pp. 9–10].

In *The Ten Books on Architecture,* Vitruvius notes:

Architects who have aimed at acquiring manual skill without scholarship have never been able to reach a position of authority to correspond to their pains, while those who relied only upon theories and scholarship were obviously hunting the shadow, not this substance. But those who have a thorough knowledge of both, like men armed at all points, have the sooner attained their object and carried authority with them (Vitruvius 1960).

PATTERN 16: REVIEW THE ARCHITECTURE

Problem: Blind spots in the architecture and design

Context: A software artifact whose quality is to be assessed for improvement.

Forces:
- Architecture decisions affect many people over a long time. Individual Architects and Designers can develop tunnel vision. A shared architectural vision is important.

- Even low-level design and implementation decisions matter.
- All things are deeply intermingled (Ed Yourdon).

Solution: All architectural decisions should be reviewed by all Architects. Architects should review each others' code. The reviews should be frequent—even daily—early in the project. Reviews should be informal, with a minimum of paperwork.

Resulting Context: This pattern sets the context for Mercenary Analyst. It will also solve potential problems that have been pointed out for Code Ownership.

The intent of this pattern is to increase coupling between those with a stake in the architecture and implementation, which solves the stated problem indirectly.

Rationale: QPW; a successful object-oriented project in AT&T.

Pattern 17: Code Ownership

Problem: A Developer cannot keep up with a constantly changing base of implementation code.

Context: A system with mechanisms to document and enforce the software architecture, and developers to write the code.

Forces:
- Something that's everybody's responsibility is no one's responsibility.
- You want parallelism between developers, so multiple people can be coding concurrently.
- Most design knowledge lives in the code; navigating unfamiliar code to explore design issues takes time. Provisional changes never work.
- Not everyone can know everything all the time.

Solution: Each code module in the system is owned by a single Developer. Except in exceptional and explicit circumstances, code may be modified only by its owner.

Resulting Context: The architecture and organization will better reflect each other. Related patterns include Architect Also Implements, Organization Follows Market, and Interrupts Unjam Blocking.

The pattern Review the Architecture helps keep Designers and Architects from developing tunnel vision from strict application of this pattern.

Rationale: Lack of code ownership is a major contributor to discovery effort in large-scale software development today. Note that this goes hand-in-hand with architecture: to have ownership, there must be interfaces. This is a form of Conway's-law-in-the-small (see also Architect Also Implements).

Arguments against code ownership have been many, but empirical trends uphold its value. Typical concerns include the tendency toward tunnel vision, the implied risk of having only a single individual who understands a given piece of code in-depth, and breakdown of global knowledge. Other patterns temper these problems (see Review the Architecture, and Engage Customers).

Tim Born argues that there is a relationship between code ownership and encapsulation, in the sense that C++ protection keeps one person from accessing the implementation of another's abstraction. Law is property, and the lack of identifiable property leads to anarchy (Rousseau et al.).

It has been argued that code ownership should be applied only to reusable code. Such a constraint would be worthy of consideration if someone comes up with a good distinction between usable code and reusable code.

Pattern 18: Application Design is Bounded By Test Design

Problem: When do you design and implement test plans and scripts?

Context: A system with mechanisms to document and enforce the software architecture, and developers to write the code. A Testing role is being defined.

Forces:
- Test development takes time, and cannot be started just when the system is done ("when we know what we have to test").
- Scenarios are known when requirements are known, and many of these are known early.
- Test implementation needs to know the details of message formats, interfaces, and other architectural properties in great details (to support test scripts and test jigs). Implementation changes daily;

there should be no need for test designs to track ephemeral changes in software implementation.

Solution: Scenario-driven test design starts when scenario requirements are first agreed to by the customer. Test design evolves along with software design, but only in response to customer scenario changes: the source software is inaccessible to the tester. When development decides that architectural interfaces have stabilized, low-level test design and implementation can proceed.

Resulting Context: This provides a context for Engage QA and for Scenarios Define Problem.

Rationale: Making the software accessible to the tester causes them to see the developer view rather than the customer view, and leads to the chance they may test the wrong things, or at the wrong level of detail. Furthermore, the software will continue to evolve from requirements until the architecture gels, and there is no sense in causing test design to fishtail until interfaces settle down. In short, test design kicks off at the end of the first major influx of requirements, and touches base with design again when the architecture is stable.

This is related to the (yet unspecified) pattern, "Testing first in last out," to the pattern Engage QA, and to the pattern Scenarios Define Problem.

PATTERN 19: ENGAGE QA

Problem: How do you guarantee product quality?

Context: A set of roles in a development organization, and a customer, with a need for some filter between them to ensure the quality of the product.

Forces:
- Developers feel they get everything right. Perfect software is hard.
- Quality is too often deferred. Success depends on high quality. Early feedback is important for fundamental quality problems.

Solution: Make QA a central role. Couple it tightly to development as soon as development has something to test. Test plan development can proceed in parallel with coding, but Developers declare the system ready for test.

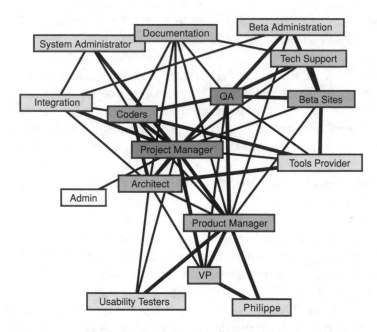

FIGURE 3   The development organization for Borland's Quattro Pro for Windows. Quality Assurance (QA) was central to the development of Quattro Pro (see Pattern 19).

The QA organization should be outside the context of the project: the planning and reporting of tests should not be accountable to the development organization.

Resulting Context: Having engaged QA, the project will be ready to approach the Customer. With QA and the Customer engaged, the quality assurance process can be put in place (use cases gathered, etc.).

Rationale: There are at least two reasons for making QA a separate organization from that holding Developers' allegiance. First, test development shouldn't be blind-sided by the Developer perspective. If both the Developer and QA perform their own tests, testing becomes a double-blind experiment with the software as a subject. Second, QA should be put outside the domain of influence by the development organization in the interest of objectivity.

This is an obvious pattern in QPW. See also Application Design is Bounded By Test Design.

PATTERN 20: ENGAGE CUSTOMERS

Problem: Maintaining customer satisfaction

Context: A quality assurance function exists, and needs input to drive its work.

Forces:
- Developers used to be called "loose cannons on deck."
- Requirements changes occur even after design reviews are complete and coding has started.
- Missing customer requirements is a serious problem. Customers are traditionally not part of the mainstream development, which makes it difficult to discover and incorporate their insights.
- Trust relationship between managers and coders.

Solution: Make Customer a role that is closely coupled to the Developer and Architect, not just to QA.

Resulting Context: The new context supports requirements discovery from the customer, as required by the pattern Scenarios Define Problem, and the pattern Prototype. Other patterns like Firewalls and unspecified also build on this pattern.

Rationale: QPW. Also, see [Floyd] and in particular the works of Reisin and Floyd therein.

Some processes and methods are founded on customer engagement, such as IBM's Joint Application Development. Other methods are conducive to customer engagement, such as Beck's CRC design technique. Other methods, particularly many CASE-based methods, are indifferent or harmful to customer engagement.

The pattern is "Engage Customers", in the plural, to support a domain view and to avoid being blind-sided by a single customer.

The project must be careful to temper interactions between Customer and Developer, using the patterns mentioned in the Resulting Context. Note that "maintaining product quality" is not the problem being solved here. Product quality is only one component of customer satisfaction. Studies have shown that customers leave one company for another when they feel they are being ignored (20% of the time), or because the attention they receive was rude or unhelpful (50% of the time). For customers having problems that cost over $100 to fix, and the company does not fix it, only 9% would buy again. 82% would do business with the company again if the problem was quickly resolved after they complained. (The source for the former pair is The Forum Corporation; for the latter pair, Traveler's Insurance Company [Zuckerman].)

Maranzano notes that this pattern probably should come earlier in the language. However, it is important that the project roles be defined first—particularly those that interact with the customer, and those that are driven by customer input (such as QA). Said in another way, the organization exists to serve the customer, so the organization should be in place before the customer is fully engaged.

PATTERN 21: GROUP VALIDATION

Problem: Ensuring product quality.

Context: The quality of analysis, design, or implementation is to be assessed.

Forces:
- The job of QA is to assess quality. QA usually assesses the quality of the end product, doing only black-box validation and verification.
- A group setting brings many insights on product problems and opportunities. Individuals may not have the insight necessary to discover the bug plaguing the system (this may be an issue of objectivity).

Solution: Even before engaging QA, the development team—including Customer—can validate the design. Techniques such as CRC cards and group debugging help socialize and solve problems. Members of a validation team can also work with QA to fix root causes attributable to common classes of software faults.

Resulting Context: A process where the quality of the system is constantly brought into focus before the whole team. In the resulting context, problems will be resolved sooner. The cost of this pattern is the time expended in group design/code debugging sessions.

Rationale: The CRC design technique has been found to be a great team-builder, and an ideal way to socialize designs. Studies of GBCS projects have found group debugging sessions to be unusually productive. Bringing the customer into these sessions can be particularly helpful.

The project must be careful to temper interactions between Customer and Developer, using the patterns mentioned in the Resulting Context.

There is an empirical research foundation for this pattern. See "An implementation of structured walk-throughs in teaching COBOL programming," *CACM,* Vol. 22, No. 6, June, 1979, which found that team debugging contributes to team learning and effectiveness. A contrary position can be found in G. J. Meyers, "A controlled experiment in program testing and code walk-throughs/inspections," *CACM,* Vol. 21, No. 9, September, 1978, though this study was limited to fault detection rates and did not evaluate the advantages of team learning.

Compare with Developing in Pairs.

Pattern 22: Scenarios Define Problem

Problem: Design documents are often ineffective as vehicles to communicate the customer vision of how the system should work.

Context: You want to engage the customer and need a mechanism to support other organizational alliances between customer and developers.

Forces:
- There is a natural business distancing and mistrust between customers and developers. Communication between developers and customers is crucial to the success of a system.

Solution: Capture system functional requirements as use cases, a la Jacobson.

Resulting Context: The problem is now defined, and the architecture can proceed in earnest. See also Mercenary Analyst, who captures scenarios and uses them for project documentation (both internal and external).

Rationale: Jacobson; also *CACM* Nov. '88 (v. 31, no. 11) pp 1268–1287, according to Ralph Johnson. Also Rubin and Goldberg, who take scenarios all the way to the front of the process, preceding even design. See also, "Formal Approach to Scenario Analysis," Pei Hsia, Jayaranan Samuel, Jerry Gao, and David Kung, *IEEE Software,* March, 1994, Vol. 11, No. 2, ff 33.

PATTERN 23: MERCENARY ANALYST

Problem: Supporting a design notation, and the related project documentation, is too tedious a job for people directly contributing to product artifacts.

Context: You are assembling the roles for the organization. The organization exists in a context where external reviewers, customers, and internal developers expect to use project documentation to understand the system architecture and its internal workings. (User documentation is considered separately).

Forces:
- If developers do their own documentation, it hampers "real" work.
- Documentation is often write-only. Engineers often don't have good communication skills.
- Architects can become victims of the elegance of their own drawings (see rationale).

Solution: Hire a technical writer, proficient in the necessary domains, but without a stake in the design itself. This person will capture the design using a suitable notation, and will format and publish the design for reviews and for consumption by the organization itself.

The documentation itself should be maintained on-line where ever possible. It must be kept up-to-date (therefore, Mercenary Analyst is a full-time job), and should relate to customer scenarios (Scenarios Define Problem).

Resulting Context: The success of this pattern depends on finding a suitably skilled agent to fill the role of mercenary analyst. If the pattern succeeds, the new context defines a project whose progress can be reviewed (the pattern Review the Architecture) and monitored by community experts outside the project.

Rationale: QPW; many AT&T projects (a joint venture based in New Jersey, a formative organization in switching support, and others). It is difficult to find people with the skills to fill this role.

Here is another liability: beautiful drawings can become ends in themselves. Often, if the drawing deceives, it is not only the viewer who is enchanted but also the maker, who is the victim of his own artifice. Alberti understood this danger and pointed out that architects should not try to imitate painters and produce lifelike drawings. The purpose of architectural drawings, according to him, was merely to illustrate the relationship of the various parts. . . . Alberti understood, as many architects of today do not, that the rules of drawing and the rules of building are not one and the same, and mastery of the former does not ensure success in the latter (Rybczynski 1989, p. 121).

PATTERN 24: FIREWALLS

Problem: Project implementors are often distracted by outsiders who feel a need to offer input and criticism.

Context: An organization of developers has formed, in a corporate or social context where they are scrutinized by peers, funders, customers, and other "outsiders."

Forces:
- Isolationism doesn't work: information flow is important.
- Communication overhead goes up non-linearly with the number of external collaborators. Many interruptions are noise.
- Maturity and progress are more highly correlated with being in control than being controlled.

Solution: Create a Manager role, who shields other development personnel from interaction with external roles. The responsibility of this role is "to keep the pests away."

Resulting Context: The new organization isolates developers from extraneous external interrupts. To avoid isolationism, this pattern must be tempered with others, such as Engage Customers and Gatekeeper.

Rationale: QPW, ATT1. See also the pattern Engage Customers, which complements this pattern. Gatekeeper is a pattern that facilitates effective flow of useful information; Firewalls restricts flow of detracting information. Sun Tzu notes: "He will win who has military capacity and is not interfered with by the sovereign."

PATTERN 25: GATEKEEPER

Problem: Balancing the need to communicate with typically introverted engineering personality types.

Context: An organization of developers has formed, in a corporate or social context scrutinized by peers, funders, customers, and other "outsiders."

Forces:
- Isolationism doesn't work: information flow is important.
- Communication overhead goes up non-linearly with the number of external collaborators. Many interruptions are noise.
- Maturity and progress are more highly correlated with being in control than being control

Solution: One project member, a Type A personality, rises to the role of Gatekeeper. This person disseminates leading-edge and fringe information from outside the project to project members, "translating" it into terms relevant to the project. The Gatekeeper may also "leak" project information to relevant outsiders. This role can also manage the development interface to marketing and to the corporate control structure.

Resulting Context: This pattern provides balance for the pattern Firewalls, and complements the pattern Engage Customers (to the degree Customers are still viewed as outsiders). Gatekeeper and Firewalls alone are insufficient to protect developers in an organization whose culture allows marketing to drive development schedules.

Rationale: Gatekeeper is a pattern that facilitates effective flow of useful information; Firewalls restricts flow of detracting information. The value of the Gatekeeper pattern has been verified in practice. In the discussion of this pattern at PLoP/94, many of the reviewers noted that creating a Gatekeeper role had served them well.

Engineers are lousy communicators as a lot; it's important to leverage the communication abilities of an effective communicating engineer when one is found.

Alexander notes that while it is important to build subcultures in a society (as we are building a subculture here in the framework of a company, or of the software industry as a whole), such a subculture should not be closed ("Mosaic of Subcultures", [Alexander 8]); also, cp. Alexander's pattern "Main Gateways" [Alexander 53]. One might muse that the Gatekeeper takes an outsider through any rites of passage necessary for more intimate access to the development team, by analogy to Alexander's "Entrance Transition" [Alexander 112]

Gatekeeper can serve the role of "pedagogue" as in Alexander's pattern "Network of Learning" [Alexander 18].

Maranzano notes that the same person often must fill both the Manager and Gatekeeper roles, because of the relationships to external people who need the info.

Pattern 26: Shaping Circulation Realms

Problem: Patterns of interaction in an organization are not as they should be, as prescribed by other patterns.

Context: This pattern is a building block for other patterns in the language, including Organization Follows Market, Developer Controls Process, Architect Also Implements, Engage QA, Engage Customers, Buffalo Mountain, and others. This pattern may also apply to circulation realms outside the project, such as Firewalls, and many others.

Forces:
- Proper communication structures between roles are key to organizational success.
- Communication can't be controlled from a single role; at least two roles must be involved.
- Communication patterns can't be dictated; some second-order force must be present to encourage them.
- Communication follows semantic coupling between responsibilities.

Solution: Give people titles that creates a hierarchy or pecking order whose structure reflects the desired taxonomy. Give people job responsibilities that suggest the appropriate interactions between roles (see also Move Responsibilities).

Physically collocate people whom you wish to have close communication coupling (this is the dual of the pattern Organization Follows Location).

Tell people what to do and with whom they should interact; people will usually try to respect your wishes if you ask them to do something reasonable that is within their purview and power.

Resulting Context: The goal is to produce an organization with higher overall cohesion, with sub-parts that are as internally cohesive and externally de-coupled as possible.

Rationale: This follows an Alexandrine pattern [Alexander 98] of the same name, and has strong analogies to the rationales of "House Cluster" [Alexander 37]. The same rationale can be found in Thomas Allen. Note that Move Responsibilities is a closely related pattern. See related notes in the Rationale for Gatekeeper.

PATTERN 27: MOVE RESPONSIBILITIES

Problem: Unscrutinized relationships between roles can lead to undesirable coupling at the organizational level.

Context: Any organization or process.

Forces:
- You want cohesive roles. You want cohesive organizations. Decoupled organizations are more important than cohesive roles. There may be fundamental trade-offs between coupling and cohesion.
- Moving an entire role from one process or organization to another doesn't reduce the overall coupling, but only moves the source.

Solution: Move responsibilities from the role that creates the most undesirable coupling, to the roles coupled to it from other processes. Simply said, this is load balancing. The responsibilities should not be shifted arbitrarily; a chief programmer team organization is one good way to implement this pattern (in the context for Developer role responsibilities).

Resulting Context: The new process may exhibit more highly de-coupled groups. It is important to balance group cohesion with the de-coupling, so this pattern must be applied with care. For example, the Developer role is often the locus for a large fraction of project responsibilities, so the role appears overloaded. Arbitrarily shifting Developer responsibilities to other

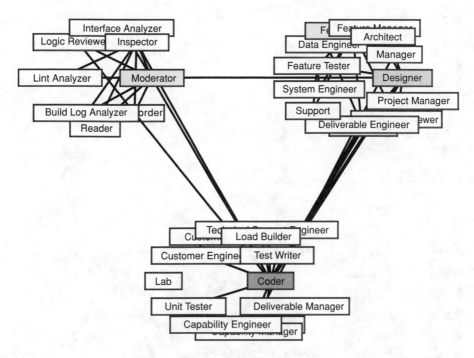

FIGURE 4   Sociogram showing clusters for activities design, coding, and review. Coupling in this partitioned design/coding process can be reduced by rearranging the Coder's responsibilities (see Pattern 27).

roles can introduce communication overhead. A chief programmer team approach to the solution helps balance these forces.

Buffalo Mountain is an alternative load-balancing pattern.

Rationale: Most of the design rationale follows from the forces themselves. This is isomorphic to Mackenzie's model that task interdependencies, together with the interdependencies of task resources and their characteristics, define project roles [Mackenzie].

PATTERN 28: BUFFALO MOUNTAIN[3]

Problem: We want to optimize communications in a large software development organization, whose members are working together on a common product.

---

[3] The pattern's name comes from the similarity between the visual graph and the characteristic shape of a mountain in Colorado, and from the analogies that can be made about the forces contributing to each.

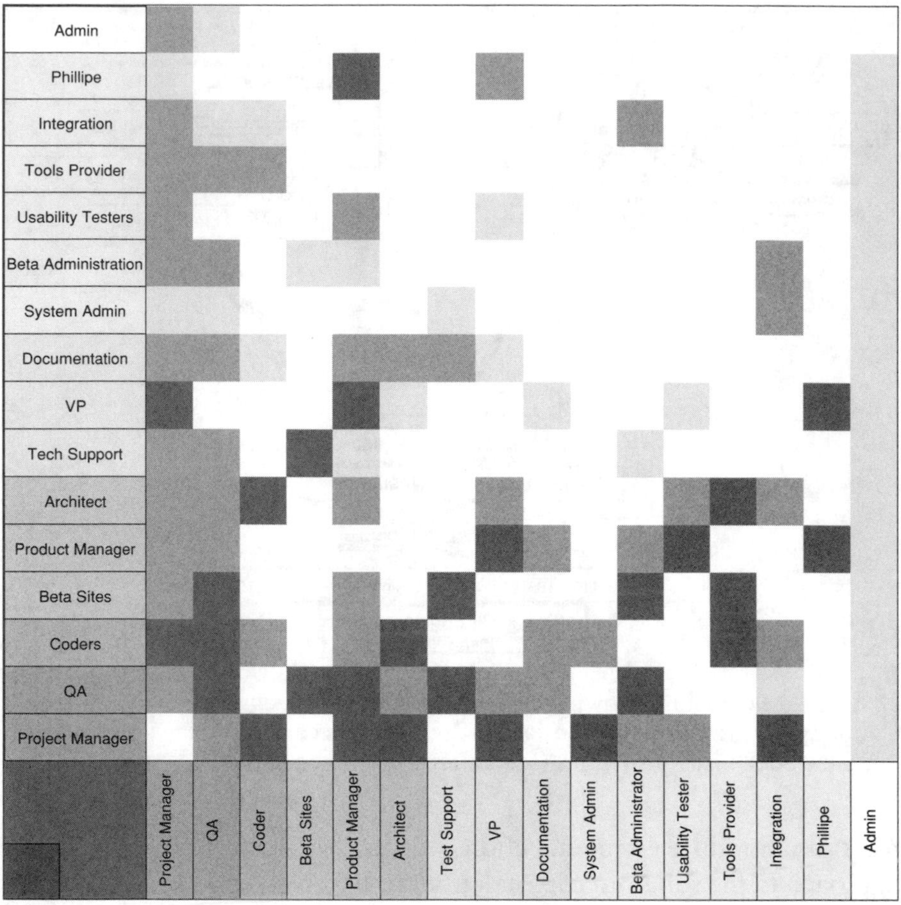

Row labels (top to bottom): Admin, Phillipe, Integration, Tools Provider, Usability Testers, Beta Administration, System Admin, Documentation, VP, Tech Support, Architect, Product Manager, Beta Sites, Coders, QA, Project Manager

Column labels (left to right): Project Manager, QA, Coder, Beta Sites, Product Manager, Architect, Test Support, VP, Documentation, System Admin, Beta Administrator, Usability Tester, Tools Provider, Integration, Phillipe, Admin

FIGURE 5   Buffalo Mountain (Pattern 28).

Context: A development organization straddling several domains, where effective interpersonal communication is key to project success. A nominal "hub" may already have been established for the organization.

Forces:
- Communication overhead goes up non-linearly with the number of people.
- Information starvation or role isolation cause people to develop unsuitable sub-products. Being a communication bottleneck leaves no time to do work.
- Communication bottlenecks cause queues in organizational work

flows that keep other people from doing work. Fully distributed control tends to lead to control breakdown.

Solution: 1. For any significant project interaction, the distance of the two collaborating roles from the "center" of the organization should sum to a distance less than the smallest distance necessary to span the entire organization.

2. Avoid coupling with neighbors (those equidistant from the center of the process as yourself; i.e., those equally coupled to the process as a whole as yourself) if you are in the outlying 50% of the organization.

3. The intensity of any interaction should be inversely proportional to the sum of the differences of the roles' distance to the center of the process.

Means A: Shuffle responsibilities between roles in a way that moves the associated collaborations, to effect the above patterns (Move Responsibilities). This is Robert Lai's idea; it's simple, but profoundly effective.

Means B: Physically relocate people to enhance their opportunity to communicate (see Work Flows Inward).

Means C: Increase span of control of a role in the project (akin to merging multiple roles into one). It is probably best to Merge Roles with Similar Responsibilities, or better, to Merge Roles with Similar Collaborations. Hey, those are patterns too!

Resulting Context: The new organization has more balanced communication across its roles.

Rationale: Most of these patterns are empirical, rather than being derived from first principles. I think it important to recognize this path to patterns as a positive and potentially fruitful one. If it works, go with it.

Subpattern 1 is empirical. It is the dominant sub-pattern. It infuses a level of "distributed control with central tendency" that lends overall direction and cohesion to an organization. Another way of stating sub-pattern 1 is that most points on the interaction grid tend to live near the axes.

Subpattern 2 avoids cliquish splinter groups. It also helps avoid linear event ordering in the distant (support) parts of a process. Linear event ordering (or pipelining) causes points on the interaction grid to line up right below the diagonal. A pattern that avoids points on the diagonal is likely to encourage more parallelism and independence.

Subpattern 3 tempers sub-pattern 1, allowing points further from the diagonal but not too far from the origin. This allows for a tight "core" at the middle of the process. It also helps to even the distribution of load across roles in the process. Many organizations are bimodal: they interact tightly in the core, and virtually not at all in the outlying roles. This evens the load across all roles.

The overall (and difficult-to-explain) nature of these sub-patterns is that they improve product quality and reduce time-to-market. They tend to correlate with high spans of control. That in turn reduces the number of people necessary to complete a project, further reducing communication overhead, improving cohesion, and causing the pattern to recursively feed on itself. It's wondrous to watch this happen in an organization.

PATTERN 29: WORK FLOWS INWARD

Problem: Work that adds value directly to the product should be done by authoritarian roles.

Context: An existing organization where the flow of information can be analyzed. The organization exhibits a management pecking order.

Forces:
- Some centralized control and direction are necessary
- During software production, the work bottleneck of a system should be at its center (in the adjacency diagram sense; see Notations). If the center of the communication center of the organization generates work more than it does work, then organization performance can become unpredictable and sporadic.
- The developer is already sensitized to market needs through Firewalls and Gatekeeper (no centralized role need fill this function).

Solution: Work should be generated by customers, filter through supporting roles, and be carried out by implementation experts at the center. You should not put managers at the center of the communication grid: they will become overloaded and make decisions that are less well-considered, and they will make decisions that don't take day-to-day dynamics into account.

Resulting Context: An organization whose communication grid has more points below the diagonal than above it.

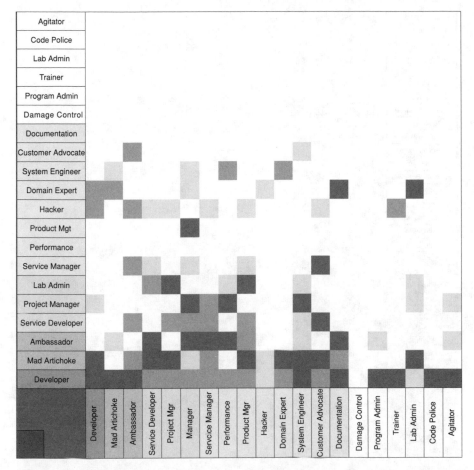

FIGURE 6   Interaction grids for two organizations (Pattern 29). The organization above has a healthy distribution of inward-directed inputs; on the following page, the center is overloaded and turns work requests outward. Above, the core roles work; on the following page they *make* work.

Rationale: Katz & Kahn's analysis of organizations shows that the exercise of control is not a zero-sum game [Katz & Kahn, p. 314]. The work should focus at the center of the process; the center of the process should focus on value-added activities (Developer Controls Process).

Organizations run by professional managers tend to have repeatable business processes, but don't seem to reach the same productivity plateaus of organizations run by engineers. In programmer-centric organizations, the value-added roles are at the center of the process (Developer Controls

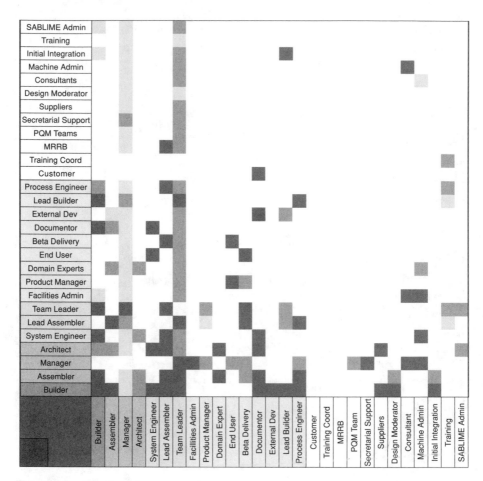

Figure 6　*Continued.*

Process; Architect Also Implements). The manager should facilitate and support these roles and their work (Patron; Firewalls).

Mackenzie characterizes this pattern using M-curves, that model the percentage of task processes of each task process law level (planning, directing, and execution) as a function of the classification [Mackenzie]

The rationale is supported with empirical observations from existing projects.

Managers should still make day-to-day decisions for the business process, and pursuant to their responsibility to "keep the pests away" (Firewalls).

PATTERN 30: THREE TO SEVEN HELPERS PER ROLE

Problem: Uneven distribution of communication.

Context: An organization whose basic social network has been built.

Forces:
- Too much coupling to any given role, and it is in overload. Too little coupling, and the role can become information-starved and under-utilized.

Solution: Ensure that each role has between 3 and 7 helpers.

Resulting Context: A more balanced organization, with better load-sharing and fewer isolated roles.

Rationale: Our empirical results from the organizations studied in the Pasteur project show that any given role can sustain at most 7 long-term relationships. In particularly productive organizations, the number can be as high as 9. Particular needs might suggest that the process designer go outside these bounds, if doing so is supported with a suitable rationale.

Communication between roles is complete in an organization if every role communicates with every other role. We can talk about the communication saturation of an organization as the ratio of the number of communication paths within the organization to the total possible number of communication paths. For a given project size, Harrison has found this ratio to be higher in highly productive organizations than in average organizations.

PATTERN 31: NAMED STABLE BASES[4]

Problem: How frequently do you integrate?

Context: A schedule framework has been determined

Forces:
- Continuous integration, and developers try to follow a moving target. Too long between integrations, and developers become blocked

---

[4] This pattern was suggested by Dennis DeBruler at AT&T.

from making progress beyond the limits of the last base.
- Stability is a good thing.
- Progress should be made. Progress must be perceived.

Solution: Stabilize system interfaces—the architecture—no more frequently than once a week. Other software can be changed (and even integrated) more frequently.

Resulting Context: The project has targets to shoot for. This affects the Customer view of the process, and has strong ramifications for the Architect as well.

Rationale: See the description of the forces. The pattern owes to Dennis DeBruler at AT&T. The main point of the pattern is that a project should schedule change introduction so the effects of changes can be anticipated. It is less important to publish the content of a change (which will go unheeded under high change volume) than for the development community to understand that change is taking place. It is important not to violate "the rule of least surprise."

It can be helpful to have, simultaneously, various bases at different levels of stability. For example, one AT&T project had a nightly build (which is guaranteed only to have compiled), a weekly integration test build (which is guaranteed to have passed system-wide sanity tests), and a (roughly biweekly) service test build (that is considered stable enough for QA's system test).

PATTERN 32: DIVIDE AND CONQUER

Problem: Organizations grow to the point where they cannot easily manage themselves (i.e., the organization's decision process breaks down).

Context: The roles have been defined for a process and organization, and the interactions between them are understood.

Forces:
- If an organization is too large, it can't be managed. Incohesive organizations are confusing and engender dilution of focus.
- Separation of concerns is good. It is useful to have organization boundaries that are somehow lightweight.

Solution: Find clusters of roles that have strong mutual coupling, but that are loosely coupled to the rest of the organization. Form a separate organization and process around those roles.

Resulting Context: Each new suborganization is a largely independent entity to which the remaining patterns in this language can be independently applied.

Rationale: See the description of the forces. Note that each sub-organizations that arises from this pattern is fodder for most other patterns, since each subsystem is a system in itself. Also, to see an organization that has been reverse engineered and redivided into new processes, see the picture for the pattern Move Responsibilities.

PATTERN 33: DECOUPLE STAGES

Problem: How do you de-couple stages (architecture, design, coding) in a development process?

Context: A design and implementation process for a well-understood domain.

Forces:
- Stages should be independent to reduce coupling and promote independence between stages. Independence hampers information flow. Independence creates opportunities for parallelism.

Solution: For known and mature domains, serialize the steps. Handoffs between steps should take place via well-defined interfaces. This makes it possible to automate one or more of the steps, or to create a pattern that lets inexpert staff carry out the step.

Resulting Context: The new organization allows for specialization in carrying out parts of the process, rather than emphasizing specialization in solving the customer problem. This approach is "safe" only for well-understood domains, where the mapping from needs to implementation is straightforward. Domains that are well-understood are also good candidates for mechanization. For less mature domains, the process should build on the creativity of those involved at each stage of the process, and there should be more parallelism and interworking.

This pattern prepares for Hub-Spoke-and-Rim

Rationale: See the forces.

PATTERN 34: HUB-SPOKE-AND-RIM

Problem: How do you de-couple stages (architecture, design, coding) in a development process?

Context: A design and implementation process. A well-understood domain. Aesthetic Pattern has been applied.

Forces:
- Stages should be independent to reduce coupling and promote independence between stages. Independence hampers information flow.
- Independence creates opportunities for parallelism.

Solution: Link each role to a central role that orchestrates process activities. Parallelism can be re-introduced if the central role pipelines activities.

Resulting Context: The process has more order and is more likely to be repeatable than Aesthetic Pattern alone. The process designer must be wary of the central role becoming a bottleneck, and address such bottlenecks with other patterns (e.g., Move Responsibilities).

Rationale: Empirical studies done on a front-end process called CNM for a large AT&T project (unpublished work); pipelining theory.

PATTERN 35: AESTHETIC PATTERN

Problem: An organization has an irregular structure

Context: The organization has been designed through preceding patterns. The project is in early development of the first release of its product. The organization must plan how to evolve itself beyond the product's first release, and eventually into the product's maintenance phase.

Forces:
- Even distribution of responsibility is good because it distributes the work load. Regular structures, such as hierarchies, can easily be

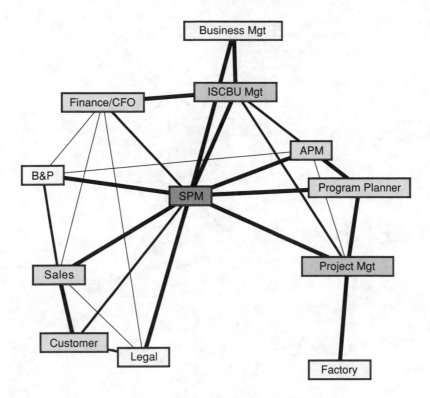

FIGURE 7   A product management organization. A single central role orchestrates this highly responsive front-end process supporting sales and marketing
activities (see Pattern 34).

grown by adding more people, without destroying the spirit of the
original structure. A regular hierarchical structure does not distribute responsibility evenly.

Solution: Make sure the organization has identifiable sub-domains that
can grow into departments of their own as the project thrives and expands
to serve a maintained market.

Resulting Context: The organization will have sub-organization foundations on which to grow.

Rationale: This is empirical from our organization studies. To this point,
patterns help ensure a functional, highly productive organization. But
work still must be done to allow the organization to grow elegantly. We

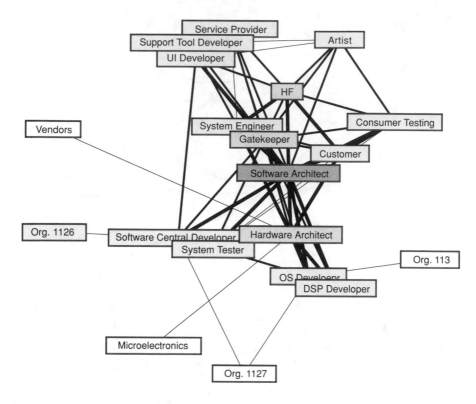

FIGURE 8   Two development organizations. The organization above has no apparent structure, and though it is productive, it is not likely to evolve well. The organization on the facing page has no well-partitioned structures, but one can identify
logical partitions within it (customer, developer, management, and so on; see
Pattern 35).

achieve that end by identifying the roots of sub-organizations in the current
organization. If we can find none, the organization may not be able to grow.
For example, it is difficult to grow a Chief Programmer Team organization.

PATTERN 36: COUPLING DECREASES LATENCY

Problem: The process is not responsive enough; development intervals
are too long; market windows are not met.

Context: A service process and, perhaps in special cases, a small design/
implementation process using an iterative or incremental approach.

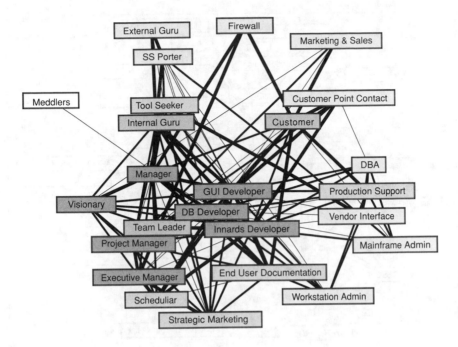

FIGURE 8   *Continued.*

Forces:
- Stages should be independent to reduce coupling and promote independence. Independence improves opportunities for parallelism. Independence hampers information flow.

Solution: Open communication paths between roles to increase the overall coupling/role ratio, particularly between central process roles. Communication between roles can be shaped using patterns such as Work Flows Inward and Move Responsibilities.

Resulting Context: Coupling of course increases dependence between roles, which may not always be a good thing. This pattern is somehow related to Interrupts Unjam Blocking.

Handoffs can increase latency. The number of "hops" between roles should be kept small for any given problem.

Rationale: Basic software engineering principle.

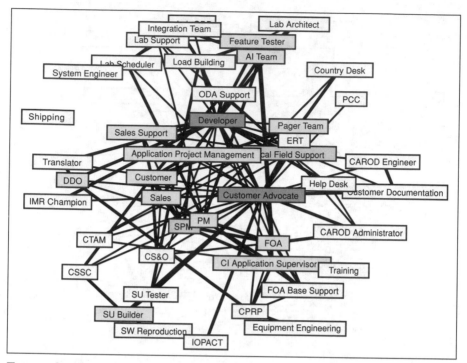

FIGURE 9   A service process. This is a highly responsive process, owing largely to its high degree of internal coupling (see Pattern 36).

PATTERN 37: PROTOTYPE

Problem: Early acquired requirements are difficult to validate without testing.

Context: Trying to gather requirements necessary for test planning, as in pattern Application Design is Bounded By Test Design, and for the architecture, as for the pattern Architect Also Implements.

Forces:
- Requirements are always changing. Written requirements are usually too ambiguous. Need to get requirements changes early. Designers and implementors must understand requirements directly.

Solution: Build a prototype, whose purpose is to understand requirements. Prototypes are particularly useful for external interfaces. Throw the prototype away when you're done.

Resulting Context: A better assessment of requirements to supplement use cases. This pattern nicely complements Engage Customers and Scenarios Define Problem.

Rationale: The processes of the visualizations used for Developer Controls Process, and the pattern Engage QA, are based largely on prototyping.

As Frank Lloyd Wright said, "The best friend of the architect is the pencil in the drafting room, and the sledgehammer on the job" (Jacobs 1978).

PATTERN 38: TAKE NO SMALL SLIPS

Problem: How long should the project take?

Context: The product is under way and progress must be tracked.

Forces:
- Too long, and developers become complacent, and you miss market windows.
- Too short, and developers become burned out, and you miss market windows.
- Projects without schedule motivation tend to go on forever, or spend too much time polishing details that are either irrelevant or don't serve customer needs.

Solution: "We found a good way to live by 'Take no small slips' from . . . 'The Mythical Man Month.' Every week, measure how close the critical path (at least) of the schedule is doing. If it's three days beyond schedule, track a 'delusion index' of three days. When the delusion index gets too ludicrous, then slip the schedule. This helps avoid churning the schedule."— Personal discussion with Paul Chisholm, June, 1994.

Resulting Context: A project with a flexible target date. Dates are always difficult to estimate; DeMarco notes that one of the most serious signs of a problem in trouble is a schedule worked backward from an end date [DeMarco].

Rationale: MIT project management simulation; QPW; [Brooks]. Most sane projects manage this way.

PATTERN 39: DEVELOPING IN PAIRS

Problem: People are scared to solve problems alone.

Context: Code ownership has been identified and development is proceeding.

Forces:
- People sometime feel they can solve a problem only if they have help. Some problems are bigger than an individual. Too many people can't sit in front of a keyboard and screen. Effort goes up nonlinearly with number of people.

Solution: Pair compatible designers to work together; together, they can produce more than the sum of the two individually.

Resulting Context: A more effective implementation process. A pair of people is less likely to be blindsided than an individual developer.

Rationale: Compare with Group Validation.

PATTERN 40: INTERRUPTS UNJAM BLOCKING

Problem: The events and tasks in a process are too complex to schedule development activities as a time-linear sequence.

Context: A high productivity design/implementation process or low-latency service process. The scheduling problem is to be addressed on a small scale (i.e., this is not scheduling entire departments, but the work of cooperating individuals).

Forces:
- Complete scheduling insight is impossible.
- The programmers with the longest development schedules will benefit if more of others' code is done before they try integrating or testing later code, and their interval can't otherwise be shortened (see Code Ownership).

Solution: If a role is about to block on a critical resource, interrupt the role that provides that resource so they stop what they're doing to keep you unblocked.

If the overhead is small enough, it doesn't affect throughput. It will always improve local latency.

Resulting Context: The process should have a higher throughput, again, at the expense of higher coupling. Coupling may have already been facilitated by earlier patterns, such as Work Flows Inward, Move Responsibilities, Buffalo Mountain, and Coupling Decreases Latency.

Rationale: See the forces. The intent is that this pattern will apply most frequently between cooperating developers working on a single project. This is supported empirically from a high productivity process in AT&T. There are strong software engineering (operating system) principles as well.

It may be useful to prioritize interrupts, and service the ones that would optimize the productivity of the organization as a whole. That is, it is better to unblock 4 people who are currently blocked than to unblock a single squeaky wheel. The decision-making process should be fast: Most of the time, it should be distributed. Where arbitration is needed, apply Patron. The Patron and Manager can help the team audit the project for blocked progress, but should defer to the Developers (or other directly impacted roles) to resolve the blockage when ever possible.

Maranzano notes a corollary to this pattern is another pattern: Don't put too many critical tasks on one person.

PATTERN 41: Don't Interrupt an Interrupt

Problem: The pattern Interrupts Unjam Blocking is causing people to thrash.

Context: Execution of pattern for Interrupts Unjam Blocking.

Forces:
- One worker will inevitably be blocked on you—you can't do both things at once.
- Complete, omniscient foresight and scheduling are unreasonable.

Solution: If a role is about to block on a critical resource, interrupt the role that provides that resource so they stop what they're doing to keep you unblocked. If the overhead is small enough, it doesn't affect throughput. It will always improve local latency.

Resulting Context: Largely unchanged from that emanating from Interrupts Unjam Blocking.

Rationale: This is a simple, though somewhat arbitrary, rule to keep scheduling from becoming an elaborate ceremony.

PATTERN 42: COMPENSATE SUCCESS

Problem: Providing appropriate motivation for success.

Context: A group of developers meeting tight schedules in a high-payoff market.

Forces:
- Schedule motivations tend to be self-fulfilling: a wide range of schedules may be perceived as equally applicable for a given task. Schedules are poor motivators. Altruism and egoless teams are quaint, Victorian notions.
- Companies often embark on make-or-break projects, and such projects should be managed differently from others.
- Disparate rewards motivate those who receive them, but may frustrate their peers.

Solution: Establish lavish rewards for individuals contributing to successful make-or-break projects. The entire team (social unit) should receive comparable rewards, to avoid de-motivating individuals who might assess their value by their salary relative to their peers.

"Very special" individuals might receive exceptional awards that are tied les strongly to team performance. A celebration is a particularly effective reward [Zuckerman and Hatala].

Resulting Context: An organization that focuses less on schedule (but see Size the Schedule) and more on customer satisfaction and systemic success. Such high rewards may cause individuals to over-extend themselves, leading to personal stress with potential risk to the project.

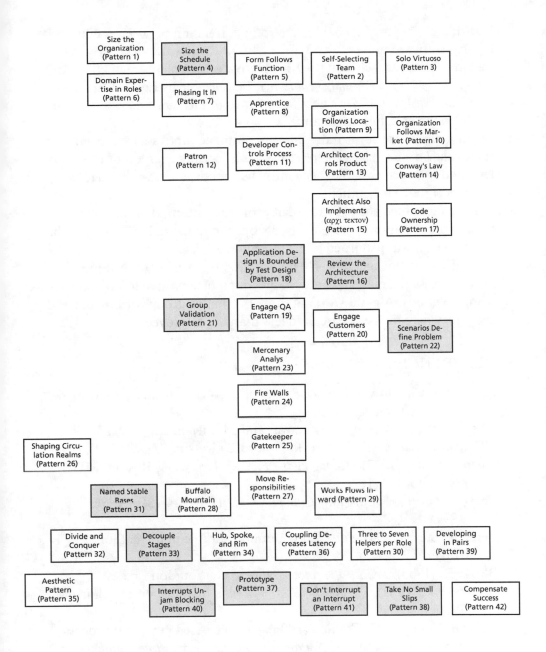

FIGURE 10   A map of the pattern language. Shaded boxes are process patterns; unshaded boxes are organizational patterns.

Rationale: Empirical. There is a strong correlation between wildly successful software projects, and a very lucrative reward structure. Cases include QPW, cases cited at the Risk Derivatives Conference in New York on 6 May 1994; see *Pay and Organization Development,* by Edward E. Lawler, Addison-Wesley, ©1981. The place of reward mechanisms is well-established in the literature [Kilmann].

High rewards to some individuals may still de-motivate their peers, but rewarding on a team basis helps remove the "personal" aspect of this problem, and helps establish the mechanism as a motivator, in addition to being just a post-mortem soother.

DeBruler noted at the PLoP review of this pattern, that most contemporary organization culture derives from the industrial complex of the 1800s, which was patterned after the only working model available at the time: military management. He notes that most American reward mechanisms are geared more toward weeding out problems than toward encouraging solutions. A good working model is that of groups of doctors and lawyers, where managers are paid less than the employees.

REFERENCES

Alexander, Christopher (1979). *The Timeless Way of Building.* New York: Oxford University Press.

Alexander, Christopher, S. Ishikawa, and M. Silverstein (1977). *A Pattern Language.* New York: Oxford University Press.

Allen, Thomas (1977). *Managing the Flow of Technology.* Boston: MIT Press, pp. 141–182.

Beck, K. (1991). "Think like an object." *UNIX Review* (September 1991).

Berczuk, Steve (1994). Personal communication with the author, August 1994.

Block, R. (1983). *Politics of Projects.* New York: Yourdon Press.

Brooks, F. P. (1982). *The Mythical Man Month.* Reading, MA: Addison-Wesley.

Cain, B. G., and J. O. Coplien (1993). "A role-based empirical process modeling environment." *Proceedings of the Second International Conference on Software Process.* Berlin, February 1993.

Carlin, Jamee (architect) (1994). Personal interview, 1 July 1994.

Chisholm, Paul (1994). Personal discussion with the author, June 1994.

Coplien, J. O. (1994a). "Borland Software craftsmanship: A new look at process, quality, and productivity." *Proceedings of the 5th Annual Borland International Conference.* Orlando, FL, June 1994.

Coplien, J. O. (1994b). "Evaluating the software development process." *Dr. Dobb's Journal* 19, 11 (October).

Curtis, B., et al. (1988). "A field study of the software design process for large systems." *CACM* 31, 11 (November): 1268–1287.

DeMarco, Tom (1993a). Personal discussion with the author, January 1993.

DeMarco, Tom (1993b). CaseWorld Converence, January 1993.

Floyd, Christiane, et al., eds. (1992). *Software Development and Reality Construction.* Berlin: Springer-Verlag.

Gabriel, Richard P. (1994). "Productivity: Is there a silver bullet?" *Journal of Object-Oriented Programming 7,* 1, pp. 89–92.

Hsia, Pei, Jayaranan Samuel, Jerry Gao, and David Kung (1994). "Forman approach to Scenario analysis." *IEEE Software* (11), 2, pp. 33ff.

"An implementation of structured walk-throughs in teaching COBOL programming" (1979). *CACM,* 22, 6, (June).

Jacobs, Herbert. (1978). *Building with Frank Lloyd Wright.* San Francisco: Chronicle Books.

Jacobson, Ivar, et al. (1992). *Object-Oriented Software Engineering.: A Use Case Driven Approach.* Reading, MA: Addison-Wesley

Johnson, Ralph. Personal communication.

Katz, Daniel, and Robert L. Kahn (1978). *The Social Psychology of Organizations,* 2d ed. New York: John Wiley.

Kerth, Norman (1994). "Caterpillar's Fate." Chapter 16, this volume.

Kilmann, R. H. (1984). *Beyond the Quick Fix.* San Francisco: Jossey-Bass.

Lawler, Edward E. (1981). *Pay and Organization Development.* Reading, MA: Addison-Wesley.

Mackenzie, K. D. (1986). "Organizing high technology operations for success." In J. R. Callhan and G. H. Haines, eds., *Managing High Technology Decisions for Success.*

Maranzano, Joe. Personal discussion with the author.

Meszaros, Gerard (1994). Personal communication at OOPSLA/94 workshop on Teams and Objects, October 24, 1994.

Meyers, G. J. (1978). "A controlled experiment in program testing and code walk-throughs/inspections." *CACM* 21, 9, (September).

Rousseau, Jean-Jacques (1972). *Discours sur l'origine de l'inégalité.* Sorbonne: Nouveaux Classiques Larrouse.

Rybczynski, Witold (1989). *The Most Beautiful House in the World.* New York: Penguin.

Sun Tzu (1983). *The Art of War.* trans. James Clavell, New York: Delacorte Press.

Swieringa, Joop, and André Wierdsma. (1992). *Becoming a Learning Organization.* Reading, MA: Addison-Wesley.

Vitruvius (1960). *The Ten Books of Architecture,* trans. Morris Morgan, New York: Dover.

Whitenack, Bruce (1994). "RAPPeL: A Requirements-Analysis Process Pattern Language for Object-Oriented Developmen." Chapter 15, this volume.

Zuckerman, M. R., and Lewis J. Hatala (1992). *Incredibly American.* Milsaukee: ASQC Quality Press, pp. 81–83.

Setting the Stage

James O. Coplien
cope@lucent.com

You've always counted on the *C++ Report* to bring you the latest tips and advice on C++. Among such articles, I consider the material on architecture and design to be the most important to the long-term success of a software project. Design encompasses all those things that help reduce the understanding of a problem to implementation (including the modified understanding along the way). Most of these tips and guidelines come in object-oriented packaging.

In the July–August 1994 issue, something decidedly un-object-oriented invaded the *C++ Report* landscape. The article "Generative pattern languages" appeared on the scene,[1] taking a niche in well-established object territory. Many of you probably wondered, "Why does the *C++ Report* have a column on *patterns*?" This month, we introduce "The Column Without a Name" (more about that later), where the theme of patterns will be taken up in coming months. Are patterns object-oriented? Just what are they doing here in the *C++ Report,* anyhow? And what do they mean to you and me?

In this column, I offer one perspective on how patterns fit in the progression of design techniques that have evolved from procedural design through object-oriented techniques in recent years. I also relate how I became interested in patterns and why I think they show promise for a new generation of software architecture.

RISING TO THE ABSTRACTION LEVEL OF PATTERNS

For years, software designers have focused on finding good classes that are understandable, useful units of software packaging. But in large systems, many important design abstractions cannot be captured within a single class, but cut across classes; the same is true in the parallel world of object instances and the relationships between them. Just as designers of the 1960s and 1970s raised the level of abstraction from procedures to procedural hierarchies and modules, so we find power in inheritance hierarchies and in object implementation hierarchies. These design techniques reflect relationships *between* classes or *between* objects, respectively. They speak more to system structure than do objects or classes alone. For example, class String or class Number offer limited understanding about the workings of a compiler that comprises them; understanding the Symbol class hierarchy offers more insight about how the compiler works. By their nature, hierarchies are more abstract than are individual classes, and they allow us to reason about more of the system at once. They also tell us about the *structure* of the system along lines of inheritance.

But for complex systems, even these techniques aren't enough. Individually, a given hierarchy is one-dimensional, and few design techniques integrate multiple perspectives into a single, unified design view. But more important, other significant hierarchies abound in complex systems. Booch's mechanisms cut across classes and objects alike. Object communities are a common design abstraction: container and iterator; handle and body; model, view, and controller. Although hierarchies are a powerful abstraction construct, the world is not fundamentally hierarchical. At best, a good world model comprises multiple interwoven hierarchies, tangled with flat clusters of related abstractions.

To me, one of the most important benefits of design patterns is that they capture not only system parts, but rich relationships between them as well. Together, these describe a system architecture that is broader than any object or class hierarchy. With the architectural tools that patterns provide, we can describe important structures and relationships at the system level and can instruct designers and implementors on how to use them. Another major benefit of patterns is that they capture emerging experience in a young domain—such as the object paradigm—so inexpert practitioners can avoid re-inventing the wheel. Pattern languages are an ideal form of documentation for frameworks, which are an important and increasingly popular software architectural packaging technique.

As described in my previous article, patterns are structured prose documents that present a solution to a problem that occurs in a given context. They describe the forces present in the problem and describe how and to what degree the pattern resolves those forces. They provide a rationale for their structure and application. The pattern form concept comes from

Christopher Alexander, who uses such formulations for the architectures of buildings and towns.

GROWING INTO PATTERNS

The work of Christopher Alexander is broadly hailed as the catalyst that precipitated the contemporary software patterns movement. However, most people involved in patterns discovered them through their experience in programming, and Alexander is regarded today as an almost quixotic guide and inspiration to the software patterns movement. Grady Booch came to patterns through his work with mechanisms (a group of objects working together on the system's behalf); Kent Beck discovered them in the elegant interworkings within Smalltalk programs.[*] An important aspect of patterns is their concreteness and their preoccupation with what we have come to refer to as *Stoff*—real stuff, not platitudes and theories.

My own experience with patterns goes back to architecture work I did with my colleague, Tom Burrows, at Bell Laboratories in the early 1980s. Tom assembled architectural principles that integrated demand-driven data flow and objects. We felt that his vision was well-suited to the problems of high-availability systems. We developed software and hardware designs in parallel to support that vision.[2] We often had difficulty allocating a given architectural feature to hardware or software. Each of these media had its respective building blocks (objects in software, modular subassemblies in hardware) and integration fabric (backplanes in hardware, data flow "ports" in software); in Tom's paradigm, the design rules for both were the same. In both domains, objects were of secondary interest for real-time and high availability; the important functionality was in the connection between them. As with most data flow architectures, the focus was on the flow of information through the system as a whole. The scheduling of real-time events and propagation of changes entailed other important nonmodular abstractions. The term *pattern* was not yet in popular use;[†] we gave the name *foils* to these recurring interconnecting structures. The term comes from the patterns of connecting metal on printed-circuit boards, a metaphor for the backplane interconnect of a hardware bus architecture.

---

[*] Such motivations have been explored in several forums, including "Coping with Grady and Kent" which took place at the Borland International Conference, Orlando, FL. June 6, 1994.

[†] Tom, in his discussions and writings, employed analogies between this work and creations made on the loom that fills one of the rooms of his home: a harbinger of patterns?

We had several pet names for this non-object-based approach to design, many of them (curiously enough, as we will see later) with roots in Eastern schools of thought. One such term was *Madhyamika,* a "middle way" of thinking, intermediate between a highly unified world-view and a world reduced to a rubble of objects.

As the data flow work reached its peak in about 1988, I had already been an active user of C++ for five years. Object-oriented programming had been the focus of many C++ users from the start, and object-oriented design started making inroads into the C++ community in about 1986. Even before published object-oriented design techniques saw wide use, programmers across the industry were discovering techniques to solve specific C++ design problems. I saw the same tricks recurring in the work of my colleagues, in early papers on C++, and in my own work. It struck me that what it took to be a professional C++ programmer wasn't in any of the books yet and that any project that started off without knowing how to use simple constructs like *handle* and *body* classes would soon be struggling. I prepared notes on effective use of such "tricks" and used them to bring new projects up to speed as they anticipated using C++. The notes grew into a comprehensive collection of the constructs whose use separated "native speakers" of C++ from those who were just learning it as a second (or first) language. After much polishing and review, the notes appeared as *Advanced C++ Programming Styles and Idioms* in 1991.[3]

The constructs were called idioms because, again, the term *patterns* was not yet in vogue. Furthermore, idioms aren't full-fledged patterns. Idioms are language-specific; patterns are broader design constructs with broader applicability across programming languages. Yet idioms captured design practices necessary to effective C++ programming; they described how to build abstractions that don't just fall out of an object-oriented analysis; most of them described symbiotic relationships between several objects. These characteristics of idioms foreshadowed what was to come in patterns.

About this time, my career focus turned from object-oriented technology to software development organization and process. Rather than follow the prevailing focus of the process community on process sequencing and intervals, I chose to assess processes indirectly by studying the architecture of their organizations. Key to this technique was the use of visual patterns (yes, there's that word) to identify instrumental organizations in development cultures. An instrumental organization is a self-organizing group of people with close ties and mutual interests, which may (and usually does) cut across institutional organization boundaries. The concept is known to cultural anthropology, which, after all, concerns itself largely with patterns of interaction in a culture. Cultural interaction patterns throw a powerful spotlight on the organization and its processes.

Kent Beck invited me into the patterns dialogue in mid-1993. At that time, a small patterns movement had already established its identity through the Software Architecture Workshop at OOPSLA, under the direction of Bruce Anderson and Peter Coad. I joined a subset of that group that met in Colorado in August 1993 to lay the groundwork for generative software patterns based on Alexander's work. Members of that group, which took the name The Hillside Group, continue to foster and shepherd software design patterns today through electronic forums, a conference, talks, and publications.

I started digesting the works of Christopher Alexander in earnest and exchanging patterns and pattern critiques through an ever-growing electronic mailing list. I saw The Hillside Group's patterns not only as the extrapolation of idioms into something much broader—like Burrows' data flow architecture vision—but also as a perfect expression of the recurring structures, practices, and interactions I found in software development organizations. Furthermore, I saw the opportunity to use patterns not only for analysis, but for synthesis as well. Today, I study patterns not only as a means to capture and shape software architecture, but also as a way to understand and shape organizational architecture. I may address both in this column but will focus on software patterns relevant to programmers using C++ (and other programming languages).

THE COLUMN WITHOUT A NAME

I decided to call this column "The Column Without a Name" after a suggestion made by Ken Auer of KSC,‡ a member of The Hillside Group. The name clearly takes its cue from Alexander's writings, and his quest for "The Quality Without a Name." Alexander measures architecture by this Quality, which applies to the result of any creative process. He describes the Quality in broad terms of systems' ability to "be alive": to be a part of, and to support, our lives. This Quality happens when the forces in a system are resolved. At a cruder level, this Quality is utilitarian, aesthetically pleasing, robust, and whole. But Alexander notes that any attempt to name or measure the Quality is futile, that all words confuse more than they explain.[4]

---

‡ The naming of things is likely to be a recurring theme in future installations of this column.

(Can you think of any programming language which, at some time, was not the subject of an obfuscation contest?)

Alexander in turn draws on more ancient sources for this phrase. The intrigue of names is an important aspect of our fascination with human language, and has been throughout history. In some cultures, names and their invocation have the power to invoke their subject; the name and the thing are inseparable. In other cultures and world-views, names are ephemeral human creations, conventions by which we understand an amorphous reality. The classic Chinese writer Lao-Tzu notes that "the Tao which can be named is not the true Tao."[5] Indeed, the role that language itself plays in communication can be brought into question. Voltaire wryly notes that "mankind was given speech so that he may better hide his thoughts." We must look beyond language to find the expressions that separate survival from greatness. In architecture, for example, we need to capture the architectural intent that goes beyond the language of the blueprints if we are to build great buildings.

If this is so with natural language, why not view computer languages with the same suspicion? Each language has its own modes of expression—both its native "primer" forms of expression and its idioms, as discussed earlier. But such expression goes only so far. C++ can't tell us why the designer chose a given idiom, what problem it solves, what other idioms might apply if circumstances change, or indeed whether a given collection of code is idiomatic at all. These are crucial design considerations that deserve structured linguistic expression.

Pattern languages provide a framework to capture such design considerations. A pattern language is not a programming language, but a structured collection of natural language blocks that give the inexpert designer some modest expert insights. For me, patterns are an opportunity to take the next logical step in the progression from C++, past object-oriented design, through idioms, and into the next generation of software design. This column is both a vehicle to share such patterns and a prod to think about design and programming in new ways. It is no less so for you than it will be for me. Our search for patterns in our respective realms of expertise will be a search within ourselves to understand how we think about design and to find expression for those thoughts so others can take advantage of our experience. If this column succeeds, it will help the experts among you discover and articulate the magic already within you that makes your great software great. If you do not consider yourself a software virtuoso, then this column might take you to a new level of design understanding, particularly for the systems you implement in C++.

Those who follow this column should understand that this is new terrain. We have witnessed some small successes with patterns (small in the sense of either scope or scale), but a full-fledged endorsement and blueprint of patterns would be premature at this point. Through this column, I wish to broaden the scope of the dialogue about patterns in the industry, hoping that the dialogue that follows will hone and shape the direction of patterns. It is my wish not to incite readers to premature practice. It is important to let the dialogue educate us, as an industry, to the point where development projects can invest in their use with confidence.

MAPPING OUT THE PATTERNS COLUMN

I could continue to tell you about patterns in future appearances of this column (as I have done so far in this issue): Much is being said these days about the value of context and history in understanding new software languages and tools. At the Conference on Pattern Languages of Programming in Illinois this past August, attendees had the opportunity to relive some of the same experiences that shaped the philosophy of The Hillside Group. But just as the best way to learn a new programming language is by writing programs in it, the best way for you and me to learn patterns together is to write patterns instead of just writing or reading about patterns. Many in The Hillside Group—and Kent Beck in particular—have established a stigma against "going meta." We want to grapple with the *Stoff* of patterns before moving on to generalities and platitudes.

I resolve these forces by making this a dual-purpose column. The first part of the column will be about patterns, including tips and techniques, new developments, answers to commonly asked questions, and much about the relationship between software patterns and techniques from other disciplines. The second part of the column will contain one or more patterns. These will almost always be software patterns, and almost all of them will have direct applicability for C++ programmers.

As opportunities arise to do so, I would like to use the column as a forum for two-way dialogue. If you have thoughts or questions on patterns, send them to me at cope@research.att.com. I will consider reprinting questions or discussions on issues of sufficiently broad interest.

A PATTERN AS PROMISED

Over the next few months, I will present a series of patterns that build a simple pattern language. These patterns are all relevant to C++, and they come from the established body of idioms currently in common use in the C++ community. One might jump to the conclusion that little is to be gained from re-casting well-known idioms as patterns. My experience suggests that the exercise is worthwhile. It reinforces the pattern form, building on what people know about the techniques to extrapolate to what they may not know about the form. And, for some, the light will come on, and they will see the patterns' applicability and purpose for the first time, or they may see it in a new light: Experience has borne this out.

In last month's article, we started this trend with the pattern *C++ Type Promotion*. I end this month's column with a pattern called *The Counted Body Pattern*.§ This pattern applies to classes to which the basic handle/body pattern has been applied. It forms the basis for patterns that will follow in future columns:

Name: Counted Body Pattern

Problem: Naive implementations of assignment in C++ are often inefficient or incorrect.

Context: A design has been transformed into body/handle C++ class pairs (Handle/Body pattern). The pattern may be relevant to other object-based programming languages.

Forces: Assignment in C++ is defined recursively as member-by-member assignment with copying as the termination of the recursion; it would be more efficient and more in the spirit of Smalltalk if copying were rebinding.

- Copying of bodies is expensive.
- Copying can be avoided by using pointers and references, but these leave the problem of who is responsible for cleaning up the object and leave a user-visible distinction between built-in types and user-defined types.
- Sharing bodies on assignment is usually semantically incorrect if the shared body is modified through one of the handles.

Solution:

- A reference count is added to the body class to facilitate memory management.

---

§ In their forthcoming book, Gamma, Helm, Johnson, and Vlissides describe related patterns based on their Bridge pattern. Watch for this book at a technical bookstore near you soon this fall.

- Memory management is added to the handle class, particularly to its implementation of initialization, assignment, copying, and destruction.
- It is incumbent on any operation that modifies the state of the body to break the sharing of the body by making its own copy. It must decrement the reference count of the original body.

Forces Resolved:

- Gratuitous copying is avoided, leading to a more efficient implementation.
- Sharing is broken when the body state is modified through any handle. Sharing is preserved in the more common case of parameter passing, etc.
- Special pointer and reference types are avoided.
- Smalltalk semantics are approximated; garbage collection is driven off of this model.

Design Rationale: Reference counting is efficient and spreads the overhead across the execution of real-time programs. This implementation is a variation of shallow copy with the semantics of deep copy and the efficiency of Smalltalk name-value pairs.

Example:

```
class String {
private:
    class StringRep {
    friend class String;
        StringRep(const char *s):count(1)
        {
            strcpy(rep=new char[strlen(s)
                +1], s);
        }
        ~StringRep() { delete rep; }
        int count; char *rep;
    } *rep;
public:
    String():rep(new StringRep("")) { }
    String(const String &s):
        rep(s.rep) { rep->count++; }
```

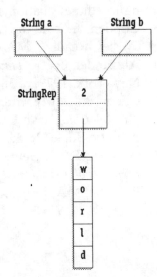

```
String &operator=(const String &s){
    s.rep->count++;
    if(—rep->count <= 0) delete rep;
    rep = s.rep;
    return *this;
}
~String() {
    if(—rep->count <= 0) delete rep;
}
String(const char *s):
    rep(new StringRep(s)) { }
. . . .
};

int main() {
    String a = "hello", b = "world";
    a = b;
    return 0;
}
```

REFERENCES

1. Coplien, J. O. Generative pattern languages, *C++ Report,* 6(6), 1994.
2. Coplien, J. O. ISHMAEL: An integrated software/hardware maintenance and evaluation system, *AT&T Technical Journal,* 70(1), 1991.
3. Coplien, J. O. *Advanced C++ Programming Styles and Idioms,* Addison-
   Wesley, Reading, MA, 1992.
4. Alexander, C. *The Timeless Way of Building,* Oxford University Press,
   New York, 1979, p. 38.
5. Cheng, M.-J. My words are very easy to understand, *Lectures on the
   Tao Teh Ching* (translated from the Chinese by T.C. Gibbs). North
   Atlantic Books, Richmond, CA, 1981, ch. 1.
6. Gamma, E., R. Helm, R. Johnson, and J. Vlissides. *Design Patterns:
   Elements of Reusable Object-Oriented Software,* Addison-Wesley,
   Reading, MA, forthcoming.

Software Design Patterns: Common Questions and Answers

James O. Coplien

cope@lucent.com

WHAT IS A PATTERN?

The term *pattern,* as adopted by contemporary software designers exploring its benefits, is both part of a system and a description of how to build that part of the system. Patterns usually describe software abstractions used by advanced designers and programmers in their software. As abstractions, patterns commonly cut across other common software abstractions like procedures and objects, or combine more common abstractions in powerful ways. For example, using one object as an iterator that non-destructively visits every element of a collection object is a simple pattern.

The term *pattern* applies both to the thing (for example, a collection class and its associated iterator) and the directions for making a thing. In this sense, software patterns can be likened to a dress pattern: the general shape is in the pattern itself, though each pattern must be tailored to its context.

WHERE DOES THIS USE OF THE TERM "PATTERN" COME FROM?

In the 1960s, building architects were exploring the issues of design in its broadest sense, and investigating automated, computerized building design.

There was keen interest in rules and algorithms that could transform requirements into a configuration of building modules. The mainstream of this movement moved on to what we know as modular construction. The architect Christopher Alexander broke with that movement, noting that the great architectures of history were not made from rigorous, planned designs, but that their pieces were custom-fit to each other and to the building's surroundings. He also noted that some buildings were more aesthetically pleasing than others, and that these aesthetics were often attuned to human needs and comforts. He found recurring themes in architecture, and captured them into descriptions (and instructions) that he called patterns. The term "pattern" appeals to the replicated similarity in a design, and in particular to similarity that makes room for variability and customization in each of the elements. Thus, *Window on Two Sides of Every Room* is a pattern, yet it prescribes neither the size of the windows, the distance between them, their height from the floor, nor their framing (though there are other patterns that may refine these properties).

Software designers have discovered (and rediscovered) analogies between Alexandrian patterns and software architecture patterns over the past decade.

WHAT IS THE DIFFERENCE BETWEEN A NON-GENERATIVE PATTERN AND A GENERATIVE PATTERN?

We observe patterns everywhere as we interact with the world around us. There are patterns in building architecture, patterns in nature, and patterns in the software people write. Recent work in software visualization is striving to bring out the patterns in software.[1] Not all these patterns are "good": for example, such research has found that people copy code from one place in a system to another, instead of generalizing the original code and reusing it in-place.

Patterns that we observe in a system that has already been built are nongenerative, and are sometimes called *Gamma patterns,* after the pioneering work of Erich Gamma.[2] Such patterns are descriptive and passive.

That we can find these patterns doesn't imply any rationale behind them, and not every pattern leads to desirable results. What we want to do is capture the patterns that are "good" and codify them, so people can use them when building systems. These patterns *generate* systems, or parts of systems. We can observe the patterns (in other words, see their structure or their effects) in the systems they generate. Patterns designed to shape system architectures are called *generative patterns.* They are prescriptive, and active.

WHAT IS "ALEXANDRIAN FORM"?

We express most patterns in a format called *Alexandrian form*. Alexandrian form tells what is contained in a pattern. As described above, a pattern is both the thing and the instructions for making the thing. The form of pattern expression makes them particularly useful. The form draws on constructs used by Christopher Alexander to describe his patterns.

There are variants on Alexandrian form, but most look like this:

- *The pattern name:* A name by which the pattern is called. For example, we might create a pattern called *C++ Type Promotion,* just so we can refer to it conveniently.
- *The problem the pattern is trying to solve:* If people know what problem the pattern solves, they'll know when to apply it. For example, *Type Promotion* solves the problem of promotion between objects of different C++ types, zero or one of which is a built-in type, or a type exported by a library for which the programmer does not have source.
- *Context:* A pattern solves a problem in a given context, and it may not make sense elsewhere. For example, C++ type promotion applies to C++, and potentially to other object-oriented languages with strong compile-time type systems; the decision of which promotion to apply is made at compile time; and the context is inadequate to apply built-in translation rules (e.g., from a derived class to one of its public base classes).
- *Forces, or tradeoffs:* Not all problems are clear-cut. Forces make clear the intricacies of a problem. For example, in *Type Promotion,* we need to point out the tension between using constructors and using conversion operators. We must also point out that we can redefine some properties for class types that we cannot redefine for built-in types. A good pattern resolves one or more forces.
- *Solution:* This describes the structure, behavior, etc., of the solution, which is often tantamount to telling how to build the solution. For *Type Promotion,* a program should promote class objects to built-ins using a member conversion operator, and should use constructors for all other promotions.
- *Examples* are present in all good patterns. *Visual analogies* are also powerful and frequent adornments for a pattern: you can draw a picture for most (but not all) good software patterns.

- *Force resolution, or resulting context:* Few patterns are perfect or stand on their own. A good pattern tells what forces it leaves unresolved, or what other patterns must be applied, and how the context is changed by the pattern.
- *Design rationale:* This tells where the pattern came from, why it works, and why experts use it. Good designers are most effective when they apply patterns insightfully, and that means being able to understand how the patterns work.

WHAT IS A "PATTERN LANGUAGE"?

A pattern language is a structured collection of patterns that build on each other to transform needs and constraints into an architecture. It is not a programming language in any ordinary sense of the term, but is a prose document whose purpose is to guide and inform the designer. Patterns rarely stand alone. Each pattern works on a context, and transforms the system in that context to produce a new system in a new context. New problems arise in the new system and context, and the next "layer" of patterns can be applied.

We usually use (or imply) the term "generative" when speaking of pattern languages. Just as the English language can generate all possible papers in conference proceedings, so a pattern language can generate all sentences in a given domain. Good pattern languages guide the designer toward useful architectures and away from architectures whose literary analogies are gibberish or unartful writing. Good architectures are durable, functional, and aesthetically pleasing, and a good combination of patterns can balance the forces on a system to strive toward these three goals. A good pattern language gives designers freedom to express themselves and to tailor the solution to the particular needs of the context where the patterns are applied.

Pure Alexandrian pattern languages uniquely specify the order in which patterns can be applied (though one may choose any one from a fixed set of patterns at any point in a given design). For software design patterns, we are finding that a more iterative approach makes better sense.

WHY AM I HEARING ABOUT PATTERNS AT OBJECT CONFERENCES?

Probably because that's where the focus of software design lies today, which in turn owes to the tremendous economic forces behind object-oriented programming languages, tools, and methods. Patterns are riding the wave of the object movement, driven by individuals commonly associated with object-oriented analysis and design (Beck, Cunningham, Johnson, Coad, Booch), but there is nothing intrinsically object-oriented about patterns. Patterns aspire to rise above object-level abstractions to more subtle structures, threads of execution, arrangements, and transformations in software. Such patterns are present in most object-oriented systems, but good patterns can be found in programs written in most programming languages under many design regimens.

Many current design patterns are expressed in terms of objects or object-oriented constructs, but good designers should introspect about how they use other paradigms effectively as well.

WHY SHOULD I BE INTERESTED IN THEM?

Because they are gaining visibility, applicability, and momentum in the object movement, which is where the action seems to be right now in software. People advocating patterns also think they are valuable (me among them), but the newcomer to patterns shouldn't expect to find volumes of material they can take home and use immediately. The best advice right now is to stay tuned, so you'll be better positioned to use patterns when they come of age.

WHAT IS THE DIFFERENCE BETWEEN "PATTERNS" AND "PARADIGMS"?

The pattern approach is a paradigm only in the most abstract, almost philosophical sense of the word. The goal of most popular paradigms is to make a complex work understandable by organizing it into separable parts, each of which can be separately understood. Patterns try to describe relationships within and between the parts, not just the parts themselves. This is why patterns are truly an architectural technique, not just a divide-and-conquer technique.

The insightful might note that Webster gives *pattern* as one definition of *paradigm*.

AREN'T PATTERNS JUST RULES?

Rules aren't commonly supported by a rationale, nor put in context. A rule may be part of the solution in a pattern description, but a rule solution is neither sufficient nor necessary. Patterns aren't designed to be executed or analyzed by computers, as one might imagine to be true for rules; patterns are to be executed by architects with insight, taste, experience, and a sense of aesthetics.

HOW ARE PATTERNS AND IDIOMS RELATED?

Idioms are special kinds of patterns that are tied to a specific programming language. I have discovered that recasting idioms in pattern form often makes them more accessible to moderately experienced C++ programmers. For example, compare the pattern form of *C++ Type Conversion* that follows, with the less structured discussion on pages 54 through 58 of my advanced C++ text.[3]

HOW DO PATTERNS RELATE TO CREATIVITY?

Design is a creative act; so is the creation or application of a design pattern. If design is codified in patterns, does the need for creativity go away? Can we replace high-priced expensive designers with less sophisticated programmers who are guided by patterns? The answer is that creativity is still needed to shape the patterns to a given context. Just as a dressmaker tailors a pattern to an individual customer, and perhaps to a specific event where the dress is to be worn, so designers must be creative when using patterns. Patterns channel creativity; they neither replace nor constrain it.

WHERE CAN I FIND PATTERNS?

Numerous articles and papers have now appeared both in published journals and in the trade press; in particular, see those by Beck,[4] Booch,[5] Gabriel,[6] and Johnson.[7] Watch for my forthcoming column on pattern in the *C++ Report*. Also, get plugged into the upcoming Patterns Conference in August in Illinois: PLoP (Pattern Languages of Programs). Send me an electronic mail inquiry if you are interested in more information.

HOW DO I GET STARTED WRITING PATTERNS?

Introspect about what makes your designs great in areas where you have recognized expertise or specialization, *and write them down* in Alexandrian form. Try them out on your friends.

Pattern Name: Type Promotion

Problem: Promotion between objects of different but related C++ types, zero or one of which is a built-in type, or a type exported by a library for which the programmer does not have source.

Context: The pattern applies to C++ and potentially to other object-oriented programming languages. The decision of which promotion to apply is made at compile time. The context is inadequate for the compiler to apply built-in translation rules, as would be possible for conversion between built-in types, or between a derived class and one of its base classes.

Forces:
- The implementation of promotion from an object of one type to an object of another type is usually coupled to the implementation of both types.
- The C++ language lets the programmer associate such an implementation with only one of the participating types.
- The type containing the conversion implementation must be a class object type, since the programmer cannot redefine the implementation of built-in types or types exported by object-code-only libraries.
- Two language mechanisms support user-defined conversions: constructors and conversion operators. Individually, each is an equally suitable solution in some circumstances, but use of both leads to an irreconcilable ambiguity.

Solution:
- A program should promote a class object type to a built-in type or a type exported from a library using a member conversion operator:
  ```
  class RationalNumber {
  public:
      operator float () const;
      . . . .
  } ;
  ```
- A program should use constructors for all other promotions:
  ```
  class Complex {
  public:
      Complex (const RationalNumber&) ;
      Complex (double) ;
      . . . .
  } ;
  ```

Force Resolution:
- Coupling between types (and, in general, friend relationships) is still necessary between types; the force is resolved only to the extent that the conversion is firmly associated with a single type. The pattern does guarantee that the type bearing the conversion is always a class object type, however.
- The pattern avoids most conversion ambiguities. An additional pattern must deal with the case:

```
struct S {
        operator int() const;
        operator float () const;
} ;
void f ( int ) ;
void f ( float ) ;
main () {
        S s;
        f ( s ) ; / / error: ambiguous call: f ( struct S )
}
```

Design Rationale: A given type cannot know about every (more general) type in the universe whose instances might be created as generalizations of itself; the onus is on the type of the newly created object to understand its own initialization parameters. Primitive types form an exceptional sub-pattern because their semantics are built into the compiler for efficiency, and their semantics are not as generally subject to change as for user-defined types.

REFERENCES

1. Church, Kenneth Ward, and Jonathan Isaac Helfman. "Dotplot: A Program for Exploring Self-Similarity in Millions of Lines for Text and Code." American Statistical Association, Institute of Mathematical Statistics and Interface Foundations of North America, Vol. 2, No. 2, pp. 153–174.
2. Gamma, Erich. "Design Patterns—Abstraction and Reuse of Object-Oriented Designs." In *Proceedings of the European Conference on Object-Oriented Programming,* Oscar Nierstrasz, ed. Berlin: Springer-Verlag, 1993.
3. Coplien, James O. *Advanced C++ Programming Styles and Idioms.* Reading, MA: Addison-Wesley, 1992.

4. Beck, Kent. "Patterns and Software Development." *Dr. Dobb's Journal,* Vol. 19, No. 2, pp. 18–23.
5. Booch, Grady. "Patterns." *Object Magazine,* Vol. 3, No. 2, SIGS Publications, New York, NY.
6. Gabriel, Richard. "Pattern Languages." *Journal of Object-Oriented Programming,* Vol. 6, No. 2, p. 14, Jan. 1994. SIGS Publications, New York, NY.
7. Johnson, Ralph E. "Documenting Frameworks using Patterns." *ACM SIGPLAN Notices,* Vol. 27, No. 10, Oct. 1992, ff. 63.

Software Development as Science, Art, and Engineering

James O. Coplien
cope@lucent.com

This month marks the first anniversary of pattern material in the *C++ Report*. I hope that those who follow this column can forgive the occasional appearance of an essay here. It's been a while since I've used this column to explore the roots and ties of patterns in the liberal arts, and I've taken the liberty to do so again this month; a year's experience and reflection provide a useful framework to step back and do so.

TECHNOLOGY, CUSTOMERS, CREATIVITY: THE FORCES THAT AFFECT OUR WORK

There's an old joke that you can tell whether something is a science by whether it has the word "science" in it's name. Is computer science a science? By no means: it has science in its name. The same can wryly be claimed for social science and political science. Physics, or chemistry: now those are sciences!

The joke aside, programmers (most of whom claim some tie to computer science) think of themselves as scientists. You can't miss the aspirations to formalism and proofs in prestigious literature of leading software conferences and scholarly publications. Software development cultures attach the same scientific mystique to metrics; we even have Halstead's *Software Science*,[1] which has been with us these many years and which still enjoys occasional invocation.

It certainly is true that science and technology are closely linked, and that there would be little place for programmers were it not for the technological revolutions and inventions that make computing environments what they are today. The same is true in building architecture: new technology supports architectural styles (for example, beams to support skyscraper construction) that would be otherwise intractable. We should look to applicable technologies when they suit our needs. Through several small essays in this article, I hope to put technology in its proper perspective as a means and not as an end, and to explore the relationship between formal and technological concerns, and the concerns of the pattern community.

While formalism and technology provide an infrastructure for our work, our ultimate focus is to delight a customer. (This term, "delight," as it has crept into management circles, will resurface later in this article.) That means dealing with people and understanding their needs, which is hardly an exact science. To solve customer problems, we need a little technological invention, but as Edison inferred, much of it is just hard work, and much of our work is to reconcile the customer world with the technological infrastructure. Focusing on that transition, and on the customer world itself, comprises the bulk of design. We must understand how customers will use our systems and how they will want us to change them. We also need to understand how we work as teams, so we can organize ourselves and our software to meet the needs of our paying customers, while meeting our own needs as well. Most software problem-solving extends far beyond the axiomatic safety of scientific method and formalism, and squarely into the realm of the arts, or at least of the "soft sciences."

Patterns draw on the arts and soft sciences, building on principles of good literature and of architectural aesthetics to serve the practical needs of programmers and software architects. That, in turn helps them better meet software consumer needs through a common language that helps the creators and users of software to communicate with each other. These were the forces that brought the Hillside Group together to explore and support software patterns. When asked about the goal of the Hillside Group, Richard Gabriel replied:

> We are trying to bring people and humanity into the software design and development process. I think this is the goal because it's the key Alexandrian idea. If you look at his patterns, each or nearly all talk about the context and forces in terms of what people need to do to live fully and to be fully alive. So far our patterns are not like this (when I get a spare moment, I will write out and send some very, very simple

patterns I have that focus on people as the context and forces and which have a technical thing as their "solution"). I believe we need to get clear on this before we subject ourselves to too much togetherness with the outside world—because this position is probably considered nuts to the theoretical community we might deal with.

The first people to offer concerns about patterns are those who can't easily attach them to a method or scientific model; they appeal to the intuitive mind first, and to the evaluative mind second. Design is and always has been an essentially creative activity even in building architecture. Even Alexander railed against those who would transform his design visions into a method. In the preface to the paperback edition of *Notes on Synthesis of Form*,[2] he states:

> Poincaré once said: "Sociologists discuss sociological methods; physicists discuss physics." I love this statement. Study of method by itself is always barren, and people who have treated [*Notes on Synthesis*] as if it were a book about "design method" have almost always missed the point of the diagrams, and their great importance, because they have been obsessed with the details of the method I propose for getting at the diagrams.

Alexander reminds us not only that design is more than rote and method, but also that it is about "stuff." For the programmer, the design lives in the code. Our studies of development organizations show again and again that despite the best intentions and strongest methodologies to support notations, documents, and abstract design, people still spend about half their design time exploring source code. That's where the design is, the good stuff—not in the methodology or in the bubble-and-arrow diagrams.

Patterns fill an interesting role in the contemporary spectrum of software practices and technologies. They take art (and in particular, literature and architecture) instead of science as their foundation. The identification of patterns with art, with the "soft side" of development, is at odds with the prevailing mores of the scientific community. Where will patterns find a home in industrial research laboratories? How will they affect undergraduate software education? Will it be possible for someone to do a pattern thesis to qualify for a Ph.D. in computer science, or only in art, or in philosophy?

To understand the importance of patterns to computer science, it is important to understand software development in terms of its "soft science" components. Though it is difficult to miss the influence of the soft sciences on the vocabulary of software development—system *architecture*, software *engineering,* computer *science,* computational *linguistics,* and even *The Art of Computer Programming*[3]—we too often dismiss the core principles of this heritage and acknowledge only a superficial influence. It pays to dig deeper.

ARCHITECTURE AND ART

Just what is architecture? Goethe described architecture as "frozen music," a definition with a strong and clear artistic overtone. Witold Rybczynski[4] notes that *Webster* defines art as creative work, and that architecture is listed among the fine arts that we distinguish from the merely useful arts on the basis of their aesthetic purpose.

Software architecture is an art, too. Can we capture art, and the process of the creative human mind, in a pattern? There are certainly many intangibles at work in the minds of software architects that will always defy capture. But creativity may be much less mysterious than we think. A friend of mine, Bill Hopkins, recently pointed me to a book with the dubious title, *Creativity as an Exact Science.*[5] The book was originally written in Russian and relates experiences with the corpus of Soviet patents from the 1920s through recent years. They found that they could organize patents by structure: their internal relationships of substances and fields. It is essentially a book about patterns. It shows how to mechanically draw new inventions from the structures of existing patents. Far-fetched? Read it for yourself and see. I was intrigued by the strong parallels with what we aspire to do with generative patterns.

ARCHITECTURE, DESIGN, AND PROGRAMMING

Computer *science* is about programming. The science of software deals with algorithms, N–P completeness, computational complexity, proving correctness, and the like. We usually call these *formal* activities. If you study what real programmers do, you'll find that they spend little time worrying about formalisms, and in fact spend little time programming. Programmers occupy themselves with *design:* coding is less than 10% of the effort in a typical development project.

The phrase "God is in the details" is attributed to the architect Mies van der Rohe. This harks back to our reading in Alexander about the importance of "stuff." Much of the true beauty of systems is in the code, where a critical eye can assess the difference between an artisan and a hacker. But I prefer Alexander's admonition to that of Mies van der Rohe, because we find aesthetics in grand architectural patterns as well as in the craftsmanship of module design and code. Though they differ in scale or magnitude, both are still "stuff" and exhibit an elegance we would find in no architectural method or software blueprint.

We find both science and art at both extremes of the software abstraction spectrum. However, the formal foundations of computer science are more difficult to find at the architecture end of the spectrum than in programming. That is a shame, given the predominant leverage of architecture and design in the software life cycle. There have been many attempts to introduce formalism in architecture and design, but it is more often in the dictionary sense of formal as "methodical" (having form or rote) rather than "conventional" (following rules or axioms). The analogous practice in building design—an architectural methodology—was the target of Alexander's railing in the second edition of *Notes on Synthesis*. Worse yet, "formal" too often takes on its dictionary sense of "ceremonial" in many so-called formal methods. Here, again, we find analogies in building architecture. Rybczynski[4] writes:

> Here is another liability: beautiful drawings can become ends in themselves. Often, if the drawing deceives, it is not only the viewer who is enchanted but also the maker, who is the victim of his own artifice . . . Alberti understood, as many architects of today do not, that the rules of drawing and the rules of building are not one and the same, and mastery of the former does not ensure success in the latter (p. 121).

We'll have more to say about that when we talk about software engineering, the home of CASE tools, below.

Formal science is rooted in the scientific method, pioneered by Descartes in the 17th century. Scientific method likes to compartmentalize things, to understand systems by decomposing them into their smallest understandable parts. Scientific method presumes that the understanding of the whole follows from the understanding of the parts (though most modern expositions of the Cartesian method focus only on his reductionist strategy, and omit his final and important strategy of integration and performing a system-level audit of reasoning).

We can see this reductionism in computer science when it separates architecture, design, and implementation as separate phases of development. Hence, the term "architecture" evokes the image of something abstract and divorced from technology or engineering. It has not always been so. Palladio,[6] one of the most influential building architects of all time, was obsessed with understanding the nature and quantity of the materials used in his work, largely so he could gauge cost and avoid waste:

> But an architect is very often obliged, to conform more to the will of those who are at the expense, than to that which ought to be observed.

A true architect is a carpenter who has learned to abstract. Alberti,[7] the original translator of the classic Roman architectures of Vitruvius, placed construction concerns in the scope of design: architects must know the means by which their designs will be implemented. Alberti notes:

> The construction of a building does not just entail setting stone on stone, and aggregate upon aggregate, as the ignorant may imagine; for, because the parts are different, so too the materials and methods of construction vary quite radically.

And Vitruvius[8] himself wrote:

> . . . [A]rchitects who have aimed at acquiring manual skill without scholarship have never been able to reach a position of authority to correspond to their pains, while those who relied only upon theories and scholarship were obviously hunting the shadow, not the substance. But those who have a thorough knowledge of both, like men armed at all points, have the sooner attained their object and carried authority with them.

Patterns give dignity to practices that don't necessarily draw on scientific foundations. Patterns not only amplify system-level architectures, but also bring a new focus to the craft of implementation. Earlier in this article, I noted Richard Gabriel's concern for the end user in his patterns, a consideration clearly within the architect's purview. Gabriel also takes the implementor under his wing, and starts with coding standards as a foundation for good system abstraction. The patterns have architectural overtones, even when talking about code. Here is the first and most straightforward of Gabriel's[9.] patterns:

PATTERN: SIMPLY UNDERSTOOD CODE

> . . . at the lowest levels of a program are chunks of code. These are the places that need to be understood to confidently make changes to a program, and ultimately understanding a program thoroughly requires understanding these chunks.
>   In many pieces of code the problem of disorientation is acute. People

have no idea what each component of the code is for and they experience considerable mental stress as a result.

Suppose you are writing a chunk of code that is not so complex that it requires extensive documentation or else it is not central enough that the bother of writing such documentation is worth the effort, especially if the code is clear enough on its own. How should you approach writing this code?

People need to stare at code in order to understand it well enough to feel secure making changes to it. Spending time switching from window to window or scrolling up and down to see all the relevant portions of a code fragment takes attention away from understanding the code and gaining confidence to modify it.

People can more readily understand things that they can read in their natural text reading order; for Western culture this is generally left to right, top to bottom.

If code cannot be confidently understood, it will be accidentally broken.

Therefore, *arrange the important parts of the code so it fits on one page. Make that code understandable to a person reading it from top to bottom. Do not require the code to be repeatedly scanned in order to understand how data is used and how control moves about.*

This pattern can be achieved by using the following patterns: *Local Variables Defined* and *Used on One Page,* which tries to keep local variables on one page; *Assign Variables Once,* which tries to minimize code scanning by having variables changed just once; *Local Variables Re-assigned Above their Uses,* which tries to make a variable's value apparent before its value is used while scanning from top to bottom; *Make Loops Apparent,* which helps people understand parts of a program that are nonlinear while retaining the ability to scan them linearly; and *Use Functions for Loops,* which packages complex loop structure involving several state variables into chunks, each of which can be easily understood.

Let's pull some of the key words from this pattern: "confidently," "stress," "secure," "culture," "understand," etc. These appeal to the "soft" side of development. This pattern is about the impact of a software practice on the people who use it—a metric I resolve to use to judge the Quality of patterns I write.

ARCHITECTURE AND ENGINEERING

Software engineering was all the rage during the 1980s. As I watched this culture emerge, and watched the term come in vogue, I struggled with how to reconcile it with my own engineering background. Engineering is a kind of informed cleverness; etymologically, it comes from the same root as "ingenious." That didn't capture what I saw emerging in the CASE tools and "formalisms" of the software engineering crowd.

Building architecture is supported by many engineering disciplines, yet buildings are more than the sum of their engineering efforts. Software architecture likewise builds on so-called software engineering principles, but are more than the result of an informed cleverness. How do we describe architecture in terms of its relationship to engineering? Somewhere along the line, I picked up the formulation:

Engineering + culture = architecture.

This is an insightful model for me. Buildings encode cultural mores and expectations; their design suggests the functions and activities that "happen there," to use a favorite Alexandrian phrase. Those functions and activities have strong cultural ties. Software is much the same way: though we have design principles (like those of OOD) that stand as architectural principles, the architecture is as much a product of the market and implementation technology that make up its context than it is of the design method used. The intended use of a piece of software should be evident from its structure. In many cases, the implementation technology is visible in its structure as well (Smalltalk and C++ programs will have quite different internal structures to serve the same end use).

Vitruvius, the classic Roman architect, defined architecture in terms of three principles joined together: Utilitas-firmitas-venustas—Commodity, Firmeness, and Delight (yes, there's that word again). "Firmeness" is an engineering concern, whereas commodity and delight are cultural. Culture evokes history and conventions that give *meaning* to architecture and the creation that embodies it. Rybczynski[10] again:

> The communication of meaning, more than beauty, distinguishes architecture from engineering. A bridge must be solid, functional, and attractive; a good public library must be all of these, but it also carries cultural baggage. Its architecture defines our attitude toward reading and celebrates a sense of civic pride. A library is more than a warehouse for books; it is a built evocation of intellectual ideal.

"Meaning" hints at some intellectual legacy. Beauty and endurance, we can attribute to mimicry, rote, or the skills of an idiot-savant. We are quick to credit the success of great programmers to their methods, their programming languages, or their managers. Too often, we don't look far enough to see the *meaning* programmers add to the body of literature we call system software. Good patterns explore their own meaning, largely through their rationale and resulting context. Look again at Gabriel's pattern: not only does it touch on cultural issues as it stands (linguistic and human factors issues), but anyone applying the pattern must explore local mores (natural language and programming language) to apply it well. Exploring this cultural sensitivity brings out the meaning of the pattern to a given project or individual. Patterns bring honor and dignity to everyday software developers by recognizing their intellectual and artistic legacies.

The meaning of our programs, and the importance of capturing that, is something we don't learn in our computer science curricula. How can we address this? Perhaps if computer science curricula incorporated more material from the arts, and vice versa, computer scientists would appreciate the important "stuff" that lies beyond the method and language wars. Much of this "stuff" is down-to-earth, like Simply Understood Code. What a concept! There is beauty in being down-to-earth, as my friend Bruce Anderson has often told me.

For an excellent collection of essays on meaning and software, see *Software Development as Reality Construction*.

WILL PATTERNS HELP?

Perhaps someday computer science will have more science, and we will be able to focus our artistic energies on loftier issues. But there will be patterns there as well. Even today, patterns provide a vocabulary and a foothold to study a complex and little understood domain. We really don't understand software architecture in a scientific sense; the control variables for commodity, firmness, and delight are too numerous, too dependent on each other, and too subjective to support a thorough formal treatment.

Ben Schneiderman[12] provides a rationale supporting this research methodology, both in his generic discussion of research methods, and in his discussion of research methods suitable to team organizations and group processes. He suggests that case studies might be a good springboard for experimental science. And at the recent ICSE, Manny Lehman made some remarks that underscored the need for a "gestalt" approach to research that balances experience studies with experimental methods. Patterns are the case studies that can help us survive in the absence of formalism, where it is premature to formulate scientifically testable hypotheses, and particularly in artistic areas where formalisms may have limited influence or worth.

It may be an uphill journey. Disciplines entrenched in formalisms have a history of not dealing well with approaches outside their sphere of experience. Doppler didn't employ the formal mathematical methods in popular use at his university in Austria when he formulated the Doppler effect. Though he was able to make a compelling argument, it was nonetheless an unconventional compelling argument. He was barred from tenure and lived out the rest of his life in disgrace. Because Laplace bore the credentials of a mathematician, he was credited with the transform that bears his name; a prior derivation by Oliver Heaviside was dismissed because he was only an electrical engineer.

We shouldn't pretend that pattern languages will completely fill the artistic needs of design. On one hand, aesthetics are important: software is read ten times as often as it is written. A pleasing and lucid style simplifies the life of the maintenance engineer, as Gabriel's patterns point out. But it is a long way from a good literary coding style to "commodity," and there are many other factors that are important to graceful program evolution. Aesthetics are a deeply human thing that we cannot always codify. We see this in Alexander's work: though his pattern approach produces architectures that are functional and resilient, many claim that they are aesthetically "funky." Perhaps the funkiness would not have been there had the architects gone beyond commodity, firmeness, and delight, to struggle with the cultural meaning of the buildings they built. Software pattern languages will be the same way.

Most contemporary patterns focus on the engineering side of software architecture, on the commodity and firmness of the Vitruvian triad. Patterns in and of themselves may delight us, as I have been delighted by Ward Cunningham's "CHECKS" language and by Gerard Meszaros' "Half Object + Protocol" (both in *Pattern Languages of Program Design*[13]). These patterns are elegant in their own right, as literature, and evoke a response in the reader that propels effective use of the pattern. These patterns' generativity and elegance as solutions suggests they might contribute to the architectural aesthetics of the product, just as Corinthian pillars contribute to the majesty of institutional buildings that employ them. But the elegance of those patterns individually doesn't portend for aesthetics in the program as a whole. A system has the Quality Without a Name only if the designer uses the right patterns, balances engineering concerns with formal constraints, and weaves a deeply human sense of aesthetics into the system structure.

Palladio, following Vitruvius, was adamant that great architecture depended on the independent presence of commodity, firmness, and delight. Good form does not follow function alone, and beauty does not promise utility. The great designer demonstrates judgment and balance between all three, and goes beyond even utility to incorporate the taste of cultural sensitivity, taste that gives an architecture meaning. As an industry, we have invested a lot of effort into firmness, begrudgingly acknowledge commodity, and puzzle at delight. Patterns provide an opportunity to raise the level of architectural aesthetics by focusing on commodity, and by giving meaning and an unnamed Quality to our programs.

SIGNPOSTS

In the October 1995 issue I will probably relate some experiences with putting a pattern culture in place in an existing organization.

The PLoP/94 proceedings are now available as *Pattern Languages of Program Design.*

REFERENCES

1. Halstead, M. H. *Elements of Software Science,* Elsevier, New York, 1977.
2. Alexander, C. *Notes on Synthesis of Form* (eighth printing, 1974) Harvard University Press, Cambridge, MA, 1964.
3. Knuth, D. E. *The Art of Computer Programming,* Addison-Wesley, Reading, MA, 1981.
4. Rybczynski, W. *The Most Beautiful House in the World,* Viking, New York, 1989, p. 283.
5. Altshuller, G. S. *Creativity as an Exact Science,* Gordon and Breach, New York, 1988.
6. Palladio, A. *The Four Books of Architecture,* ch. 1, Isaac Ware ed., printed for R. Ware, London, 1738.
7. Alberti, L. B. *Ten Books of Architecture: The 1755 Leoni Edition,* Dover, Mineola, NY, 1986, p. 41.
8. Pollio, V. *Vitruvius: The Ten Books of Architecture,* translated by Morris Hickey Morgan, Dover, New York, 1960.
9. Gabriel, Richard. Electronic mail message, 11 April 1995.
10. Rybczynski, W. *Looking Around: A Journey through Architecture,* Viking, New York, 1992, 266–267.

11. Floyd et al. *Software Development as Reality Construction,* Springer-Verlag, Berlin, 1992.
12. Schneiderman, B. *Software Psychology,* Winthrop, Cambridge, MA, 1980, Sections 2.2 and 6.5.
13. Coplien, J., and D. Schmidt, Eds., *Pattern Languages of Program Design,* Addison-Wesley, Reading, MA, 1995.

The Failure of Pattern Languages

Richard P. Gabriel
rpg@steam.stanford.edu

We have been following the Christopher Alexander saga for a while and it might surprise some to learn that Alexander completed by the early 1970s all the work I've so far reported—in what some would call the infancy of computer science. People have read his work and taken off from it—the Hillside Group and others are writing patterns, thinking they are doing something worthwhile—and they are. But are they doing for software what Alexander set out to do for architecture—find a process to build artifacts possessing the quality without a name? Or is the quality unimportant to what they are doing? Is it important only that they are accomplishing something good for software, and Alexander's original goal is unimportant, merely a catalyst or inspiration—the way fine drizzle drawing his eyes low, narrowing streetlights to a sheltering fog, can inspire a poet to write a poem of intimacy and its loss? Or the way an inept carpenter building an overly sturdy birdcage can inspire another person to construct a tiger's cage?

I think the quality without a name is vital to software development, but I'm not yet sure how. I'm not sure because I am not clear on what the quality without a name is in the realm of software. It sits zen in the midst of a typhoon frenzy of activity both in architecture and software. Alexander's story does not end with the publication of *A Pattern Language*[1] in 1977. It went on and still goes on. And Alexander did not sit still after he wrote the patterns. Like any scientist he tried them out.

And they did not work. Read Alexander's own words:

All the architects and planners in christendom, together with *The Timeless Way of Building*[2] and the *Pattern Language*,[1] could still not make buildings that are alive because it is other processes that play a more fundamental role, other changes that are more fundamental.[3]

Alexander reached this conclusion after completing some specific projects. One was the Modesto Clinic. In this project an architect from Sacramento used Alexander's pattern language to design and build a medical clinic in Modesto (in the Central Valley of California). The building was a success in the sense that a building was actually constructed and its plan looked good on paper. Alexander says:

> Up until that time I assumed that if you did the patterns correctly, from a social point of view, and you put together the overall layout of the building in terms of those patterns, it would be quite alright to build it in whatever contemporary way that was considered normal. But then I began to realize that it was not going to work that way.[3]

Despite the fact that the Sacramento architect tried hard to follow the patterns, the result was dismal. Alexander says of the Clinic:

> It's somewhat nice in plan, but it basically looks like any other building of this era. One might wonder why its plan is so nice, but in any really fundamental terms there is nothing to see there. There was hardly a trace of what I was looking for.[3]

This wasn't an isolated failure, but one that was repeated frequently by other people trying to use the pattern language from bootlegged copies of *A Pattern Language:*

> Bootleg copies of the pattern language were floating up and down the West Coast and people would show me projects they had done and I began to be more and more amazed to realize that, although it worked, all of these projects basically looked like any other buildings of our time. They had a few differences. They were more like the buildings of Charles Moore or Joseph Esherick, for example, than the buildings of S.O.M. or I. M. Pei; but basically, they still belonged perfectly within the canons of mid-twentieth century architecture. None of them whatsoever crossed the line.[3]

Alexander noticed a more bizarre phenomenon than the fact that the buildings were no different from their contemporaries—the architects believed they were different, vastly and remarkably different. Alexander says:

They thought the buildings were physically different. In fact, the people who did these projects thought that the buildings were quite different from any they had designed before, perhaps even outrageously so. But their perception was incredibly wrong; and I began to see this happening over and over again—that even a person who is very enthusiastic about all of this work will still be perfectly capable of making buildings that have this mechanical death-like morphology, even with the intention of producing buildings that are alive.

So there is the slightly strange paradox that, after all those years of work, the first three books are essentially complete and, from a theoretical point of view, do quite a good job of identifying the difference but actually do not accomplish anything. The conceptual structures that are presented are just not deep enough to actually break down the barrier. They actually do not do anything.[3]

Alexander determined the failure was because the geometry of the buildings was not as different from the old geometry as it needed to be to generate the quality. His reaction was to consider the *process* of building: the mortgage process, the zoning process, the construction process, the process of money flowing through the system, the role of the architect, and the role of the builder. But he never lost sight of geometry. He says:

> . . . the majority of people who read the work, or tried to use it, did not realize that the conception of geometry had to undergo a fundamental change in order to come to terms with all of this. They thought they could essentially graft all the ideas about life, and patterns, and functions on to their present conception of geometry. In fact, some people who have read my work actually believe it to be somewhat independent of geometry, independent of style—even of architecture.[3]

From the time when buildings routinely possessed the quality without a name to the present when almost no buildings possess that quality, the process of building has changed from the so-called "renaissance building paradigm" to the current "industrial building paradigm," from one in which building was a decentralized activity where the architect, if one was used, was closely associated with the building or even participated in the building and material was hand-crafted on site to one in which an architect might design hundreds of homes that were then built by a contractor buying and using modular parts, perhaps minimally customizing them—for example, cutting lumber to the proper length. At the same time, because building became a high-volume activity, the process of funding building changed so that, now, a large sum of money needs to be allocated to produce any homes at all.

As I mentioned in "Habitability and piecemeal growth" (JOOP 5[9]), one problem with the building process is *lump-sum development*. In such development few resources are brought to bear on the problems of repair and piecemeal growth. Instead, a large sum of money is dedicated to building a large artifact, and that artifact is allowed, somewhat, to deteriorate, and anything that is found lacking with the design or construction is ignored or minimally addressed until it is feasible to abandon the building and construct a replacement. This phenomenon also occurs in the mortgage process. The bank loans someone, say, a developer, a large sum of money to construct a home. A homebuyer purchases this home by assuming a large debt. The debt is paid off over time, with the early payments dedicated mostly to paying the interest, which accumulates, and only at the end of the mortgage period is the principal taken down. The result is that a homeowner might pay $1,000,000 for a house that cost $400,000 to build. The problem with this— aside from all the problems you can easily identify yourself—is that the additional $600,000 paid for the house is not available for repair and piecemeal growth. It is a fee to the bank. And the house is not improved in any way or only minimally during the payment period— 10–30 years—at which point the house is sold to someone else who pays another (or the same!) bank another enormous fee. The key ingredient to long-term development—piecemeal growth—is thwarted.

Alexander started a lengthy process himself of constructing arguments to show that process itself was the root cause for the practical failure of his theory of the quality without a name and of his particular pattern language— that the process of construction encompassed so many things controlling geometry that the outcome had to be as flawed and disappointing as what he saw in the early, uncontrolled experiments.

First he needed to convince himself that process could be the primary determiner of the outcome of a generative process. He got this from D'Arcy Thompson; Alexander says:

> What Thompson insisted on was that every form is basically the end result of a certain growth process. When I first read this I felt that of course the form in a purely static sense is equilibrating certain forces and that you could say that it was even the product of those forces— in a non-temporal, non-dynamic sense, as in the case of a raindrop, for example, which in the right here and now is in equilibrium with the air flow around it, the force of gravity, its velocity, and so forth—but that you did not really have to be interested in how it actually got made. Thompson however was saying that everything is the way it is today

because it is the result of a certain history—which of course includes how it got made. But at the time I read this I did not really understand it very well; whereas I now realize that he is completely right.[3]

It's somewhat amazing that Alexander would fail to understand this right off, because his theory—patterns generating the quality without a name—is an example of it. His error, if there was one, was to not go far enough with his theory. Once he latched onto this insight he went hog wild. First he examined the process closely, identifying places where its details do not serve the quality without a name and geometry. Second, he performed several important experiments in which he controlled or nearly controlled the entire process.

These experiments were based on an alternative process developed by Alexander which he called the "Grassroots Housing Process." The basic idea is that a sponsor—a group of people, a corporation—would provide land at a reasonable price. There would be a builder who is actually an architect, builder, and manager rolled into one. Families would get an allotment of money to begin construction. The builder would help and with the pattern language each family would build its own home. Each family pays a fee per year with the following characteristics. The fee is based on square footage and the fee declines from a very high rate in the early years to very low in later years. It is assumed to take around 13 years to pay off things. Materials for building are free to families (of course, it is paid for by the fees). This means that families are encouraged to initially build small homes. Because materials are free and the only fees are for square footage, each family is encouraged to improve or embellish its existing space and the cluster's common space. As time goes on and the fees drop in later years, homes can be enlarged. These clusters nested in the sense that there would be a larger "political" unit responsible for enhancing structures larger than any particular cluster. For example, roads would be handled this way and the political unit would be a sort of representative government.

The existence of free materials and nested clusters would, Alexander hoped, create a mechanism for planning within a community and with a nearby or enclosing community.

The builder helps the families do their own building by instruction and by doing the jobs requiring the most skill. Each builder has several apprentices who are trained on the job. A builder works with a cluster of families and, over time, the builder gradually moves on to service another cluster, at which point the first cluster becomes self-sufficient.

The way this scheme works, of course, is the same way the banks work, but with a lesser fee and with the community—the cluster—acting as the bank. Profits from the process are used to sponsor other clusters.

Christopher Alexander was shocked to be quizzed about his views on Marxism after presenting this proposed process. Nevertheless two important concepts came out of it: the nested cluster with shared common areas and the architect-builder.

This led to several projects. One was to see whether local politics could be changed to support this new building process. To this end he managed to get passed a Berkeley referendum in the early 1970s that put a moratorium on new construction and established a commission to look into a new master plan based on participatory planning of the sort talked about in *The Oregon Experiment*.[4] The result was not quite what he had in mind: There was a new master plan, but one in which local neighborhoods were asked about which streets could be closed, and some of them were—if you drive through Berkeley today, you can still experience the results.

The most ambitious experiment was to build a community in Mexicali. The Mexican government became convinced that Alexander would be able to build a community housing project for far less than the usual cost. So they gave him the power he needed to organize the project as he felt proper. The land was provided in such a way that the families together owned the encompassed public land and each family owned the land on which their home was built. The point of the experiment was to see whether, with a proper process and a pattern language, a community could be built that demonstrated the quality without a name. Because of the expected low cost of the project and the strong recommendation of the University of Mexico regarding Alexander's work, the Mexican government was willing to allow Alexander to put essentially his grassroots system of production into practice. The details of this system hinged on the answers to the following questions, to which I have added the software development equivalents:

1. *What kind of person is in charge of the building operation itself?* An architect-builder is in charge—this corresponds to the master architect of a software system who also participates in coding and helps his co-developers with their work.

2. *How local to the community is the construction firm responsible for building?* Each site has its own builder's yard, each responsible for local develop-

ment—this corresponds to putting control of the computer and software resources for each small project within that project. Local control and physically local resources are important.

3. *Who lays out and controls the common land between the houses, and the array of lots and houses?* This is handled by the community itself, in groups small enough to come to agreement in face-to-face meetings—this corresponds to small group meetings to discuss and negotiate interfaces in a project. There is no centralized decision-maker, but a community of developers sits down and discusses the best interfaces as a group.

4. *Who lays out the plans of individual houses?* Families design their own homes—this corresponds to each developer designing his or her own implementations for a component.

5. *Is the construction system based on the assembly of standard **components**, or is it based on acts of creation which use standard **processes**?* Construction is based on a standard process rather than by standard components—this goes against one of the supposed tenets of the object philosophy in which standardized class libraries are de rigueur. Nevertheless, many experiences show that the true benefits of reuse come from reuse within a project and not as much from between projects. Such successful reuse is based on being able to model the domain of the project so that classes defined to represent aspects of the domain can be used for several purposes within that same model. Typically such a model is called a *framework*.

6. *How is cost controlled?* Cost is controlled flexibly so that local decisions and trade-offs can be made—this corresponds to giving a project a total budget number rather than breaking it down too far, such as a budget for hardware and another for developers.

7. *What is the day-to-day life like, on-site, during the construction operation?* It is not just a place where the job is done, but a place where the importance of the houses themselves as homes infuses the everyday work—developers need to have their own community in which not only the work but the lives of the developers are shared: common meals, rest time together in play. It's called team-building in the management literature, but it's more than that and every development manager worth paying knows that this is one of the most important parts of a project.

You might wonder why Alexander (or I, for that matter) considers the day-to-day life of a project important. It's because the quality of the result depends on the quality of communication between the builders or developers, and this depends on whether it is fun to work on the project and whether the project is important to the builder or developer in a personal sense and not just in a monetary or job sense.

Alexander tells the story of this project—including the sorts of meals the families had and their celebrations after completing major projects—in *The Production of Houses*.[5] At the end of that book Alexander tells about the failures of the project as seen close-up—that is, before he was able to sit back and look at the results objectively. He says there were a number of failures. First, the Mexican government lost faith in the project and pulled the plug after 5 houses were built, leaving 25 unbuilt. Partly they lost faith because the buildings looked so "traditional" rather than modern. Alexander says:

> The almost naive, childish, rudimentary outward character of the houses disturbed them extremely. (Remember that the families, by their own frequent testimony, love their houses.)[5]

Another reason was that the government was dismayed by the experimentation that Alexander did with construction systems. The government felt that, because Alexander was a world authority on architecture and building, he was simply going to apply what he knew to produce beautiful homes cheaply and rapidly.

A failure that seemed to disturb Alexander was that the builder's yard was abandoned within three years of the end of the project. He felt that the process would have continued without his involvement once the families saw that they could control their own living spaces.

But did the buildings and the community have the quality without a name? Alexander said at the time:

> The buildings, for example, are very nice, and we are very happy that they so beautifully reflect the needs of different families. But they are still far from the limpid simplicity of traditional houses, which was our aim. The roofs are still a little awkward, for example. And the plans, too, have limits. The houses are very nice internally, but they do not form outdoor space which is as pleasant, or as simple, or as profound as we can imagine it. For instance, the common land has a rather complex shape, and several of the gardens are not quite in the right place. The freedom of the pattern language, especially in the hands of our apprentices, who did not fully understand the deepest ways of making buildings simple, occasionally caused a kind of confusion compared with what we now understand, and what we now will do next time.[5]

This chilling reference to the deep understanding required to build buildings with the quality without a name is echoed in the discussion of the builder's yard:

> When their [the government's] support faded, the physical buildings of the builder's yard had no clear function, and, because of peculiarities in the way the land was held, legally, were not transferred to any other use, either; so now, the most beautiful part of the buildings which we built stand idle. And yet these buildings, which we built first, with our own deeper understanding of the pattern language, were the most beautiful buildings in the project. That is very distressing, perhaps the most distressing of all.[5]

Later, after some reflection, Alexander became more harsh:

> There was one fact above everything else I was aware of, and that was that the buildings were still a bit more funky than I would have liked. That is, there are just a few little things that we built down there that truly have that sort of limpid beauty that have been around for ages and that, actually, are just dead right. That's rare; and it occurred in only a few places. Generally speaking, the project is very delightful—different of course from what is generally being built, not just in the way of low-cost housing—but it doesn't quite come to the place where I believe it must.
>   . . . But what I am saying now is that, given all that work (or at least insofar as it came together in the Mexican situation) and even with us doing it (so there is no excuse that someone who doesn't understand it is doing it), it only works partially. Although the pattern language worked beautifully—in the sense that the families designed very nice houses with lovely spaces and which are completely out of the rubric of modern architecture—this very magical quality is only faintly showing through here and there.[3]

Alexander noticed that there is a problem with using the word "simplicity" to refer to the fundamental goal of the patterns. He says:

> We were running several little experiments in the builder's yard. There is an arcade around the courtyard with each room off of the arcade designed by a different person. Some of the rooms were designed by my colleagues at the Center and they also had this unusual funkiness—still very charming, very delightful, but not calm at all. In that sense, vastly different from what is going on in the four-hundred year old Norwegian farm where there is an incredible clarity and simplicity that has nothing to do with its age. But this was typical of things that were happening.

Here is this very sort of limpid simplicity and yet the pattern language was actually encouraging people to be a little bit crazy and to conceive of much more intricate relationships than were necessary. They were actually disturbing. Yet in all of the most wonderful buildings, at the same time that they have all of these patterns in them, they are incredibly simple. They are not simple like an S.O.M. building—sometimes they are incredibly ornate—so I'm not talking about that kind of simplicity. There is however a kind of limpidity which is very crucial; and I felt that we just cannot keep going through this problem. We must somehow identify what it is and how to do it—because I knew it was not just my perception of it.

The problem is complicated because the word simplicity completely fails to cover it; at another moment it might be exactly the opposite. Take the example of the columns. If you have the opportunity to put a capital or a foot on it, it is certainly better to do those two things than not—which is different from what the modern architectural tradition tells you to do. Now, in a peculiar sense, the reasons for it being better that way are the same as the reasons for being very simple and direct in the spacing of those same columns around the courtyard. I'm saying that, wherever the source of that judgment is coming from, it is the same in both cases. . . . The word simplicity is obviously not the relevant word. There is something which in one instance tells you to be simple and which in another tells you to be more complicated. It's the same thing which is telling you those two things.[3]

Another part of the problem he saw with the Mexicali project had to do with the level of mastery needed in the construction process. At the start of the project he felt that merely having the same person do the design and the construction was enough, so that the important small decisions dictated by the design were made correctly. But during the project and later on Alexander learned that the builder needed more. He says:

Only recently have I begun to realize that the problem is not merely one of technical mastery or the competent application of the rules—like trowelling a piece of concrete so that it's really nice—but that there is actually something else which is guiding these rules. It actually involves a different level of mastery. It's quite a different process to do it right; and every single act that you do can be done in that sense well or badly. But even assuming that you have got the technical part clear, the creation of this quality is a much more complicated process of the most utterly absorbing and fascinating dimensions. It is in fact a major creative or artistic act—every single little thing you do—and it is only in the years since the Mexican project that I have begun to see the dimensions of that fact.[3]

Not only must you decide to build the right thing but you must build it with skill and artistry. This leads to an obvious question: Can it be that buildings with the quality without a name are just too hard to put together deliberately, and the fact that they exist in older societies is that they were created by chance and survive because of the quality? Or, even more cynically, could it be that there really is a form of nostalgia at work in which everything old is revered, having come from a more innocent and noble age?

Perhaps, but this should not dissuade us from considering how to create things with the quality without a name.

It is easy to see that the process of constructing buildings has an obvious correspondent in software—the process of software construction is the single most important determining factor in software quality. Alexander's building process adapted to software could be called a form of incremental development because it advises the use of small groups with autonomy, architect-builders at the helm.

But what of geometry? Alexander always goes back to this. And one of his key questions is this: What is it that dictates geometry possessing the quality without a name—what is that thing that is falsely called "simplicity"?

What corresponds to geometry for us?

I think it is the code itself. Many talk about the need for excellent interfaces and the benefits of separating interface from implementation so that the implementation may vary. But few people talk seriously about the quality of the code itself. In fact, most theorists are eager to lump it into the category of things best not discussed, something to be hidden from view so that it can be changed in private. But think of Alexander's last remarks above: the quality comes in nearly equal part from the artistry and creativity of the builder, who is the one whose hands most directly form the geometry that gives the building its quality and character. Isn't the builder the coder? And isn't the old-style software methodology to put design in the hands of analysts and designers and to put coding in the hands of lowly coders, sometimes offshore coders who can be paid the lowest wages to do the least important work?

Patterns can help designers and designer-coders to make sure they put the right stuff in their software, but it takes a coder with extraordinary mastery to construct software with the quality without a name.

And what of simplicity? Can it be that blind subservience to simplicity in software development can lead to the same "death-like morphology" that it causes in architecture?

Alexander's story is nearly up to date, but to many it disappears at the point we've left him here. Our modern-day pattern-writers are content to stop with *A Pattern Language* and *The Timeless Way of Building* and to go off writing patterns. They ignore the failures that Alexander himself saw in his own processes at that point. The next chapter of his story takes him back to geometry and art. It's probably a story that has only the most metaphorical application to software because it has to do with beads, beauty, art, geometry, and Turkish carpets.

REFERENCES

1. Alexander, C. *A Pattern Language,* Oxford University Press, New York, 1977.
2. Alexander, C. *The Timeless Way of Building,* Oxford University Press, New York, 1979.
3. Grabow, S. *Christopher Alexander: The Search for a New Paradigm in Architecture,* Oriel Press, Stocksfield, UK, 1983.
4. Alexander, C. *The Oregon Experiment,* Oxford University Press, New York, 1978.
5. Alexander, C. *The Production of Houses,* Oxford University Press, New York, 1985.

Potential Pattern Pitfalls, or How to Jump on the Patterns Bandwagon Without the Wheels Coming Off

Neil B. Harrison

cnbh@drmail.dr.lucent.com

By now, most software developers have heard something about patterns. It's hard not to. Books about patterns are popular, and are some of the better sellers among professional software books.[2,3,7,8,12–14] Articles are common; some journals have devoted entire issues to patterns.[4,10] In the object-oriented community, patterns are particularly strong. The *C++ Report* has a regular feature on patterns, authored alternately by Jim Coplien and John Vlissides. And at OOPSLA96, there were (count 'em) seven tutorials and four workshops on patterns. The keynote speaker was Christopher Alexander, the author of books on architectural patterns of buildings and communities[1] and an inspiration to many software pattern writers. Patterns are a big deal.

But are patterns here to stay? The patterns discipline is growing rapidly, but it is still very young and immature. We don't fully understand the benefits of patterns, their use, and even their form and content. In spite of this, some people are touting patterns as the next great panacea. If expectations are built up and patterns fail to live up to them, they will be viewed in the same vein as AI, CASE, and even to some extent Object-Oriented Programming (OOP)—as yet another wreck on the side of the road to excellence in software development.

From the early beginnings of patterns, the practitioners have recognized the seductive nature of patterns and have sought to keep patterns at the highest ethical level. In fact, at the first Conference on Pattern Languages of Programs (PLoP), a full session was devoted to issues such as overblown expectations, hype, profiteering from patterns, and giving credit where credit is due. In the two intervening years, many of us have been pleased at the growth of patterns. But we are also sobered by the great deal of hype that patterns have received. Our fears at the first PLoP may well have been justified.

Here are some of the pitfalls that we might fall into as we write and use patterns. Perhaps you can already see some of these in your own organization. The suggestions given with each pitfall will help you combat them.

PATTERN MADNESS

For many software professionals, the first reaction to patterns is to sit down and write some patterns. After all, most of us are just full of good ideas, particularly if we have been at our jobs for some time. Besides, we in the software industry have shown a strong preference for creation over reuse. So before long, we end up with a mountain of patterns. Some organizations have come up with well over a hundred patterns, just for their own project! And look at the books; there are already hundreds of patterns that have been published.

Is it a bad thing to have so many patterns? Certainly not; there is a great deal of knowledge to be captured and shared through patterns. However, it is fraught with problems. How do you organize a sizable collection of patterns? How do you find the ones you need? More importantly, how do you know which patterns are the good ones? With so many patterns, some people may just not bother with patterns. Above all, the real power of patterns is unleashed when we have them at our fingertips; each person needs a conceptually manageable working set for their domain.

The solution is not to stifle the writing of patterns, but to identify and organize the best patterns. Therefore, each project or community of interest should have a writers' workshop that can serve as a forum to collect and organize patterns. They could organize them by degree or confidence, frequency of use, and expertise of the source.[5]

Ideally, the set of patterns for a given domain should be kept to a number that the users can memorize, because people are much more likely to use a pattern they have at their fingertips than one they have to look up. Only when patterns can be immediately called to memory is their full power unleashed. Note that the book *Design Patterns*[8] has 23 patterns and *Pattern-*

Oriented Software Architecture[3] has 25 patterns. A group of 23–25 patterns appears to be a reasonable size for a collection of general purpose patterns.

An aid to memorization is descriptive but concise names for patterns; Ralph Johnson noted that one of the hardest parts of writing the book *Design Patterns*[8] was coming up with good names for the patterns.[9] Interestingly, some of the conversation in the patterns discussion group has focused on alternative names for the Template pattern in the *Design Patterns* book.

A SILVER BULLET UNDER EVERY ROCK

The hype has begun. Patterns are going to solve the software crisis! It happens to nearly every new software development technology. This author recently attended a meeting where patterns were being presented to management. One person noted that the projected benefits from patterns were based on speculation, and the speaker agreed, saying that he expected the benefits to be *much* (his emphasis) greater than what he had indicated.

Let's put these benefits into perspective. Most patterns affect software design, only one activity among many. In addition, some studies have shown that in some projects, software developers spend only 40% of their time actually doing software development; the rest of the time is eaten up by meetings, communication, etc. Now suppose that using patterns reduces software development effort by a factor of four, which is no small feat. Then the overall benefit to the total effort is only 30%. The systemic problems of software development are much broader than design, coding, and testing.

To many of us, the overselling of patterns is a serious concern. We know well that patterns won't save the world. We freely admit that the benefits of patterns have not been quantified yet, and may never be quantified. For patterns have little to do with lines of code, but everything to do with transferring knowledge. What units do you use to measure the flow of knowledge from person to person?

WHAT ARE PATTERNS, ANYWAY?

As a concept, patterns are so general that anything can be a pattern. Indeed, much of the inspiration for software patterns has come from building architectural patterns.[1] This is both a blessing and a curse. People are already writing patterns for many different aspects of software, and even patterns of the software development organizations.[6] This is leading to confusion about what patterns are and where and how they can be applied.

This problem is largely one of management, organization, and education. One approach is for people to limit their pattern study to a single domain; where this is not practical, they should carefully organize patterns so as to help others assimilate them effectively. Of course, we like to have patterns which are applicable across a large set of domains; in fact, we hope that others will use our patterns in domains we never thought of. But we need to start learning the patterns in the domains with which we are familiar. As we present our patterns to others, they will see applications of these patterns in their domains.

This problem is also undoubtedly linked to the newness of patterns as a software discipline. It may go away as the discipline matures. We can help attain that maturity by sharing and improving patterns through writers' workshops and similar activities.

THE "SO WHAT" SYNDROME

Let's assume that you have a set of design patterns, and you have just finished teaching a group of designers your patterns. Someone in the back stands up and says, "I don't see what is so great about patterns. I've been using these in my designs for years now. I didn't need formal patterns before, and can work perfectly well without them." Of course, the person who says this is one of the best and most respected designers in the company. Aside from the PR problems, you fear that there is a lot of truth in that statement. What do you do?

Remember that patterns capture existing, well proven design experience. The patterns *should* look familiar, especially to the senior designers. We expect them to already know the patterns. The written patterns give the non-expert designers some reusable building blocks for software development. They also provide a common vocabulary and understanding of design principles. Finally, they can capture some of the most important intellectual assets of your company—information which must be kept and passed on to the next generation of programmers.

GUILT BY ASSOCIATION

One of the largely unfulfilled promises of OOP is that of code reuse. OOP was supposed to produce large libraries of objects one could use, as well as sets of base classes that would provide foundations for specialized applications. Most of us are still waiting.

The promises of patterns are not all that different from those of code reuse. To be sure, patterns are not dependent on a particular hardware platform, nor do they have to be compiled. But patterns are often associated with reuse, because they do provide reuse of concepts, insights, and information. Some people expect them to enable reuse of code as well.

On the other side from code reuse lurk design documents. They are supposed to be a way to encode design information in such a way that it can be used again and to provide a way of understanding the elements of the design. These expectations have largely gone unfulfilled. Most design documents do not express elements of the software well,[11] and few design documents are even read after they have been written. Patterns can easily suffer the same fate.

So how can we keep patterns from sliding into the abyss of ineffective design documentation, and keep out of the code reuse morass? It's simple. The patterns have to be genuinely useful. This means, first, that the patterns must capture those things that have stood the test of time. Shame on the person who writes an unproven idea and tries to peddle it as a pattern! Pattern writers should also strive to capture the insightful ideas in patterns, the ones that make you stop and say, "I wish I'd thought of that!"

Of course, patterns must be easily understandable too. Therefore, patterns must be reviewed for clarity and style; pattern writers have adopted writers' workshops from the literature community to aid in this goal.

Finally, most new technologies require champions, who doggedly pursue the implementation of that technology in their company. Patterns are no different. You will probably have to beat the patterns drum in your organization to make it happen.

A PATTERN PRIESTHOOD

In order to use a pattern, it is necessary to understand it. If patterns are too complex, then only a select few can use them effectively. These few are often the top individuals in the project, the ones who know the patterns already. Maybe they wrote the patterns. This may lead to a cultural elitism, which is in total opposition to the goals of patterns.

To combat this, remember that patterns are for the express purpose of sharing insight and knowledge. Keep this in mind when holding writers' workshops. In addition, enlist the experts to teach others about the patterns they find most useful. Teaching breaks down many walls.

Work to keep patterns simple. Some, of course, are complex by nature. Just remember the words of Einstein: "Everything should be as simple as possible, but no simpler." This leads us to the next point.

THE LAW OF CONSERVATION OF COMPLEXITY

The law of conservation of complexity states that the essential complexity of a problem does not go away. It may change form, but it still stays around. (The companion Law of Software Entropy states that the complexity of a solution contains at least the complexity of the problem, and naturally increases over time.) The implications for patterns are twofold. First, the essential complexity of large systems means that its patterns will also be either complex, or many, or both! The only way to avoid this is to stick to simple systems! Second, the application of patterns does not mean that software design suddenly becomes easy. Patterns don't make the hard stuff go away. Instead, they will help people understand the complex problems, so they can be more easily tackled. They also free people from repeatedly solving the easy problems, allowing them to tackle the interesting hard problems. Remember, too, that patterns capture existing knowledge, so they can help with novel problems to the extent that the new solution builds on existing solutions.

The law of conservation of complexity serves as a balance to the Pattern Priesthood. It becomes important to select patterns which contain enough substance as to be worth the effort, but at the same time are not so complex that only the elite understand them. Further experience may help us in this area.

IS THERE ANY HOPE?

So what does the future hold for patterns? With such obstacles, do patterns stand a chance of becoming an important software design and development tool? Of course they do. In fact, some organizations are reporting that they have reaped benefits in design, coding, and maintenance through using patterns.

The pitfalls outlined above are not new; they have applied to many technologies over the years. Our experience in the introduction of previous technologies can serve us well as we attempt to avoid the same pitfalls with patterns.

So what should we do? Yes, we should be active with patterns. There is great potential there. But we must not, in our haste, lose our way. Everyone should be encouraged to write patterns. The people who are best at writing good patterns will continue to write them. We will select the best ones for our pattern collections. Writers' workshops are invaluable for evaluating technical merit and for improving the literary quality of patterns—for the patterns must stand on their own as literature.

We must take an active role in teaching the patterns to others, and provide follow up support as they begin to use them. We will help ourselves in both these efforts if we use a good pattern language, and if we organize patterns in a way that helps the users understand them.

Finally, we should resist the urge to preach patterns from the rooftops. After all, there are already enough pattern preachers. Instead, we should spread patterns through excellence, both in writing and in using patterns. Our experience will give us stories that will ring more solidly than the hollow peal of the huckster's chimes. If patterns live up to our expectations, the stories will come. If they don't, no amount of hyping will make them so.

REFERENCES

1. Alexander, C. et al, *A Pattern Language,* Oxford University Press, New York, 1977.
2. Beck, Kent, *Smalltalk Best Practice Patterns,* Prentice Hall, Upper Saddle River, N.J., 1997.
3. Buschmann, F. et al, *Pattern-Oriented Software Architecture—A System of Patterns,* Wiley and Sons Ltd., October 1995.
4. Communications of the ACM, Issue on Software Patterns, October 1996, vol 39, no 10, New York, 1996.
5. Coplien, J. O., Personal communication, April 11, 1995.
6. Coplien, J. O., "A Development Process Generative Pattern Language," in *Pattern Languages of Program Design,* Addison-Wesley, Reading, Mass., 1995.
7. Gabriel, Richard P., *Patterns of Software: Talks from the Software Community,* Oxford University Press, New York, 1996.
8. Gamma, E. et al, *Design Patterns: Elements of Reusable Object-Oriented Software,* Addison-Wesley, Reading, Mass., 1995.
9. Johnson, R., Personal communication at PLoP '94, August 1994.
10. *Object Magazine.* March 1997, vol. x, no. x, 1997.
11. Parnas, D. L. and D. M. Weiss, "Active Design Reviews: Principles and Practices," *Proc. 8th Intl. Conf. on Software Engineering,* London, 1985, pp. 132–136.

12. *Pattern Languages of Program Design,* Addison-Wesley, Reading, Mass., 1995.
13. *Pattern Languages of Program Design 2,* Addison-Wesley, Reading, Mass., 1995.
14. *Pattern Languages of Program Design 3,* Addison-Wesley, Reading, Mass., 1995.

An Introduction to Patterns

Ralph E. Johnson

johnson@cs.uiuc.edu

Analysis and design methods tend to focus more on notation and less on what is written in the notation. But experts not only know how to use a notation, but they also remember past models and designs, and they often solve a problem by recalling similar situations from the past and reusing old solutions in the new context. These problem/solution pairs tend to fall into families of similar problems and solutions, with each family exhibiting a pattern in both the problems and the solutions. An expert knows and uses a set of these patterns, which have been learned from experience and from other people. This applies to experts in areas other than object-oriented analysis and design, of course, but it applies as much to us as it does to anyone else.

There have been people in the object-oriented community who have been trying to describe and organize patterns since the late 1980s. My work has been especially influenced by that of Kent Beck, Ward Cunningham, and Erich Gamma. But recently a community of like-minded people has formed, mostly because of a series of OOPSLA workshops. This has led to workshops such as "Towards an Architecture Handbook," which was organized by Bruce Anderson in 1991; a continuation of that workshop and the creation of one on "Patterns" that was organized by Peter Coad in 1992; and a pattern workshop in 1993 in which the two joined forces. Kent Beck organized the Hillside Group to promote the explicit use of patterns in designing software, which is sponsoring a conference this August [1994] on Pattern Languages of Programs. Several books are in the works, and several people from this community teach courses on patterns. Many groups are using patterns explicitly in software projects.

I intend to use this column to share some of the pattern-related work that is going on. The column will not only describe particular patterns that have been discovered, but also will describe some of the issues involving patterns, such as how to use them, how to find them, and how they change the way we develop software. Because discovering and documenting patterns is a group activity, occasionally other members of the pattern community will write the column.

THE COMPOSITE PATTERN

All experts use patterns. But usually these patterns don't have names, are not written down, and so are hard to teach to nonexperts. Giving these patterns names lets us talk about them, which is not only useful for teaching them to newcomers, but also lets experts quickly describe their models and designs to each other. Our patterns become a kind of language that we can use to document our systems and to think about our designs.

The Composite pattern is so common that probably all of you have used one form of it. But there are many variations of it, and some of them are better than others. There are also common mistakes that people make when they use the Composite pattern. If you know the pattern and the kind of mistakes that you are likely to make when you use it, then you can check for those mistakes and will be able to catch errors earlier. Thus, using the Composite pattern explicitly can lead to more reliable systems, as well as to systems that are easier to understand. After all, if you are going to use a pattern, you should use it correctly.

The problem that leads to Composite is that there are complex objects that form part-whole or containment hierarchies. For example, a document processing system might have documents that contain chapters that contain sections that contain paragraphs. A company might have divisions that contain departments that contain projects. A user interface might have windows that contain subwindows. All these examples have part-whole hierarchies that can be arbitrarily deep.

The key to the Composite pattern is objects that form a tree. You won't necessarily want to use Composite to represent a car just because it contains an engine, wheels, and doors, but you might want to if the car's engine contains pistons and spark plugs. When objects form deep part-whole hierarchies, we usually want to treat individual objects and composite objects in the same way. The Composite pattern lets us do so. Larry Williams told me that this pattern is taught at ObjectTime with the motto, "Make a composite like its components." But knowing that you want to make a composite like its components is only half the battle; you also have to know how to do it.

USING THE COMPOSITE PATTERN

The first step in using the Composite pattern is to make three kinds of classes: Component, Composite, and Leaf. Figure 1 shows the relationship of these classes using OMT notation. Component is an abstract class that defines the interface of all components. Composite represents a component with components. Leaf represents a component without components. There are usually several Leaf classes. In a document processing system, the Component class might be called "TextElement," the Composite class "CompositeTextElement," and the Leaf classes might be "Paragraph" and "Figure."

The next step in using the Composite pattern is to make sure that the Leaf and Composite classes have the same interface and to describe that interface with the Component class. There are two sides to this step: making the Composite class support all the operations that any other component supports and making the Component class support operations that are needed to use Composite.

A Composite class usually implements component operations by delegating them to its components. It may only need to use a few of its components. For example, a text component probably needs to know its starting line number and its ending line number. A composite text element can use the starting line number of its first component and the ending line number of its last component as its own. More often, a composite will implement an operation by iterating over its components, performing the same operation on each. For example, a composite text element will display itself by displaying its components.

Usually, a composite supports operations for adding a component, removing a component, and enumerating its components. Some of these must be supported by the component interface, too. The main composite operation that must be defined in class Component is iteration. It is easy to support, because a component that is not a composite will iterate over its components by iterating over the null set. Other composite operations are both harder to implement for leaf components and also less important. They are harder to implement because it isn't possible to add a component to a leaf without making it no longer a leaf, and deleting a component from a leaf is always an error. One solution is to define default versions of the add and remove operations in class Component that always generate a

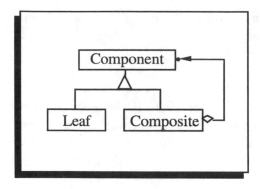

FIGURE 1   The composite pattern.

run-time error, but this defeats static type-checking. Fortunately, it is usually not necessary to implement these operations in Component, because you can redesign your system so that they are always performed on an object known to be a composite, never on just a component. For example, a text editor could have context-sensitive menus so that the only place you could add an element would be in a composite. This not only solves a problem in the design of the program, but it also makes the design of the user interface better.

COMMON VARIATIONS ON THE COMPOSITE PATTERN

The main variation with the Composite pattern is whether a component knows its parent. If a component does not know its parent, then the resulting design is simpler, and it is possible for an object to be the component of several composites. In other words, the component hierarchy will be a directed acyclic graph instead of a tree. However, components often need to know their composite. For example, if a component knows its composite, then we can delete an element from a composite by asking the component to delete itself instead of asking a composite to remove a component.

If each component knows its parent, then:

- a component will have a "parent" or "container" variable that indicates its composite,
- a component will ensure that it is removed from any previous parent before it is added to another, and
- when a composite adds a component to itself, it will always register itself as the component's parent.

This will solve one of the common errors with composite objects, namely, situations in which one of the composite's components has the wrong parent.

COMMON MISTAKES WITH THE COMPOSITE PATTERN

One common mistake is merging the Composite and Component classes. If the Component class defines a collection of components, then every component becomes a composite. Although this eliminates the problem of deciding what part of the Composite interface will be supported by all components, it means that every leaf component can have components, which doesn't make sense. In fact, many of the component classes will never have components, but they will still inherit everything that they need to have components.

A classic example of this mistake is class View in the original Model/View/Controller. Instead of having a separate View and CompositeView class, View defined an instance variable for subviews, so each view could have subviews. Most subclasses of View, such as TextView and ListView, could never have subviews, but they did not enforce this restriction, so it was easy for a programmer to mistakenly give them subviews, with odd results. ParcPlace fixed this problem when they rewrote Model/View/Controller as part of Release 4.0, and so now CompositeView is a subclass of VisualComponent (VisualComponent is a generalization of View).

I made the same mistake in an early version of Accounts, a framework for accounting. Accounts can be nested, because accounts for particular inventory items can be nested in accounts for a department, which can be nested in accounts for stores, which can be nested in a single account for the entire company. In spite of the fact that I know the Composite pattern well and have taught it to many people, we made it possible for every account to have components. When I realized that we should be using the Composite pattern, we quickly redesigned Accounts to have an abstract class Account, with subclasses SimpleAccount and CompositeAccount. In fact, we ended up with two kinds of composite accounts and one leaf account (SimpleAccount), which is unusual, but it still fits the pattern perfectly. This example shows that just knowing a pattern isn't enough; you have to recognize when to apply it. Knowing the pattern makes it a lot easier to see where to apply it, of course, and it was not hard to apply once we saw we needed it.

Another common mistake is for the Composite class not to be a subclass of Component but to be an unrelated class. This makes it impossible to recursively embed a composite inside a composite. This can lead to a proliferation of composite classes that are very similar to each other. For example, Chapter, Section, Subsection, and Subsubsection could all be different classes, or there could be a CompositeTextElementWithTitle class that could be used to implement all of them.

Sometimes it takes a conceptual breakthrough to realize that you should use the Composite pattern when the classes that should be composite and component are unrelated.

For example, the RTL System is a compiler back-end written in Smalltalk that represents a program as a collection of register transfers. It converts register transfers into machine instructions by combining register transfers and checking whether they are a legal machine instruction. An early version of the RTL System had three kinds of classes for representing register transfers; RegisterTransfer represented a single register transfer, RTLList represented a list of register transfers, and RTLRecord represented a list of register transfers that matched a machine instruction. In addition to an RTLList, an RTLRecord kept track of the machine instruction that the register transfers matched and the dependencies between the register transfers in the RTLList and those in other RTLRecords.

The design was greatly simplified when we realized that most RTLLists had only one register transfer in them, and we should treat the rest as exceptions by representing them with CompositeRegisterTransfer. This let us realize that dependencies and machine instructions should really be the responsibility of RegisterTransfers, thereby eliminating two kinds of objects from the design and reducing the size of the design.

Note that both "Everything is a composite" and "Composite and component are different" are not really faulty versions of the Composite pattern, they are just different patterns. "Everything is a composite" works well when you don't want different kinds of elements to have different behaviors, and so want to represent all elements with a universal "tree node" class. When you start making different kinds of elements, then some of them will never have components, and it will be confusing for them to be a subclass of a class that does. "Composite and component are different" usually models the world better than the Composite pattern; skin, blood, arms, and cells are all part of a human body, but it is pretty artificial to have an abstract "body part" class.

Giving composites and components the same interface makes the systems that use them more extensible and makes those parts more reusable. Thus, we use the Composite pattern when we are more concerned with making our artificial world powerful than with trying to perfectly model the real world.

CONCLUSION

Nearly every large object-oriented system I've seen has used the Composite pattern. It was rarely pointed out. Instead, I had to reverse-engineer it from the design. It is a lot easier for me to understand a system once I can see patterns like this in it, because each pattern explains and influences a large part of the system.

There are many advantages to explicitly using patterns like Composite. It helps us document the systems we build, it helps us build better systems, it prevents common mistakes. But we will lose these advantages if we don't name and describe these patterns and if we expect people to learn them by example instead of by teaching them directly.

POSTLUDE

The Composite pattern is described in *Design Patterns: Elements of Object-Oriented Software Architecture,* by Erich Gamma, Richard Helm, Ralph Johnson, and John Vlissides (Addison-Wesley; to appear later in 1994). There is an Internet mailing list on patterns: contact patterns-request@cs.uiuc.edu to join.

How Patterns Work in Teams

Ralph E. Johnson

My first column introduced patterns and described one of the most common object-oriented design patterns, Composite. I claimed that experts organized their knowledge as patterns, and that if we wrote down the patterns that we used and gave names to them, then we could communicate our models and designs more efficiently, we could think about them better, and we could train new analysts and designers faster. However, I only gave one example of a pattern, and many of you probably didn't think it was very compelling. A single example is rarely compelling, and even less so with patterns, because the power of patterns comes in the way sets of patterns work together, not in the power of a single pattern. This column will describe how a set of patterns works together.

Each pattern solves a particular problem. Composite solved the problem of how to represent part–whole hierarchies with as little duplication as possible by making the composite like the components. The Decorator pattern makes it easy to add an attribute to an object at runtime. The Strategy pattern makes it easy to change the way an object responds to a particular request. Once you learn a large enough set of patterns, you will find that design becomes easier because most of the design problems you face can be solved with one of the design patterns you already know. Thus, you don't have to solve your problems from first principles but can reuse old solutions.

AN EXAMPLE

Consider a document processing system in which a document might contain chapters, sections, subsections, figures, paragraphs, and so on. One way to represent a book is to make a Book class, a Chapter class, a Paragraph

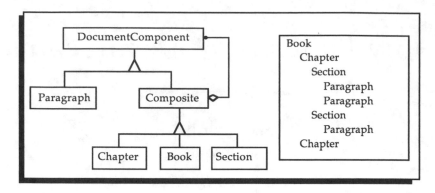

FIGURE 1   The DocumentComponent class and instance hierarchy.

class, and so on. Each Book would contain a list of Chapters, and a Chapter would contain a list of Sections, Figures, and Paragraphs. Since a book consists of a large whole–part hierarchy, it makes sense to apply the Composite pattern. The result would be a DocumentComponent class with subclasses Paragraph, Figure, and Composite, in which Chapter, Section, and the other composite classes would all be subclasses of Composite. Applying the Composite pattern reduces the duplication between the various classes and makes it easier to mix and match components to make a book, but it doesn't reduce the number of classes.

However, it is possible to reduce the number of subclasses of DocumentComponent substantially. Consider a Chapter, a Section, and a Subsection. Each of them has a title. They can all be optionally numbered. A Chapter starts on a new page, while the others don't. A Chapter is level 1 in the tree, while a section is level 2 and a Subsection is level 3. But most of their functionality consists of having components that are Paragraphs, Figures, etc., and that is inherited from Composite. Thus, they will not necessarily be very different.

One solution is to give Composite a title, level, and optional number. Sections and subsections would then be normal instances of Composite. Chapter would need to be a subclass of Composite so that a Chapter would also start a new page. However, most of the other classes of Composite would no longer be needed.

How do we specify whether a Composite is numbered? One alternative is for each one to have a Boolean that indicates whether it is numbered. But a better solution is for a Composite to contain an object that is responsible for keeping track of the numbering scheme. An object that represents an algorithm is called a Strategy. There are at least two Strategies for numbering parts of a Document: one for parts that are numbered (NumberStrategy), and one for parts that are unnumbered (NoNumberStrategy). A part's NumberStrategy can also keep track of its number. This way, we only have to allocate space for a variable when it is needed.

A third way to specify whether a Composite is numbered is to use the Decorator pattern. Instead of making the algorithm for numbering a part be stored in the part, we can "decorate" the part with the algorithm. A DocumentComponent decorator is a subclass of DocumentComponent that has a DocumentComponent as a component. It will add an attribute or change a property of its component. In this case, NumberDecorator will add a number to the component that it decorates.

Earlier, we made the title be a part of the Composite. But the title could be a decoration, too. We could either make the title be part of the NumberDecorator, since we never number a component unless it has a title, or we could have a separate TitleDecorator class. We'll probably need a separate TitleDecorator class, because many components with titles are never numbered. It might make sense to give every NumberDecorator a title anyway, but we will not do that to ensure that we see an example of one of the strengths of the Decorator pattern, which is the ability to recursively embed decorators.

Decorator and Strategy are classic patterns that are alternatives to each other. The main advantage of Decorator is that it lets you customize every component and it can be more space efficient when components are usually not decorated. The Decorator pattern makes it easy to put a number and title on any component, such as a Paragraph or a Picture, not just on a Composite. The main disadvantage is that recursive decorators can be hard to understand, especially when they are several layers deep. The Strategy pattern usually results in designs that are easier to understand. If you never want to give a paragraph a title and if every section and subsection has a title, then it is probably better to use the Strategy pattern.

There is a fourth alternative, which is to make the title and number be a normal DocumentComponent that is the first element of a Chapter or a Section. This alternative can't be used when the property you want to add must apply to the entire component. However, titles and numbers always show up at the beginning of a Section, so this alternative will work fine for representing titles.

Which of these alternatives is best? As usual, it depends on what you want to do with the design. For example, a design based on the Decorator

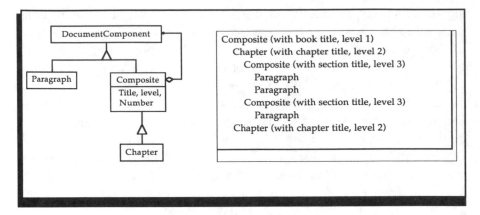

FIGURE 2   Distinguishing components by attributes, not classes.

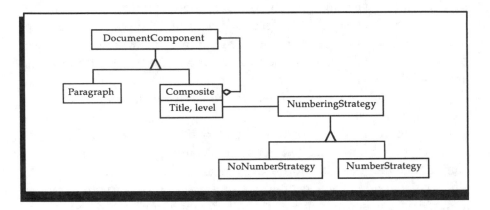

FIGURE 3   Class hierarchy using Strategy.

or Strategy pattern makes it easier to implement an outline mode that lets you move a section by dragging its title. A design based on making the title be a normal DocumentComponent would make it easy for the user to decide not to have a Section title by deleting the title. Nearly any feature could be implemented with any design. However, each design alternative makes some features easier to implement.

THE PROTOTYPE PATTERN

The last three designs all let you create new kinds of document components by composing existing ones. You can design a sub-sub-sub-sub Section by

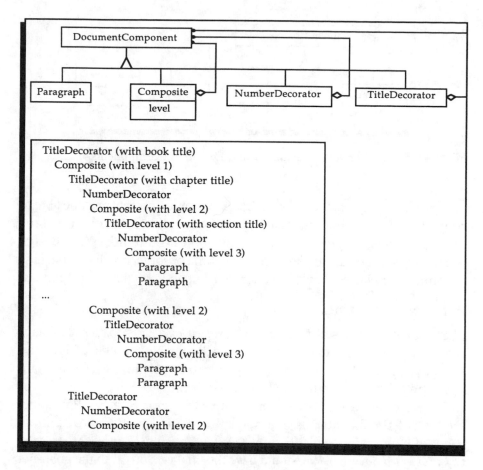

FIGURE 4 Class & Instance hierarchies using Decorator.

putting a Composite six levels down from the top of the document instead of by making a new class. An editor will probably have menu items for things like "add a section," and these menu items can't hardcode the class of the object to create, because there will be no Section class. Instead, the menu item will be associated with an example or prototype of the object to be added. "Add a chapter" will copy the object being used as a prototype of chapters and add it to the document. You can make a new kind of object to be added to your document by creating an object and adding it to the menu as a prototype.

The Prototype pattern is common in compositional designs because it lets the user make new kinds of objects by composing existing kinds of objects. The major disadvantage of the Prototype pattern is that it requires

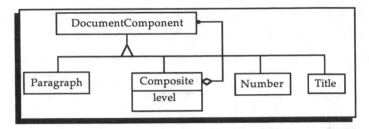

FIGURE 5   Class hierarchies using normal DocumentComponents.

that each object be able to copy itself, and complex objects must be able to copy all their components, ensuring that any relationships between the original objects are present between the copies. But unlike some design patterns, it does not add any inefficiency in time or space, nor does it increase the number of classes. Thus, it is an important and popular design pattern.

PATTERN LANGUAGES

The usual name for a set of patterns is a *pattern language*. A pattern language is more than just a set of patterns that work together, though. There is an order to a pattern language, and the goal is to be able to use a pattern language by going through it from beginning to end.

The patterns I've discussed (Composite, Decorator, Strategy, Prototype) are four of the 23 patterns in a book I'm writing with Erich Gamma, Richard Helm, and John Vlissides (*Design Patterns: Elements of Reusable Object-Oriented Software*). We should have the final version off to the publisher before this column is printed.

Our patterns are not a pattern language, because we do not impose an order on them. We describe how patterns like Decorator and Strategy are competitors, and we describe how patterns like Composite and Prototype work together, but we don't tell you the order that you should apply the patterns. One of the reasons is that we disagree about the order. For example, I tend to apply Prototype late in the design of a system, while John tends to apply it early. This is probably because he mostly uses C++, while I mostly use Smalltalk. Prototype is more important in C++ than in Smalltalk because it makes it easy to parameterize an object with the kinds of objects it will create, while Smalltalk programmers can use classes for that purpose. Probably each of us has our own pattern language, influenced partly by the environment we work in and by our past experience. This makes it hard to develop a common pattern language.

```
Composite (with level 1)
    TitleDecorator (with book title)
    Composite (with level 2)
        TitleDecorator (with chapter title)
        NumberDecorator
        Composite (with level 3)
            TitleDecorator (with section title)
            NumberDecorator
            Paragraph
            Paragraph
...
        Composite (with level 3)
            TitleDecorator
            NumberDecorator
            Paragraph
            Paragraph
        Composite (with level 2)
            TitleDecorator
            NumberDecorator
```

FIGURE 6   Instance hierarchies using normal DocumentComponents.

It isn't obvious that there ever will be a complete pattern language for developing software. Writing a compiler is different from writing a word processor, and they are both different from writing an accounting system. Many principles apply to all three, of course, but the theory of parsing only applies to compilers, user interface design principles are more important to a word processor, while database design is important for an accounting system. Although we could try to combine patterns for all these kinds of designs into one pattern language, it would seem to be better to keep them separate.

PATTERNS ARE NOT JUST FOR DESIGN

The patterns I have discussed are all design patterns. It would be easy to think that patterns are just about design. But there are many kinds of patterns, and they don't have to be about designing an object-oriented program or any kind of program. Christopher Alexander's *A Pattern Language* is about designing communities and buildings. Hal Hildebrand has developed a pattern language for using Tensegrity, his company's ODBMS. Kent Beck is working on a pattern language for using CRC cards. Jim Coplien is working on a pattern language for designing software development organizations. I had a paper in OOPSLA'92 about a pattern language for using

HotDraw. Patterns and pattern languages are useful ways of organizing all kinds of how-to information.

I think that pattern languages will eventually play a central role in software engineering. We will use pattern languages to write architecture handbooks, user manuals for frameworks and other software packages, and specifications of our software processes. We will describe our systems in terms of an underlying pattern language.

But we aren't there yet. None of the pattern languages for software that I mentioned is as well-developed as it should be. Developing a pattern language is difficult. But even the relatively unorganized sets of patterns in the design pattern catalog are extremely valuable. Even when patterns are not organized into a language, they still can be used together synergistically. As we organize them and add to them, they will become even more valuable.

A Report on PLoP'94

Ralph E. Johnson

johnson@cs.uiuc.edu

A conference titled Pattern Languages of Programs was held August 4–6 at Allerton Park in Monticello, Illinois. The goal of this conference, the first of its kind, was to expand the literature on patterns of programs and to explore the best form for describing software patterns. It succeeded, producing 30 papers on a wide range of topics in a wide range of styles. Twelve of the papers described pattern languages, while the others presented a single pattern in detail, described a set of related patterns without trying to structure them into a language, analyzed some existing patterns, or discussed some other aspect of patterns.

I'm going to describe a few of the papers on pattern languages so you can get an idea of what people interested in patterns are thinking about. (At the end of this article, you will find information on how you can get copies of the papers.)

A PATTERN LANGUAGE FOR CLIENT/SERVER APPLICATIONS

One of the papers I found most interesting was by Kirk Wolf and Chamond Liu. It contained a pattern language for frameworks for workstations communicating with legacy database systems. Lots of people are building applications like this, which accounts for a lot of my interest. But I learned something about the pattern form from the paper, too.

Wolf and Liu's pattern language says that the main jobs of a workstation client are searching for business objects, viewing them, and updating and creating them. It says to implement search with a Search object that represents both a search operation and its status. Search objects use mega-scrolling—they only return small collections of objects and so must be repeatedly invoked until the entire result is received. The pattern language says to ensure loose coupling between business objects and their views by using the Factory Method pattern and the Observer (also called the Dependency pattern). In addition, its says to avoid the time-and-screen real estate expense of creating new windows by using a singleton "window keeper" to keep track of windows that have already been created. After explaining how data is exchanged between the database and the client using Proxy, Requests as Objects, and Objects from Records, the pattern language says to use the Observer pattern again to propagate updates from the client to the server.

I'm always interested in comparing other people's patterns with the ones I have found.

Some of the patterns in the paper, such as Proxy, Observer, Singleton, and Factory Method, are in the design pattern catalog; still others are special cases of patterns in the catalog; still others are completely different or are higher-level patterns than are those in the catalog.

The Search object is a special case of the Command pattern. A Command is an object that represents an invocation of an operation. Before a Command is invoked, a program can modify its parameters. It can be passed as an argument to the point at which it is finally invoked, and it is often saved after it is invoked in case it needs to be undone. Commands are often used to represent operations in menus or in key maps.

A Search object defines the criteria for a search. Although it makes no sense to undo a search, a Search object is often created in one place and invoked in another. Search objects can be reused on different Files by passing them to those files. Searches can return a large number of objects. To keep from running out of memory, Search objects store the state of a search and let you retrieve the results a little at a time. It is unusual for a Command to be reused with different parameters or to return its results incrementally, so a Search object is not the most typical example of Command, but it seems to me to fit, since it represents the invocation of a search operation on a database.

The Exception pattern from Wolf and Liu's paper is common and would be a good candidate for the design pattern catalog. The Objects from Records pattern describes how to map data from the client to the host; therefore, it is more specialized than the patterns in the catalog. However, it is about the same level of abstraction as those patterns. Other patterns, such as the Viewing pattern, are both more specialized and more complex and are at a different level of abstraction.

I learned several things about patterns from this paper. Almost all the papers presented a pattern language top down. This has the advantage that early patterns set the context for later ones, but the disadvantage is that there are many forward references. This paper presented the patterns bottom up; I decided I like top down better. Context is more important than closure. If patterns have good names, I don't mind forward references, but I always want to know why a pattern is relevant, which means knowing its context.

I also learned something about the difference between a framework and a pattern language. Patterns and frameworks are obviously related, since they are both ways of conveying design information and are reusable. I usually say that frameworks are bigger, more domain specific, more complex, and more concrete than patterns, but this is not very precise. A better distinction might be that a framework *is* a design, while a pattern language tells you how to make one. A framework is like the standard house plans that many builders use. You can move some rooms around, customize the kitchen, and add a patio, but the basic design is fixed. A pattern language says what an architect will do when you tell him that you have eleven kids and your mother-in-law lives with you.

Given a choice between a framework and a pattern language, you should probably pick a framework. Frameworks provide more reuse and require less work to use. Pattern languages teach you how to do something, frameworks do it for you. On the other hand, pattern languages are more adaptable than frameworks. Frameworks are written in particular languages and often depend on a particular operating system. Moreover, frameworks don't solve all your problems. Sometimes you have to understand why the framework was designed the way it is, and you have to learn how to use the framework before it does you any good. Patterns can help you learn both how to use a framework and why it was designed the way it is.

In my opinion, Wolf and Liu's paper really describes a framework, not a pattern language. It describes the framework in terms of patterns, it describes a bunch of new patterns, and it uses the pattern form; so, it looks a lot like a pattern language. But it tells you exactly how many objects to have and how they interact. It doesn't provide choices but always follows the same path. The paper probably should have followed the form of "Patterns Generate Architectures," from ECOOP'94.

I hope I don't sound like I'm griping. I got a lot out of their paper. Now I have a much better idea how to build client/server systems. And I learned some new things about patterns. The purpose of PLoP was to generate papers like this. The art of writing patterns is still new, and we need a lot of experimentation. Since it is new, nearly everything we will do will need some improvement, and there is no way to avoid that.

A PATTERN LANGUAGE FOR CHECKING FOR INPUT ERRORS

Ward Cunningham wrote a pattern language called Checks that is about checking for errors in input data. Checks ensures data integrity while minimizing the number of checks in a program. Putting lots of checks in a program makes it large and inflexible, but not checking input data will corrupt your database. The pattern language resolves these opposing forces.

Checks starts with a fundamental pattern of object-oriented design, Whole Value. This pattern says to represent the meaningful quantities of your domain with special classes. In other words, don't represent money with integers, use a Money class. Don't use a string to represent a telephone number unless you are never going to do anything except display it. Interface widgets should produce and accept these values directly and not just edit numbers and strings.

Although Whole Value is more fundamental than checking input data, it is crucial to data integrity. All the other patterns in Checks build on it. The next two patterns give more information about these values and how they should behave. Exceptional Value says that each kind of data should allow exceptional values to represent errors. Interface widgets produce exceptional values on blank input and should produce blank output when given an exceptional value. Meaningless Behavior says that you shouldn't try to write methods that work under all conditions. Instead, meaningless behavior should result in exceptional values or should raise an exception, and the interface widgets should be expected to recover.

About half the patterns in Checks are about user interface design. Only one (Deferred Validation) is entirely about checking data. The strategy of the pattern language is to design a user interface in which most errors are detected automatically by the user, reducing the need for a lot of error checking. Deferred Validation says that detailed validation of a domain model should be deferred until an action is requested. This might be when a transaction is posted, or it might be when the user asks, "Is this OK?"—but it will always be at a time when the user will expect it. The pattern language sets the context for Deferred Validation, making it the only part of the program with explicit checks.

The patterns in Checks are very different from the patterns in the design pattern catalog, most of which are what Booch calls *mechanisms*. The design patterns are patterns of relationships between objects. But Checks is more about the design of a user interface than it is about the design of objects that implement it. I like Checks partly because it is so different (and thus shows the paper of the pattern form) and partly because it is so useful. Error checking is an important part of most designs, but it is a part that is usually ignored.

A PATTERN LANGUAGE FOR A SOFTWARE DEVELOPMENT GROUP

There were several more pattern languages that were not about design patterns, including one by Bruce Whitenack on requirements analysis and one by Norm Kerth on transforming analysis to design. Perhaps the most far out (and the most intriguing!) was written by Jim Coplien. To most people, Jim is known as the author of *Advanced C++ Programming,* but to the patterns community he is known as the "process guy." He has been using object-oriented analysis techniques to study the roles people play in software development teams. He has found some patterns that typify productive teams. He combined those patterns (as well as a lot of well-known patterns) to form a pattern language for a development process.

It is interesting to compare the software development patterns with design patterns. Some are a little like the patterns in the design pattern catalog. For example, Gatekeeper says that one of the project members should disseminate leading-edge information from outside the project-to-project members. Firewall says that the job of the manager is to shield other development personnel from being bothered by funders, customers, and other outsiders. These patterns are a lot like the Facade pattern, in which an object acts as the interface to a subsystem or framework. But most of the patterns in his language are not like any object-oriented design patterns. There are patterns about who writes documentation, who can be an architect, and how information flows from the customer to the developer. In contrast to most of what is written about the software development process, I found that Jim's paper told me what do do, and it made sense. That doesn't mean that it is right, of course. But it is at least testable, and as we use it, we can find out what works and what doesn't.

By the time you read this, the design pattern catalog should be at a bookstore near you. It is *Design Patterns: Elements of Reusable Object-Oriented Software,* by Erich Gamma, Richard Helm, Ralph Johnson, and John Vlissides. It is published by Addison-Wesley.

Patterns and Frameworks

Ralph E. Johnson

johnson@cs.uiuc.edu

I'm often asked, "What is the difference between a pattern and a framework?" According to the dictionary definition of a pattern, there isn't much difference. The *World Book Dictionary* gives 11 noun definitions for pattern, including the following: "A model or a guide for something to be made," which certainly matches a framework. But even a macro or a C++ template is a pattern according to that definition, and that is too broad to be useful.

The definition of a pattern that I use (which is Christopher Alexander's definition) is based on the realization that the reason there are reoccurring *solutions* is because there are reoccurring *problems.* Thus, the problem that a pattern solves is just as much a part of the pattern as is the particular arrangement of objects that makes up the solution. A pattern is therefore a solution to a problem in a context. This influences the way we describe them, and patterns are usually described using a form that points out the solution, problem, and context.

A framework like Model-View-Controller or InterViews is more than just a pattern—it is also code. It is a reusable design expressed as a set of abstract classes (i.e., code) and the way that instances of those classes interact. Since it includes the way instances of those classes interact, it is the collaborative model or pattern of object interaction as much as it is the kinds of classes in the design. A single framework will contain many of the patterns in *Design Patterns: Elements of Reusable Object-Oriented Software.*[1] Moreover, those patterns cannot be expressed as C++ or Smalltalk classes and then just reused by inheritance or composition. So, those patterns are both smaller and more abstract than frameworks.

The first part of this article will describe how Model-View-Controller is made up of simpler design patterns. It will reuse a couple of patterns I've talked about already and describe some new ones. The second part will revisit Model-View-Controller and try to find what someone might mean by "the MVC pattern."

MODEL-VIEW-CONTROLLER

MVC is probably the earliest framework that was recognized to be a framework. It was part of Smalltalk-80 and was the inspiration for later user interface frameworks like MacApp and the Andrew Toolkit, which in turn inspired Interviews, ET++, OWL, MFC, and all the other modern user interface frameworks. It has evolved a lot since its earliest days but still consists of three main classes: Model, View, and Controller. The Model is the application object, and represents the data that the program manipulates. The View manages a region of the display and is responsible for making sure that the region contains a picture that is a function of the state of the model. When the model changes state, the view must redraw the part of the screen that it manages. The Controller translates user actions (like pressing a key or moving the mouse) into operations on the View or the Model. Thus, it is responsible for user input.

MVC is usually treated as a single mechanism, but it is useful to break it down into smaller patterns. These patterns are easier to understand in isolation, they are often reused in other contexts, and it is easier to precisely define their purpose. There are three main patterns: Observer, which describes the relationship between Models and Views; Composite, which describes the relationship between Views and their subviews; and Strategy, which describes the relationship between Views and Controllers.

THE OBSERVER PATTERN

One of the most important steps in making reusable user interface components is to separate the application data from the user interface objects. A common way to do this is to make an object for each component of the user interface that we can see on the screen. In other words, buttons, input fields, scroll bars, and lists are all objects. But an application doesn't consist of buttons, input fields, and scroll bars. An invoice has a vendor, a due date, a total amount, and a list of items purchased. The objects in the interface have to be tied to the application objects in some way so that an invoice's vendor is displayed as a label or in an input field of the user interface for an invoice. When the vendor name or total amount changes in the application, the corresponding user interface objects must change their appearance.

How does a change in an application object cause a user interface object to change its appearance? There are lots of ways to accomplish this: user interface objects can register their interest in global "events," and application objects can notify user interface objects directly or indirectly. For the Observer pattern, observers (like user interface objects) register with subjects (like application objects) and are then notified when the subjects change their state. Each subject keeps track of its observers, and each time it changes state, the subject will notify all its observers. Although there is a kind of coupling between subject and observer, it does not cause trouble in practice, because it is quite abstract. A subject does not know the concrete class of its observer, though an observer often knows the class of its subject. The Subject class just supports a few operations to add an observer, to remove an observer, or to notify its observers. The Observer class only needs to support one operation: Update.

Here is a description of the Observer pattern, in pattern form. Note that it does not mention user interfaces. The Observer pattern can be used for more than just user interfaces.

- *Context.* Two objects must be synchronized. Changes in one object must be reflected in the other.
- *Problem.* If changing one object requires changing another then there is a constraint between them. But we don't want every client to have to know about this constraint. Moreover, we aren't even sure how many objects need to be changed when the first object is changed. Different instances of the same class might have different numbers of dependents, or the dependents might change over time.
- *Constraints.* To make objects as reusable as possible, we do not want to hard-code constraints into them. Objects should be responsible only for their own state, not for the state of other objects. On the other hand, if there is a constraint between the states of two objects, then that constraint must be recorded somewhere. In some way, changes to the first object must be translated into changes to the second.

Therefore:

- *Solution.* Have an object involved in a constraint and keep a list of dependents. Each time it changes, it notifies all its dependents.

> When an object is notified that something it depends on has changed, it takes appropriate action. In general, an object can have many dependents, and a change to the object will require only some of its dependents to change. But each dependent will be able to determine whether the change to the object was significant and can ignore those that are not.

In practice, the Observer pattern leads to loosely linked objects that communicate indirectly.

It is easy to write new observers or to add new observers to an existing design, because the observers just have to support the Update operation, and a new observer just has to register itself with the subject it is observing. However, it can be hard to design Subject classes correctly, because they must be written to notify their observers whenever there is a significant change. The biggest problem, however, is that the abstract coupling makes it hard to imagine the effects of a change to a design. For example, if you give a subject a new operation that makes several changes to its state, you might end up notifying its observers several times, which might be inefficient or result in annoying redraws of the screen. Although the loose coupling makes most changes easy, when a change leads to unpredicted behavior, it can be hard to figure out why. Although the Observer pattern causes problems as well as solving them, its advantages are strong enough that it is used in most user interface frameworks.

There are many variations on the Observer pattern. In the Smalltalk-80 dependence mechanism, class Object supports both the Observer and the Subject protocol. Thus, any object can be an observer or a subject, and sometimes an object is both. Class Model is a subclass of Object that implements the Subject interface more efficiently. Class View is the Observer. In C++, where it is unlikely that you will have a universal Object class, you will probably have a separate Subject and Observer class. Another design choice is what the arguments of the Notify operation will be. In Smalltalk-80, where the operation is called update:, this argument is traditionally a symbol, which denotes the aspect of the state of the observer that changed. This does not have much expressive power, so often there is a new class hierarchy for describing update events.

MVC eliminates some of the potential pitfalls of the Observer pattern. In particular, you don't have to worry about registering or unregistering observers when you use MVC, because a view will automatically register itself as a dependent of its model.

The Composite pattern

I've said a lot about the Composite pattern in earlier articles, so I won't say much about it here. In short, the Composite pattern lets you group a set of objects together and treat them as a single object. The main use of Composite in MVC is to let you group a set of views together and treat them as a single view. In the original MVC, every view had a set of subviews, so any view could be used as a composite. However, most subclasses of View never had any subviews and never would. Thus, the original design was a mistake, and it was changed so that instead of View having a set of subviews, there was a class CompositeView that had a set of subviews. Now, you can make a set of radio buttons by creating a CompositeView and giving it some Buttons as subviews. The Buttons all have the same model, but each has a different value that they will give to their model if they are pushed. When the state of the model changes, they compare the new value with their value to see whether they are pressed.

MVC uses some other patterns that are closely related to Composite. It uses Decorator (called Wrapper in Smalltalk) to add borders or scroll bars to Views or to change the way they are clipped or positioned. It uses Adaptor to customize the interface between Views and Models, thereby making Views more reusable. It uses Abstract Factory to create views, thereby making it easier to change the look and feel of an application. But all these patterns are enhanced by the fact that there is a universal View interface and that a set of views can be treated as a single view, so in some sense they all follow from the Composite pattern.

THE STRATEGY PATTERN

Many user-interface frameworks do not separate views from controllers but instead have a single user interface object. A common criticism of MVC is that views and controllers are tightly coupled, and you cannot mix views and controllers arbitrarily. A text controller only works with a text view, and a list controller only works with a list view. A critic might claim that it is misleading to provide two separate class hierarchies when there is only one way to combine them.

The best way to think about controllers is that they are components of views. A view delegates to its controller responsibility for handling user input. The original MVC hid this fact, because a controller would communicate with other controllers (the controllers of its subclass's subviews, to be exact). But the current version of MVC routes all operations to the view, which then delegates them to its controller. Thus, it is easier to see that the controller is just a component of the view.

Separating controllers from views sometimes lets you mix and match them. For example, you can give any view a NoController as a controller, and it will then ignore all user input. It also divides the responsibility of a view into two pieces along a natural boundary, making each easier to understand. The view keeps track of screen real estate and knows how to translate data elements to screen coordinates and vice versa, while the controller keeps track of the mouse and keyboard and translates user events into operations on the view and model.

THE MODEL-VIEW-CONTROLLER PATTERN

The patterns I've described don't completely cover Model-View-Controller. For example, they don't tell you that it is not all that common to subclass View and Controller, that in practice you can usually just combine instances of existing classes to make a user interface. Some of the things you need to know about MVC come from the design of individual classes rather than from the framework as a whole. So, what is the MVC pattern? Does it just consist of a set of simpler patterns, or is it something different?

In *Patterns Generate Architecture,*[2] Kent Beck and I described the MVC pattern in the following way:

1. Model-View-Controller.
   Context. A system is going to have a graphical user interface.
   Problem. Graphical user interfaces can be hard to build. Users demand programs that are easy to use, easy to learn, and power-ful, and a good user interface is necessary to achieve these goals. How should the responsibilities of implementing a user interface be divided between objects?
   Constraints. Modern graphical user interfaces have a small number of recurring visual elements. Because user interfaces need to be consis-tent, we depend on a few interaction techniques, such as menus, buttons, scrollbars, and lists. The effort that someone puts into learn-ing how to use one program, or one part of one program, should apply to other programs and other parts of the same program.
   A user interface design must strike a balance between one that uses many objects but is difficult to learn and one that uses few

objects and sacrifices flexibility. One axis of flexibility is the information that is displayed. A second axis of flexibility, independent of display, is interpreting user gestures and mapping them into state changes. A third degree of freedom is the ability to put multiple user interfaces on the same information. This leads us to the following:

Solution. Divide your system into three objects: a Model, a View, and a Controller. The Model is responsible for maintaining state and surfacing the behavior necessary to support the user interface. The View is responsible for displaying an up-to-date version of the Model. The Controller is responsible for mapping user gestures to changes of state in the model.

This is a higher level pattern than the ones described earlier, but it is still a design pattern. It focuses on the kinds of objects you should have, and it could be described by an object diagram. It is possible to think of MVC not as a design pattern, but as a development strategy. In fact, I think this is a more accurate description of why people use MVC.

2. Model-View-Controller.

Context. You are a Smalltalk-80 application programmer.

Problem. You need to build a graphical user interface, but none of the existing components provide what you need.

Constraints. If none of the existing components provide what you need, it might be easier to build them from scratch than to try to modify MVC to support your needs. On the other hand, your user interface should fit in with that of the rest of the system. Your system needs to be maintainable, reusable, and reliable. You aren't in the user-interface framework business, but in the application business, so any time you spend writing your own user interface components is time you don't spend on your real business. Therefore . . .

Solution. Use MVC. Don't create a new user-interface framework unless you are willing to support it and to rewrite it for each new version of Smalltalk.

In my opinion, the main reason that people use MVC is because it is the standard user interface framework of the environment in which they are programming. People who are not using Smalltalk don't use MVC, they use whatever user-interface framework they can get their hands on. People do not pick MVC because its design is perfect, they pick it because it is good enough, it is available, and they know how to use it. Thus, the real pattern that people are following is the second one. Or maybe I'm just cynical!

Frameworks are a kind of pattern. But they are not patterns on the same level the design patterns are. They are composed of many design patterns, they are represented by code, and they are much more complex. In fact, it can take a whole set of patterns just to describe how to use a single framework, as I showed in "Documenting Frameworks with Patterns."[3]

Given a choice between solving a problem using a framework and solving it using some other kind of pattern, I usually go with a framework. Because frameworks are code, you can reuse them by calling or including the code in your program. Patterns that are not code have to be understood and then followed. I'd rather reuse a text editor than follow patterns for building a text editor and build it from scratch. But there are many problems that can't be solved by building a framework. One of them is obviously how to use the framework. Frameworks are expensive to build and not always worth the effort. Thus, there are many times that you have to reuse knowledge instead of reusing code. Both ways of reusing design are important.

REFERENCES

1. Gamma, E., R. Helm, R. Johnson, and J. Vlissides. *Design Patterns: Elements of Object-Oriented Software Architecture,* Addison-Wesley, Reading, MA, 1995.
2. Beck, K., and R. Johnson. Patterns generate architectures, ECOOP '94 Proceedings, *Springer-Verlag Lecture Notes in Computer Science* #821:139–149, July 1994.
3. Johnson, R. Documenting frameworks with patterns, OOPSLA '92 Proceedings, *SIGPLAN Notices,* 27(10):63–76, Vancouver, BC, October 1992.

Patterns and Antipatterns

Andrew Koenig

ark@research.att.com

Every once in a while an idea comes along that promises to be widely influential, even though in retrospect it seems obvious. Such ideas often attract hype, precisely because of their promise: people see an opportunity to profit from them and take it. Sometimes the hype can even obscure the original idea. Still, the mere presence of hype surrounding an idea does not mean that the idea is not worthwhile. Otherwise, we would have to abandon useful ideas as soon as enough other people discovered them.

The idea in this case is simple to describe: write down things good designers do, to help other people do similar things. I've been doing that in some of my columns. But until recently, I haven't been aware of any systematic effort to find such things and present them in the form of a catalog.

That is no longer true. I recently received a copy of a new book by Erich Gamma, Richard Helm, Ralph Johnson, and John Vlissides called *Design Patterns—Elements of Reusable Object-Oriented Software* (Addison-Wesley, 1995), which is primarily a catalog of useful design techniques.

Before continuing, I have three confessions to make. First, I have not read the entire book. This article is therefore not a book review in the ordinary sense. Instead, it is a discussion of ideas and a suggestion that this book, and other related things that will surely come along, will probably interest people who are interested in this discussion.

Second, although I do not consider myself a member of the community that produced this book, I am not a disinterested observer either. This work was first brought to my attention by Jim Coplien, an AT&T colleague of long standing. He has also written a book, called *Advanced C++ Programming Styles and Idioms* (Addison-Wesley, 1992), which is one of the few books with "advanced" in its title that truly means it. It was Jim who introduced me to the notion of design patterns and the book by that name. If even a small fraction of potential readers share his enthusiasm, I expect the book and the ideas will be very influential indeed.

Finally, because I am a newcomer to this community, I'm sure that some readers will find familiar some of the things that follow. Some ideas are worth encountering several times, however, and the notion of a pattern is probably one of them.

WHAT IS A PATTERN?

A pattern is a useful way of thinking about and solving a particular class of problem in a context. Moreover, as described in the design patterns book, every pattern has a name. Names are important in general, and if we can get into the habit of assigning widely accepted names to important design or programming techniques, we will have a much easier time talking about them.

For example, people talking about abstract algorithms use names for particular classes of algorithms. An example is the idea of a *maximal munch* algorithm in lexical analysis, which is what decrees that

```
x=y/*p;
```

does not divide y by the object pointed to by p but instead begins a comment. The idea behind maximal munch is that the lexical analyzer consumes as many characters as can possibly be part of a token, regardless of whether the resulting token makes sense in the surrounding context. Maximal munch, in turn, is an example of a *greedy algorithm,* which is a term used to describe algorithms that try to extend things as much as they can right away. Another kind of algorithm is *divide and conquer.* Such algorithms solve problems by reducing them to subproblems and then solving those, usually recursively. When thinking about what algorithm to use to solve a particular problem, a hint like "a greedy algorithm won't work here because . . ." may be just the thing one needs to find the right solution.

In addition to having a name, a pattern describes a problem, a solution, and the consequences of using the pattern. By "consequences" I mean the things that make the problem a problem and the solution a solution. In practice it is rare for solutions to be "right" or "wrong." Instead, a proposed solution will typically do some things well and other things less well. We can imagine that there are several desirable states of affairs that cannot all be true at once, so we have to trade one off against another.

AN EXAMPLE OF A PATTERN

One pattern the book describes is called Factory Method. The description runs to 10 pages, including examples and diagrams, so I won't try to present it in full detail. Instead, I will try to capture its essentials and refer interested readers to the book.

One useful way of organizing extensible systems in object-oriented languages, including C++, is as *application frameworks.* An application framework is a skeletal application made up of a collection of classes, with the idea that the user will use inheritance (or other techniques such as template parameterization) to define new classes that will add flesh to the skeleton. For example, a framework for applications with graphical user interfaces might contain classes that display menus and react to menu selections and then leave it to the programmer (that is, to the user of the framework, not the user of the finished application) to say what specific menu selections this particular application should offer and what they should do.

Such a framework may also have classes that represent the data structure common to all applications. Again, these classes will presumably represent only the common parts, with the assumption that the programmer will define specific classes that will implement the data structures needed for the specific applications.

Among other things, then, an application framework is a collection of classes that can be simultaneously extended along two or more dimensions. This presents an interesting problem: how can those extensions be made aware of each other?

To make this question concrete, I'll use the example from the book. Suppose we are writing an application framework for dealing with various kinds of documents. The data structures will then include documents, so we will define a class Document. We will also have a class Application, and we will tell people that they should write their own applications by deriving from class Application. Of course, there are some things that every application should be able to do. One of these things is creating a new document. We would therefore like to include in our Application class code for creating a new Document.

But that will never do. Class Document exists only as a base class for others to derive from. Indeed, it is likely that class Document will be an abstract base class. So the obvious solution, namely saying something like:

```
Document* dp = new Document;
```

inside some member of class Application, won't work. At best, it will fail to compile because Document is an abstract base class. At worst, it will do the wrong thing because it will create a Document object instead of an object of the appropriate derived class.

So what do we do? The Factory Method pattern tells us that we should first take the notion of creating a document and make it a class. We give that class a member function to do the creating and make that member function virtual:

```
class DocumentCreator {
public:
    virtual Document* create();
};
```

This means that if we have a pointer to a DocumentCreator object called, say, cp:

```
DocumentCreator* cp;
```

then we can create a Document by saying

```
Document* dp = cp->create();
```

The point of this is that what we are creating need no longer be of class Document. Instead, it can be of any class derived from Document. For example, an application for dealing with newspapers might say something like this:

```
class Newspaper: public Document {
    // ...
};
class NewspaperCreator:
    public DocumentCreator {
public:
    // This overrides DocumentCreator::create
    Document* create() {
        return new Newspaper;
    }
};
```

and if cp points at a NewspaperCreator object, then dp will point at a newly created Newspaper object. The point is that when writing:

```
Document* dp = cp->create();
```

it is unnecessary to know anything about the Newspaper or NewspaperCreator classes, or even that they exist at all.

This technique makes it possible to create various kinds of documents directly within class Application. It only requires that whoever extends class Application ensure that the appropriate variable of type DocumentCreator has the appropriate value—and of course that would be necessary anyway.

The description of Factory Method is, of course, much more detailed than I have given here. There is a full page of motivation, including a diagram, followed by a paragraph that describes when Factory Method is applicable. Then comes another diagram that describes the solution, a half page explaining the structure of the solution, and another half page explaining the advantages and disadvantages of the technique.

The next five and a half pages give implementation details, both in C++ and Smalltalk, including complete C++ code examples. Finally, there is a half page of pointers to places where this pattern has been used successfully and a few pointers to related patterns.

ANTIPATTERNS

There is a rapidly growing community of people who are intensely involved in finding and cataloging new patterns. While I do not consider myself a member of that community, I would like to make a suggestion that I hope will turn out to be worthwhile.

The suggestion is inspired by a story told about Thomas Edison. While he was trying to build the first electric light, he tried hundreds of possible materials for filaments. Every experiment came out a failure. At some point, someone remarked to him that all those failures must be discouraging. He responded that he was not discouraged—after all, he now knew hundreds of things that didn't work.

If one does not know how to solve a problem, it may nevertheless be useful to know about likely blind alleys. This is particularly true when something appears at first to be a solution but further analysis proves it is not. Even if one knows the right answer, however, it may be important to point out particular hazards associated with that answer or seemingly trivial variations of that answer that turn solutions into non-solutions.

I have coined the term *antipattern* to refer to such non-solutions. An antipattern is just like a pattern, except that instead of a solution it gives something that looks superficially like a solution but isn't one. If an antipattern is coupled with a pattern, it might be tempting to think of it as a pattern-antipattern pair. This would impart a certain energy to the situation.

Here is an example of an antipattern. The problem is defining comparison in a dynamically typed programming language, particularly one that has types including strings and integers. Because the language is dynamically typed, it is not possible to tell until execution time just what kind of comparison is being done. For example, if we have an expression like x<y, the < could conceivably mean completely different things depending on whether x and y are numbers, strings, or one of each.

If x and y are both numbers, comparison is trivial: There is no question about what it means to compare numbers. If x and y are both strings, comparison is slightly less trivial, but dynamically typed languages usually define string comparison in terms of character comparison by using a notion of "dictionary order." The algorithm is to scan the strings from left to right, a character at a time, looking for a character of x that is different from the corresponding character of y. One of the following three things will happen:

- Such a character will be found. In that case, the result of the string comparison is the result of comparing the relevant characters. Thus, for example, temerity is less than temporary because e is less than p.
- We will run out of characters in one string while there are still characters in the other. Then we say the shorter string is a *prefix* of the other and define that one as being the smaller of the two. Thus short is less than shorter.
- We will exhaust both strings at the same time, in which case they are equal.

We know how to compare two numbers and how to compare two strings. What about comparing a number to a string? Here is where the antipattern part comes in. There are a number of reasonable ways to answer this question, but one way is both obvious and wrong: convert the number to a string and compare the strings.

We note first that doing it the other way doesn't work. We can't convert the string to a number because not every string can be converted to a number. But people convert numbers to strings all the time and, in most such languages, every number can be converted to a string. What is wrong with just comparing the strings?

The answer is that such a rule results in a comparison operator that is not an order relation. In particular, it does not have the desirable property of *transitivity:* if x<y and y<z then x<z. The first sign of trouble is to note that

when treating numbers as strings, the leading digits are compared with each other. So, for example, although 3<20 when treated as numbers, "3">"20" when treated as strings because the comparison finds an inequality at the first character of each string.

If we were dealing only with strings, this would not be a problem: defining < this way might look a little weird to strings that happen to look like numbers, but it would still define an order relation. The trouble comes when the "same" value is treated as a number in one context and a string in the other.

To expose the problem, let's try to find three values that violate transitivity. To do that, we will have to have a mixture of numeric and string comparisons. If two of our values were strings, every comparison would have to be a string comparison, so two of them will have to be numbers. If they were all numbers, we would have no string comparisons, so we must look for two numbers and one string.

The obvious way to exploit the ambiguity is to pick a pair of numbers that will compare one way as numbers and the other way as strings. We already have two such, namely 3 and 20. We need only find a string s such that "3">s and s>"20". One such string is "21".

Let's check if this works (fails?) the way we want. First we will compare 3 with "21". This involves converting 3 to a string, and sure enough we find that "3">"21". Next we will compare "21" and 20, which must be converted to a string. Sure enough, "21">"20". Finally, of course, 20>3.

If you don't think this is a problem, find a language that does comparisons this way and try sorting an array that contains these three values.

I suspect it is going to be more difficult to catalog antipatterns than patterns. For one thing, people would rather boast about successes than about failures. Still, I am completely serious when I say that it can be useful to know about things that look like they should work but don't.

CONCLUSION

I have no doubt that in the next year or two, the work "pattern" will start springing up everywhere. We will see all kinds of things having to do with patterns: books, papers, conferences, software, and maybe even mugs and T-shirts. If this happens, try not to let the hype overwhelm the fact that there is real substance here.

Design is hard, and good design even harder. If I can obtain a collection of design techniques, well explained, that have proven to be useful in practice, I'm willing to ignore quite a bit of hype to get it.

Design Reuse:
Chemical Engineering vs.
Software Engineering

Paul Kogut

kogut@Paoli.ATM.LMCO.COM

INTRODUCTION

In mature engineering disciplines (e.g., chemical and civil engineering), systems (e.g., chemical plants and buildings) are commonly developed from reusable architectures and designs. Software engineering began implementing reuse at the code level but, in order to get higher leverage, software engineering is now beginning to develop and adopt architecture level reuse techniques that are characteristic of mature engineering disciplines. The key to design reuse is the use of models to capture design knowledge and facilitate early analyses of system properties. This paper will examine how design models are used in chemical engineering to gain insight that can be applied to software engineering.

ENGINEERING DESIGN

In mature engineering disciplines, most design is routine rather than innovative.[1] Figure 1 shows the design knowledge evolution process. Innovative designs are often prototyped and then implemented in one or more full-scale systems before becoming routine. The knowledge for routine design is captured, organized, and shared in the form of handbooks, published designs, and design standards. Handbooks are used by practitioners and students in the engineering community. Detailed designs are published in books/journals and they are often licensed. Design standards are used to share design knowledge in an organization or corporation. These design

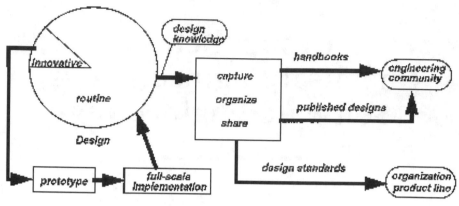

FIGURE 1   Design knowledge evolution process.

standards are often proprietary and very specific to product lines. These design knowledge dissemination techniques lead to extensive design reuse.

The distinction between routine and innovative design is obviously not binary. The distinction can be further understood in terms of the problem space (i.e., application functionality) and the solution space (i.e., the actual design). In mature engineering disciplines most design is routine both in the problem space and the solution space. In software engineering, more than 85% of the problem space is routine (i.e., not "unique, novel, and specific to individual applications") but much of the solution space in many domains (except e.g., compilers) is innovative because designs are not systematically reused.[2] When designs are reused in software engineering, it is often by default (i.e., blind application of old designs) and reuse depends heavily on the knowledge in the head of a human expert because of the lack of handbooks, published designs, and design standards.

ARCHITECTURE ANALOGIES

In order to study design in mature engineering disciplines, it is necessary to make analogies that help overcome the differences in concepts and terminology. The primary concept for design reuse in software engineering is software architecture. In this paper a software architecture is loosely defined as the organizational structure of a software system including components, connectors, and constraints.[3,4]

Software architectures, building architectures, chemical processes, and other kinds of architectures are all systems that are "wholes" which are "more than the sum of their parts."[5] The analogies of software architecture to computer architecture and network architectures are natural for those in computer science. However, Perry and Wolf[3] point out that these analogies are limited because they have a small number of component types and topologies compared to software architecture.

The currently popular building architecture analogy for software architecture is informative. Both architects and civil engineers are involved in designing a building. Architects do the preliminary conceptual and spatial design of a building, while civil engineers do the detailed design including structural analysis. The perspective from civil engineering is quite valuable because of the emphasis on design reuse and analytical methods for validating designs. The perspective from architects is less informative in that they place too much emphasis on aesthetics, which is not a major factor for software architecture. Architects are also heavily concerned with analyzing the requirements for the building rather than the detailed design. The current fad in the object-oriented community is to cite the work of Christopher Alexander an architect, writer, and mathematician.[6] The main valuable insight from Alexander is his emphasis on the use of patterns for design, which is cognitively realistic. Recognition and manipulation of patterns is as important in design as it is in almost any complex human activity (e.g., music).

The analogy between a chemical process and a software architecture is even more informative than the building architecture analogy. A chemical process has inputs (often with random variations within a certain range), processing (often continuous), and the outputs (under user control). A building is fairly static in comparison. A chemical process has a rich set of component types (called unit operations) and topologies. Graph theory has been applied to represent chemical processes[5] as well as software architectures.

Figure 2 shows a typical chemical process. Chemical processes are made up of unit operations and material flows. This alcohol distillation process takes an alcohol-water mixture as an input feed and processes it into absolute alcohol (100% ethanol). Benzene is added to help the distillation columns (A, C, and D in Figure 2) do this separation process. The process shown in Figure 2 along with other supporting data and guidelines is a generic design for a family of chemical plants. Each plant may differ in capacity, design of the individual unit operations, and composition of raw material and product streams, but they would all be derived from the same generic design. The chemical process is analogous to the domain specific software architectures found in software engineering such as object-oriented frameworks.[8,9] Table 1 shows the mapping between chemical process

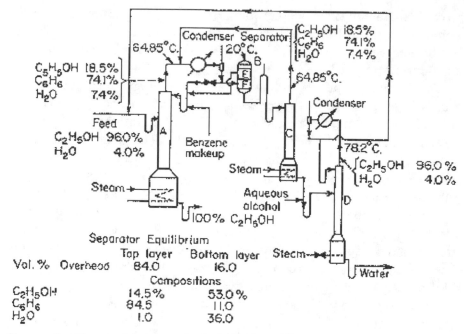

FIGURE 2   Chemical process: alcohol distillation.[*]

terminology and software architecture terminology. Most unit operations have complicated scalable internal designs but they are treated like black boxes. Unit operations are designed and built by specialized niche companies. The situation is similar to niche companies for components found in software engineering (e.g., database management systems). The process is organized based on constraints and the mode of operation. The process is represented in a standard flowchart format (i.e., a graphical/textual language that is not specific to a particular chemical process). Chemical engineers frequently apply an abstraction of a set of functionally related unit operations called a "system" when describing a process (a process usually has more than one system—see section on Patterns that follows). These systems perform a certain abstract functionality which is useful for the production of many different kinds of chemicals. A specific process (e.g., sulfur burning contact sulfuric acid process) includes specific unit operations (e.g., burner, absorbing tower) connected in a constrained but not fixed topology. A great deal of domain specific knowledge is associated with the specific process[*] (e.g., control parameters, maintenance schedules).

---

[*] From Perry, Chilton.

TABLE 1   Mapping of Terminology

Chemical Process Terms	Chemical Process Examples	Software Architecture Terms	Software Architecture Examples
Unit operations	Heat exchanger	Components	Database
Material flows	Pipes, conveyors	Connectors	Pipes, messages
Operation	Batch, continuous	Architecture styles	Batch sequential, pipes & filters
Constraints on choice and placement of unit operations	A mixer must precede a settler in an extraction system	Constraints on choice and placement of components	Lexical analyzer must precede a parser in a compiler
Systems (subprocesses)	Extraction, distillation	Patterns (microarchitectures)	Object oriented patterns
Process flowchart standard	See symbols in Figure 2	Architecture representation language	Rapide[29]
Specific chemical process	Sulfur burning contact sulfuric acid process	Domain specific software architecture	Generic command center architecture
Chemical plant	Sulfuric acid plant	Application system	Command center

The remaining sections of this paper will discuss how chemical engineers reuse design through handbooks, published processes, and corporate design standards based on the above analogy. These practices will be compared to current and emerging practices in software engineering.

HANDBOOKS

Handbooks are a pervasive technique for sharing design knowledge in mature engineering disciplines. Chemical engineering has one main handbook (usually referred to as Perry's Handbook)[7] that has more breadth and depth than any of the fragmented set of existing software engineering handbooks/textbooks[10-20] (this is not an exhaustive list). Perry's Handbook has over 1000 "telephone book" style pages. It is updated about every 10 years and it is now on its 6th edition.

PERRY VS. KNUTH . . .

Perry's Handbook gives comprehensive coverage of most unit operations and material flow equipment, including background knowledge, formulas, data, and extensive design guidelines. It contains enough information to do a complete routine design from a published process (see section on Routine Design that follows) and is a good starting point for synthesizing a new process (innovative design). Some of the existing software engineering handbooks cover certain types of components and algorithms in detail.[10,13,17] Most, but not all (e.g., *Datapro Reports*[16]) software engineering handbooks deal with small grained components/algorithms (vs. large grained components like databases) that are at a lower level of abstraction than unit operations. Other handbooks focus on design methods,[12] design analysis methods,[18] or design patterns.[19] None of these books individually, or even all the books collectively, match the level of information in Perry's. It is interesting to note that Perry's Handbook has over 100 authors due to the amount of expertise required (a true community effort). The software engineering handbooks do not have near this level of community participation.

Perry's Handbook is a good model for how a handbook should be written and organized. It is organized into sections with functionally grouped categories of unit operations, each covering principles followed by design guidelines. The handbook format supports quick location and understanding of design information. The existing software engineering handbooks are sometimes more like textbooks for sequenced learning or they are hard to use collections of detailed information.

Perry's has a section on cost and profitability estimation based on the plant design. This demonstrates the emphasis on economics in mature engineering fields. Many software engineering handbooks only address processing and memory resources rather than cost. Software engineering cost estimating techniques are not yet as directly tied to design factors.

KNOWLEDGE REPRESENTATION

There are 2 main facilitators for design knowledge sharing that exist in Perry's Handbook and other chemical engineering literature: a common language and a shareable ontology. The common language of chemical engineering is mathematics and chemistry. Many design notions are communicated in the form of equations with well-defined variables. The language of chemical formulas is also pervasive. There are also fairly standard graphical symbols for unit operations in process flowcharts. In software engineering there is a proliferation of design notations (e.g., Booch diagrams, Object Modeling Technique diagrams, Statecharts), development standards (e.g., IEEE, DOD), and programming languages (e.g., Ada, C++). This language problem has been recognized by others (e.g., Booch[21]) and must be overcome in order to reduce the barriers to design reuse.

Perry's Handbook defines a shareable ontology for the field of chemical engineering. This ontology is a common model of the domain which goes beyond a common language. An ontology is an explicit specification of a simplified view of the world including the objects, concepts, and relations that are assumed to exist in some domain.[22] Recent work in the ARPA Knowledge Sharing Initiative at Stanford has focused on the design of ontologies that promote sharing of knowledge between knowledge based systems. These shareable ontologies also promote sharing of knowledge between humans. A shareable ontology is an ontology that meets the following design criteria:[22]

- clarity—unambiguous definitions
- coherence—internally consistent
- extensibility—anticipate uses
- minimal encoding bias—doesn't lock into one language
- minimal ontological commitment—doesn't make too many assumptions

Perry's Handbook defines commonly accepted ontologies of unit operations and material flows. These ontologies are well documented, although they might not meet all the criteria for a shareable ontology. The following is an example of an ontology found in Perry's: Columns and heat exchangers are two types of unit operations. Shell and tube, air cooled, and evaporators are types of heat exchangers. Fixed tube sheet and U tube are types of shell and tube heat exchangers. Shell and tube heat exchangers have different functionnaire categories including chiller, condenser, superheater, and cooler. Perry's Handbook is also based on the common ontology of chemistry.

Ontologies of varying levels of formality exist in software engineering and computer science. These include fragmented ontologies for components (e.g., relational and object-oriented are two categories of database management systems) and other design entities (e.g., features or parameters that distinguish instances of components). However they are not as standardized and documented as in chemical engineering. Existing ontologies cover only a few very common component types (e.g., compilers, databases).

Features of certain component types are scattered throughout the literature (e.g., *Datapro Reports*[16] lists features used for comparing certain types of component products). There are many problems with developing a common ontology for software components and other design entities. Software tends to reflect the application domain. There is no consistency of component names between and within application domains. The common features of components evolve rapidly. Reuse libraries have had a difficult time classifying components. Part of the reason for this was their early focus on small grained components. It is also difficult to determine when a component is generic enough to warrant classification.[23]

Patterns

Another important design reuse facilitator found in Perry's Handbook are systems of unit operations. These show the typical pattern or context in which the unit operation is used. These systems show how certain types of unit operations collaborate to do a certain stage of a process. They allow the designer to understand a process by providing an abstraction. These systems are also building blocks for synthesizing new processes or modifying existing ones. Figure 3 shows a good example of systems or patterns of unit operations that are interspersed in Perry's with unit operations design guidance. Liquid extraction systems take advantage of differences in solubility to extract a liquid from a solution. A discussion of heuristics and design trade-offs related to these patterns is also found in the handbook.

Software engineering is just beginning to capture and organize a wide range of information about patterns. Textbooks generally contain a few patterns to illustrate some typical designs in a domain (e.g., compilers) or the effective use of a certain programming language. The object-oriented community is currently cataloging patterns of objects that recur in real systems.[24,25] These patterns or "micro-architectures" are being categorized in a taxonomy and documented in a descriptive framework (e.g., intent, applicability, participants, collaborators, diagram). The term micro-architecture is used because they are a configuration of objects and classes which would be combined with other micro-architectures to synthesize and understand an application system in the same way that is done with patterns of unit operations in chemical engineering. This pattern cataloging is a great step toward design reuse in software engineering. In the future these patterns should move up a level of abstraction to large grained components instead of the fine grained implementation oriented objects that are currently being cataloged.

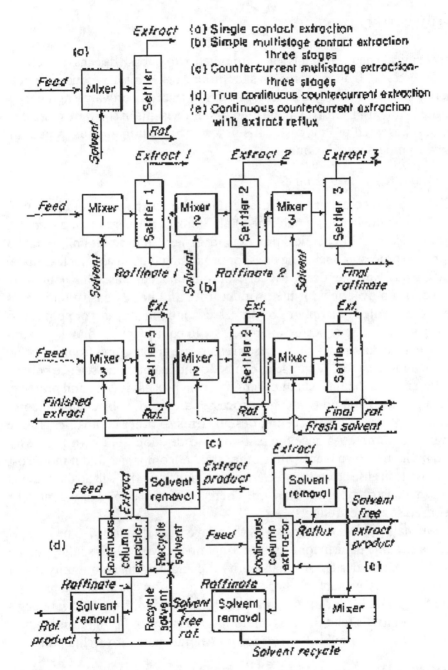

(a) Single contact extraction
(b) Simple multistage contact extraction
       three stages
(c) Countercurrent multistage extraction-
       three stages
(d) True continuous countercurrent extraction
(e) Continuous countercurrent extraction
       with extract reflux

FIGURE 3   Patterns—liquid extraction systems.*

* From Perry, Chilton.

PUBLISHED DESIGNS

In chemical engineering it is standard practice to publish designs (i.e., chemical processes). Industrial processes for producing chemical products are published more frequently and in more detail than in software engineering (note "industrial"—many published system designs in software engineering are research prototypes). This practice has a tremendous impact on how routine design is done.

PUBLISHING MECHANISMS

Chemical processes are published in handbooks, patents, and journals. There is a widely known published handbook of processes that covers the entire spectrum of chemical process industries.[26] It describes more than a hundred processes, including ones for producing fuels, glass, nuclear materials, acids, agrichemicals, rubber, and pharmaceuticals. This handbook serves as an overview for the product lines and has extensive references to more detailed descriptions of processes found in journals or pointers to companies who may license the process. No equivalent handbook for software engineering exists, although some software architectures from a specific application area (e.g., compilers) can be found in computer science books.

Patenting a detailed chemical engineering process is common practice. Both patented and non-patented processes are licensed by chemical companies or chemical engineering design firms to other companies. Large chemical companies have the resources to develop their own processes and build their own plants while other smaller companies find it more cost effective to license processes from an engineering firm who will do the detailed design, construction, and start-up. There are few examples of patented or licensed software architectures.

Journals publish new processes that have been developed. The journal serves as a mechanism for disseminating innovative designs so they can be used in routine design. Journals notify the engineering community that a new process is available for licensing. Figure 4 is an example of a process, which is available for license, that was found in a journal. Software engineering journals tend to focus on design methods and programming languages instead of publishing industrial strength software architectures.

ROUTINE DESIGN

The existence of published and licensable processes leads to a routine design approach that emphasizes the engineering mindset of composing

S&W and Chevron licensing deal

The end of October saw more activity in hydrotreating technology. Stone & Webster won exclusive rights to offer Chevron's established Vacuum Gas Oil hydrotreating and mild hydrocracking processes.

These fixed-bed, mixed-phase technologies are well proven. Chevron has 79 installations worldwide. The systems are based on nobel metal catalysts.

Don Mulraney, S&W's director of process engineering, says: 'Chevron has been a world leader in this area for some time. They are now directing any enquiries to us. We are forecasting a continuing high level of interest, with one or more awards [projects] in 1994.'

Chevron's schemes boast particular attention to energy efficiency, safe plant layout and equipment reliability.

Stone & Webster expects most of the business from the deal to come in from outside the US market.

211 on enquiry card

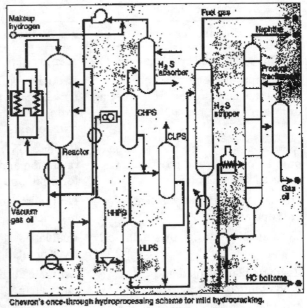

Chevron's once-through hydroprocessing scheme for mild hydrocracking.

FIGURE 4   Licensable process.[*]

solutions from past experience. Table 2 shows the analogy of routine design by refining a published process[27,28] to routine design by refining a domain specific software architecture (DSSA) based on detailed requirements (not yet standard practice). The design steps in the table do not have to be performed in the strict order shown.

Identifying an appropriate chemical process may require a significant amount of research and negotiation but often a company sticks with a product line which it is familiar with. The identification of appropriate DSSAs is either trivial or fruitless based on the scarcity of DSSAs currently available and in use; however, this is expected to change in the future. The synthesis of a new chemical process from unit operation patterns and lab data is straightforward (but not easy). Until software design patterns are available in cataloged form and are systematically used, software will continue to be synthesized from individual small grained components.

Refining a published process involves adjusting the unit operation configuration based on the requirements for production rate (e.g., tons/year), raw material composition, and specified product purity. Refining the DSSA

---

[*] From *Process Engineering*, Dec. 1993.

TABLE 2   Routine Design

Chemical Engineering	Software Engineering (Future)
Identify appropriate process	Identify appropriate DSSA
If no appropriate process then synthesize new process from existing unit operation patterns	If no appropriate DSSA then synthesize new DSSA or single system design from existing design patterns and components
Refine published process based on production rates and product/raw material specifications	Refine DSSA based on concept of operation and detailed requirements for input and output
Do sizing (preliminary design) of unit operations	Do preliminary selection of component instances
Evaluate plant design by simulation	Evaluate system design by architecture level simulation or analytical techniques
Estimate plant capital and production/operating costs	Estimate costs for integration, maintenance, and licenses
Calculate return on investment—will this plant be profitable?	Calculate return on investment—is this level of automation worth it?
Optimize for energy efficiency, emissions . . .	Optimize for efficiency, reliability . . .
Do detailed design of unit operations, process controls, and piping	Do detailed design of system specific code
Build plant	Integrate and test

may involve adding/deleting components from the DSSA based on functional requirements and input/output content and format. Preliminary design of unit operations involves choosing from and specifying the size of a set of characteristic features. Preliminary selection of software component instances (e.g., commercial off the shelf components or components in a reuse library) is a very similar task (the features can be qualitative or quantitative).

Evaluating the designed system before it is built is also part of the engineering mindset. Sophisticated simulation and optimization programs have been used in chemical engineering since the early 1960s.[27,28] These are important tools which are used to analyze and improve the design before the plant is ever built. Steady-state analysis is used to calculate the material and energy balances based on models of the preliminary design unit operations. Dynamic simulation programs check the behavior of the process in various conditions such as start-up, shut-down, changes in raw material composition, and equipment disturbances.

Tools for evaluating the designed system before it is built are not widely used yet in software engineering. Analytical tools like rate monotonic analysis[18] are now available. Rate monotonic analysis helps to predict the ability to satisfy scheduling deadlines in a real time system. Advanced tools for dynamic simulation are beginning to emerge.[29] These dynamic simulation tools help to predict how the system will behave in various conditions and scenarios.

In chemical engineering there is a large emphasis on calculating the return on investment (ROI). Given a preliminary design for a process, a cost estimation (for capital equipment and production costs, e.g., utilities) and economic evaluation program produces data for decision making and analyzing alternatives. No equivalent methods or tools exist for software engineering. Function points may be the closest thing but this method is not detailed enough to allow you to compare software architecture alternatives. There is an obvious lack of emphasis on calculating the ROI for a software engineering design. To calculate ROI, you would need to determine the dollar value of a certain level of automation provided by a software system.

CORPORATE DESIGN STANDARDS

Design standards are a key way to reuse design knowledge within an organization, domain, or product line. The use of design standards shows management commitment to design reuse. Design standards in chemical engineering capture and organize experience/knowledge of corporate engineers in the product lines of the company. Chemical engineering design standards include:

- specific recommended design equations
- design guidelines for equipment, e.g., "Avoid thin wall tubes"
- guidelines for parameter estimation
- example calculations
- chemical data for company specific products

These corporate design standards go beyond handbooks in helping to design unit operations and refine processes. These standards often contain proprietary details which may be licensable with a process.

The equivalent of corporate design standards in software engineering would be a set of documented corporate standard software designs and components used in all systems in each application domain. This would include a detailed domain model and DSSA. The technology books at Schlumberger are a good example of on-line corporate design standards for software.[30] Technology books are a representation of reusable design information in structured form with a graphical user interface. They include:

- formal consolidated analysis & design models
- non-functional requirements analysis (e.g., processing and memory resources)
- domain specific code components
- design rationale composition

The technology book environment provides a domain-specific information workspace and efficient access to the best information available in the organization. This is much more than software development process definitions and coding standards. Unfortunately the technology book approach is not yet standard practice in software engineering.

CONCLUSIONS

The comparison of design reuse in chemical engineering to design reuse in software engineering points the way for software engineering to become a mature engineering discipline. Design reuse in software engineering is progressing toward the types of design reuse found in chemical engineering (e.g., domain specific software architectures, object-oriented frameworks and design patterns, design analysis/simulation techniques, and on-line domain/design models). The efforts have to be coalesced and the gaps have to be filled. The comparison would have been easier if there were a common language and ontology for engineering design in general.

We need to start developing a "Perry's Handbook" for software engineering to serve as a baseline for good design. Due to the cooperative and dynamic nature of a software handbook it should be available on-line via the internet and eventually the national information infrastructure. One of the first areas that should be focused on is developing a common language and ontology for software design.

We need to start developing mechanisms (e.g., books, journals) for publishing and licensing software architectures. Domain specific software architectures and associated tools should be available for license on the internet. Standards and tools should be developed to support the sharing of domain specific design knowledge within an organization and throughout the whole engineering community. We need to examine the business, organizational, and management aspects of software design reuse. We should facilitate the reorganization of the current software industry to one based on design and component reuse facilitated by internet.

Finally, we need software architecture based cost estimation tools and return on investment tools.

ACKNOWLEDGMENTS

Special thanks to Kurt Wallnau, Mary Shaw, Anne Quinn, and Sholom Cohen for providing feedback.

REFERENCES

1. Shaw, M. *Prospects for an Engineering Discipline of Software* IEEE Software Nov. 1990.
2. Capers Jones, *Reusability in Programming: A Survey of the State of the Art* IEEE Trans. on Software Eng. Sept. 1984.
3. Perry, Wolf, *Foundations for the Study of Software Architecture* ACM SIGSOFT Software Engineering Notes Oct. 1992.
4. Shaw and Garlan, *Software Architecture: Perspectives on an Emerging Discipline,* Prentice Hall 1996.
5. Mah, *Chemical Process Structures and Information Flows* Butterworths 1990.
6. Lea, *C., Alexander: An Intro for OO Designers* ACM SIGSOFT Software Engineering Notes Jan. 1994.
7. Perry, Chilton editors *Chemical Engineers' Handbook,* 5th ed. 1973.
8. Buschmann Rational architectures for object-oriented software systems *Journal of Object-Oriented Programming,* Sept. 1993.
9. Peterson, A. Spencer, and Stanley, Jay L. Jr. *Mapping a Domain Model and Architecture to a Generic Design* (CMU/SEI-94-TR-8). Pittsburgh, Pa.: Software Engineering Institute, Carnegie Mellon University, May 1994.
10. Knuth, *The Art of Computer Programming* vols. I–III Addison Wesley 1973.
11. Booch, *Software Components with Ada* Benjamin Cummings 1987.

12. Booch, *Object Oriented Analysis and Design with Applications* Benjamin Cummings 1993.
13. Sedgewick, *Algorithms in C* Addison Wesley 1990.
14. Sedgewick, *Algorithms in C++* Addison Wesley 1992.
15. Dumas, *Designing User Interfaces for Software* Prentice Hall 1988.
16. Datapro *Reports on . . .* Datapro Research Corp.
17. Barr, Feigenbaum, Cohen, *The Handbook of Artificial Intelligence* vols. I-IV Morgan Kaufman 1981–1989.
18. Klein, Ralya, Pollak, Obenza, Gonzalez, and Harbour, *Practitioner's Handbook for Real-Time Analysis, A Guide to Rate Monotonic Analysis for Real-Time Systems* Kluwer 1993.
19. Gamma, Helm, Johnson, and Vlissides, *Design Patterns: Elements of Reusable Object-Oriented Software* Addison Wesley 1994.
20. Lane, *A design space and design rules for user interface software architecture* CMU/SEI-90-TR-22.
21. Booch, *Next Generation Methods—Bringing Order out of the Chaos* Journal of Object Oriented Programming—Supplement on OO Analysis and Design July/August 1993.
22. Gruber, *Toward principles for the design of ontologies used for knowledge sharing* unpublished report Stanford Univ. Jan. 1993.
23. Buck, *Knowledge for sale: The advent of industry-specific class libraries* IEEE Expert Oct. 1993.
24. Gamma, Helm, Johnson, and Vlissides, *Design Patterns: Abstraction and Reuse of Object-Oriented Design* In European Conference on OOP July 1993—Lecture Notes in CS #707 Springer Verlag.
25. Dutton, Sims, *Patterns in OO Design and Code Could Improve Reuse* IEEE Software May 1994.
26. Shreve, Brink, *Chemical Process Industries*, 4th ed. McGraw Hill 1977.
27. Evans, *CAD: Advances in Process Flowsheeting Systems* in Liu, McGee, Epperley, *Recent Developments in Chemical Process and Plant Design* Wiley 1987.
28. Leesley, *Computer-Aided Process Plant Design* Gulf 1982.
29. Luckham, Kenney, Augustin, Vera, Bryan, and Mann, *Specification and Analysis of System Architecture Using Rapide* IEEE Transactions on Software Engineering, April 1995.
30. Arango, Schoen, and Pettengill, *A Process for Consolidating and Reusing Design Knowledge* Proceedings of The 15th International Conference on Software Engineering May 1993.

Christopher Alexander:
An Introduction for
Object-Oriented Designers

Doug Lea

dl@cs.oswego.edu

Software developers lament *"If only software engineering could be more like X . . .",* where X is any design-intensive profession with a longer and apparently more successful history than software. It is therefore both comforting and troubling to discover that the same fundamental philosophical, methodological, and pragmatic concerns arise in all of these Xs (see, for example,[18,23,33,43,45,46,48,50]). In part because it is considered as much artistry as engineering, writings about architecture have most extensively explored and argued out the basic underpinnings of design. Even within this context, the ideas of the architect Christopher Alexander stand out as penetrating, and bear compelling implications for software design.

Alexander is increasingly well-known in object-oriented (OO) design circles for his influential work on "patterns." This paper considers patterns within a broader review of Alexander's prolific writings on design. These include core books *Notes on the Synthesis of Form,*[1] *The Timeless Way of Building,*[5] and *A Pattern Language*[4] (hereafter abbreviated as Notes, Timeless, and Patterns respectively), other books based mostly on case studies,[3,6–8,15] related articles,[2,9] and a collaborative biography.[29]

This review introduces some highlights of Alexander's work. The format is mainly topical, roughly in historical order, interspersed and concluded with remarks about connections to software design. It focuses on conceptual issues, but omits topics (e.g., geometry and color) that seem less central to software. Some discussions are abstracted and abbreviated to the point of caricature, and in no case capture the poetry of Alexander's writings that can only be appreciated by reading the originals, or the concreteness and practicality of pattern-based development that can only be conveyed through experience.

QUALITY

Alexander's central premise, driving over thirty years of thoughts, actions, and writings, is that there is something fundamentally wrong with twentieth century architectural design methods and practices. In *Notes,* Alexander illustrates failures in the sensitivity of contemporary methods to the actual requirements and conditions surrounding their development. He argues that contemporary methods fail to generate products that satisfy the true requirements placed upon them by individuals and society, and fail to meet the real demands of real users, and ultimately fail in the basic requirement that design and engineering improve the human condition. Problems include:

- Inability to balance individual, group, societal, and ecological needs
- Lack of purpose, order, and human scale
- Aesthetic and functional failure in adapting to local physical and social environments
- Development of materials and standardized components that are ill suited for use in any specific application
- Creation of artifacts that people do not like.

Timeless continues this theme, opening with phenomenologically toned essays on "the quality without a name," the possession of which is the ultimate goal of any design product. It is impossible to briefly summarize this. Alexander presents a number of partial synonyms: *freedom, life, wholeness, comfortability,* and *harmony.* But no single term or example fully conveys meaning or captures the force of Alexander's writings on the reader, especially surrounding the human impact of design, the feelings and aesthetics of designers and users, the need for commitment by developers to obtain and preserve wholeness, and its basis in the objective equilibrium of form. Alexander has been working for the past twelve years on a follow-up book, *The Nature of Order,* devoted solely to this topic.[9,29]

METHOD AND STRUCTURE

Notes is Alexander's most conventional and still most frequently cited book, and most clearly reflects Alexander's formalist training. (He pursued architecture after obtaining science and mathematics degrees. He is also an artist, a Turkish carpet collector, and a licensed contractor.) It has much in common with other works on systems, design, and engineering that appeared in the late 1950s and early 1960s attempting to integrate ideas from cybernetics, discrete math, and computing, exuding an optimistic tone that real progress was being made.

Notes[12,15,40] describes how, before the advent of modern architectural methods, artifacts tended not to suffer from adaptation, quality, and usability failures. The "unselfconsciously" constructed artifacts of tradition are produced without the benefit of formal models and methods. Instead, a system of implicit and often inflexible rules for design/construction progress in an evolutionary fashion. Over time, natural forces cause successive artifacts to better adapt to and mesh with their environments, almost always ultimately finding points of equilibrium and beauty, while also resulting in increasingly better rules applied by people who do not necessarily know why the rules work.

Historically, the modern "rational" design paradigm was both a contributing factor towards and a byproduct of the professionalization of design.[18,37] Rational design is distinguished from traditional craftsmanship by its "self-conscious" separation of designs from products (or, to continue the evolutionary analogy, genotype from phenotype), its use of analytic models, and its focus on methods that anyone with sufficient formal training may apply. Analytic designers first make tractable models (from simple blueprints on up) that are analyzed and manipulated into a form that specifies construction.

Rational design was in many ways a major advance over traditional methods. However, as discussed in *Notes,* the notions of analysis and synthesis are badly, and harmfully, construed in architecture and artifact design, leading to the sterile study of methods that have no bearing on the vast majority of artifacts actually built or the work involved in developing them. (Wolfe[51] provides a breezier account of some of this territory, but focusing on the schools and cults of personality found in modern architecture, that luckily have few parallels in software engineering.)

The main problem lies in separating activities surrounding analysis and synthesis rather than recognizing their duality. While it is common to exploit the symmetries between form and function (roughly translatable as system statics versus dynamics), further opportunities for integrating views become lost. Like an organism, a building is more than a realization of a design or even of a development process. Model, process, context, and artifact are all intertwined aspects of the same system. Artificial separations of models, phases, and roles break these connections. One consequence is that abstract representations lose details that always end up mattering, but each time in different ways. The micro-adaptations of tradition are lost, and resist model validation efforts in those rare cases in which they are performed. Alexander provides examples from houses to kettles in which fascination with the form of detached, oversimplified, inappropriate models leads to designs that no user would want.

In *Notes,* Alexander argues that the key to methodological continuity, integration, and unification is to temper, or even replace intensionally defined models with reliance upon complete, extensionally described sets of constraints, specific to each design effort. To match its context, a solution must be constructed along the intrinsic fractures of the problem space. This ecological perspective generates design products that are optimally adapted to the microstructure of local conditions and constraints, without the "requirements stress" characteristic of the products of classic methods.

Notes includes presentation of a semiformal algorithmic method that helps automate good partitioning under various assumptions. To use it, one first prepares an exhaustive list of functional and structural constraints. The major illustrations employ 33 and 141 constraints respectively, each collected and refined over periods of months. The algorithm takes as input a boolean matrix indicating whether any given pair of constraints interact—either positively or negatively, although concentrating on the negative since "misfits" are easier to identify and characterize. The method results in indications of groupings that minimize total requirements interaction and resulting complexity. This statistical clustering algorithm arrives at subsystems by minimizing the interaction of problem requirements that each one deals with. The goal is to mirror the microstructure that each part in a well-adapted unselfconsciously designed system would possess. This method relies upon a consideration of all such constraints, again leading him to argue for empirically and experientially guided analysis.

Even though exemplified with architectural artifacts, Alexander's concerns and methods apply equally well to software systems, subsystems, objects, etc. While there are many obvious differences between houses and software, most are matters of degree at this level of discussion. Consider, for example:

- Software entities engage in greater dynamic interaction (e.g., send messages to each other).
- Sometimes, describing software is the same as constructing it (as in programming).
- More of a software design is hidden from its users.

- Software generally has many fewer physical constraints.
- Some software requirements are allegedly more explicit and precise than "build a house here."

None of these have much bearing on methodological issues. As noted by Dasgupta,[18] Alexander's early writings on structure and method have influenced designers in all realms, including computer scientists ranging from Herbert Simon to Harlan Mills. Variants of Alexander's decomposition algorithm have been applied to OO software.[13] One can find passages in standard presentations of OO decomposition[14] that surely have indirect roots in this work. Although apparently independently conceived, Winograd & Flores[50] is especially close in spirit, and includes discussions that Alexander might have written had he been dealing with software:

> Many of the problems that are popularly attributed to "computerization" are the result of forcing our interactions into the narrow mold provided by a limited formalized domain.
> The most successful designs are not those that try to fully model the domain in which they operate, but those that are "in alignment" with the fundamental structure of that domain, and that allow for modification and evolution to generate new structural coupling.

These themes form a basis for most of Alexander's later writings. However, later efforts are also in large part a response to failures in the methods and algorithms presented in *Notes*, as discovered by Alexander and others.[2,29,33,38,49] While they remain useful guides and tools, the methods encounter problems including the possibility of missing relevant constraints, assumptions that requirements are completely knowable beforehand, ignoring the intrinsic value-ladenness of requirements specifications, inability to deal with relative weights among constraints or higher-level interactions, failure to accommodate the fact that design components may interact in ways that requirements do not, and inflexibility in adapting to future constraints. These problems, along with observations that people blindly following such methods do not always create better products, led to work increasingly removed from mainstream architectural design practices.

PATTERNS

Timeless and *Patterns* were written as a pair, with the former presenting rationale and method, and the latter concrete details. They present a fresh alternative to the use of standardized models and components, and accentuate the philosophical, technical, and social-impact differences between analytic methods and the adaptive, open, and reflective (all in several senses) approach to design that Alexander is reaching for.

The term *pattern* is a preformal construct (Alexander does not ever provide a formal definition) describing sets of forces in the world and relations among them. In *Timeless,* Alexander describes common, sometimes even universal patterns of space, of events, of human existence, ranging across all levels of granularity.

Patterns contains 253 pattern entries. Each entry might be seen as an in-the-small handbook on a common, concrete architectural domain. Each entry links a set of forces, a configuration or family of artifacts, and a process for constructing a particular realization. Entries intertwine these "problem space," "solution space," and "construction space" issues in a simple, down-to-earth fashion, so that each may evolve concurrently when patterns are used in development.

Entries have five parts:

Name. A short familiar, descriptive name or phrase, usually more indicative of the solution than of the problem or context. Examples include *Alcoves, Main entrance, Public outdoor room, Parallel roads, Density rings, Office connections, Sequence of sitting spaces,* and *Interior windows.*

Example. One or more pictures, diagrams, and/or descriptions that illustrate prototypical application.

Context. Delineation of situations under which the pattern applies. Often includes background, discussions of why this pattern exists, and evidence for generality.

Problem. A description of the relevant forces and constraints, and how they interact. In many cases, entries focus almost entirely on problem constraints that a reader has probably never thought about. Design and construction issues sometimes themselves form parts of the constraints.

Solution. Static relationships and dynamic rules (microprocess) describing how to construct artifacts in accord with the pattern, often listing several variants and/or ways to adjust to circumstances. Solutions reference and relate other higher- and lower-level patterns.

But not everything of this form counts as a pattern. Ideally, pattern entries have the following properties:

Encapsulation. Each pattern encapsulates a well-defined problem/solution (cf.,[41,42]). Patterns are independent, specific, and precisely formulated enough to make clear when they apply and whether they capture real problems and issues, and to ensure that each step of synthesis results in the construction of a complete, recognizable entity, where each part makes sense as an in-the-small whole.

Generativity. Each entry contains a local, self-standing process prescription describing how to construct realizations. Pattern entries are written to be usable by all development participants, not merely trained designers. Many patterns are unashamedly "recipes," mirroring the "unselfconscious" procedures characteristic of traditional methodless construction. An expert may still use a pattern in the same way that an expert chef uses a cooking recipe—to help create a personal vision of a particular realization, while still maintaining critical ingredients and proportions.

Equilibrium. Each pattern identifies a solution space containing an invariant that minimizes conflict among forces and constraints. When a pattern is used in an application, equilibrium provides a reason for each design step, traceable to situational constraints. The rationale that the solution meets this equilibrium may be a formal, theoretical derivation, an abstraction from empirical data, observations of the pattern in naturally occurring or traditional artifacts, a convincing series of examples, analysis of poor or failed solutions, or any mixture of these. Equilibrium is the structural side of optimality notions familiar in computing, and can be just as hard to find a basis for, meet, or approximate.[28] Alexander argues for establishment of objective equilibria based in the "quality without a name" even (or especially) when surrounding aesthetic, personal, and social factors. He also notes the elusiveness of this goal—artifacts more often than not fail to achieve this quality despite the best of efforts.

Abstraction. Patterns represent abstractions of empirical experience and everyday knowledge. They are general within the stated context, although not necessarily universal. (Each entry in *Patterns* is marked with a "universality" designation of zero to two stars.) Pattern construction (like domain analysis[44]) is an iterative social process collecting, sharing, and amplifying distributed experience and knowledge. Also, patterns with a structural basis in or similarity with natural and traditionally constructed artifacts exploit well adapted partitionings of the world. Sometimes, patterns may be constructed more mechanically, by merging others and/or transforming them to apply to a different domain. And some patterns are so tied to universals that they emerge from introspection and intuition uncontaminated by formalism. Heuristics based on participatory design, introspection, linkage to existing artifacts, and social consensus all increase the likelihood of identifying central fixed and variable features, and play a role even when that environment is purely internal and/or artificial, but where each part helps generate a context for others.

Openness. Patterns may be extended down to arbitrarily fine levels of detail. Like fractals, patterns have no top or bottom—at the lowest levels of any design effort, some are merely opaque and/or fluid (e.g., plaster, concrete). Patterns are used in development by finding a collection of entries addressing the desired features of the project at hand, where each of these may in turn require other subpatterns. Experimentation with possible variants and examination of the relationships among patterns that together form the whole add constraints, adjustments, and situation-specific specializations and refinements. For example, while only a small set of patterns would typically apply in the design of a certain housing community, each house will itself be unique due to varying micro-patterns. Because the details of pattern instantiations are encapsulated, they may vary within stated constraints. These details often do impact and further constrain those of other related patterns. But again, this variability remains within the borders of higher-level constraints.

Composibility. Patterns are hierarchically related. Coarse grained patterns are layered on top of, relate, and constrain fine grained ones. These relations include, but are not restricted to, various whole–part relations.[16] Most patterns are both upwardly and downwardly composible, minimizing interaction with other patterns, making clear when two related patterns must share a third, and admitting maximal variation in sub-patterns. Pattern entries are arranged conceptually as a *language* that expresses this layering. Because the forms of patterns and their relations to others are only loosely constrained and written entirely in natural language, the pattern language is merely analogous to a formal production system language, but has about the same properties, including infinite nondeterministic generativity.

PROCESS

Patterns includes brief recipe-like accounts on how to apply and compose patterns. However, Alexander discourages slavish conformance, and describes development mainly through concrete examples illustrating how groupings at different levels of hierarchies tend to be based upon different levels of concerns. Coarser-grained patterns are less constraining in detail than finer-grained ones. Exact commitments are postponed until the consequences of lower-level construction and/or experimentation can be assessed.

Even though high-level patterns hold throughout development, this process need not, for example, generate a classic blueprint drawing before construction. Also, because the relations among larger and smaller patterns do not always represent strict containment, there may be interactions among subpatterns and other higher-level interactions requiring experimentation and resolution. *Patterns* includes entries (e.g., *Site repair*) describing how to deal with particular kinds of interactions. All "joints," "transitions," and "spaces" among components are explicitly designed using other patterns that balance the needs of the parts versus the needs of the whole.

Pattern-based design activities resist accommodation within a linear development process, and raise challenges in the construction of suitable process models that still meet costing, predictability, and control criteria. Since the early 1970s Alexander has experimented with several overall development processes that preserve the integrity and promises of pattern-based design, as applied to projects at all scales, including houses, a cafe, a medical facility, apartments, two universities, a rural housing community, and an urban community.[3, 5–9, 29] The resulting process principles and development patterns include:

Collective Development. Development is a social process. Participation from all levels (users, policy-makers, etc.) is required for decisions affecting multiple parts or users, as well as those concerning future growth and evolution. Rather than a plan, a group adopts a (stateful) process that balances collective and individual needs, and preserves the rationale for particular decisions.

Participatory Design. Users can help design things that they really need and want, that are better adapted to their surroundings, and that are more aesthetically pleasing.[34,40,47] Even if the design participants are not the permanent, ultimate users, participation by someone impacted by the artifact is better than the alternative. Architects may reject user requests only when their knowledge of local constraints is demonstrably greater.

Responsibility. Architects hold financial and legal charge for the consequences of their activities, and control corresponding cash flow. This provides both authority and responsibility for adaptation across development.

Decentralization. Larger efforts can be subdivided into expanding centers or domains that increasingly influence one another in the course of growth. Localized experimentation, discovery, and change are intrinsic to such adaptation. This includes situations in which conditions change and designs evolve. The diagnosis and local repair of problems with existing parts are part of any design effort.

Integration of Roles. Designers operate at several levels. Primary roles should be assigned with respect to problem task or domain, not phase or level. Architects must sometimes be builders, and vice versa. They cannot otherwise get things right. Intimacy with all aspects of an effort allows the builder-architect to firsthand discover constraints, needs, and desires.

Integration of Activities. Design is interwoven with synthesis in a mainly bottom-up fashion. Construction proceeds in an order governed by pattern interdependencies, the continuous analysis and repair of failures, and commitment to detail, variety, experimentation, and wholeness. Concurrent development of mostly independent parts allows construction to branch out from multiple centers, ultimately "stiffening" into final form.

Stepwise Construction. Artifacts are constructed one pattern at a time, each of which results in a complete, recognizable form adapted to other already-constructed artifacts and partially committed plans. Efforts are focused upon operations, not components. Each operation is complete in itself. Creativity and accomplishment are maintained at all levels of this process.

PATTERNS AND OO DESIGN

The form and features of patterns, and the methods and processes surrounding them, are in no way special to architectural design. The entries in *Patterns* represent "special theories" of the world. Alexander notes[29] that his characterization of patterns meshes well with common definitions of scientific theories. The heuristics governing the construction of patterns are all but indistinguishable from those for theories. (See also Dasgupta,[18] March,[38] and Steddman,[49] who note that while such correspondences add an aura of respectability, they also open up design to the controversies surrounding modern scientific method.) Patterns are less general than descriptions of the base semantics of the pattern language itself, yet equally far removed from the realm of "neat tricks." The careful interplay between contexts, problem-space forces, and constructive solutions make this framework an ideal basis for capturing other kinds of design knowledge and practices as well.

In fact, Alexander's patterns bear a straightforward relation to OO constructs. Patterns may be viewed as extending the definitional features of classes. In OO design, classes have two principle aspects, analogous to those of patterns:

- The external, problem-space view: Descriptions of properties, responsibilities, capabilities and supported services as seen by software clients or the outside world.
- The internal, solution-space view: Static and dynamic descriptions, constraints, and contracts among other components, delegates, collaborators, and helpers, each of which is known only with respect to a possibly incomplete external view (i.e., a class, but where the actual member may conform to a stronger subclass).

The best classes also share the properties of appropriate abstraction, encapsulation, openness, and equilibrium. Like patterns, classes are normally generative, supporting parameterized instance construction as well as higher-order instantiation in the case of generic (template) classes. Classes are intrinsically composible, although these compositions need not always be expressed as classes, e.g., at topmost decomposition levels.

Indeed, since patterns can describe concepts and structures (e.g., coordinated groups) that are not themselves objects, the term *pattern* may be more fitting than *class* (or alternatively, the notion of a class should be broadened) at least at the level of OO design variously termed "abstract," "architectural," and/or "functional."[20] Patterns can thus raise the expressiveness and level of description supported by familiar OO constructs. Conversely, OO concepts may be applied to strengthen pattern-based design notions:

Languages and Tools. Alexander grammatically arranges pattern entries (although in an implicit fashion) to exploit the generative properties of formal languages.[29] In computing, just about every possible formal, semi-formal, and informal set of constructs have been collected as a language of some sort. For example, as shown in the Demeter project,[36] a set of OO classes may be represented grammatically using rewrite rules denoting pattern-like compositional layering. However, it is unnecessary to construe a collection of patterns or classes themselves *as* a language. In programming, it is usually more convenient to express descriptions *in* a broader language, to facilitate manipulation, compilation, etc. Extensions of OO modeling, design and/or programming languages may serve well in representing patterns. Such formalization also allows for construction of design tools. Several Computer Aided Architectural Design (CAAD) systems have represented Alexander's patterns in software. Most recently, Galle[24,25] has described a CAAD framework supporting pattern-based design built as a partially object-oriented expert system. Aspects of this system might be abstracted as patterns and used in the construction of similar CASE design tools. However, it will surely take some time before OO design tools and books reach the utility and authoritativeness of *Patterns*.

Subclassing and Refinement. In addition to supporting compositional relations, all OO notations include a second kind of structuring rule to describe possible alternative paths though a set of concepts, capturing both the composition/decomposition and abstraction/refinement design spectra within a linguistic framework. OO methods and languages thus add a new set of concepts to this aspect of Alexander's framework. While the notion of variability within broad classifications permeates his writings, Alexander does not explicitly employ the idea of structured refinement through subclassing. This probably stems from the fact that there is no good reason for formalizing the concept in architectural design, where there is little use in explicitly capturing the refinements between a pattern and its realization. Instead, the pattern is (often gradually) *replaced* by its realization. However, in software, these intermediate forms can play all sorts of roles in development, including use as branch points for alternative specializations, bases for differential design, descriptions of common protocols in OO frameworks, and a means for swapping in one component for another.

Inheritance and Delegation. OO design techniques incorporating various subclassing, delegation, and composition constructs conquer a potential obstacle found in the application of pattern-based design in other realms. Alexander's patterns provide a basis for *design* reuse without any necessary implications for *component* reuse, thus limiting the routine generation and predictable use of standardized components with known cost and properties, and running into quality-control problems intrinsic to reliance on one-shot implementations. This is generally not the case in OO design. Even when an existing or standard component isn't what you want, it often happens that alternative specializations, delegation structures, and/or subclasses can share much code via standard OO programming tactics. In fact, this happens so often that OO programmers are surprised, complain, and are sometimes unable to cope when it does not (e.g., fairly often in concurrent OO programming).[39]

Adaptation and Reflection. Further out, OO concepts may also help crystallize the senses of methodological unity, adaptation, openness, and reflection that pervade Alexander's work. The lack of a crisp distinction between software "design" and "manufacturing" already makes development practices harder to classify along the continuum from craftsmanship to analytic engineering.[34] This becomes accentuated when software systems themselves include provisions for self-adaptation and redesign. So while it sounds overly metaphysical to, for example, view buildings as clever devices to propagate architects or blueprints (cf.,[19,21,49]), in software these dualities have very practical consequences. Work in OO and AI[30,31,35,50] has led to reification and metalevel reasoning constructs that, although by no means completely understood, allow creation of useful systems in which the borderlines between designer, model, design, and product nearly vanish, as is necessary for example in computer assisted manufacturing (CAD/CAM/CIM),[11] where the market-driven trend has been to move away from systems that merely increase productivity or reduce defects in mass-produced products. Instead, systems must rely on both adaptive development methods and adaptive software mechanisms to enable the reconfigurability required to obtain flexibility and user-perceived quality in manufacturing small runs.

Process Integration. While OO process models remain underdeveloped, their potential synergy with pattern-based models is obvious. The average OO developer personifies the builder-architect (hacker-designer?) ethic at the heart of pattern-based development processes. More than anything else, *experiences* with OO versions of patterns have been the driving force leading OO researcher-practitioners to examine and exploit the many relationships between the semantic bases, usages, activities, and processes of OO and pattern-based development. Most work is still in the exploratory phase, including reconceptualizations of basic OO techniques and idioms (e.g., those found in Booch,[14] Coplien,[17] and de Champeaux et al.[20]), OO frameworks[32] and micro-architectures,[10,26,27] as well as the methods, processes, tools, formalizations, development patterns, education, and social contexts best supporting their development. It may yet turn out that the ideas that have long isolated Alexander from the mainstream commercial architectural community[9, 22] will find their widest and most enduring impact in object-oriented software engineering.

REFERENCES

1. Alexander, C., *Notes on the Synthesis of Form,* Harvard University Press, 1964.
2. Alexander, C., "A Refutation of Design Methodology" (Interview with Max Jacobson), *Architectural Design,* December 1971.
3. Alexander, C., M. Silverstein, S. Angel, S. Ishikawa, & D. Abrams, *The Oregon Experiment,* Oxford University Press, 1975.
4. Alexander, C., S. Ishikawa, & M. Silverstein, *A Pattern Language,* Oxford University Press, 1977.
5. Alexander, C., *The Timeless Way of Building,* Oxford University Press, 1979.
6. Alexander, C., *The Linz Cafe,* Oxford University Press, 1981.
7. Alexander, C., *The Production of Houses,* Oxford University Press, 1985.
8. Alexander, C., *A New Theory of Urban Design,* Oxford University Press, 1987.
9. Alexander, C., "Perspectives: Manifesto 1991," *Progressive Architecture,* July 1991.
10. Anderson, B., & P. Coad (Organizers), "Patterns Workshop," *OOPSLA '93.*
11. Ayers, R., & D. Butcher, "The Flexible Factory Revisited," *American Scientist,* September-October 1993.
12. Basalla, G., *The Evolution of Technology,* Cambridge University Press, 1988.
13. Bonine, J., "A Theory of Software Architecture Design," unpublished draft manuscript, 1993.
14. Booch, G., *Object Oriented Design with Applications,* 2nd ed., Benjamin Cummings, 1993.
15. Chermayeff, S., & C. Alexander, *Community and Privacy: Toward a New Architecture of Humanism,* Doubleday, 1963.

16. Civello, F., "Roles for Composite Objects in Object Oriented Analysis and Design," *Proceedings, OOPSLA'93,* ACM, 1993.
17. Coplien, J., *Advanced C++: Programming Styles and Idioms,* Addison-Wesley, 1991.
18. Dasgupta, S., *Design Theory and Computer Science,* Cambridge University Press, 1991.
19. Dawkins, R., *The Selfish Gene,* Oxford University Press, 1976.
20. de Champeaux, D., D. Lea, & P. Faure, *Object Oriented System Development,* Addison-Wesley, 1993.
21. Dennett, D., *The Intentional Stance,* Bradford Books, 1987.
22. Dovey, K., "The Pattern Language and its Enemies," *Design Studies,* vol 11, p. 3–9, 1990.
23. French, M. J., *Invention and Evolution: Design in Nature and Engineering.* Cambridge, 1988.
24. Galle, P., "Alexander Patterns for Design Computing: Atoms of Conceptual Structure?" *Environment and Planning B: Planning and Design,* vol 18, p. 327–346, 1991.
25. Galle, P., "Computer Support of Architectural Sketch Design: A Matter of Simplicity?" *Environment and Planning B: Planning and Design,* vol 21, 1994.
26. Gamma, E., R. Helm, R. Johnson, & J. Vlissides, "Design Patterns: Abstraction and Reuse of Object-Oriented Designs," *Proceedings, ECOOP '93,* Springer-Verlag, 1993.
27. Gamma, E., R. Helm, R. Johnson, & J. Vlissides, *Design Patterns,* Addison-Wesley, forthcoming.
28. Garey, M., & D. Johnson, *Computers and Intractability,* Freeman, 1979.
29. Grabow, S., *Christopher Alexander: The Search for a New Paradigm,* Oriel Press, 1983.
30. Hamilton, G., M. Powell, & J. Mitchell. *Subcontract: A Flexible Base for Distributed Programming.* Sun Microsystems Laboratories Technical Report TR-93-13, 1993.
31. Hewitt, C., P. Bishop, & R. Steiger, "A Universal Modular ACTOR Formalism for AI," *Third International Joint Conference on Artificial Intelligence,* Stanford University, August 1973.
32. Johnson, R., "Documenting Frameworks Using Patterns," *Proceedings, OOPSLA 92,* ACM, 1992.
33. Jones, J. C., *Design Methods,* 2nd ed., Van Nostrand, 1992.
34. Karat, J. (ed), *Taking Software Design Seriously: Practical Techniques for Human-Computer Interaction Design,* Academic Press, 1991.

35. Kiczales, G., J. des Rivieres, & D.G. Bobrow, *The Art of the Metaobject Protocol,* MIT Press, 1991.
36. Lieberherr, K., & I. Holland, "Assuring Good Style for Object-Oriented Programs," *IEEE Software,* September 1989.
37. Lucie-Smith, B., *A History of Industrial Design,* Van Nostrand, 1983.
38. March, L. (ed), *The Architecture of Form,* Cambridge University Press, 1976.
39. Matsuoka, S., K. Taura, & A. Yonezawa, "Highly Efficient and Encapsulated Reuse of Synchronization Code in Concurrent Object-Oriented Languages," *Proceedings, OOPSLA '93,* ACM, 1993.
40. Norman, D., *The Psychology of Everyday Things,* Basic Books, 1988.
41. Parnas, D., "On the Criteria to be Used in the Decomposition of Systems into Modules," *Communications of the ACM,* December 1972.
42. Parnas, D., "Designing Software for Ease of Extension and Contraction," *IEEE Transactions on Software Engineering,* March 1979.
43. Petroski, H., *To Engineer is Human,* St. Martin's Press, 1982.
44. Prieto-Diaz, R., & G. Arango (eds.), *Domain Analysis: Acquisition of Reusable Information for Software Construction,* IEEE Computer Society Press, 1989.
45. Rowe, P., *Design Thinking,* MIT Press, 1987.
46. Schön, D., *Educating the Reflective Practitioner,* Jossey-Bass, 1987.
47. Schuler, D., & A. Namioka, *Participatory Design,* Lawrence Erlbaum, 1993.
48. Simon, H., *The Sciences of the Artificial,* MIT Press, 1981.
49. Steadman, P., *The Evolution of Designs,* Cambridge University Press, 1979.
50. Winograd, T., & F. Flores, *Understanding Computers and Cognition: A New Foundation for Design,* Addison-Wesley, 1986.
51. Wolfe, T., *From Our House to Bauhaus,* Pocket Books, 1981.

Patterns: PLoP, PLoP, Fizz, Fizz

Robert Martin
rmartin@oma.com

O n August 4–6, I attended the first conference on Pattern Languages of Programming (PLoP). This was a conference for people to get together and discuss the topic of "design patterns" (e.g., see Coplien[1]).

The conference was held at the Robert Allerton Park and Conference Center in Monticello, IL, which belongs to the University of Illinois. The setting was reminiscent of an English manor. There were elaborate gardens decorated with old, weathered statuary. There were winding paths that wandered by reflection pools, gardens, or the acres of deep woods that surround the park. All in all, it was quite nice.

I do have one complaint about the setting, however: there were no phones in the rooms. In fact, the only phones around were payphones. Let me tell you, there were lots of people running helter skelter looking for modem connections and wondering how they were going to get their next "net fix," or at least their email. When you are strung out from "net-withdrawal" all the reflection pools in the world don't make up for it.

The list of O-O celebrities that attended this conference was impressive, and many are well known to the readers of this magazine, including Richard Gabriel, Ralph Johnson, John Vlissides, Tom Cargill, Sam Adams, Doug Lea, Doug Schmidt, Mary Shaw, Jim Newkirk, and James Coplien, just to mention a few. From this list, one could expect that things were lively indeed.

WHAT IS A PATTERN?

I will tell you more about PLoP presently. But first a discussion about patterns is warranted.

In 1979, an architect (the kind that designs buildings) named Christopher Alexander wrote a couple of books: *The Timeless Way of Building* and *A Pattern Language*. In these books, amongst an incredible amount of philosophical and pseudo-religious babbling, was an idea. A pretty good idea, too.

Alexander noticed that there were techniques and principles in "good" architecture that tended to recur. For example, a well-designed doorway generally had some kind of transitional area that separated the outside of the door from the outside world in general. Whether it was a little path with bushes, or a porch with hanging plants and swings, or even just a little landing with a chair, the transition itself gave the doorway a "nice" quality.

Alexander called these repeating techniques "patterns." He named and catalogued quite a few of them and arranged them into something that he called a "pattern language." A pattern language is a group of interacting patterns. These patterns depend upon each other and build upon each other to create a particular style of building. For example, one pattern language might be used to build a French village, and another to build an American city.

SOFTWARE PATTERNS

What has all this to do with software? It turns out that upon examining well-designed software, certain techniques can be seen to recur. For example, in C++, if we want to break a dependency between a client class and a server class we can use inheritance as follows:

```
class Client
{
  public:
    void Use(AbstractServer& s) {s.Serve();}
};

class AbstractServer
{
  public:
    virtual void Serve() = 0;
};

class Server : public AbstractServer
{
  public:
```

```
virtual void Serve()
    {// actually perform service}
};
```

The Client and Server classes both depend upon the AbstractServer class. However, Client does not depend upon Server, and so the Server class can be changed; e.g., private members can be added or deleted without forcing Client to be recompiled.

The use of inheritance in this fashion is an instance of a pattern named *Bridge*. This pattern and many others are described in a new book: *Design Patterns: Elements of Reusable Object-Oriented Software* by Erich Gamma et al.[2]

Other patterns in this book include:

- *Composite*—A pattern for giving a container the same interface as the objects it contains, thus preventing clients from knowing whether they deal with one object or many.
- *Prototype*—A pattern for creating objects by cloning a single prototype object of the correct type, thus preventing clients from having to know the exact type of the object they are creating.
- *State*—A pattern for modeling the state variable of a Finite State Machine as an object, thus preventing the client of a finite state machine from knowing the specific state of that machine.
- *Factory*—A pattern for using an abstract class which supplies an object creation interface. Users can create objects without depending upon their absolute type.
- *Visitor*—A pattern for polymorphically invoking behaviors which are specific to a class, but defined outside the class.

and there are several dozen more . . .

THE USEFULNESS OF PATTERNS

For some of us, the patterns in Gamma's book are not new ideas. We have been using techniques like them for years. What is new, however, is the notion of giving them names and standard forms and putting them in a catalog. This allows us to reason about them and use them as formal components in our designs. Cataloging them makes them accessible to those of us who have not stumbled across the techniques on our own.

Thus, I think that Gamma's book is an important piece of work, and that the notion of patterns will be of benefit to all software engineers. By making use of these patterns we may be able to reason about our designs at a higher level of granularity.

Consider Figure 1, a class diagram from a payroll example. It shows a very clear instance of the Bridge pattern. The Employee class acts as the client while the three derivatives of PaymentMethod are the potential servers. The Employee class can use these three derivatives, but does not depend upon any of them. Instead, Employee and all three derivatives depend upon the abstract class PaymentMethod.

PATTERN EXAMPLE

Following is one of the patterns, the *Three Level Finite State Machine,* from a paper that I submitted at PLoP. It shows one of the common styles for documenting a pattern. Notice that the pattern first presents a problem, discusses the forces that motivated a solution, and then presents the solution in terms of techniques that are independent of language or application domain.

NAME

Three Level Finite State Machine

INTENT

To create finite state machines (FSMs) whose behavior is independent of their logic. This allows them to be derivable and extensible.

MOTIVATION

Finite state machines are often used to describe the logic that an application uses to convert its incoming events to its resultant behaviors. When the logic and behaviors are intermixed in the same algorithms, they become difficult to change and subject to error.

It is difficult to separate control from logic because they often form a closed loop. The logic of the FSM invokes a behavior that, in turn, invokes another event in the FSM. Thus, even when behavior and control are separated into two classes, as in the *Objects For States* pattern, the two classes have source-code dependencies on each other and it is difficult to use the behavior class with a different control class.

SOLUTION

Describe the finite state machine in three layers of inheritance. The first layer supplies interfaces and implementations for the behaviors of the

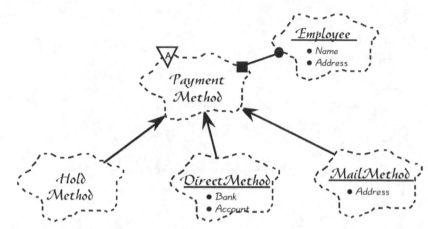

FIGURE 1   Payroll class diagram.

FSM. However, the events of the FSM are not known at this level, so this class is independent of control. This means that any behaviors that subsequently invoke events will be implemented as pure virtual functions at this level.

The second layer is derived from the first and adds the functions that respond to the events of the FSM. It also employs the *Objects For States* pattern or the *Strategy* pattern to implement the control logic of the FSM. It is possible for this level to be automatically generated from a state table or STD because, except for their names, this layer is independent of the behaviors.

The third layer derives from the second and supplies those behaviors that must invoke subsequent events.

Thus, because the first layer is completely independent of the control mechanisms of the FSM, it can become the base class for derivations that alter or extend the behaviors. It can also be used with different finite state machines by the derivation of another second and third layer.

STRUCTURE

The structure is shown in Figure 2.

IMPLEMENTATION

The following code examples show a typical implementation of the three levels. The second level has been automatically generated by a finite state machine compiler that employs the *Objects For State* pattern.

The finite state machine for this example is a model of a subway turnstyle. The state table input to the finite state machine compiler is shown in Listing 1.

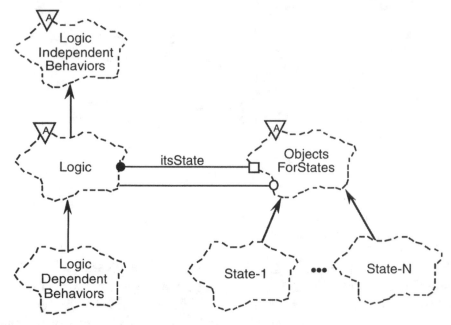

FIGURE 2   Structure of the *Three Level Finite State Machine* pattern.

This is a simple state machine. It starts out in the Locked state. If a coin is detected, it transitions into the Unlocked state. When the turnstile detects the person has passed (Pass) through, it returns to the Locked state. If, while in the Locked state, the person forces his way through, then it stays in the Locked state, but sounds the alarm. If, while in the Unlocked state, the person deposits another coin, it lights up a little "Thankyou" light.

Whenever we enter the Locked state, we invoke the Lock action. This action can fail, resulting in a Failed event. Likewise, whenever we enter the Unlocked state, we call the Unlock function. This function can fail, resulting in a Failed event.

Upon failure, the FSM enters the Broken state. Upon entry into this state, the OutOfOrder function is invoked, lighting a little light warning people away from the turnstile. When the repairman fixes the turnstile, the Fixed event occurs and the system returns to the Locked state. Upon exiting the Broken state the system calls the InOrder function, which turns off the out-of-order light.

Level 1—Behaviors independent of logic. The first level is a class that defines the interfaces for all the behaviors of the turnstile. It also provides implementations for most of those behaviors. Only the Lock and Unlock functions

Listing 1. State table.

```
Context TurnStyleLevel1        // the name of the context class
FSMName TurnStyleLevel2        // the name of the FSM to create
Initial Locked                 // Initial state.
{
  Locked < Lock // Lock upon entry
  {
     Coin    Unlocked          {}
     Pass    *                 Alarm
     Failed  Broken            LockError // indicate can't lock.
  }
  Unlocked <Unlock
  {
     Coin    *                 Thankyou
     Pass    Locked            {}
     Failed  Broken            UnlockError // indicate can't unlock
  }

  Broken <OutOfOrder >InOrder
  {
     Fixed    Locked           {}
  }
}
```

remain unimplemented because they must invoke the Failed event, which has not been defined at this level.

```
class TurnStyleLevel1
{
  public:
     virtual void Lock() = 0;
     virtual void Unlock() = 0;

     virtual void Alarm();
     virtual void LockError();
     virtual void UnlockError();
     virtual void Thankyou();
     virtual void OutOfOrder();
     virtual void InOrder();
  protected:
     bool LockAndCheck();
     bool UnlockAndCheck();
};
```

The last two member functions, LockAndCheck and UnlockAndCheck, provide implementations for the Lock and Unlock functions. However, the bool that these functions return must be translated to an event for the finite state machine. This translation will occur at level 3.

Level 2—The control logic. This level has been entirely generated by a finite state machine compiler from the text shown above in the state table. The implementation is shown in Listing 2.

Level 3—Behaviors dependent upon control. Finally, level 3 derives from level 2 and implements those behaviors that must invoke events in the FSM. These functions are Lock and Unlock, which must call the LockAndCheck and UnlockAndCheck functions, respectively, and then invoke the Failed event if the functions return false.

```
class TurnStyleLevel3 : public TurnStyleLevel2
{
  public:
    virtual void Lock()
    {
      if (!LockAndCheck()) Failed();
    }
    virtual void Unlock()
    {
      if (!UnlockAndCheck()) Failed();
    }
};
```

Because the first level provides all the substantial behaviors that the finite state machine controls, yet in no way depends upon any particular state machine, it can be reused by many state machines. It can also be the target of derivation so that its behaviors can be overridden or extended.

APPLICABILITY

Use this pattern in any context where behaviors may be controlled by more than one finite state machine, or where such behaviors need to be overridden and/or extended through inheritance.

CONSEQUENCES

Virtual deployment of the action functions may add a small amount of execution time overhead. Also, the *Objects For States* pattern used in level 2 can

Listing 2. The control logic.

```cpp
class TurnStyleLevel2;
class TurnStyleLevel2State
{
    public:
    virtual const char* StateName() const = 0;
    virtual void Coin(TurnStyleLevel2&);
    virtual void Pass(TurnStyleLevel2&);
    virtual void Failed(TurnStyleLevel2&);
    virtual void Fixed(TurnStyleLevel2&);
};
class TurnStyleLevel2BrokenState : public TurnStyleLevel2State
{
    public:
    virtual const char* StateName() const
        {return "Broken";}
    virtual void Fixed(TurnStyleLevel2&);
};
class TurnStyleLevel2UnlockedState : public TurnStyleLevel2State
{
    public:
    virtual const char* StateName() const
        {return "Unlocked";}
    virtual void Coin(TurnStyleLevel2&);
    virtual void Pass(TurnStyleLevel2&);
    virtual void Failed(TurnStyleLevel2&);
};
class TurnStyleLevel2LockedState : public TurnStyleLevel2State
{
    public:
    virtual const char* StateName() const
        {return "Locked";}
    virtual void Coin(TurnStyleLevel2&);
    virtual void Pass(TurnStyleLevel2&);
    virtual void Failed(TurnStyleLevel2&);
};
class TurnStyleLevel2: public TurnStyleLevel1
{
    public:
    // Static State Variables
    static TurnStyleLevel2BrokenState Broken;
    static TurnStyleLevel2UnlockedState Unlocked;
    static TurnStyleLevel2LockedState Locked;
    TurnStyleLevel2(); // Default Constructor
    // Event functions
    void Coin() {itsState->Coin(*this);}
    void Pass() {itsState->Pass(*this);}
    void Failed() {itsState->Failed(*this);}
    void Fixed() {itsState->Fixed(*this);}
    // State Accessor Functions
    void SetState(TurnStyleLevel2State& theState)
        {itsState = &theState;}
    TurnStyleLevel2State& GetState() const {return *itsState;}
    private:
    TurnStyleLevel2State* itsState;
};
TurnStyleLevel2BrokenState TurnStyleLevel2::Broken;
TurnStyleLevel2UnlockedState TurnStyleLevel2::Unlocked;
TurnStyleLevel2LockedState TurnStyleLevel2::Locked;
void TurnStyleLevel2State::Coin(TurnStyleLevel2& s) { }
void TurnStyleLevel2State::Pass(TurnStyleLevel2& s) { }
void TurnStyleLevel2State::Failed(TurnStyleLevel2& s) { }
void TurnStyleLevel2State::Fixed(TurnStyleLevel2& s) { }
void TurnStyleLevel2BrokenState::Fixed(TurnStyleLevel2& s)
{
    s.SetState(TurnStyleLevel2::Locked);
    s.InOrder();
    s.Lock();
}
void TurnStyleLevel2UnlockedState::Coin(TurnStyleLevel2& s)
{
    s.Thankyou();
}
void TurnStyleLevel2UnlockedState::Pass(TurnStyleLevel2& s)
{
    s.SetState(TurnStyleLevel2::Locked);
    s.Lock();
}
void TurnStyleLevel2UnlockedState::Failed(TurnStyleLevel2& s)
{
    s.UnlockError();
    s.SetState(TurnStyleLevel2::Broken);
    s.OutOfOrder();
}
void TurnStyleLevel2LockedState::Coin(TurnStyleLevel2& s)
{
    s.SetState(TurnStyleLevel2::Unlocked);
    s.Unlock();
}
void TurnStyleLevel2LockedState::Pass(TurnStyleLevel2& s)
{
    s.Alarm();
}
void TurnStyleLevel2LockedState::Failed(TurnStyleLevel2& s)
{
    s.LockError();
    s.SetState(TurnStyleLevel2::Broken);
    s.OutOfOrder();
}
TurnStyleLevel2::TurnStyleLevel2() : itsState(&Locked)
{
    Lock();
}
```

add lots of classes (one per state). Fortunately, because those classes can be generated by a state machine compiler, they do not need to add to the programmer's conceptual burden.

RELATED PATTERNS

Related patterns include *Objects For States* and *Strategy.*

BACK TO PLoP

I arrived at PLoP with high hopes of a very dynamic and information-packed conference. I wanted to hear about all the patterns that people had found, and how they had been using them. I was expecting a pragmatic conference.

In many ways, this is just what I got. The majority of the papers presented were well done and worth reading. They documented patterns that people had found useful in one context or another. The patterns ranged from finite state machines to concurrent processes, from validating user interfaces to building networking products, from strategies for structuring low-level code to strategies for structuring development organizations. The proceedings from this conference will be published soon, and will provide a rich source of information for those who read it.

THE WRITER'S WORKSHOP APPROACH

The papers for PLoP were presented in what I found to be a very unique manner. Authors did not stand at an overhead projector and drone on about their papers while flipping slide after slide before a sleeping audience. Instead, authors remained utterly silent while listening to a group of preselected reviewers discuss the paper—saying what they liked, what they didn't like, and making suggestions for revision.

I found this format extremely successful. There was a great deal of participation amongst the reviewers and amongst the audience, and the presenter went away richer for the experience. I believe it worked very well as a presentation strategy, and I hope to see a repeat at the next PLoP as well as at other shows.

DISAPPOINTMENTS

Although I generally enjoyed the conference, there were several things that bothered me. As I said before, I was looking for a certain level of pragmatism.

I wanted to hear people discuss their own successes and failures with certain patterns. I wanted to see and experience the kind of synergy that a group of practitioners can achieve when they begin discussing their fields. However, there was far too little of this kind of discussion for my tastes.

Instead, there seemed to be a lot of folks at the conference who felt that "patterns" are "the way," the "solution," the long-sought "magic bullet" for software design. Excitement was high, but in many cases substance was low.

Instead of talking about *particular* patterns, there was a tendency to talk about patterns in general, as if there was some spiritual significance in the word "pattern." At one point I overheard a young pattern philosopher say: "We don't truly know what patterns are yet." I found this statement to be simultaneously amusing and disturbing.

WARNING! SOAP-BOX

The last thing the software industry needs at this juncture is another source of fantastic and impossible claims. Patterns are undoubtedly in danger of becoming just that. Preventing this is probably impossible, yet I must rail at the Fates by publishing the appropriate counterclaims. Patterns are *not* some new thing that will save software engineering from its long, slow decline into chaos. The use of patterns will *not* dramatically shorten your development times or dramatically increase your productivity. A catalog of patterns will *not* turn new grads into consummate software designers overnight. Aliens from Arcturus did not beam the notion of patterns into Christopher Alexander's mind twenty years ago.

Patterns *are* a way to capture good design principles, and they are good techniques. They *may* be useful to teach the principles of software design. They *may* be helpful to designers who would like to look up potential solutions to particular problems. They *are* an effective way to communicate solutions to problems.

OFF THE SOAP-BOX AND BACK TO PLoP

I had hoped that people would be talking about which patterns they had found best in certain circumstances, or how a particular pattern can be modified to work in an unanticipated way. Instead, people talked about how to categorize patterns, how to merge two pattern languages, how to document patterns, or which were the fundamental O-O patterns. While these kinds of discussions are necessary, useful, and to be expected at a conference about patterns, I was disturbed that they were so dominant. Where were the practitioners? Why weren't they displaying their patterns for all to see? With the exception of the papers, these practitioners were all but silent.

And so, aside from the generally high quality of the papers themselves, and the unique and effective way in which they were presented, I found the conference to be just a little tedious. Don't get me wrong. I enjoyed it, and I intend to attend again. Furthermore, I can recommend the conference as a learning experience. It's just that, next time, I hope there will be a little less philosophy, a little less of the search for the holy grail, and a little more pragmatism. Oh, and perhaps some phones, too.

REFERENCES

1. Coplien, J.O. Software design: The emerging pattersn, *C++ Report* 6(6), 1994.
2. Alexander, C. *The Timeless Way of Building,* Oxford University Press, New York, 1979.
3. Alexander, C. *A Pattern Language,* Oxford University Press, New York, 1979.
4. Gamma, E. et al. *Design Patterns: Elements of Reusable Object-Oriented Software,* Addison-Wesley, Reading, MA, 1994.

A Design Patterns Experience Report

Russell L. Ramirez
ramirez@vnet.ibm.com

This column has introduced readers to design patterns and pattern languages, described how patterns and frameworks relate to each other, and given a glimpse of a pattern community that is working to move this technology into the mainstream. What I am going to describe is a small project within the context of a much larger one that applied design patterns exclusively to solve some of the common problems encountered in framework construction and object orientation in general.

But first, some background. The project on which I was first exposed to design patterns was part of a multimillion line of code rewrite of the Licensed Internal Code of AS/400 for 64-bit RISC hardware, most of which was in C++. The first release became available this past October [1994] to support the System/36 OS for the Advanced Series model 236.* Our part of that project was to provide an object-oriented (O-O) framework for analyzing hardware errors and passing the results to the operating system to aid in problem resolution. The framework is comprised of seven classes, three of which are abstract and are intended for subclassing concrete implementations to support error analysis for the various pieces of hardware in a system.

GROPING

I spent the first four months of last year groping my way through what would accomplish all of my goals: understandability, extensibility, etc.—

---

* AS/400 and System/36 are trademarks of IBM Corporation.

you know, all the "-bilities" that object-oriented designs (OODs) are supposed to have. Then there were all those practical goals like small memory footprint and optimum runtime efficiencies. Why did it seem that there were so many forces at work keeping me from reaching framework nirvana? Lack of domain expertise wasn't the problem. Thirteen years seemed like enough; in fact, it tended to get in the way of creating a good mental model because it was easy to put myself in the end-user's shoes and be demanding of the design. Every time I did this though, I ran into some new design/implementation issues, and some of them were not pretty.

A few years previously we had built a house for the first time, and the two experiences seemed to be very similar, except for one very important difference—while there are constraints that limit what *is* possible to build, what is possible is pretty well known and understood, and even a totally custom-built house doesn't take special architectural innovations or several years to build. So why are buildings relatively easy to deal with and software so difficult? Well, I suppose one obvious answer is that you can see buildings on paper and while they are being constructed, but is this the only difference?

This was not the first time I had made this analogy to myself, so once again I was wondering what was missing. I have to admit that I was disappointed in O-O technology at this point because the same old problems seemed to be getting worse instead of better.

HITTING THE "WALL"

The process of error or exception analysis is generally straightforward. An event is labeled an exception by some piece of code that is usually trying to process a command of some sort. The system then has the task of handling, or at least reporting, the situation. Quite often the exception is not life-threatening to the task responsible for its handling, so the task merely logs the information. Each exception is typically preassigned a unique integer value so it can be easily identified. The exception can be examined later by one central entity that will determine if some external action needs to be taken, e.g., modifying an operational parameter of a communications subsystem. In its simplest form, error analysis can be performed as a table look-up operation using the integer representation as an index. A table can be constructed that contains message numbers, possible causes, network alerts, etc., for each error. However, there are cases in error analysis, many of them unique, where complex decision-making logic is required.

I believed that I had two design options. I could solve the problem with a pool of unique coarse-grained objects, each being assigned to analyze a logical grouping of errors. Another option would be to define a set of reusable fine-grained objects that would work collaboratively to perform analysis. Neither approach was adequate though. A set of coarse-grained objects might be appropriate, or at least justifiable, for the complex cases. The fine-grained objects were better suited for the simpler cases because of the uniformity possible in processing tables. It appeared that I needed some of the attributes of both approaches in just the right combination.

I had other design constraints to consider as well. The logging interface was the common point that all errors passed through and I needed access to it, but it was already defined and implemented. I had to find a way to accommodate the logging design while minimizing changes to it, and I did not want its clients to be aware of the analysis process. The error data was encapsulated in a log object; however, it only provided dozens of get/set methods and I wanted a better abstraction that would hide future changes.

So I had several forces at work here pushing against each other. I knew it was too complex a task for a human to simultaneously resolve all the various forces, so I needed to tackle them individually with an organized process. As an engineer, this situation was hardly new to me, but I didn't have a computer-aided design program or even an analytical technique to help me. I had no luck in applying the popular OOD techniques of the time. I thought I should be able to apply a technique that dealt directly with the forces and constraints that I had identified, but none were known to me. Consequently, I was unable to progress any further and just hit a wall.

A LITTLE HELP

In April of last year I was exposed to the Gamma et al. patterns catalog[1] and Jim Coplien's *Advanced C++* book[2] as part of an internal pilot class I was attending. The project I was in charge of needed to deliver code in a matter of a few months so I didn't want to risk using a new technique. The design was to be handed over to five folks whose collective O-O experience totaled just a few months, so I felt that understandability was crucial if the rest of the team was going to have any chance of coming up to speed on my design quickly enough to do a good job of writing the code. Further, what I was really groping for, but did not realize at the time, was a reusable framework.

By the end of the class, the last week of April, I was convinced for various reasons (maybe desperation was one of them!) that I should attempt to map some of the design patterns and idioms I had just learned to my current design.

One of the first patterns I tried was *strategy* because I was trying to avoid the excessive reuse of control structures in the decision-making flow (I thought the encapsulation of the error analysis algorithms would lead to better code organization) and because the pattern seemed to fit my problem domain. As it turned out though, I missed a key point about the strategy pattern. All the encapsulated algorithms need to have a common purpose that just needs to be applied in different ways for different contexts of the same problem. Since I didn't pay close attention to this detail, I ended up with strategy objects that required different interfaces. Okay, a rookie mistake, but I learned that the subtle distinctions between some of the patterns in the catalog that many of us in the classroom environment didn't see the first or second time around were *very* important indeed.

I also had a working model written in C++ running on my workstation that was being used to "kick the tires" of each iteration of my design. So when I wanted to try something out, I was able to see the results quickly. I think this was a key reason that the light bulb finally came on for me. It was easier to see what a pattern was about when I tried to apply it to my design model. Nothing revolutionary about that.

ENLIGHTENMENT

As I successfully applied various patterns, the design started to take the form of something I had not seen before. I began to say "Wow!" a lot because it was as if I was being guided by something acting as a mentor.

I started with the interface to the logging function. The *facade* pattern seemed like an obvious choice. I wanted a simple interface to the logging function that would hide the details of the analysis process, and the applicability section for facade was a perfect match. Next, I looked for something to hide the interface of the log object better. The *wrapper* (currently called adapter) pattern sounded like the trick, but since I had already learned from the strategy pattern experience that haste makes waste, I carefully examined its applicability section. It also turned out to be a great way to solve another problem. What I later found out was that the applicability section in the patterns catalog was a way to document, in as general a way as possible, the forces that are at work in one's design problems. Works for me!

I now had a good way to get to the objects that would do the actual processing. What I wanted was a class that I could subclass concrete implementations from and use dynamic binding as part of the runtime selection mechanism. I had initially chosen the strategy pattern in part for this reason. However, with strategy I was trying to split the analysis process at the point where a different isolation technique (strategy) might be called for under different circumstances. I realized that I was paying as much attention to the "few" cases as to the "many." I made a major breakthrough when I just tried to solve the most common cases first, working the exceptions in later. I then opted for a two-object design, one class to coordinate the process and another to isolate the errors to specific probable causes. The two objects always had to exist in a pair. I remembered an idiom from the course called "shadow hierarchy," where object sets were called for in cases like mine. A factory was used as part of the set to make construction of the objects simple, so I now had three classes for every implementation. *Abstract factory* essentially describes the same phenomenon as shadow hierarchy.

By the time I had finished the first pass, several big problems had just "disappeared." I had the same experience that probably everyone has had when they "see" the answer to a problem or puzzle that they have spent a great deal of time on; i.e., when you finally see the way to solve the problem, you work at an incredibly accelerated rate because you now know every move you need to make. Using the patterns catalog is a lot like having a cheat sheet! Of course this was just the beginning, but I felt I had made genuine progress at last.

I threw all my code away and implemented a new model in about two hours (virtually all typing time). I understood what I was doing so well that there were only a few typo-related compile errors for approximately 1K of code. It was the same experience as writing a program a second time with some minor changes; it goes quickly. However, this was the first time I had written this code. Even though my new design was pattern based, the C++ idioms I had learned did not go to waste. In fact, I was also amazed at how obvious their use became as I implemented this new model.

Several more iterations occurred because I was now able to move past my initial assumptions and on to new problems. However, I noticed that the new problems were easily solved either by applying another pattern or by simply using a language idiom. So in a very real sense, my problems became small ones that were easy to solve. It was now the middle of May. I was becoming aware that I had built a framework and that all of my original goals had been met with a few additions that I hadn't even thought of.

SUCCESS!

I handed the design over to the team for implementation in June. I had expressed the design in a standard way (class responsibilities, members, storage semantics, etc.) as well as in terms of the patterns used. I noticed that the folks who had also attended the OOD class in April, and were somewhat comfortable with the pattern concept, understood what I had designed much better than I had anticipated. I began to realize that we were now almost overstaffed because the level of ability to understand design was far greater than I had anticipated. Needless to say, the effort put into the design paid off throughout the fall, and virtually all of our problems were unrelated to design (the C++ code we wrote lives in the kernel of our operating system, so the build and debug process was not a pleasant experience compared to my workstation environment). We delivered our code ahead of schedule by one month!

Not surprisingly, I have attributed much of our success to my exposure to the design patterns catalog. Ever since I attended graduate classes in the early '80s in software engineering, I have wondered why mankind is unable to build software—let alone estimate the work for building—the way we build houses. I knew that when a builder takes on a job with an architecture he's never worked with before, he still knows enough about what it will take to give a good estimate—I also never believed the argument that experience was the sole explanation for why this is possible. Now that I am a student of patterns, I know from Alexander's work[3] why architects and builders can do what they do so well—they follow patterns passed down through generations. Now some of those patterns for success have been passed down to me.

CONCLUSION

Since this project was completed I have spent many hundreds of hours studying design patterns in more depth. At this point I have at least convinced myself that I understand why I had the successes I did. I think the strongest selling point for design patterns is the fact that exceptional results occur very quickly, even before you start to think you know what you are doing. However, I think it is impossible to understand design patterns unless you have actually applied them to real problems. Of course, some people have used design patterns without knowing it, but most of us need to experiment with them before we can internalize their applicability and value. Therefore, if you are new to object-oriented programming, expect to spend some time with the design pattern book before you can fully understand it.

Now that I have more experience, I find myself thinking in terms of patterns, looking for them right away as I shift back and forth between the problem domain and the implementation space. I can now only imagine how I would design without having been exposed to design patterns—oh wait, that's right, the way I used to fumble my way around.

REFERENCES

1. Gamma, E., R. Helm, R. Johnson, and J. Vlissides. *Design Patterns: Elements of Reusable Object Oriented Software,* Addison-Wesley, Reading, MA, 1995.
2. Coplien, J.O. *Advanced C++ Programming Styles and Idioms.* Addison-Wesley, Reading, MA, 1992.
3. Alexander, C. *The Timeless Way of Building,* Oxford University Press, New York, 1979.

Design Patterns to Construct the Hot Spots of a Manufacturing Framework

Hans Albrecht Schmid
schmidha@rz-uxazs.fh-konstanz.de

INTRODUCTION

The design of a framework is usually fairly complex [JF88] as a result of the considerable variability required, since a framework represents not just a solution to a given application problem, but a family of solutions for the application domain. Our experience in developing the black-box framework, OSEFA, for automated control of a subdomain of manufacturing systems [S95b], has shown that framework design is made easier by performing a sequence of transformation steps on a simple, specialized domain model. Each transformation is guided by a design pattern [GHJV94] [BeJ94]. In this paper, which extends the work in [S95b], we generalize our experience and show how design patterns are useful for framework design.

Before designing a domain-specific framework, a domain analysis must be done. Its objective is to identify the fixed aspects or frozen spots, common to all applications in the domain, and the variable aspects, where applications may differ, called hot spots after [P94]. Note that we use the term *hot spot* in a slightly more general way.

In a framework, each hot spot is represented by a subsystem that hides the variability of the aspect from the rest of the framework. Developing a detailed structure for each hot spot subsystem of the framework may be complicated. Design patterns are ideally suited to help with this work. Most of the design patterns presented in [GHJV94] provide a different

---

This article was originally published in a somewhat different form.

kind of flexibility. The Adapter pattern, for example, provides flexibility with regard to different implementation classes with differing interfaces.

A hot spot requires a certain variability or flexibility, so when implementing a hot spot of a framework, we should look for the pattern that provides this flexibility. The pattern then provides the architectural design for the hot spot.

The hot spot design is incorporated into the framework design as follows. We start with a basic domain-specific model, which does not provide any variability, but is strictly tailored toward a specific configuration. This model is obtained by an object-oriented analysis of a single, specific configuration. In subsequent transformation steps, the model is generalized to incorporate domain variability. For each hot spot, a transformation step is performed. Each transformation introduces a flexible subsystem, where the detailed design is determined by a pattern.

We describe in the Frameworks section the characteristics of different kinds of frameworks and their impacts on framework design. In Hot Spot Subsystem Design with Design Patterns, we relate hot spots with their required variability to the general structure of a hot spot subsystem and show how the detailed design is done with design patterns. After a description of the manufacturing subdomain in the Variability of the Manufacturing Subdomain section, we begin Basic Model of a Manufacturing Application with a simple domain-specific model, the result of an object-oriented analysis for a particular manufacturing configuration. A sequence of transformation steps, described in Machine Variability Hot Spot, Business Task Variability Hot Spot, Processing Sequence Variability Hot Spot, and Variability of the Business Services Hot Spot, is applied for each hot spot to create the class structure of the framework.

Each transformation step for a hot spot is based on generative design patterns, which provide a rule to be applied dynamically for when and how to apply a pattern, the "why" of a design [BeJ94]. It has seven sections, which describe:

- the variable aspect of the hot spot
- the problems related to the variability
- the requirements for the solution
- the hot spot design, i.e., the subsystem structure that covers the variability of the hot spot in a transparent way, and how it relates to existing classes
- the hot spot subsystem base class and the derived classes
- their cooperation with other classes.

FRAMEWORKS

A framework [JF88] [JR91] provides functionality, with fixed aspects that cannot be changed and variable aspects that can be changed. Different systems may be created from a framework depending on how the variable aspects are configured. Thus, a framework defines a family of programs. Following [P94], we call the variable aspects the hot spots of a framework and the fixed aspects the frozen spots. Each hot spot incorporates a single, variable aspect of the application domain.

Frameworks comprise a set of cooperating classes [JF88]. The interactions of these classes are, typically, part of the frozen spots of a framework. The high-level design of a system, which defines the components of the solution, their interfaces and their interactions, is reused within a framework, and since complete classes or methods of classes belong to the frozen spots of the . framework, detailed design and code are also reused. By combining the reuse of high-level design, detailed design and code, frameworks promise high reuse rates, i.e., the ratio of reused code to the total code.

Frameworks are classified according to their subject area, as application or domain-specific frameworks, and according to the way in which an application is created, as white-box or black-box frameworks.

Application frameworks provide basic functionality for similar kinds of applications in different application domains. Specific application content that models the application domain is missing. For this reason, it might be better to call these application-enabling frameworks. Most of the well-known frameworks like ET++ [WGM89] [G92] [P94] and Taligent's Commonpoint belong to this category. They provide mainly a GUI-functionality for the representation, administration, and storage of application-specific data.

Domain-specific frameworks, with which there is still not a lot of experience, model specific functionality of an application domain with generic business process and business objects. Usually, the business process is generic in that it may be performed in different configurations from the domain. A developer creates an application from a domain-specific framework by implementing a particular configuration based on business objects and binding the generic business process to this configuration. The example we describe in this paper is a part-processing manufacturing process from the metal industries, which may be performed in many different configurations of manufacturing cells and manufacturing systems.

White-box frameworks, the predominant type, provide classes that are incomplete for the hot spots. A developer completes or specializes these classes by completing or redefining their methods. The developer must have considerable knowledge of the framework code. Different approaches have been proposed to alleviate the task of developing an application from a framework [J92] [P94], but it is not yet clear how successful they will be.

For this reason, we advocate the use of black-box frameworks. A black-box framework contains the complete code. To provide an adaptation, the framework contains, for each hot spot, a set of alternative and sometimes complementary classes (see Fig. 1). For example, if the aspect is the machining of parts, the subsystem will provide different classes of machines suitable for the machining of parts. An application developer will select, for each hot spot, one or more of these classes, possibly parameterize it, and configure it. There is no need to do any programming, and the task requires less knowledge of software engineering than the application domain.

Development of black-box frameworks is more expensive than that of white-box frameworks, for two reasons. One is that variable aspects have to be separated from each other so the resulting elementary variable aspects are orthogonal (see Fig. 2). For example, suppose there are three related, but independent variable aspects, with ten, ten, and twenty choices, respectively. When the three aspects are included in one hot spot, the framework would have to provide 2,000 alternatives for the hot spot, which is practically impossible. When the variable aspects are separated, and each elementary aspect is included in a hot spot of its own, the framework has to provide only 40 alternatives, which is realistic. For a white-box framework, the problem does not exist, since it does not provide alternatives for a hot spot, but just leaves the hot spot open for completion by the framework user. It is not possible to reduce the initial design effort for black-box frameworks. On the other hand, it has been shown that this effort pays off [BrJ94].

The second reason for the expense of black-box framework development is that all alternative realizations of each variable aspect must be provided. One approach, as we have done in our project, is to provide only those alternatives required for the few first uses of the framework. Later, the framework may be supplemented on demand. In this way, the initial investment may be reduced considerably.

There is not necessarily a strict distinction between black-box and white-box frameworks; the distance between them may be a continuum. Within a black-box framework, some alternatives may not be provided, but must be supplemented. When a white-box framework is fully orthogonalized, frequently selected alternatives may be preplanned and implemented as sub-

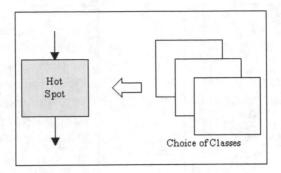

FIGURE 1   Hot spot subsystem of a black-box framework.

classes in black-box mode, whereas less frequent or unanticipated cases must be created in white-box mode by developing a new subclass.

HOT SPOT SUBSYSTEM DESIGN
WITH DESIGN PATTERNS

One of the characteristics of a black-box framework is that a new application is created from it without requiring a recompilation, by implementing each hot spot with a distinct subsystem that provides the required variability (see Fig. 3). A hot spot subsystem contains a set of alternative classes, each of which incorporates one occurrence of the variability. The application developer selects one or several classes from this set to compose an application. This binds the variability of the hot spot to the selected occurrences.

The alternative classes of a subsystem are derived from the same, typically abstract, base class, which defines the common interface. This class may also implement functionality common to all subclasses. Polymorphism and dynamic binding , the distinguishing characteristics of object-orientation, are used to fix the variability of a hot spot:

- without requiring recompilation
- open to future completion with additional subclasses.

Often, a subsystem contains additional classes that may have other relationships with its subclasses.

A template method requests a service from one of the alternative subclasses of the subsystem [GHJV94] [P94]. It makes no difference, if it is a

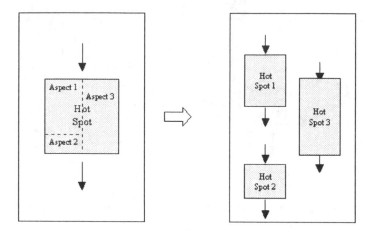

FIGURE 2   Orthogonalization of a hot spot.

member of a class outside of the subsystem, or of a class that is a part of it. The method of the subsystem base class that provides the service is called a hook method. The template method makes its request by sending a message via a polymorphic reference of the subsystem base class type. This pointer is set during the composition of an application from the framework to reference an object from one of the subsystem subclasses. Thus, the result of calling a hook method depends on the way an application has been configured from the framework.

For example, consider the transmission hot spot of a subframework that provides the connection of a machine control or a robot control via a communication line or network to a cell computer, a DNC coupling, or an RC-coupling [SP93]. The subframework is represented in Figure 4 by a Coad/Yourdon diagram [CY91]. (The Coad/Yourdon notation, generated by the tool objectiF, is explained in Box 1.) The hot spot subsystem consists of the Transmission base class and the subclasses Transmission A, B, and C. Send is the hook method. It is called by the template method Download of the class DNC-Coupling, which is exterior to the subsystem. Each of the alternative transmission classes implements the Send method with a different transmission protocol. The template method Download, which requests the service Send, is parameterized with regard to the way telegrams are transmitted. On the other hand, when we consider the SerialCom hot spot and subsystem, the previous hook method Send is a template method. It calls the hook method Put of the class SerialCom to put characters onto the transmission line.

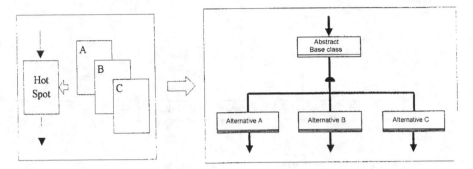

FIGURE 3   Realization of a hot spot subsystem by a base class with derived classes.

The view that all hot spots are mapped in the same way into a subsystem is high-level and coarse. Though the basic structure of a hot spot subsystem is always the same (see Fig. 3), different subsystems must be refined, and their relationship to non-subsystem classes must be elaborated in a different way, since the requirements of the different hot spots differ. We will use the term *detailed structure of a subsystem* when we mean both its refinement and its elaboration.

Our experience [S95b] is that it is useful to classify and describe the detailed structure of a hot spot subsystem according to domain-independent semantic aspects using design patterns [GHJV94]. This is different from the approach proposed in [P94], which classifies the different detailed structures of subsystems according to their syntactic characteristics; i.e., the way template methods and hook methods are related, as metapatterns. Although we did not know this approach when doing the work described in this paper, our opinion is that this approach is less suitable for the average software developer.

Consider, for example, the Adapter design pattern [GHJV94]. It provides variability with regard to the different representations and implementations of a concept, where each implementation has different responsibilities and a different interface. The Adapter pattern has as participants a client, which requests services from a target. The target is the base class of the hot spot subsystem to be introduced. Each Adapter subclass, derived from the target, adapts an adaptee—i.e., one of the different representations and implementations of the concept—to the target. Figure 5 shows how the Adapter pattern forms the hot spot subsystem of a framework and defines the relationships of the subsystem with the outside.

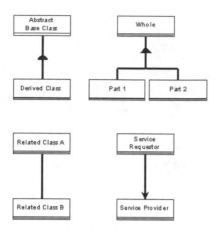

Box 1   Coad/Yourdon notation.

If the hot spot subsystems of a framework are classified after completing the development according to the design patterns used, the result is better understanding and insight, but no saving of development effort. On the other hand, considerable effort may be saved if the developer uses design patterns to design the detailed structure of the hot spot subsystems. The starting point for this approach is to collect the hot spots and to describe, for each of them, the required variability. A design pattern that provides the required variability is then selected to refine the hot spot subsystem. For example, if variability of the implementation of a concept is required under the assumption that classes with different interfaces implement the concept, a framework developer would select the Adapter design pattern to realize the hot spot subsystem.

The framework developer will usually not have to develop a solution to realize a hot spot subsystem of a framework. The design pattern provides the required variability and becomes the hot spot architectural design. In addition to the development effort saved, which might be smaller with a more experienced developer, this approach has the following advantages:

- the solution is standardized, easier to understand, document, and maintain
- the confidence in the appropriateness and correctness of the solution is much greater.

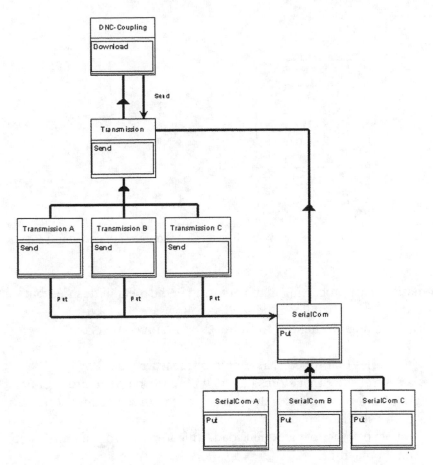

FIGURE 4   Coad/Yourdon diagram of the subsystems of a DNC/RC-coupling subframework.

VARIABILITY OF THE MANUFACTURING SUBDOMAIN

OSEFA [S95a] is a black-box framework, developed at the Fachhochschule Konstanz, that supports the creation of a family of automated control applications for a subdomain of part processing manufacturing cells or systems. In this paper we will speak of manufacturing cells when referring to cells or systems. For related work on object-oriented manufacturing cell control, see [AEM94]. OSEFA realizes a business process, which might be considered a business procedure that forms a part of a business process, in different configurations of manufacturing cells. The business process itself may vary slightly. The application domain is not the whole

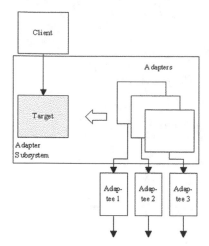

FIGURE 5   Adapter hot spot subsystem.

domain of part-processing manufacturing in the metal industries, but only a subdomain of it, which is defined as follows.

Each manufacturing cell from the subdomain consists of:

- machines that process, assemble or measure parts
- a central store that stores pallets with parts between processing
- robots or other devices that move pallets from a central store to a buffer store and back
- robots or other devices that load/unload parts from a buffer store into a machine.

Each of the machines, robots, and devices has a local control, a CNC-control (Computerized Numerical Control), a RC-control (Robot Control), or a PLC-control (Programmable Logic Control), which is coupled to the cell computer that coordinates the processing of the machines, robots, and devices of the manufacturing cell.

Together with the business process, these characteristics form the frozen spots of OSEFA. The business process is the production of parts by several machines. Parts undergo one or more processing steps on different machines. A work sheet describes, for a part, the sequence of processing steps and the resources required to perform a processing step. A machine order is an order to a machine to perform a processing step for a number of parts. The parts are on or in pallets. Before and after processing steps, a pallet with the parts is stored in a central store. For each machine, there exists a machine allocation schedule. It describes in which sequence and at which time machine orders are processed on the machine, and it provides a reference to the work sheet. The list of machine orders is created by an external control system that optimizes the work allocation, which may be a fine-grained material requirements planning or a manual shop-floor planning system.

The steps for the processing of a machine order are shown in Box 2. Together with the steps required to go from one machine order to the next, which we do not describe here for simplicity, this processing sequence describes the abstract application logic. It is simplified for easier understanding. In reality:

- It is optimized so the transport of pallets is done, when possible, in parallel with, and not between, machining steps. We try to keep expensive machines busy.
- The processing is directly coupled to the manufacturing process. It has to react to and is controlled by the technical events that originate in the manufacturing process.
- The processing sequence is performed concurrently on all machines in the manufacturing cell.

In this paper, we will not address problems related to concurrent execution.

An example of a configuration in which this business process is performed, see the manufacturing cell in Figure 6, the simplified CIM factory of the Fachhochschule Konstanz. It consists of a CNC-lathe machine with a pallet buffer store, a portal robot, and a central store for pallets. The portal robot, equipped with an effector exchange system, is a transport system

---

1. Move a pallet with raw parts from the central store to the buffer store near the machine.
2. Load a raw part from the pallet into the machine.
3. Process the part in the machine.
4. Unload the machined part from the machine into the pallet.
5. Repeat steps 2 to 4, until all parts on the pallet are processed.
6. Move the pallet back to the central store.
7. Repeat steps 1 to 6, until all pallets in a machine order are processed.

Box 2   Abstract processing sequence, or abstract business logic of the subdomain.

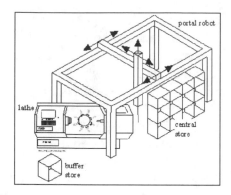

FIGURE 6   Manufacturing cell with store, buffer, lathe, and portal robot.

that moves pallets between store and buffer store, and a handling system for loading and unloading parts from the pallet into the lathe and back.

Other configurations that support the same business process, may have, at first glance, no similarity with the configuration described. Consider, for example, a manufacturing cell that contains a machining center and a numerically controlled coordinate inspection machine, the interfaces of which differ from each other and from the lathe machine. Pallets are moved by a PLC-controlled conveyor belt to the buffer stores near the machines. Each robot loads and unloads parts from the pallet to the machine. Configurations from the selected subdomain are variable with regard to the following aspects, the hot spots of OSEFA:

- the number, variety, and kinds of machines. OSEFA includes different CNC-machines, different RC-controlled assembly stations, and different PLC-controlled machines or assembly stations.
- the loading and unloading of parts. It may be performed by a different number and kind of robot or device; for example, either by one portal robot serving all machines, or by one or two smaller robots or devices for each machine.
- the geometry, topology, and kind of system that moves the pallets. The transport system may be, for example, a portal robot, as in the sample cell, or a PLC-controlled conveyor belt.
- the combination of the transport and the handling system. There may be separate transport and handling systems, or they may be combined, as in the robot of the sample cell.
- the automated processing may include only the part processing, as described in this paper, or the set-up and preparing of tools.

Whereas this configuration variability is of a global kind, there is a configuration variability of a local kind. It causes only slight differences in the sequence of processing steps, i.e., a variability of the business logic, in comparison to that described in Box 2. For example:

- A single effector or a double effector may be used for loading and unloading of parts.
- The same pallet, or two different pallets may be used for the raw and the machined parts.

The processing shown in Box 2 is done with a single effector and one pallet for both the raw and machined parts.

The hot spots of the subdomain targeted by OSEFA are represented in Figure 7, ordered according to the layer of abstraction to which each one belongs. The business services variability hot spot does not stem directly from the subdomain characteristics, but is due to framework evolution; more business services might be included in the framework (see Business Task Variability Hot Spot and Variability of the Business Services Hot Spot).

BASIC MODEL OF A MANUFACTURING APPLICATION

An object-oriented analysis of the sample application (see Fig. 6) yields a basic model of a manufacturing application. It is represented in Figure 8 by a Coad/Yourdon diagram.

The diagram says that a manufacturing cell consists of stores, buffers, robots, and lathe machines (see Fig. 6) as well as a cell operator, a processing control, a list of machine orders, and a work sheet. For each processing machine like the lathe, the processing sequence, described in Box 2, is performed concurrently with the other machines by a ProcessingControl object. Each ProcessingControl object uses its list of machine orders with information from the work sheet. It may receive service requests from a cell operator. ProcessingControl requests services from the store, the buffers, its associated lathe machine, and from the robot.

ProcessingControl performs the abstract application logic described in Box 2. Since it is bound to a particular configuration, the simplified concrete application logic shown in Box 3 looks quite different. It is easy to see that it is strongly tied to the configuration, i.e., the lathe doing the processing and the robot doing the handling and moving of pallets. The same

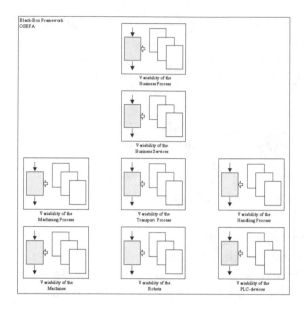

FIGURE 7   Hot spots of the manufacturing subdomain treated by OSEFA.

handling task might be performed by completely different command sequences and robot programs on different handling machines or devices.

This means that the concrete application logic, i.e., the concrete business logic, cannot be reused over different configurations. To make the concrete application logic configuration independent, we apply a sequence of transformation steps to the basic manufacturing control model. For each hot spot, a transformation step is performed. (Note that these transformation steps are a subset of the ones described in [S95b]. Some of the latter were done for structural reasons, and not to achieve flexibility or generality.) Each transformation introduces a subsystem into the basic manufacturing control model. The detailed structure of the subsystem is determined by the design pattern that covers the variable aspect of the hot spot.

The introduction of a hot spot subsystem makes the framework invariant or transparent, relative to the variability of the hot spot. The framework classes become reusable even when the variable aspect of the hot spot is changed in different configurations. After subsystems have been introduced for all hot spots of the framework, the class structure of the framework and its classes are invariant with respect to all variable aspects of the domain and thus reusable.

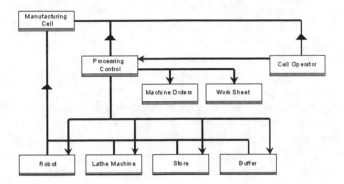

FIGURE 8   Basic manufacturing control model.

MACHINE VARIABILITY HOT SPOT

The machine variability hot spot and the robot variability hot spot (see Fig. 7) are examples of the common variability of devices. Our objective is to make this variability transparent to the other objects of the framework.

Hot spot variability. Machines and robots are configuration specific objects. Different manufacturing cell configurations contain different machines and robots from different classes, which have a similar responsibility. ProcessingControl requests services from one or several of them (see Fig. 8). Exchanging a machine of one manufacturing cell with another should be possible without modifying ProcessingControl.

Problem. Different machine classes may have different interfaces, so ProcessingControl has to adapt to these differences when a machine is exchanged.

Requirement. The client ProcessingControl must cooperate with service providing objects from different classes without having to be modified.

Hot Spot Design. The Adapter pattern [GHJV94] (see Fig. 9) allows the client ProcessingControl to request identical services from different classes or adaptees, like LatheMachine and Robot, with similar responsibilities. The adapter hot spot subsystem replaces the direct use of client and adaptee by having the client ProcessingControl request services from the base class of the hot spot subsystem to be introduced. Since the adaptees,

---

1. Request the following services from the robot (to move the pallet from the store to the buffer)
   - to download the robot program A
   - to parameterize program A with the position of the pallet in the store
   - to start program A
2. Request the following services from the robot (to load a part to the lathe machine from the buffer store)
   - to download and start a robot program B (to exchange the pallet effector with a part effector)
   - to download the robot program C (that loads the part)
   - to load parameters to parameterize (with the position of the part in the pallet)
   - to start the robot program C
3. Request the lathe machine to start the NC-program that machines the part.
4. Unloading is done similarly; see step 2.
5. Repeat steps 2 to 4, until all parts of a pallet are machined.
6. Move the full pallet back to the store as in step 1.
7. Repeat steps 1 to 6, until all pallets of a machine order are processed.

BOX 3   Concrete business logic.

the existing machines, must be adapted to the target, an adapter subclass is derived for each adaptee.

Subsystem Base Class and Derived Classes. To allow for Processing-Control to request identical services, the interfaces of the CNC-machines and robots must be standardized. We generalize and abstract from their differences by introducing an abstract base class, CNC-Machine, which defines a common interface and common internal data and services. We include robots in this class, since they have a similar behavior with regard to NC-programs, to RC-programs, and as CNC-machines. Note that generalization is a difficult and lengthy process with regard to existing real world objects and is not the topic of this paper.

To make the base class CNC-Machine cooperate with different machines, adapter classes are derived from the base class. An adapter class, like StandardizedLatheMachine or StandardizedRobot, represents a standardized machine. It contains a reference to the adaptee, the specific machine, and maps the base class interface to the interface of the specific machine class.

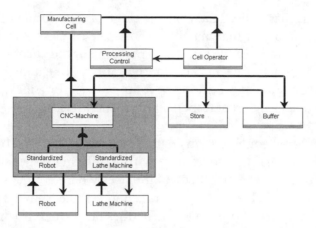

FIGURE 9   Manufacturing cell with hot spot subsystem that covers the machine variability (without machine orders and work sheet).

Cooperation with other classes. A standardized machine receives standardized service requests from ProcessingControl. It transforms a request into a robot or a lathe request, or a sequence of these requests. It forwards the requests to the specific machine that it references.

The hot spots for machines or devices controlled by a programmable logic control (PLC) and other kinds of machines and devices are standardized with separate base classes as, e.g., PLC-Device, in the same way.

BUSINESS TASK VARIABILITY HOT SPOT

The abstract business logic (see Box 2) requests the execution of business-related tasks like the movement of pallets and the handling and machining of parts. The machining, movement, and handling task hot spots (see Fig. 7) show that the implementation of business tasks may vary in different configurations. After the first transformation step, ProcessingControl requests standardized machine and device services, instead of business task related services.

Movement hot spot variability. In different configurations, different kinds of devices may perform the same business task. For example, either a robot from a CNC-Machine class or a conveyor belt from a PLC-Device class may receive the order to move a pallet.

This means that a client class has the same task performed by a configuration specific object that may be an instance of classes with different responsibilities. To have the same task performed, the client may have to request a different service for each configuration. For example, sending a message to someone may be done by a fax, a letter, or a messenger, each of which provides different responsibilities and services.

Problem. When a configuration change exchanges one kind of machine, robot, or device against another one with a differing responsibility, ProcessingControl must be modified at all places where it requests a service from an exchanged object as, e.g., a transport service from the robot. The reason for this is that ProcessingControl does not request a genuine transport service from the robot, but a specific service for a generalized machine or device. The knowledge of how a transport service is performed by the robot is incorporated in ProcessingControl's code. For example, ProcessingControl has to know which robot program performs a certain transport task, and how this robot program is parameterized with the position of the pallet. There is a strong binding between ProcessingControl and the device performing the transport task.

Requirement. To relax this binding, the transport service is realized in different configurations by different kinds of devices as, e.g., by a portal robot, modeled by a CNC-Machine, or by a conveyor belt modeled by a PLC-controlled device. ProcessingControl should request a business-task related service without regard for the device that performs this business task in a particular configuration.

Hot Spot Design. The Adapter pattern [GHJV94] (see Fig. 10) allows the client ProcessingControl, to request identical services from adaptees, different classes with different responsibilities, like a CNCMachine. It replaces the relationship between client and adaptee by having the client ProcessingControl request services defined by Transport, the newly introduced target. Transport is the base class of the hot spot subsystem to be introduced. To implement these services on the adaptees, standardized devices of different kinds like CNC-Machines or PLC-Devices, the adaptees must be adapted to the Transport interface. This is done by adapter classes, e.g., CNC-Transport or PLC-Transport, which are derived as subclasses from Transport (see Fig. 10).

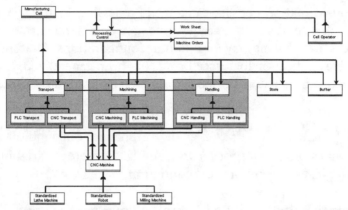

FIGURE 10   Manufacturing cell with business task related hot spot subsystems.

Subsystem Base Class and Derived Classes. To make the Processing-Control flexible with respect to a change of the transport system, we have to abstract from the particular way transport is done. To this end, we introduce a class Transport that provides genuine transport services, for example, "Move pallet x from position y in the store to the buffer store z," without considering how they are implemented.

From Transport, an adapter subclass like CNC-Transport is derived for each standardized device that provides transport services. A class like CNC-Transport is parameterizable to be adapted to different cell configurations. It contains a reference to the machine/device performing the task, a CNC-Machine (see Fig. 10) and mapping tables. These tables describe the configuration specific mapping from different transport tasks to robot programs, and from the parameters of the transport service that describe, e.g., the position of a pallet abstractly, to the concrete parameters of the robot program.

Cooperation with other classes. A CNC-Transport receives standardized requests for transport services from ProcessingControl, transforms a request using the mapping tables to one or several requests to a CNC-machine, and forwards these requests to the referenced machine.

The same approach applies to the handling and the machining hot spots. Introducing Transport, Handling, and Machining classes and applying the adapter pattern to them produces the Coad/Yourdon diagram in Figure 10. The relations among Machining, Transport, and Handling in Figure 10 show that one Transport object and one or two Handling objects provide services for a Machining object.

The transformation steps have changed ProcessingControl so it requests business task specific services, i.e., genuine transport, handling, and machining services, in the same way for different configurations. That means that the concrete application logic (see Box 3) has been generalized. It has been transformed to the subdomain-specific abstract application logic (see Box 2).

PROCESSING SEQUENCE VARIABILITY HOT SPOT

As the business logic hot spot shows (see Fig. 7), there is variability in the business logic, as a result of local configuration changes.

Hot spot variability. ProcessingControl controls the processing of the system. In different configurations, processing is done following different sequences. Consider the business logic when using an effector for single parts. A machine is unloaded before it can be loaded again (see Box 2). A completed part is put on a pallet before the next raw part is fetched. With a double effector that can grip both a raw and a machined part, loading and unloading is a combined process so the raw part is fetched before the completed part is put down.

There are a number of different algorithms embedded in a common context.

Problem. It would be expensive to provide a ProcessingControl class for each processing sequence. Also, it requires considerable knowledge of a major part of the framework to develop a new ProcessingControl, since ProcessingControl must consider more details than just the sequencing of part processing. These include the coarse-grained processing of machine orders like:

- the transition from one machine order to the next
- the fetching of information from a machine order list, work sheet, store, buffer, and pallets
- doing the set-up of machines with NC-programs, tools, and other resources,
- the binding of service requests to the objects that provide them
- the implementation of the reaction to technical events, and of the locking of concurrent accesses to shared resources like buffers or pallets.

Requirement. To separate the sequencing decisions, which vary to a great extent, from the other items which are invariant.

Hot Spot Design. The strategy pattern [GHJV94] objectifies an algorithm and separates it from its context in separate strategy classes. Concrete strategy subclasses are derived from an abstract base class strategy, ProcessingStrategy (see Fig.11).

Subsystem Base Class and Derived Classes. An abstract strategy base class, ProcessingStrategy, defines the interface of the algorithm. The interface contains a method, Process, that executes the part processing sequence. Each subclass implements the method for one local configuration (see Fig. 11).

Cooperation with other classes. The context ProcessingControl contains a reference to the strategy. Using this reference, ProcessingControl calls the Process method of ProcessingStrategy when everything is ready to produce the parts.

The ProcessingStrategy subclasses request business services like transport and handling services. When separating the ProcessingStrategy from its context, the objective is to make the strategy as simple and as abstract as possible. This means that ProcessingStrategy should describe only the variable sequencing decisions. It should not have to consider items that are the same for all strategies, for example, providing the parameters for transport and similar service requests. Therefore, these items are separated from ProcessingStrategy and added to a commonly used class.

The only candidate location for these services is ProcessingControl. ProcessingControl is complex, even though we have separated ProcessingStrategy from it. It should not have more responsibilities, but do only coarse-grained processing of machine orders. To this end, we use the mediator pattern [GHJV94]. The reason for choosing this pattern is, in contrast to our use of the other design patterns, not flexibility but clearer structuring. A mediator object, ProcessingMediator, is attached to each part processing machine and its associated ProcessingControl object.

The ProcessingMediator (see Fig. 12) enables references to objects to participate in an interaction between colleague objects: Machining, Transport, Handling, ProcessingStrategy, and MachineOrderAdministration. The ProcessingMediator provides parameterless services, e.g., UnloadMachine, ExchangePallet, DoMachining, IsCompletedPartPalletFull. ProcessingStrategy requests these services in the correct sequence. When ProcessingStrategy requests these services, ProcessingMediator adds the missing parameter values to these service requests, and forwards the requests to their destination

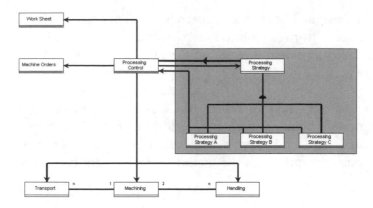

FIGURE 11   ProcessingStrategy hot spot subsystem, separated from Processing-Control (Figure does not show all classes of Fig. 10).

objects. It stores the references to the destination objects and the information to complete the parameter values.

Consider, for example, the request UnloadMachine. When Processing-Mediator receives this request from a ProcessingStrategy it adds the machine to be unloaded, the buffer into which the part is put, and the position of the part in the pallet on the buffer. It forwards the completed request to its associated handling object. ProcessingStrategy can be coded as easily as writing pseudocode, and for only one class. ProcessingControl is required for all variations of the global and local configuration.

ProcessingMediator is different from the mediator in [GHJV94]. We do not use an abstract base class with derived subclasses. The only flexibility required from ProcessingMediator is the connection to different colleagues. This flexibility is provided by setting up references to the colleagues during the manufacturing cell configuration.

VARIABILITY OF THE BUSINESS SERVICES HOT SPOT

ProcessingStrategy and ProcessingControl request business services from the business tasks. Over time, more services may be added to the manufacturing control system, as Figure 7 shows.

Hot spot variability. Requests for different kinds of services, like transport and handling services, originate in a ProcessingStrategy subclass and are forwarded via classes, like ProcessingMediator, to the service providing classes like Transport and Handling. The ability to include services,

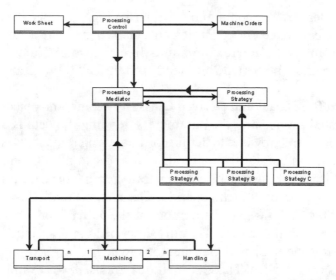

FIGURE 12   Using a Processing Mediator to simplify ProcessingControl.

which are currently not part of the system, might be required. For example, if automated tool processing were implemented, related service requests for the set-up of machines with tools would have to be added.

Problem. A number of classes provide methods for each of the services, e.g., load, unload, move pallet, even though each class handles the different services in a similar way. The service requests are queued by a class, MaterialFlow, not described in this paper, see [S95b]. This class forwards the requests to Transport or Handling. Two structural problems, not related to the variability of the hot spot, are that different methods are required to forward different services in the same way, and that service requests must be queued. The third problem, related to the variability of the services, is that if a new request is defined, the interfaces of all participating classes must be modified.

Requirement. For structural reasons, we want to:

- have a simple way to forward and queue service requests
- simplify the participating classes and make variability of services more transparent
- provide interfaces for services not dependent on number and details, i.e., the parameters, of the commands.

Hot Spot Design. The command pattern (see Fig. 13) objectifies a service request to a command object. Participants in the pattern are an abstract base class, Command; concrete commands like TransportCommand, HandlingCommand, and SetUpCommand; and the caller ProcessingStrategy.

Subsystem Base Class and Derived Classes. A command object describes the requested service and the parameters defining the details of the service. Methods are provided to define commands incrementally. The Command base class defines the methods that apply to all different services. Mainly, this is the constructor with a parameter that determines the command as, e.g., UnloadMachine, and a Get-method that allows querying it. The details, for example, the number of the buffer from which a part is loaded, vary with the service. They are described in the specific command subclass Add methods and Get methods, which allow setting or getting the details of a service. The Get methods are used, for example, by the classes that pass and forward the commands to make, when required, case distinctions based on the command contents.

Cooperation with other classes. A command object is created by the caller ProcessingStrategy, which knows the service it requests. Details are added by the ProcessingMediator before it forwards the commands to the provider of the service.

Our motivation for introducing commands differs from that in the command design pattern [GHJV94]. For further details regarding our motivation and information on the control of a directly coupled technical process, see [S95b].

The command hot spot subsystem differs from the hot spot subsystems described in the preceding sections with respect to the transparency of its variability. When we add a new Command subclass, it will probably provide new, specialized services not defined in the base class. When we add a new subclass to the hot spot subsystems defined in the preceding sections, it will probably provide a different implementation of the abstract services defined in the base class.

As a result, the objective of making the variability of the business services hot spot transparent to the other framework classes has not been met completely in this case. When we add a new command subclass, we have to add the corresponding methods to other classes outside the command hot spot subsystem, that not only forward the command, but process it. One answer to this framework evolution problem might be to provide, internally to the

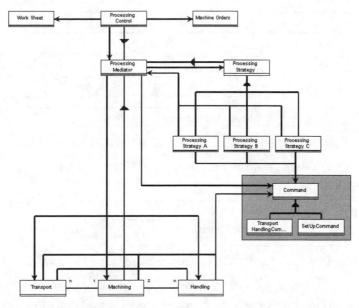

FIGURE 13   The business services (command) hot spot subsystem and its use by other classes.

classes that process commands, a class hierarchy for processing commands that parallels the command hierarchy. We have not yet investigated this question in detail, since it is currently a minor problem.

CONCLUSION

We have presented a new approach for constructing a framework and its hot spots with the use of design patterns. The example used is the manufacturing framework OSEFA, with which we have experience implementing several prototypes, since 1993, and the full version, as described in this paper, by end of 1995.

By the transformations and the introduction of the hot spot subsystems, a layered architecture, represented in Figure 14, was created for the manufacturing framework. We have added to the initial two layers, specific machines/devices and processing control, three more layers, standardized machines/devices, business objects, and part processing strategy, the latter by separating the processing control layer. Each of the new layers embeds one, or several similar, hot spot subsystems, each consisting of a new generalized concept with different alternatives for its realization. Thus, the new layers provide for the variability and flexibility of the framework.

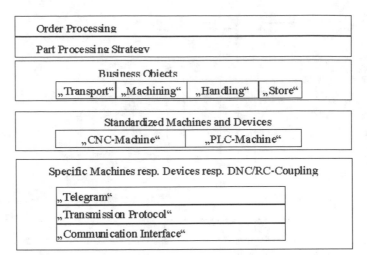

FIGURE 14   Layered architecture of the manufacturing framework.

Our approach to framework construction is similar to Pree's [P94] in that both

- center framework design around the hot spots of the framework
- provide a structure that makes the variability of a hot spot transparent to the rest of the framework. Pree's structure is a template-hook structure, our structure is a hot spot subsystem.

The differences are that

- Pree uses metapatterns, while we use design patterns, to provide the required flexibility for the hot spot design
- we use a sequence of generalizing transformation steps to develop the framework class structure. Each transformation step creates a subsystem that implements a hot spot.

Comparing the use of design patterns and of metapatterns, it seems that design patterns provide better, more concrete direction for realizing the hot spots, at least for an average software engineer. Metapatterns leave a lot of detailed design to be done by the framework developer, but provide more flexibility. The latter obviously is an advantage but may also be a disadvantage, since for similar problems, dissimilar solutions may be developed. Design patterns show promise of becoming canonical components for software engineering. Further, as the catalog of design patterns becomes more and more complete, there will be few open design problems.

There is no contradiction between the use of design patterns and that of metapatterns; they may be easily combined in the following way. When a pattern covers the variability required in a hot spot, one should use the pattern to determine an architectural hot spot subsystem design. Otherwise, if no suitable pattern is available, one should use a metapattern.

ACKNOWLEDGMENTS

Thanks are due to
- Clemens Ballarin, Francesco Indolfo, Frank Mueller and Jochen Peters, who cooperated with me to build the framework OSEFA
- to the Bundesministerium fuer Forschung, Technologie, Bildung und Wissenschaft for the support of the project in 1994/95
- to the Deutsche Forschungsgemeinschaft (DFG) for the support of the project.

REFERENCES

[AEM94] A. Aarsten, G. Elia, G. Menga: G++: A Pattern Language for Computer Integrated Manufacturing; In: J. Coplien, D. Schmidt (eds): *Proc. PLOP'94,* Addison Wesley, 1995.

[AP91] R. Prieto-Diaz, G. Arango, eds., *Domain Analysis and Soft-ware Systems Modeling,* IEEE Computer Press, Los Alamitos, 1991.

[BeJ94] K. Beck, R. Johnson: Patterns Generate Architectures; In: *Proc. ECOOP 1994,* Springer Lecture Notes in Computer Science, Berlin, 1994.

[BrJ94] J. Brant, R. E. Johnson: Creating Tools in HotDraw by Composition; in: B. Magnusson et al. (eds.): *Technology of Object-Oriented Languages and Systems TOOLS 13,* Prentice Hall, Englewood Cliffs, NJ, 1994, pp. 445–454.

[CY91] P. Coad, E. Yourdon: *Object Oriented Analysis,* Prentice-Hall, Englewood Cliffs, NJ, 1991.

[D89] L. P. Deutsch: Design Reuse and Frameworks in the Smalltalk-80 Programming System; In: Biggerstaff, Perlis, eds., *Software Reusability,* Vol. II, ACM Press, New York, 1989, 55–71.

[G92] E. Gamma: *Objektorientierte Softwareentwicklung am Beispiel von ET++;* Springer, Berlin, 1992.

[GHJV94] E. Gamma, R. Helm, R. Johnson, J. Vlissides: *Design Patterns: Elements of Reusable ObjectOriented Software;* Addison-Wesley, 1994.

[J92] R. E. Johnson: Documenting Frameworks Using Patterns; In: *Proc. OOPSLA '92,* Vancouver, Canada.

[JF88] R. E. Johnson, B. Foote: Designing Reusable Classes; *Journal of Object-Oriented Programming* Vol/No2, June 88, 22–35.

[JR91] R. E. Johnson, V. Russo: Reusing Object-Oriented Design; Tech Report UIUCCDS 91-1696, Dept. of Computer Science, Univ. of Illinois.

[P94] W. Pree: *Design Patterns for Object-Oriented Software Develop-ment;* Addison-Wesley, Reading, Mass., 1994.

[SP93] H. A. Schmid und J. Peters: Ein objektorientierten Baukasten fuer CNC-Maschinen fuer die Zellsteuerung von flexiblen Fertigungszellen; in: H. Reichel (ed.), *Informatik, Wirtschaft, Gesellschaft,* Springer, Berlin, 1993, S.407-414.

[S95a] H. A. Schmid: Entwurf eines objektorientierten Baukastens zur Automatisierung von Fertigungsanlagen; *Informatik Spektrum,* Vol18/No4, August 1995, 210–220.

[S95b] H. A. Schmid: Creating the Architecture of a Manufacturing Framework by Design Patterns; *Proc. OOPSLA '95,* SIGPLAN, ACM.

[WGM89] A. Weinand, E. Gamma, R. Marty: Design and Implemen-tation of ET++, a Seamless Object-Oriented Application Frame-work; *Structured Programming,* Vol. 10, No. 2, 1989.

Using Design Patterns to Evolve System Software from UNIX to Windows NT

Douglas C. Schmidt* and
Paul Stephenson

Developing system software that is reusable across OS platforms is challenging. Due to constraints imposed by the underlying OS platforms, it is often impractical to directly reuse existing algorithms, detailed designs, interfaces, or implementations. This article describes our experiences using a large-scale reuse strategy for system software based on design patterns. Design patterns capture the static and dynamic structures of solutions that occur repeatedly when producing applications in a particular context.[1,2] Design patterns are an important technique for improving system software quality since they address a fundamental challenge in large-scale software development: communication of architectural knowledge among developers.[3]

Our experiences with a large-scale reuse strategy based upon design patterns are described here. This strategy has been used to facilitate the development of efficient OO telecommunication system software at Ericsson. In this article, we present a case study that describes the cross-platform evolution of portions of an OO framework called the ADAPTIVE Service eXecutive (ASX).[4] The ASX framework is an integrated collection of components that collaborate to produce a reusable infrastructure for developing distributed applications.

The ASX framework supports event-driven distributed applications. One of the key components in the ASX framework is the Reactor class category.[5] The Reactor integrates the demultiplexing of events and the

* schmidt@cs.wustl.edu

dispatching of the corresponding event handlers. Event handlers are triggered by various types of events such as timers, synchronization objects, signals, or I/O operations.

We recently ported the ASX framework from several UNIX platforms to the Windows NT platform. These OS platforms possess significantly different mechanisms for event demultiplexing and I/O. To meet our performance requirements, it was not possible to directly reuse many of the components in the ASX framework across the OS platforms. However, it was possible to reuse the underlying design patterns that were embodied in the ASX framework, thereby reducing project risk.

The remainder of the article is organized as follows: the first section outlines the background of our work using OO frameworks for telecommunications system software; the second section presents an overview of the design patterns that are the focus of this article; the third section examines the issues that arose as we ported the components in the Reactor framework from several UNIX platforms to the Windows NT platform; the fourth section summarizes the experience we gained, both pro and con, while deploying a design pattern-based system development methodology in a production software environment; and concluding remarks are given in the fifth section.

BACKGROUND

The design patterns and framework described in this article are currently being applied at Ericsson on a family of client/server applications.[6] These applications use ASX framework as the basis for a highly flexible and extensible telecommunication system management framework. The ASX framework enhances the flexibility and reuse of system software that monitors and manages telecommunication switch performance across multiple hardware and software platforms.

The system software we are developing provides essential services and mechanisms used by higher-level application software. Our system software frameworks are comprised of components that access and manipulate hardware devices (such as telecommunication switches) and software mechanisms residing within an OS kernel (such as alarms, interval timers, synchronization objects, communication ports, and signal handlers).

In general, developing system software that is capable of being directly reused on different OS platforms is challenging. Several factors complicating cross-platform reuse of system software are outlined as follows.

- *Efficiency:* Since applications and other reusable components will be layered upon system software, the techniques used to develop system software must not degrade performance significantly. Otherwise, developers will reinvent special-purpose code rather than reuse existing components, thereby defeating a major benefit of reuse.
- *Portability:* To meet performance and functionality requirements, system software often must access nonportable mechanisms and interfaces (such as device registers within a network link-layer controller or event demultiplexing mechanisms) provided by the underlying OS and hardware platform.
- *Lack of functionality:* Many OS platforms do not provide adequate functionality to develop portable, reusable system components. For example, the lack of kernel-level multithreading, explicit dynamic linking, and asynchronous exception handling (as well as robust compilers that interact correctly with these features) greatly increases the complexity of developing and porting reusable system software.
- *Need to master complex concepts:* Successfully developing robust, efficient, and portable system software requires intimate knowledge of complex mechanisms (such as concurrency control, interrupt handling, and interprocess communication) offered by multiple OS platforms. It is also essential to understand the performance costs associated with using alternative mechanisms (such as shared memory versus message passing) on different OS platforms.

There are trade-offs among the factors described above that further complicate the reuse of system software across OS platforms. Often, it may be difficult to develop portable system software that does not significantly degrade efficiency or subtly alter the semantics and robustness of commonly used operations. For instance, many traditional OS kernels do not support pre-emptive multithreading. Therefore, writing a portable user-level threads mechanism may be less efficient than programming with thread mechanisms supported by the kernel.[7] Likewise, user-level threads may reduce robustness by restricting the use of OS features such as signals or synchronous I/O operations.

DESIGN PATTERN OVERVIEW

A design pattern is a recurring architectural theme that provides a solution to a set of requirements within a particular context.[1] Design patterns facilitate architectural level reuse by providing "blueprints" or guidelines for defining, composing, and reasoning about the key components in a software system. In general, a large amount of reuse is possible at the architectural level. However, reusing design patterns does not necessarily result in direct reuse of algorithms, detailed designs, interfaces, or implementations.

OO frameworks typically embody a wide range of design patterns. For example, the ET++ graphical user-interface (GUI) framework[8] incorporates design patterns (such as Abstract Factory[1]) that hide the details of creating user-interface objects. This enables an application to be portable across different window systems (such as X windows and Microsoft Windows). Likewise, the InterViews[9] GUI framework contains design patterns (such as Strategy and Iterator[1]) that allow algorithms and/or application behavior to be decoupled from mechanisms provided by the reusable GUI components.

In the context of distributed applications, OO toolkits such as the Orbix CORBA object request broker[11] and the ADAPTIVE Service eXecutive framework[4] embody many common design patterns. These design patterns express recurring architectural themes (such as event demultiplexing, connection establishment, message routing, publish/subscribe communication, remote object proxies, and flexible composition of hierarchically related services) found in most distributed applications.

This article focuses on two specific design patterns (the Reactor[5] and Acceptor patterns) that are implemented by the ASX framework. Components in the ASX framework have been ported to a number of UNIX platforms, as well as Windows NT. The ASX components, and the Reactor and Acceptor design patterns embodied by these components, are currently used in a number of production systems. These systems include the Bellcore Q.port ATM signaling software product, the system control segment for the Motorola Iridium global personal communications system, and a family of system/network management applications for Ericsson telecommunication switches.[6]

The design patterns described in the following section provided a concise set of architectural blueprints that guided our porting effort from UNIX to Windows NT. In particular, by employing the patterns, we did not have to rediscover the key collaborations between architectural components. Instead, our development task focused on determining a suitable mapping of the components in the pattern onto the mechanisms provided by the different OS platforms. Finding an appropriate mapping was nontrivial, as we describe later. Nevertheless, our knowledge of the design patterns significantly reduced redevelopment effort and minimized the level of risk in our projects.

THE REACTOR PATTERN

The Reactor pattern is an object behavioral pattern.[1] This pattern simplifies the development of event-driven applications (such as a CORBA ORB,[10] an X-windows host resource manager, or a distributed logging service[5]). The Reactor pattern provides a common infrastructure that integrates event demultiplexing and the dispatching of event handlers. Event handlers perform application-specific processing operations in response to various types of events. An event handler may be triggered by different sources of events (such as timers, communication ports, synchronization objects, and signal handlers) that are monitored by an application. The callback-driven programming style provided by a Motif or Windows application is a prime example of the Reactor pattern.

The Reactor pattern provides several major benefits for event-driven distributed applications:

- *Improve performance:* it enables an application to wait for activity to occur on multiple sources of events simultaneously without blocking or continuously polling for events on any single source.
- *Minimize synchronization complexity:* it provides applications with a low-overhead, coarse-grained form of concurrency control. The Reactor pattern serializes the invocation of event handlers at the level of "event demultiplexing and dispatching" within a single process or thread. For many applications, this eliminates the need for more complicated synchronization or locking.
- *Enchance reuse:* it decouples application-specific functionality from application-independent mechanisms. Application-specific functionality is performed by user-defined methods that override virtual functions inherited from an event handler base class. Application-independent mechanisms are reusable components that demultiplex events and dispatch pre-registered event handlers.

Figure 1 illustrates the structure of participants in the Reactor pattern.* The Reactor class defines an interface for registering, removing, and dispatching

---

* Relationships between components are illustrated throughout the article via Booch notation.[11] Dashed clouds indicate classes; nondashed directed edges indicate inheritance relationships between classes; dashed directed edges indicate a template instantiation relationship; and an undirected edge with a solid bullet at one end indicates a composition relation. Solid clouds indicate objects; nesting indicates composition relationships between objects; and undirected edges indicate some type of link exists between objects.

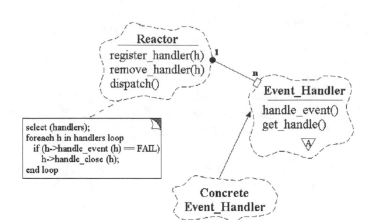

FIGURE 1   The structure of participants in the reactor pattern.

Event_Handler objects. An implementation of the Reactor pattern provides application-independent mechanisms that perform event demultiplexing and dispatch application-specific concrete event handlers. The Reactor class contains references to objects of Concrete_Event_Handler subclasses. These subclasses are derived from the Event_Handler abstract base class, which defines virtual methods for handling events. A Concrete_Event_Handler subclass may override these virtual methods to perform application-specific functionality when the corresponding events occur.

The Reactor triggers Event_Handler methods in response to events. These events may be associated with handles that are bound to sources of events (such as I/O ports, synchronization objects, or signals). To bind the Reactor together with these handles, a subclass of Event_Handler must override the get_handle method. When the Reactor registers an Event_Handler subclass object, the object's handle is obtained by invoking its Event_Handler::get_handle method. The Reactor then combines this handle with other registered Event_Handlers and waits for events to occur on the handle(s).

When events occur, the Reactor uses the handles activated by the events as keys to locate and dispatch the appropriate Event_Handler methods. The code annotation in Figure 1 outlines the behavior of the dispatch method. The handle_event method is then invoked by the Reactor as a "callback." This method performs application-specific functionality in response to an event. If a call to handle_event fails, the Reactor invokes the handle_close method. This method performs any application-specific cleanup operations. When the handle_close method returns, the Reactor removes the Event_Handler subclass object from its internal tables.

An alternative way to implement event demultiplexing and dispatching is to use multitasking. In this approach, an application spawns a separate thread or process that monitors an event source. Every thread or process blocks until it receives an event notification. At this point, the appropriate event handler code is executed. Certain types of applications (such as file transfer, remote login, or teleconferencing) benefit from multitasking. For these applications, multithreading or multiprocessing helps to reduce development effort, improves application robustness, and transparently leverages off of available multiprocessor capabilities.

Using multithreading to implement event demultiplexing has several drawbacks, however. It may require the use of complex concurrency control schemes; it may lead to poor performance on uniprocessors›; and it may not be available on widely available OS platforms (such as many variants of UNIX). In these cases, the Reactor pattern may be used in lieu of, or in conjunction with, OS multithreading or multiprocessing mechanisms, as described in the next section.

THE ACCEPTOR PATTERN

The Acceptor pattern is an object creational pattern[1] that decouples the act of establishing a connection from the service(s) provided after a connection is established. Connection-oriented services (such as file transfer, remote login, distributed logging, and video-on-demand) are particularly amenable to this pattern. The Acceptor pattern simplifies the development of these services by allowing the application-specific portion of a service to be modified independently of the mechanism used to establish the connection. The UNIX "superserver" inetd is a prime example of an application that uses the Acceptor pattern.

To build upon the interfaces and mechanisms already provided by the Reactor pattern, the Acceptor class inherits the Event_Handler's demultiplexing and dispatching interface (shown in Figure 1). Figure 2 illustrates the structure of participants in the Acceptor pattern. The open method in template class Acceptor initializes a communication endpoint and listens for incoming connection requests from clients. The get_handle method returns the I/O handle corresponding to the communication endpoint.

When a connection request arrives from a client the Reactor triggers a callback on the Acceptor's handle_event method. This method is a *factory* that dynamically produces a new SVC_HANDLER object. In the example in Figure 2, SVC_HANDLER is a formal parameterized type argument in the Acceptor template class. The Instantiated_Acceptor class supplies an actual Svc_Han-

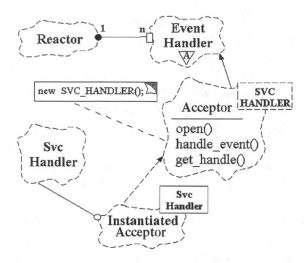

FIGURE 2   The structure of participants in the acceptor pattern.

dler class parameter. The Svc_Handler parameter implements a particular application-specific service (i.e., transferring a file, permitting remote login, receiving logging records, sending a video sequence, etc.).

Note that the Acceptor pattern does not dictate the behavior or concurrency dynamics of the Svc_Handler service it creates. In particular, a dynamically created Svc_Handler service may be executed in any of the following ways:

- *Run in the same thread of control:* This approach may be implemented by inheriting the Svc_Handler from Event_Handler and registering each newly created Svc_Handler object with the Reactor. Thus, each Svc_Handler object is dispatched in the same thread of control as an Acceptor object. The implementation described in the third section uses this single-threaded behavior.
- *Run in a separate thread of control:* In this approach, the Reactor serves as the master connection dispatcher within an application. When a client connects, the Acceptor's handle_event method spawns a separate thread of control. The Svc_Handler object then processes messages exchanged over the connection within the new slave thread. Threads are useful for cooperating services that frequently reference common memory-resident data structures shared by the threads within a process address space.[7]
- *Run in a separate OS process:* This approach is similar in form to the previous bullet. However, a separate process is created rather than

a separate thread. Network services that base their security and protection mechanisms on process ownership are typically executed in separate processes to prevent accidental or intentional access to unauthorized resources. For example, the standard UNIX super-server, inetd, uses the Acceptor pattern in this manner to execute the standard Internet ftp and telnet services in separate processes.[12]

The ASX framework[4] provides mechanisms that support all three of these types of concurrency dynamics. Moreover, the selection of concurrency mechanism may be deferred until late in the design, or even until run-time. This flexibility increases the range of design alternatives available to developers.

In addition, the Acceptor pattern may be used to develop highly extensible event handlers that may be configured into an application at installation-time or at runtime. This enables applications to be updated and extended without modifying, recompiling, relinking, or restarting the applications at runtime. Achieving this degree of flexibility and extensibility requires the use of OO language features (such as templates, inheritance, and dynamic binding), OO design techniques (such as the Factory Method or Abstract Factory design patterns[1]), and advanced operating system mechanisms (such as explicit dynamic linking and multithreading[4]).

EVOLVING DESIGN PATTERNS ACROSS OS PLATFORMS

Motivation

Based on our experience at Ericsson, explicitly modeling design patterns is a very beneficial activity. In particular, design patterns focus attention on relatively stable aspects of a system's software architecture. They also emphasize the strategic collaborations between key participants in the architecture without overwhelming developers with excessive detail. Abstracting away from low-level implementation details is particularly important for system software since platform constraints often preclude direct reuse of system components.

In our experience it is essential to illustrate how design patterns are realized in actual systems. One observation we discuss in the fourth section is that existing design pattern catalogs[1,2] do not present "wide spectrum" coverage of patterns. Often, this makes it difficult for novices to recognize how to apply patterns in practice on their projects. We believe the development sequence that unfolds in this section will provide a technically rich, motivating, and detailed (yet comprehensible) roadmap to help shepherd other developers into the realm of patterns.

With these goals in mind, this section outlines how the Reactor and Acceptor design patterns were implemented and evolved on BSD and System V UNIX, as well as on Windows NT. The discussion emphasizes the relevant functional differences between the various OS platforms and describes how these differences affected the implementation of the design patterns. To focus the discussion later, C++ is used as the implementation language. However, the principles and concepts underlying the Reactor and Acceptor patterns are independent of the programming language, the OS platform, and any particular implementation. Readers who are not interested in the lower-level details of implementing design patterns may wish to skip ahead to the fourth section, where we summarize the lessons we learned from using design patterns on several projects at Ericsson.

The Impact of Platform Demultiplexing and I/O Semantics

The implementation of the Reactor pattern was affected significantly by the semantics of the event demultiplexing and I/O mechanisms in the underlying OS. In general, there are two types of demultiplexing and I/O semantics: *reactive* and *proactive*. Reactive semantics allow an application to inform the OS which I/O handles to notify it about when an I/O-related operation (such as a read, write, and connection request/accept) may be performed without blocking. Subsequently, when the OS detects that the desired operation may be performed without blocking on any of the indicated handles, it informs the application that the handle(s) are ready. The application then "reacts" by processing the handle(s) accordingly (such as reading or writing data, accepting connections, etc.). Reactive demultiplexing and I/O semantics are provided on standard BSD and System V UNIX systems.[12]

In contrast, proactive semantics allow an application to proactively initiate I/O-related operations (such as a read, write, or connection request/accept) or general-purpose event-signaling operations (such as a semaphore lock being acquired or a thread terminating). The invoked operation proceeds asynchronously and does not block the caller. When an operation completes, it signals the application. At this point, the application runs a completion routine that determines the exit status of the operation and potentially starts up another asynchronous operation. Proactive demultiplexing and I/O semantics are provided on Windows NT[13] and VMS.

For performance reasons, we were not able to completely encapsulate the variation in behavior between the UNIX and Windows NT demultiplexing and I/O semantics. Thus, we could not directly reuse existing C++ code, algorithms, or detailed designs. However, it was possible to capture and reuse the concepts that underlay the Reactor and Acceptor design patterns.

UNIX EVOLUTION OF THE PATTERNS

Implementing the reactor pattern on UNIX. The standard demultiplexing mechanisms on UNIX operating systems provide reactive I/O semantics. For instance, the UNIX select and poll event demultiplexing system calls inform an application which subset of handles within a set of I/O handles may send/receive messages or request/accept connections without blocking. Implementing the Reactor pattern using UNIX reactive I/O is straightforward. After select or poll indicate which I/O handles have become ready, the Reactor object reacts by invoking the appropriate Event_Handler callback methods (i.e., handle_event or handle_close).

One advantage of the UNIX reactive I/O scheme is that it decouples 1) event detection and notification from 2) the operation performed in response to the triggered event. This allows an application to optimize its response to an event by using context information available when the event occurs. For example, when select indicates a "read" event is pending, a network server might check to see how many bytes are in a socket receive queue. It might use this information to optimize the buffer size it allocates before making a recv system call. A disadvantage of UNIX reactive I/O is that operations may not be invoked asynchronously with other operations. Therefore, computation and communication may not occur in parallel unless separate threads or processes are used.

The original implementation of the Reactor pattern provided by the ASX framework was derived from the Dispatcher class category available in the InterViews OO GUI framework.[9] The Dispatcher is an OO interface to the UNIX select system call. InterViews uses the Dispatcher to define an application's main event loop and to manage connections to one or more physical window displays. The Reactor framework's first modification to the Dispatcher framework added support for signal-based event dispatching. The Reactor's signal-based dispatching mechanism was modeled closely on the Dispatcher's existing timer-based and I/O handle-based event demultiplexing and event handler dispatching mechanisms.[†]

[†] The Reactor's interfaces for signals and timer-based event handling are not shown in this article due to space limitations.

The next modification to the Reactor occurred when porting it from SunOS 4.x (which is based primarily on BSD 4.3 UNIX) to SunOS 5.x (which is based primarily on System V release 4 (SVR4) UNIX). SVR4 provides another event demultiplexing system call named poll. Poll is similar to select, though it uses a different interface and provides a broader, more flexible model for event demultiplexing that supports SVR4 features such as STREAM pipe band-data.[12]

The SunOS 5.x port of the Reactor was enhanced to support either select or poll as the underlying event demultiplexer. Although portions of the Reactor's internal implementation changed, its external interface remained the same for both the select-based and the poll-based versions. This common interface improves networking application portability across BSD and SVR4 UNIX platforms.

A portion of the public interface for the BSD and SVR4 UNIX implementation of the Reactor pattern is shown as follows:

```
// Bit-wise "or" these values to check
// for multiple activities per-handle.
enum Reactor_Mask { READ_MASK = 01,
    WRITE_MASK = 02, EXCEPT_MASK = 04 };
class Reactor
{
public:
    // Register an Event_Handler object according
    // to the Reactor_Mask(s) (i.e., "reading,"
    // "writing," and/or "exceptions").
    virtual int register_handler (Event_Handler *,
                Reactor_Mask);
    // Remove the handler associated with
    // the appropriate Reactor_Mask(s).
    virtual int remove_handler (Event_Handler *,
                Reactor_Mask);
    // Block process until I/O events occur or
    // a timer expires, then dispatch Event_Handler(s).
    virtual int dispatch (void);
// ...
};
```

Likewise, the Event_Handler interface for UNIX is defined as follows:

```
typedef int HANDLE; // I/O handle.
class Event_Handler
{
```

```
protected:
        // Returns the I/O handle associated with the
        // derived object (must be supplied by a subclass).
        virtual HANDLE get_handle (void) const;
        // Called when an event occurs on the HANDLE.
        virtual int handle_event (HANDLE, Reactor_Mask);
        // Called when object is removed from the Reactor.
        virtual int handle_close (HANDLE, Reactor_Mask);
    // ...
    };
```

The next major modification to the Reactor extended it for use with multi-threaded applications on SunOS 5.x using Solaris threads.[7] Adding multi-threading support required changes to the internals of both the select-based and poll-based versions of the Reactor. These changes involved a SunOS 5.x mutual exclusion mechanism known as a "mutex." A mutex serializes the execution of multiple threads by defining a critical section where only one thread executes the code at a time.[7] Critical sections of the Reactor's code that concurrently access shared resources (such as the Reactor's internal dispatch table containing Event_Handler objects) are protected by a mutex.

The standard SunOS 5.x synchronization type (mutex_t) provides support for *nonrecursive* mutexes. The SunOS 5.x nonrecursive mutex provides a simple and efficient form of mutual exclusion based on adaptive spin-locks. However, nonrecursive mutexes possess the restriction that the thread currently owning a mutex may not reacquire the mutex without releasing it first. Otherwise, deadlock will occur immediately.

While developing the multithreaded Reactor, it quickly became obvious that SunOS 5.x mutex variables were inadequate to support the synchronization semantics required by the Reactor. In particular, the Reactor's dispatch interface performs callbacks to methods of pre-registered, application-specific event handler objects as follows:

```
void Reactor::dispatch (void)
{
    for (;;) {
    // Block until events occur.
    this->wait_for_events (this->handler_set);
    // Obtain the mutex.
    this->lock->acquire ();

    // Dispatch all the callback methods
```

```
    // on handlers who contain active events.
    for each handler in this->handler_set {
    if (handler->handle_event
        (handler, mask) == FAIL)
    // Cleanup on failure.
        handler->handle_close (handler);
    }
    // Release the mutex.
    this->lock->release ();
    }
}
```

Callback methods (such as handle_event and handle_close) defined by Event_Handler subclass objects may subsequently re-enter the Reactor object by calling its register_handler and remove_handler methods as follows:

```
// Global per-process instance of the Reactor.
extern Reactor reactor;

// Application-specific method called
// back by the Reactor.

int Acceptor::handle_event (HANDLE handle,
                            Reactor_Mask)
{
    Concrete_Event_Handler *new_handler =
        new Concrete_Event_Handler;

    *new_handler = this->accept (handle);

    // Re-enter the Reactor object.
    reactor.register_handler (new_handler,
                        READ_MASK);
    // ...
}
```

In this code fragment, nonrecursive mutexes will result in deadlock since 1) the mutex within the Reactor's dispatch method is locked throughout the callback and 2) the Reactor's register_handler method tries to acquire the same mutex.

One solution to this problem involved recoding the Reactor to release its mutex lock before invoking callbacks to application-specific Event_Handler methods. However, this solution was tedious and error-prone. It also increased synchronization overhead by repeatedly releasing and reacquiring mutex locks. A more elegant and efficient solution used *recursive* mutexes to prevent deadlock and to avoid modifying the Reactor's concurrency control scheme. A recursive mutex allows calls to its acquire method to be nested as long as the thread that owns the lock is the one attempting to re-acquire it.

The current implementation of the UNIX-based Reactor pattern is about 2,400 lines of C++ code (not including comments or extraneous whitespace). This implementation is portable between both BSD and System V UNIX variants.

Implementing the Acceptor Pattern on UNIX. To illustrate the Reactor and Acceptor patterns, consider the event-driven server for a distributed logging service shown in Figure 3. Client applications use this service to log information (such as error notifications, debugging traces, and status updates) in a distributed environment. In this service, logging records are sent to a central logging server. The logging server outputs the logging records to a console, a printer, a file, or a network management database, etc.

In the architecture of the distributed logging service, the logging server shown in Figure 3 handles logging records and connection requests sent by clients. These records and requests may arrive concurrently on multiple I/O handles. An I/O handle identifies a resource control block managed by the operating system.[‡]

The logging server listens on one I/O handle for connection requests to arrive from new clients. In addition, a separate I/O handle is associated with each connected client. Input from multiple clients may arrive concurrently. Therefore, a single-threaded server must not block indefinitely reading from any individual I/O handle. A blocking read on one handle may significantly delay the response time for clients associated on other handles.

A highly modular and extensible way to design the server logging daemon is to combine the Reactor and Acceptor patterns. Together, these patterns decouple 1) the application-independent mechanisms that demultiplex and dispatch preregistered Event_Handler objects from 2) the application-specific connection establishment and logging record transfer functionality performed by methods in these objects.

Within the server logging daemon, two subclasses of the Event_Handler base class (Logging_Handler and Logging_Acceptor) perform the actions required

---

[‡] Different operating systems use different terms for I/O handles. For example, UNIX programmers typically refer to these as file descriptors, whereas Windows programmers typically refer to them as I/O HANDLEs. In both cases, the underlying concepts are the same.}

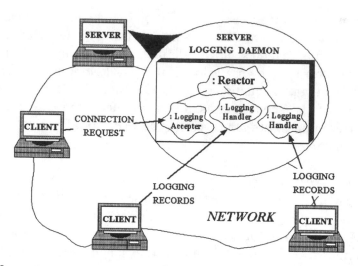

FIGURE 3

to process the different types of events arriving on different I/O handles. The Logging_Handler event handler is responsible for receiving and processing logging records transmitted from a client. Likewise, the Logging_Acceptor event handler is a factory that is responsible for accepting a new connection request from a client, dynamically allocating a new Logging_Handler event handler to handle logging records from this client, and registering the new handler with an instance of a Reactor object.

The following code illustrates an implementation the server logging daemon based upon the Reactor and Acceptor patterns. An instance of the Logging_Handler template class performs I/O between the server logging daemon and a particular instance of a client logging daemon. As shown in the following code, the Logging_Handler class inherits from Event_Handler. Inheriting from Event_Handler enables a Logging_Handler object to be registered with the Reactor. This inheritance also allows a Logging_Handler object's handle_event method to be dispatched automatically by a Reactor object to process logging records when they arrive from clients. The Logging_Handler class contains an instance of the template parameter PEER_IO. The PEER_IO class provides reliable TCP capabilities used to transfer logging records between an application and the server. The use of templates removes the reliance on a particular IPC interface (such as BSD sockets or System V TLI).

```
template <class PEER_IO>
class Logging_Handler
    : public Event_Handler
```

```
{
public:
    // Callback method that handles the reception
    // of logging transmissions from remote clients.
    // Two recv()'s are used to maintain framing
    // across a TCP bytestream.

    virtual int handle_event (HANDLE, Reactor_Mask) {
        long len;
        // Determine logging record length.
        long n = this->peer_io_.recv (&len, sizeof len);

        if (n <= 0) return n;
        else {
            Log_Record log_record;

            // Convert from network to host byte-order.
            len = ntohl (len);
            // Read remaining data in record.
            this->peer_io_.recv (&log_record, len);

            // Format and print the logging record.
            log_record.decode_and_print ();
            return 0;
        }
    }

    // Retrieve the I/O handle (called by Reactor
    // when Logging_Handler object is registered).

    virtual HANDLE get_handle (void) const {
        return this->peer_io_.get_handle ();
    }


    // Close down the I/O handle and delete the
    // object when a client closes the connection.

    virtual int handle_close (HANDLE,
                              Reactor_Mask) {
        delete this;
        return 0;
    }
```

```
private:
    // Private ensures dynamic allocation.
    ~Logging_Handler (void) {
    this->peer_io_.close ();
    }

    // C++ wrapper for data transfer.
    PEER_IO peer_io_;
}
```

The Logging_Acceptor template class is shown in the C++ code below. It is a generic factory that performs the steps necessary to 1) accept connection requests from client logging daemons and 2) create SVC_HANDLER objects that are used to perform an actual application-specific service on behalf of clients. Note that the Logging_Acceptor object and the SVC_HANDLER objects it creates run within the same thread of control. Logging record processing is driven reactively by method callbacks triggered by the Reactor.

The Logging_Acceptor subclass inherits from the Event_Handler class. Inheriting from the Event_Handler class enables an Logging_Acceptor object to be registered with the Reactor. The Reactor subsequently dispatches the Logging_Acceptor object's handle_event method. This method then invokes SOCK_Acceptor::accept, which accepts a new client connection. The Logging_Acceptor class also contains an instance of the template parameter PEER_ACCEPTOR. The PEER_ACCEPTOR class is a factory that listens for connection requests on a well-known communication port and accepts connections when they arrive on that port from clients.

```
// Global per-process instance of the Reactor.
extern Reactor reactor;

// Handles connection requests
// from a remote client.

template <class SVC_HANDLER,
        class PEER_ACCEPTOR,
        class PEER_ADDR>
class Logging_Acceptor
    : public Event_Handler
{
public:

    // Initialize the acceptor endpoint.
```

```
Logging_Acceptor (PEER_ADDR &addr)
  : peer_acceptor_ (addr) {}

// Callback method that accepts a new
// connection, creates a new SVC_HANDLER object
// to perform I/O with the client connection,
// and registers the new object with the Reactor.

virtual int handle_event (HANDLE, Reactor_Mask) {
    SVC_HANDLER *handler = new SVC_HANDLER;

    this->peer_acceptor_.accept (*handler);
    reactor.register_handler (handler, READ_MASK);
    return 0;
}

// Retrieve the I/O handle (called by Reactor
// when an Logging_Acceptor object is registered).

virtual HANDLE get_handle (void) const {
    return this->peer_acceptor_.get_handle ();
}

// Close down the I/O handle when the
// Logging_Acceptor is shut down.

virtual int handle_close (HANDLE,
                          Reactor_Mask) {
    return this->peer_acceptor_.close ();
}
private:
// Factory that accepts client connections.
PEER_ACCEPTOR peer_acceptor_;
};
```

The following C++ code shows the main entry point into the server logging daemon. This code creates a Reactor object and an Logging_Acceptor object and registers the Logging_Acceptor with the Reactor. Note that the Logging_Acceptor template is instantiated with the Logging_Handler class, which performs the distributed logging service on behalf of clients. Next, the main program calls dispatch and enters the Reactor's event-loop. The dispatch method continuously handles connection requests and logging records that arrive from clients.

The interaction diagram shown in Figure 4 illustrates the collaboration between the various objects in the server logging daemon at runtime. Note that once the Reactor object is initialized, it becomes the primary focus of the control flow within the server logging daemon. All subsequent activity is triggered by callback methods on the event handlers controlled by the Reactor.

```cpp
// Global per-process instance of the Reactor.
Reactor reactor;

// Server port number.
const unsigned int PORT = 10000;

// Instantiate the Logging_Handler template.
typedef Logging_Handler <SOCK_Stream>
    LOGGING_HANDLER;

// Instantiate the Logging_Acceptor template.
typedef Logging_Acceptor<LOGGING_HANDLER,
                SOCK_Acceptor,
                INET_Addr>
                LOGGING_ACCEPTOR;

int
main (void)
{
    // Logging server address and port number.
    INET_Addr addr (PORT);
    // Initialize logging server endpoint.
    LOGGING_ACCEPTOR acceptor (addr);

    reactor.register_handler (&acceptor, READ_MASK);

    // Main event loop that handles client
    // logging records and connection requests.
    reactor.dispatch ();
    /* NOTREACHED */
    return 0;
}
```

This C++ code example uses templates to decouple the reliance on the particular type of IPC interface used for connection establishment and communication. The SOCK_Stream, SOCK_Acceptor and INET_Addr classes used in the template instantiations are part of the SOCK_SAP C++ wrapper library.[14] SOCK_SAP encapsulates the SOCK_STREAM semantics of the socket

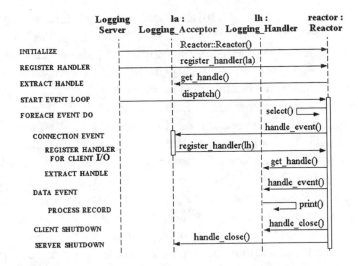

FIGURE 4   Server logging daemon interaction diagram.

transport layer interface within a type-secure, OO interface. SOCK_STREAM sockets support the reliable transfer of bytestream data between two processes, which may run on the same or on different host machines in a network.[12]

By using templates, it is relatively straightforward to instantiate a different IPC interface (such as the TLI_SAP C++ wrappers that encapsulate the System V UNIX TLI interface). Templates trade additional compile-time and linktime overhead for improved runtime efficiency. Note that a similar degree of decoupling also could be achieved via inheritance and dynamic binding by using the Abstract Factory or Factory Method patterns.[1]

EVOLVING THE DESIGN PATTERNS TO WINDOWS NT

This section describes the Windows NT implementation of the Reactor and Acceptor design patterns performed at the Ericsson facility in Cypress, CA. Initially, we attempted to evolve the existing Reactor implementation from UNIX to Windows NT using the select function from the Windows Sockets (WinSock) library.[§] This approach failed because the WinSock version of select does not interoperate with standard Win32[#] I/O HANDLEs. Our applications required the use of Win32 I/O HANDLEs to support network

---

[§] WinSock is a Windows-oriented transport layer programming interface based on the BSD socket paradigm.
[#] Win32 is the 32-bit Windows subsystem of the Windows NT operating system.

protocols (such as Microsoft's NetBIOS Extended User Interface (NetBEUI)) that are not supported by WinSock version 1.1. Next, we tried to reimplement the Reactor interface using the Win32 API system call WaitForMultipleObjects. The goal was to maintain the original UNIX interface, but transparently supply a different implementation.

Transparent reimplementation failed to work due to fundamental differences in the proactive-versus-reactive I/O semantics on Windows NT and UNIX outlined in the fourth section. We initially considered circumventing these differences by asynchronously initiating a 0-sized ReadFile request on an overlapped I/O HANDLE. Overlapped I/O is a Win32 mechanism that supports asynchronous input and output. An overlapped event signals an application when data arrives, allowing ReadFile to receive the data synchronously. Unfortunately, this solution doubles the number of system calls for every input operation, creating unacceptable performance overhead. In addition, this approach does not adequately emulate the reactive output semantics provided by the UNIX event demultiplexing and I/O mechanisms.

It soon became clear that directly reusing class method interfaces, attributes, detailed designs, or algorithms was not feasible under the circumstances. Instead, we needed to elevate the level of abstraction for reuse to the level of design patterns. Regardless of the underlying OS event demultiplexing I/O semantics, the Reactor and Acceptor patterns are applicable for event-driven applications that must provide different types services that are triggered simultaneously by different types of events. Therefore, although OS platform differences precluded direct reuse of implementations or interfaces, the design knowledge we had invested in learning and documenting the Reactor and Acceptor patterns *was* reusable.

The remainder of this section describes the modifications we made to the implementations of the Reactor and Acceptor design patterns in order to port them to Windows NT.

Implementing the Reactor Pattern on Windows NT. Windows NT provides proactive I/O semantics that are typically used in the following manner. First, an application creates a HANDLE that corresponds to an I/O channel for the type of networking mechanism being used (such as named pipes or sockets). The overlapped I/O attribute is specified to the HANDLE creation system call (WinSock sockets are created for overlapped I/O by default). Next, an application creates a HANDLE to a Win32 event object and uses this event object HANDLE to initialize an overlapped I/O structure. The HANDLE to the I/O channel and the overlapped I/O structure are then passed to the

WriteFile or ReadFile system calls to initiate a send or receive operation, respectively. The initiated operation proceeds asynchronously and does not block the caller. When the operation completes, the event object specified inside the overlapped I/O structure is set to the "signaled" state. Subsequently, Win32 demultiplexing system calls (such as WaitForSingleObject or WaitForMultipleObjects) may be used to detect the signaled state of the Win32 event object. These calls indicate when an outstanding asynchronous operation has completed.

The Win32 WaitForMultipleObjects system call is functionally similar to the UNIX select and poll system calls. It blocks on an array of HANDLEs waiting for one or more of them to signal. Unlike the two UNIX system calls (which wait only for I/O handles), WaitForMultipleObjects is a general purpose routine that may be used to wait for any type of Win32 object (such as a thread, process, synchronization object, I/O handle, named pipe, socket, or timer). It may be programmed to return to its caller either when any one of the HANDLEs becomes signaled or when all of the HANDLEs become signaled. WaitForMultipleObjects returns the index location in the HANDLE array of the lowest signaled HANDLE.

Windows NT proactive I/O has both advantages and disadvantages. One advantage over UNIX is that Windows NT WaitForMultipleObjects provides the flexibility to synchronize on a wide range Win32 objects. Another advantage is that overlapped I/O may improve performance by allowing I/O operations to execute asynchronously with respect to other computation performed by applications or the OS. In contrast, the reactive I/O semantics offered by UNIX do not support asynchronous I/O directly (threads may be used instead).

On the other hand, designing and implementing the Reactor pattern using proactive I/O on Windows NT turned out to be more difficult than using reactive I/O on UNIX. Several characteristics of WaitForMultipleObjects significantly complicated the implementation of the Windows NT version of the Reactor pattern.

First, applications that must synchronize simultaneous send and receive operations on the same I/O channel are more complicated to program on Windows NT. For example, to distinguish the completion of a WriteFile operation from a ReadFile operation, separate overlapped I/O structures and Win32 event objects must be allocated for input and output. Furthermore, two elements in the WaitForMultipleObjects HANDLE array (which is currently limited to a rather small maximum of 64 HANDLEs) are consumed by the separate event object HANDLEs dedicated to the sender and the receiver.

Second, each Win32 WaitForMultipleObjects call only returns notification on a single HANDLE. Therefore, to achieve the same behavior as the UNIX select and poll system calls (which return a set of activated I/O handles), multiple WaitForMultipleObjects must be performed. In addition, the semantics of WaitForMultipleObjects do not result in a fair distribution of notifications. In particular, the lowest signaled HANDLE in the array is always returned, regardless of how long other HANDLEs further back in the array may have been pending.

The implementation techniques required to deal with these characteristics of Windows NT were rather complicated. Therefore, we modified the NT Reactor by creating a Handler_Repository class that shields the Reactor from this complexity. This class stores Event_Handler objects that registered with a Reactor. This container class implements standard operations for inserting, deleting, suspending, and resuming Event_Handlers. Each Reactor object contains a Handler_Repository object in its private data portion. A Handler_Repository maintains the array of HANDLEs passed to WaitForMultipleObjects and it also provides methods for inserting, retrieving, and "reprioritizing" the HANDLE array. Reprioritization alleviates the inherent unfairness in the way that the Windows NT WaitForMultipleObjects system call notifies applications when HANDLEs become signaled.

The Handler_Repository's re-prioritization method is invoked by specifying the index of the HANDLE that has signaled and been dispatched by the Reactor. The method's algorithm moves the signaled HANDLE toward the end of the HANDLE array. This allows signaled HANDLEs that are further back in the array to be returned by subsequent calls to WaitForMultipleObjects. Over time, HANDLEs that signal frequently migrate to the end of the HANDLE array. Likewise, HANDLES that signal infrequently migrate to the front of the HANDLE array. This algorithm ensures a reasonably fair distribution of HANDLE dispatching.

The implementation techniques described in the previous paragraph did not affect the external interface of the Reactor. Unfortunately, certain aspects of Windows NT proactive I/O semantics, coupled with the desire to fully utilize the flexibility of WaitForMultipleObjects, forced visible changes to the Reactor's external interface. In particular, Windows NT overlapped I/O operations must be initiated *immediately*. Therefore, it was necessary for the Windows NT Event_Handler interface to distinguish between I/O HANDLEs and synchronization object HANDLES, as well as to supply additional information (such as message buffers and event HANDLEs) to the Reactor. In contrast, the UNIX version of the Reactor does not require this information immediately. Therefore, it may wait until it is *possible* to perform an operation, at which point additional information may be available to help optimize program behavior.

The following modifications to the Reactor were required to support Windows NT I/O semantics. The Reactor_Mask enumeration was modified to include a new SYNC_MASK value to allow the registration of an Event_Handler that is dispatched when a general Win32 synchronization object signals. The send method was added to the Reactor class to proactively initiate output operations on behalf of an Event_Handler.

```cpp
// Bit-wise "or" these values to
// check for multiple activities per-handle.
enum Reactor_Mask { READ_MASK = 01,
    WRITE_MASK = 02, SYNC_MASK = 04
};

class Reactor
{
public:
    // Same as UNIX Reactor...

    // Initiate an asynchronous send operation.
    virtual int send (Event_Handler *,
                    const Message_Block *);

// ...
};
```

Likewise, the Event_Handler interface for Windows NT was also modified as follows:

```cpp
class Event_Handler
{
protected:
    // Returns the Win32 I/O HANDLE
    // associated with the derived object
    // (must be supplied by a subclass).
    virtual HANDLE get_handle (void) const;

    // Allocates a message for the Reactor.
    virtual Message_Block *get_message (void);

    // Called when event occurs.
    virtual int handle_event (Message_Block *,
                            Reactor_Mask);
```

```
// Called when object is removed from Reactor.
virtual int handle_close (Message_Block *,
                          Reactor_Mask);
```

```
// Same as UNIX Event_Handler...
};
```

When a derived Event_Handler is registered for input with the Reactor an over-lapped input operation is immediately initiated on its behalf. This requires the Reactor to request the derived Event_Handler for an I/O mechanism HAN-DLE, destination buffer, and a Win32 event object HANDLE for synchro-nization. A derived Event_Handler returns the I/O mechanism HANDLE via its get_handle method and returns the destination buffer location and length information via the Message_Block abstraction.[4]

The current implementation of the Windows NT-based Reactor pattern is about 2,600 lines C++ code (not including comments or extraneous whitespace). This code is approximately 200 lines longer than the UNIX version. The additional code primarily ensures the fairness of WaitForMulti-pleObjects event demultiplexing, as discussed above. Although Windows NT event demultiplexing is more complex than UNIX, the behavior of Win32 mutex objects eliminated the need for the separate Mutex interface with recursive-mutex semantics discussed in the unix reactor section. Under Win32, a thread will not be blocked if it attempts to acquire a mutex spec-ifying the HANDLE to a mutex that it already owns. However, to release its ownership, the thread must release a Win32 mutex once for each time that the mutex was acquired.

Implementing the Acceptor Pattern on Windows NT. The following example C++ code illustrates an implementation of the Acceptor pattern based on the Windows NT version of the Reactor pattern:

```
template <class PEER_IO>
class Logging_Handler : public Event_Handler
{
public:
    // Callback method that handles the ·
    // reception of logging transmissions from
    // remote clients. The Message_Block object
    // stores a message received from a client.

    virtual int handle_event (Message_Block *msg,
```

```
                        Reactor_Mask) {
        Log_Record *log_record =
           (Log_Record *) msg->get_rd_ptr ();

        // Format and print logging record.
        log_record.format_and_print ();
        delete msg;
        return 0;
    }

    // Retrieve the I/O HANDLE (called by Reactor
    // when a Logging_Handler object is registered).

    virtual HANDLE get_handle (void) const {
        return this->peer_io_.get_handle ();
    }

    // Return a dynamically allocated buffer
    // to store an incoming logging message.

    virtual Message_Block *get_message (void) {
        return new Message_Block (sizeof (Log_Record));
    }

    // Close down I/O handle and delete
    // object when a client closes connection.
    virtual int handle_close (Message_Block *msg,
                        Reactor_Mask) {
        delete msg;
        delete this;
        return 0;
    }

private:
    // Private ensures dynamic allocation.
    ~Logging_Handler (void) {
        this->peer_io_.close ();
    }

    // C++ wrapper for data transfer.
    PEER_IO peer_io_;
};
```

The Logging_Acceptor class is essentially the same as the one illustrated in the UNIX listen section. Likewise, the interaction diagram that describes the collaboration between objects in the server logging daemon is also very similar to the one shown in Figure 4.

The application is the same server logging daemon presented in the UNIX listen subsection. The primary difference is that Win32 Named_Pipe C++ wrappers are used instead of the SOCK_SAP socket C++ wrappers in the main program as shown here:

```
// Global per-process instance of the Reactor.
Reactor reactor;

// Server endpoint.
const char ENDPOINT[] = "logger";

// Instantiate the Logging_Handler template
typedef Logging_Handler <NPipe_IO>
    LOGGING_HANDLER;

// Instantiate the Logging_Acceptor template
typedef Logging_Acceptor<LOGGING_HANDLER, NPipe_Acceptor,
                    Local_Pipe_Name>
    LOGGING_ACCEPTOR;

int
main (void)
{
    // Logging server address.
    Local_Pipe_Name addr (ENDPOINT);
    // Initialize logging server endpoint.
    LOGGING_ACCEPTOR acceptor (addr);

    reactor.register_handler (&acceptor,
                        SYNC_MASK);

    // Arm the proactive I/O handler.
    acceptor.initiate ();

    // Main event loop that handles client
    // logging records and connection requests.
    reactor.dispatch ();
    /* NOTREACHED */
    return 0;
}
```

The Named Pipe Acceptor object (acceptor) is registered with the Reactor to handle asynchronous connection establishment. Due to the semantics of Windows NT proactive I/O, the acceptor object must explicitly initiate the acceptance of a Named Pipe connection via an initiate method. Each time a connection acceptance is completed, the Reactor dispatches the handle_event method of the Named Pipe version of the Acceptor pattern to create a new Svc_Handler that will receive logging records from the client. The Reactor will also initiate the next connection acceptance sequence asynchronously.

LESSONS LEARNED

Our group at Ericsson has been developing OO frameworks based on design patterns for the past two years.[6] During this time, we have identified a number of pros and cons related to using design patterns as the basis for our system design, implementation, and documentation. We have also formulated a number of "workarounds" for the problems we observed using design patterns in a production environment. This section discusses the lessons we have learned thus far.

PROS AND CONS OF DESIGN PATTERNS

Ironically, many pros and cons of using design patterns are "duals" of each other, representing "two sides of the same coin:"

Patterns are underspecified. They generally do not overconstrain an implementation. This is beneficial since it permits flexible solutions that may be customized according to application requirements and the constraints imposed by the OS platform and network environment.

On the other hand, it is important for developers and managers to recognize that understanding a collection of design patterns is no substitute for design and implementation skills. For example, recognizing the structure and participants in a pattern (such as the Reactor or Acceptor patterns) is only the first step. As we describe in the fourth section, a major development effort is often required to fully realize the pattern correctly and efficiently.

Patterns enable large-scale architectural reuse. Even if reuse of algorithms, implementations, interfaces, or detailed designs is not feasible. Understanding these benefits was crucial in the design evolution we presented in the fourth section. Our task became much simpler when we recognized how to leverage off our prior development effort and reduce risk by reusing the Reactor and Acceptor patterns across UNIX and Windows NT.

It is important, however, to manage the expectations of developers and managers, who may have misconceptions about the fundamental contribution of design patterns to a project. In particular, patterns do not lead to automated code reuse. Neither do they guarantee flexible and efficient design and implementation. As always, there is no substitute for creativity and diligence on the part of developers.

Patterns capture implicit knowledge that is implicitly understood. Our experience has been that once developers are exposed to, and properly motivated by, the concepts of design patterns, they are generally very eager to adopt the nomenclature and methodology. Patterns tend to codify knowledge that is already understood intuitively. Therefore, once basic concepts, notations, and pattern template formats are mastered, it is straightforward to document and reason about many portions of a system's architecture and design using patterns.

The downside of the intuitive nature of patterns is a phenomenon we termed "pattern explosion." In this situation, all aspects of a project become expressed as patterns, which often leads to relabeling existing development practices without significantly improving them. We also noticed a tendency for developers to spend considerable time formalizing relatively mundane concepts (such as binary search, a linked list, or opening a file) as patterns. Although this may be intellectually satisfying, it does not necessarily improve productivity or software quality.

Patterns help improve communication within and across software development teams: Developers share a common vocabulary and a common conceptual "gestalt." By learning the key recurring patterns in their application domain, developers at Ericsson elevated the level of abstraction by which they communicated with their colleagues. For example, once our team understood the Reactor and Acceptor patterns, they began to use them in many other projects that benefited from these architectures.

As usual, however, restraint and a good sense of aesthetics is required to resist the temptation of elevating complex concepts and principles to the level of "buzz words" and hype. We noticed a tendency for many developers to get locked into "pattern-think," where they would try to apply patterns that were inappropriate simply because they were familiar with the patterns. For example, the Reactor pattern is often an inefficient event demultiplexing model for a multiprocessor platform since it serializes application concurrency at a very coarse-grained level.

Patterns promote a structured means of documenting software architectures. This documentation may be written at a high-level of abstraction, which captures the essential architectural interactions while suppressing unnecessary details.

One drawback we observed with much of the existing pattern literature[1,2] however, is that it is often *too* abstract. Abstraction is a benefit in many cases since it avoids inundating a casual reader with excessive details. However, we found that in many cases that overly abstract pattern descriptions made it difficult for developers to understand and apply a particular pattern to systems they were building.

Solutions and Workarounds

Based on our experiences, we recommend the following solutions and workarounds to the various traps and pitfalls with patterns mentioned previously.

- *Expectation management:* Many of the problems with patterns we discussed previously are related to managing the expectations of development team members. As usual, patterns are no silver bullet that will magically absolve managers and developers from having to wrestle with tough design and implementation issues. At Ericsson, we have worked hard to motivate the genuine benefits from patterns, without hyping them beyond their actual contribution.
- *Wide-Spectrum pattern exemplars:* Based on our experience using design patterns as a documentation tool, we believe that pattern catalogues should include more than just object model diagrams and structured prose. Although these notations are suitable for a high-level overview, we found in practice that they are insufficient to guide developers through difficult design and implementation tradeoffs. Therefore, it is very useful to have concrete source code examples to supplement the more abstract diagrams and text.

Hypertext browsers, such as Mosaic and Windows Help Files, are particularly useful for creating compound documents that possess multiple levels of abstraction. Moreover, in our experience, it was particularly important to illustrate multiple implementations of a pattern. This helps to avoid "tunnel vision" and overconstrained solutions based upon a limited pattern vocabulary. The extended discussion in the third section is one example of a wide-spectrum exemplar using this approach. This example contains in-depth coverage of tradeoffs encountered in actual use.

- *Integrate patterns with OO frameworks:* Ideally, examples in pattern catalogs[1,2] should reference (or better yet, contain hypertext links to) source code that comprises an actual OO framework. We have begun building such an environment at Ericsson, in order to disseminate our patterns and frameworks to a wider audience. In addition to linking on-line documentation and source code, we have had good success with periodic design reviews where developers throughout the organization present interesting patterns they have been working on. This is another technique for avoiding "tunnel vision" and enhancing the pattern vocabulary within and across development teams.

CONCLUSION

Design patterns facilitate the reuse of abstract architectures that are decoupled from concrete realizations of these architectures. This decoupling is useful when developing system software components and frameworks that are reusable across OS platforms. This article describes two design patterns, Reactor and Acceptor, that are commonly used in distributed system software. These design patterns characterize the collaboration between objects that are used to automate common activities (such as event demultiplexing, event handler dispatching, and connection establishment) performed by distributed applications. Using the design pattern techniques described in this article, we successfully reused major portions of our telecommunication system software development effort across several diverse OS platforms.

This case study describes how an OO framework based on the Reactor and Acceptor design patterns evolved from several UNIX platforms to the Windows NT Win32 platform. Due to fundamental differences between the platforms, it was not possible to directly reuse the algorithms, detailed designs, interfaces, or implementations of the framework across the different OS platforms. In particular, performance constraints and fundamental differences in the I/O mechanisms available on Windows NT and UNIX platforms prevented us from encapsulating event demultiplexing functionality within a directly reusable framework. However, we were able to reuse the underlying design patterns, which reduced project risk significantly and simplified our redevelopment effort.

Our experiences with patterns reinforce the observation that the transition from OO analysis to OO design and implementation is challenging.[11] Often, the constraints of the underlying OS and hardware platform influence design and implementation details significantly. This is particularly problematic for system software, which is frequently targeted for particular platforms with particular nonportable characteristics. In such circumstances, reuse of design patterns may be the only viable means to leverage previous development expertise.

The UNIX version of the ASX framework components we described here are freely available via anonymous ftp from the Internet host ics.uci.edu (128.195.1.1) in the file gnu/C++_wrappers.tar.Z. This distribution contains complete source code, documentation, and example test drivers for the C++ components developed as part of the ADAPTIVE project[4] at the University of California, Irvine and Washington University.

REFERENCES

1. Gamma, E., R. Helm, R. Johnson, and J. Vlissides. *Design Patterns: Elements of Reusable Object-Oriented Software,* Reading, MA, Addison-Wesley, 1994.
2. Buschmann, F., R. Meunier, H. Rohnert, and M. Stal. *Pattern-Oriented Software Architecture—A Pattern System,* Wiley, New York, 1995.
3. Coplien, J. O. A development process generative pattern language, in *Pattern Languages of Programs,* J. O. Coplien and D. C. Schmidt, Eds., Addison-Wesley, Reading, MA, June 1995.
4. Schmidt, D. C. ASX: An object-oriented framework for developing distributed applications, *Proceedings of the 6th USENIX C++ Technical Conference,* Cambridge, MA, USENIX Assoc., Apr. 1994.
5. Schmidt, D. C. Reactor: An object behavioral pattern for concurrent event demultiplexing and event handler dispatching, in *Pattern Languages of Programs,* J. O. Coplien and D. C. Schmidt, Eds., Addison-Wesley, Reading, MA, June 1995.
6. D. C. Schmidt and P. Stephenson. An object-oriented framework for developing network server daemons, *Proceedings of the 2nd C++ World Conference,* Dallas, TX, SIGS, Oct. 1993.
7. Eykholt, J., S. Kleiman, S. Barton, R. Faulkner, A. Shivalingiah, M. Smith, D. Stein, J. Voll, M. Weeks, and D. Williams. Beyond

multiprocessing . . . Multithreading the SunOS kernel, *Proceedings of the Summer USENIX Conference,* San Antonio, TX, June 1992.

8. Weinand, A., E. Gamma, and R. Marty. ET++—An object-oriented application framework in C++, *Proceedings of the Object-Oriented Programming Systems, Languages and Applications Conference,* ACM, Sept. 1988, pp. 46–57.

9. Linton, M. A., J. Vlissides, and P. Calder, Composing User Interfaces with InterViews, *IEEE Computer,* vol. 22, pp. 8–22, Feb. 1989.

10. S. Vinoski, Distributed object computing with CORBA, *C++ Report,* 5(6), July/August 1993.

11. Booch, G. *Object Oriented Analysis and Design with Applications,* 2nd ed., Benjamin/Cummings, Redwood City, CA, 1993.

12. Stevens, W. R. *UNIX Network Programming,* Prentice Hall, Englewood Cliffs, NJ, 1990.

13. Custer, H. *Inside Windows NT,* Microsoft Press, Redmond, WA, 1993.

14. Schmidt, D. C. IPC_SAP: An object-oriented interface to interprocess communication services, *C++ Report,* 4(6), Nov./Dec. 1992.

Pattern Hatching—
Perspectives from the
"Gang of Four"

John Vlissides
vlis@watson.ibm.com

Jim Coplien has laid the groundwork for all sorts of discussions on software patterns in "The Column Without a Name." In this column I'll offer another perspective on this emerging discipline, one that reflects my experience as a member of the "Gang of Four." I'm referring not to some group of malefactors, I think, but to Erich Gamma, Richard Helm, Ralph Johnson, and myself. Together we authored *Design Patterns: Elements of Reusable Object-Oriented Software,* a book of 23 patterns distilled from numerous object-oriented software systems.[1]

In *Design Patterns* we've tried to describe recurring snippets of object-oriented design that impart those elusive properties of good software: elegance, flexibility, extensibility, and reusability. We've recorded these snippets in a form that, although different from Alexander's,[2] is nevertheless faithful to pattern ideals. More on our pattern form later.

The patterns in the book come from many application domains, including user interfaces, compilers, programming environments, operating systems, distributed systems, financial modeling, and computer-aided design. That's not to say design patterns are domain-specific, however. We were careful to include only proven designs we'd seen again and again across domains.

We call our patterns "design patterns" for at least a couple of reasons. Our work has its roots in Erich Gamma's doctoral dissertation, where he coined the term.[3] He wanted to emphasize that he was capturing *design* expertise as opposed to other software development skills, such as domain analysis or implementation. Another reason is that "pattern" alone means different things to different people, even among pattern aficionados. Prepending "design" provides some needed qualification. But since I'll be talking mostly about design patterns in this column, I'll dispense with the "design" prefix whenever I can get away with it.

As for the title of this column, I chose "Pattern Hatching" initially for its similarity to a familiar concept in computer science. (Besides, all the good titles were taken.) But I've come around to thinking that it captures my intent for this column rather well. "Hatching" doesn't suggest that we are creating anything. It implies development from preexisting rudiments. That happens to be appropriate: *Design Patterns* is our incubator of eggs, as it were, from which much new life will hopefully emerge. (I trust we won't have opportunity to take this analogy too much further.)

The "Pattern Hatching" column will not merely echo the book. My aim is to build on what's in the book, to leverage its concepts so that we can learn from them and improve on them.

DESIGN PATTERNS VERSUS ALEXANDER'S PATTERNS

Design patterns have a substantially different structure from Alexander's patterns. Basically, Alexander starts with a short statement describing the problem, followed by an example that explains and resolves the forces behind the problem, and culminates in a succinct statement of the solution. Except for a few typographical embellishments, the pattern looks much like conventional prose. It invites reading through from start to finish. The down side is that this structure is rather coarse; there's no structure at a finer level, just narration. If for example you need detailed information about a particular "force" in the pattern, you have to scan through a lot of text.

Design patterns are more highly structured by comparison. They have to be. They contain more material than Alexander's patterns: the average design pattern is 10 pages, compared to four (smaller) pages for its Alexandrian counterpart. Design patterns also describe in detail how you might implement the pattern, including sample code and a discussion of implementation trade-offs. Alexander seldom deals with construction details on a comparable level.

We could have presented this material using a more Alexander-like structure, but we wanted to allow quick reference in the heat of design or implementation. Since we don't prescribe an order in which to apply the patterns (as would a true pattern language in the Alexandrian tradition), there's less to guide you to the right pattern. Even if you know which pattern you want, its size could make it hard to find the detail that interests you. We had to make it fast and easy for designers to find the patterns that are appropriate to their problems. That led us toward a finer-grained pattern structure.

DESIGN PATTERN STRUCTURE

A design pattern has the following 13 sections:

1. Name
2. Intent
3. Also Known As
4. Motivation
5. Applicability
6. Structure
7. Participants
8. Collaborations
9. Consequences
10. Implementation
11. Sample Code
12. Known Uses
13. Related Patterns

The first three sections identify the pattern. Section 4 approximates the content of an Alexandrian pattern: It gives a concrete example that illustrates the problem, its context, and its solution. Sections 5–9 define the pattern abstractly. Most people seem to understand things better when they're explained in concrete terms first, followed by more abstract terms. That's why a design pattern considers the problem and its solution concretely before describing them in the abstract. Section 10 gets concrete again, and section 11 is the most concrete of all. Section 12 is bibliographic, and section 13 provides cross-references.

BUILDING WITH COMPOSITES

Let's take the Composite pattern as an example. Its intent is twofold: Compose objects into tree structures to represent part–whole hierarchies, and give clients a uniform way of dealing with these objects whether they are internal nodes or leaves. To motivate the pattern, let's consider how we might design a hierarchical file system. For now I'll focus on just two particularly important aspects of the design. I'll build on this example in subsequent columns as a way of showing you how other patterns address design issues.

From the user's perspective, the file system should handle file structures of arbitrary size and complexity. It shouldn't put arbitrary limits on how wide or deep the file structure can get. From the implementor's perspective, the representation for the file structure should be easy to deal with and extend.

Suppose you are implementing a command that lists the files in a directory. The code you write to get the name of a *directory* shouldn't have to be different from the code you write to get the name of a *file*—the same code should work for both. In other words, you should be able to treat directories and files uniformly with respect to their names. The resulting code will be easier to write and maintain. You also want to accommodate new kinds of files (like symbolic links, for example) without reimplementing half the system.

It's clear that files and directories are key elements in our problem domain and that we need a way of introducing specialized versions of these elements after we've finalized the design. An obvious design approach would be to represent these elements as objects, as shown in Figure 1.

How do you implement such a structure? The fact that we have two kinds of objects suggests two classes, one for files and one for directories. We want to treat files and directories uniformly, which means they must have a common interface. In turn, that means the classes must be derived from a common (abstract) base class, which we'll call "Node." We also know that directories aggregate files. Together, these constraints essentially define the class hierarchy for us:

```
class Node {
public:
    // declare common interface here
protected:
    Node();
};

class File : public Node {
public:
    File();

    // redeclare common interface here
};

class Directory : public Node {
public:
```

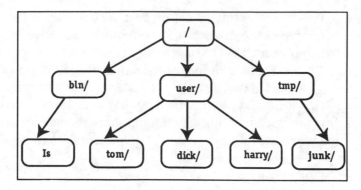

FIGURE 1

```
    Directory();

    // redeclare common interface here
private:
    List<Node*> _nodes;
};
```

The next question to consider concerns the makeup of the common interface. What are the operations that apply equally to files and directories? Well, there are all sorts of attributes of interest, like name, size, protection, and so forth. Each attribute can have operations for accessing and modifying its value(s). Operations like these that have clear meaning for both files and directories are easy to treat uniformly. The tricky issues arise when the operations don't seem to apply so clearly to both.

For example, one of the most common things users do is ask for a list of the files in a directory. That means that Directory needs an interface for enumerating its children. Here's a simple one that returns the *n*th child:

```
    virtual Node* GetChild(int n);
```

GetChild must return a Node*, because the directory may contain either File objects or Directory objects. The type of that return value has an important ramification: It forces us to define GetChild not just in the Directory class but in the Node class as well. Why? Because we want to be able to list the children of a subdirectory. In fact, the user will often want to descend the file system structure. We won't be able to do that unless we can call GetChild on the object GetChild returns. So, like the attribute operations, GetChild is something we want to be able to apply uniformly.

GetChild is also key to letting us define Directory operations recursively. For example, suppose Node declares a Size operation that returns the total number of bytes consumed by the directory (sub)tree. Directory could define its version of this operation as a sum of the values that its children return when their Size operation is called:

```
long Directory::Size () {
    long total = 0;
    Node* child;

    for (int i = 0; child = GetChild(i); ++i) {
        total += child->Size();
    }

    return total;
}
```

Directories and files illustrate the key aspects of the Composite pattern: It generates tree structures of arbitrary complexity, and it prescribes how to treat those objects uniformly. The Applicability section of the pattern echoes these aspects. It states that you should use Composite when

- you want to represent part–whole hierarchies of objects.
- you want clients to be able to ignore the difference between compositions of objects and individual objects. Clients will treat all objects in the composite structure uniformly.

The pattern's Structure section presents a modified OMT diagram of the canonical Composite class structure (see Fig. 2). By "canonical" I mean simply that it represents the most common arrangement of classes that we (the Gang of Four) have observed. It can't represent the *definitive* set of classes and relationships, because the interfaces may vary when we consider certain design or implementation-driven trade-offs. (The pattern will spell those out, too.)

Figure 2 shows the classes that participate in the pattern and their static relationships. Component is the abstract base class to which our Node class corresponds. Subclass participants are Leaf (which corresponds to File) and Composite (corresponding to Directory). The arrowhead line going from Composite to Component indicates that Composite contains instances of type Component. The ball at the tip of the arrowhead indicates more than one instance; if the ball were omitted, it would mean *exactly* one instance. The diamond

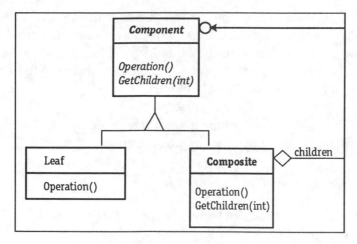

FIGURE 2   OMT structure diagram for Composite.

at the base of the arrowhead line means that the Composite aggregates its child instances, which implies that deleting the Composite would delete its children as well. It also implies that components aren't shared, thus assuring tree structures. The Participant and Collaboration sections of the pattern explain the static and dynamic relationships, respectively, among these participants.

Composite's Consequences section sums up the benefits and liabilities of the pattern. On the plus side, the pattern supports tree structures of arbitrary complexity. A corollary of this property is that a node's complexity is hidden from clients: they can't tell whether they're dealing with a leaf or a composite component, because they don't have to. That makes client code more independent of the code in the components. The client is also simpler, because it can treat leaves and composites uniformly. No longer do clients have to decide which of multiple code paths to take based on the type of component. Best of all, you can add new types of components without touching existing code.

Composite's down side, however, is that it can lead to a system where the class of every object looks like the class of every other. The significant differences show up only at run-time. That can make the code hard to understand, even if you are privy to class implementations. Moreover, the number of objects may become prohibitive if the pattern is applied at a low level or at too fine a granularity.

As you might have guessed, implementation issues abound for the Composite pattern. Some of the issues we address include:

- when and where to cache information to improve performance,
- what if any storage the Component class should allocate,
- what data structure(s) to use for storing children, and
- whether or not operations for adding and removing children should be declared in the Component class.

Since I'm rapidly running out of space, I'll take a closer look at these and other implementation questions in future columns.

WINDING DOWN

People tend to react to design patterns in one of two ways, which I'll try to describe by way of analogy.

Picture an electronics hobbyist who, though bereft of formal training, has nevertheless designed and built a slew of useful gadgets over the years: a ham radio, a Geiger counter, a security alarm, and many others. One day the hobbyist decides it's time to get some official recognition for this talent by going back to school and earning a degree in electronics. As the course-work unfolds, the hobbyist is struck by how familiar the material seems. It's not the terminology or the presentation that's familiar but the underlying concepts. The hobbyist keeps seeing names and rationalizations for stuff he's used implicitly for years. It's just one epiphany after another.

Cut now to the first year undergraduate taking the same classes and study-ing the same material. The undergrad has no electronics background—lots of rollerblading, yes, but no electronics. The stuff in the course is intensely painful for him, not because he's dumb, but because it's so totally new. It takes quite a bit more time for the undergrad to understand and appreciate the material. But eventually he does, with hard work and a bit of perseverance.

If you feel like a design pattern hobbyist, then more power to you. If on the other hand you feel more like the undergrad, take heart: the invest-ment you make in learning good patterns will pay for itself each time you apply them in your designs. That's a promise.

But maybe electronics, with its "techie" connotations, isn't the best anal-ogy for everyone. If you agree, then consider something Alfred North Whitehead said in 1943, admittedly in a different context, which might nonetheless make a more appealing connection:

> Art is the imposing of a pattern on experience, and our aesthetic enjoy-ment in recognition of the pattern.

REFERENCES

1. Gamma, E., R. Helm, R. Johnson, J. Vlissides. *Design Patterns: Elements of Reusable Object-Oriented Software,* Addison-Wesley, Reading, MA, 1995.
2. Alexander, C., et al. *A Pattern Language,* Oxford University Press, New York, 1977.
3. Gamma, E. *Object-Oriented Software Development Based on ET++: Design Patterns, Class Library, Tools,* (in German), PhD thesis, University of Zurich Institut für Informatik, 1991.

APPENDIX A:
ANNOTATED
BIBLIOGRAPHY

The annotated bibliography serves several purposes. I wanted to include as many of my colleagues as possible in this book. Many of them didn't have much time for writing in the heat of deadlines, so sharing their feelings about a particular book gave them a chance to contribute. These reviews will also provide you with down-to-earth opinions about the growing stack of books about patterns. Most of us have bought most of these books but none of us has all of them. Our company library does have copies for all interested readers, but most of these, to be really useful, should sit at the ready on your desk. We all have a copy of *Design Patterns* (Gamma, Helm, Johnson, & Vlissides, 1994) but after that the commonality drops off. Some of us are interested in Alexander's books, some are interested in data bases, some look at organizational and process issues. We've tried to answer the questions you might ask as you consider your own purchases.

REFERENCE

Gamma, E., Helm, R., Johnson, R., & Vlissides, J. (1994). *Design patterns: Elements of reusable object oriented software*. Reading, MA: Addison-Wesley.

The Timeless Way of Building
Christopher Alexander
Oxford University Press, 1979

A Pattern Language
Christopher Alexander, et al.
Oxford University Press, 1977

The Oregon Experiment
Christopher Alexander, et al.
Oxford University Press, 1975

Reviewed by Russell Corfman

It has been a long while since I took the responsibility for reviewing these works of Christopher Alexander and his colleagues. I have thought about what to write numerous times and have sat down and made several attempts, all to no avail. Finally, as the eleventh hour is upon me, as Mr. Deadline knocks at my door, I am forced to collect my thoughts and set them down for you to read and for the Editor to breathe a sigh of relief.

I know the source of my hesitation. How can I do justice to these wonderful books? Almost everyone who writes about software patterns will cite at least one of these volumes, most likely two if not all three. With all these citations, they must be important to us, and they are.

Why is the work of this architect and his colleagues important to us? We design software systems, not buildings. We are interested in software design patterns, not patterns for placing building entrances. The curious thing is that Alexander's work on patterns for constructing towns, buildings, and gardens has had a profound effect on software design patterns and may very well be the catalyst that is moving them to the mainstream.

The Timeless Way of Building begins by describing a special quality that Alexander calls "the quality without a name." This quality is nameless because there is no one word that captures its meaning. Words such as alive, whole, comfortable are examined but they carry other meanings that get in the way of truly expressing this quality.

Alexander describes how this quality is central to all good things in life, to things that make us happy and alive, and how it is central to those activities that make us feel alive and the places where we do those activities. These activities and their locations are inexorably tied together. They cannot be separated, so to truly be alive we need to live in places that contain this quality.

How do we construct homes that contain this quality? On a larger scale, how do we build towns or societies that contain this quality, this ability to let us truly live? Simply speaking, we need to know what gives things this quality.

What is it that, using one of Alexander's examples, gives one entryway that quality while another entryway doesn't have it? To find out, we need to examine many different entryways and search for the attributes that are invariant in all the entryways that contain the quality. We need to discover the pattern that makes them good.

These patterns are the core to the timeless way of building. Alexander describes how they are the gate to constructing things that contain this quality, this ability to make us come alive. A pattern helps resolve the forces of a particular problem and finds its solution. The solution will create new problems to resolve. Patterns are not autonomous; they are tied together in a network of patterns that Alexander calls a pattern language. Using this language, we first confront the large scale problems and work our way down to the details.

A Pattern Language describes one such pattern language that Alexander and his colleagues developed over many years of research. It contains 253 patterns for a geographic region, a town, communities and neighborhoods, parks, private lands, building complexes, buildings and rooms, gardens and paths, small rooms and closets, construction materials and configuration, construction details, and decoration. This pattern language is an example of one possible pattern language. It shouldn't be considered complete or static. The component patterns can be modified as conditions change, new patterns can be added, or existing patterns can be replaced. The language should be dynamic.

Most of these patterns are well developed. They are good examples of the things that software design patterns should contain, such as developing the context of the problem, explaining the forces that affect the solution the pattern proposes, the proposed solution, how the pattern resolves the forces, and the context that results once the pattern is applied.

It was more than a year or so after I had read *The Timeless Way of Building* and *A Pattern Language* before I had the opportunity to read *The Oregon Experiment,* the final volume of this series. It is a small book and not nearly as popular as the first two. It describes how a pattern language was applied at the University of Oregon. I wish I had been able to read it earlier. It helped clarify many of the things that are presented in *The Timeless Way of*

Building. It details items that are mentioned but brushed over, such as "organic order" and "piecemeal growth." Reading what Alexander meant by these concepts and their importance helped tie together things in the earlier volumes.

I highly recommend reading these books. Besides the benefit of becoming more familiar with and learning a lot about patterns and the concepts behind them, these books are just plain enjoyable to read. It is especially fun thumbing through the various patterns in *A Pattern Language* and dreaming about building your own perfect community and home. I ran to my wife several times to show her a pattern. She especially liked the forces described in "137 Children's Realm." There are a number of little gems scattered about waiting to be found. For example, all the solutions presented in the patterns begin with "therefore . . ." except one, "186 Communal Sleeping."

Pattern-Oriented Software Architecture: A System of Patterns
Frank Buschmann, Regine Meunier, Hans Rohnert,
Peter Sommerlad, and Michael Stal
John Wiley & Sons, 1997

Reviewed by David E. DeLano
Published in *C++ Report,* December 1996

The apparent trend of the publishing industry is to push words like "patterns" and "object-oriented" into the titles of books and magazine articles to get the items noticed and sold. It is perceived that these words represent the current trend of the software development industry, and thus have an influence on the spending habits of the technical community. Many of the works containing these words in the title have little or nothing to do with patterns or OO. The title of this book combines the two concepts into "pattern-oriented." Fortunately the title conveys the true contents of the book. This is a book about and containing patterns.

Another trend is to produce an overwhelming number of books on a selling topic. For example, there are many books currently available on the topic of C++ and one need only pick and choose between them according to preference. *Pattern-Oriented Software Architecture: A System of Patterns* is not a substitute for other pattern texts currently available. The book contains information about patterns that complements the information found in *Design Patterns: Elements of Reusable Object-Oriented Software,* by Gamma et al., but it in no way replaces it. In fact, some knowledge of the patterns in *Design Patterns* is needed in order to read and understand the patterns contained in this text. Other pattern texts, such as the Pattern Languages of Program Design series, present a wide variety of mostly unique patterns. Where the patterns from these texts overlap with the patterns contained in this book, they are noted. Some existing patterns are restated to aid the reader in understanding this text.

The book is essentially comprised of three sections: an introduction to patterns, the patterns introduced in the book, and a discussion of pattern topics. Several chapters make up each part of the book, further defining each of the three areas. This type of layout enables the text to serve as both a tutorial and reference to patterns.

Chapter one of the text, along with the two introductory pieces entitled "About this Book" and "Guide to the Reader," serves as an introduction to patterns. The preliminary pieces are recommended reading as they lay the groundwork for the book and give a brief history of the patterns movement. The first chapter lays out the definition and makeup of a pattern. The chapter also lays out a categorization of patterns based on the level of design abstraction represented by the pattern. This categorization is refined to architectural patterns, design patterns, and idioms, which could also be called implementation patterns. These three categories are then used to group the patterns presented in the subsequent chapters.

The remainder of chapter one provides more information on using patterns and presents the template for the patterns contained in the book. The tutorial information makes worthwhile reading even to those experienced in patterns literature, though the template could have been placed earlier in the chapter and tends to break up the rest of the information.

The pattern description template is explained well and is similar to other pattern templates that have been influenced by James Coplien. The template is not of the canonical form used by Christopher Alexander, but is closer to the template used in *Design Patterns*. This type of template can initially detract from the flow of the pattern text, but it makes the patterns far more useful as a reference. The differences between this template and the template used in *Design Patterns* further enhance the usefulness of the text as a reference.

The template uses two widely recognized notations to aid in the documentation and introduces a third notation. The solution of the patterns is supplemented with a CRC-card for each participating component. The structure of the pattern contains an OMT class diagram. The dynamics of the pattern is illustrated with scenarios using an Object Message Sequence

Chart (OMSC). A brief overview of each notation is given in the "Notation" appendix. The OMSC notation has been adopted by Booch, Jacobson, and Rumbaugh for inclusion in their Unified Modeling Language.

The next three chapters contain the actual patterns presented in the book. A chapter is given for each of the categories identified earlier in the book. The capabilities of modern technology have allowed many of the patterns contained in these chapters to be reviewed by pattern readers throughout the world. They were posted for reading on the World Wide Web, and discussions about the patterns took place on a dedicated newsgroup and via email. This allowed the authors to receive much more feedback on their works than is usually available in the process of writing a book. Comparisons with early versions of the patterns shows that this widespread review contributed greatly to the refinement of the patterns.

The architectural patterns are further broken down into categories of "From Mud to Structure," "Distributed Systems," "Interactive System," and "Adaptable Systems." These patterns are not intended to be an exhaustive collection of architectural patterns; rather they serve as examples of good architectures. The patterns are not sufficient for creating an entire system architecture, but are intended to form a framework around which a software system can be built.

The design patterns are further categorized as "Structural Decomposition," "Organization of Work," "Access Control," "Management," and "Communication" patterns. Of the three pattern categories, this one contains patterns that are the closest to those contained in the *Design Patterns* text.

The idioms chapter contains only one pattern which is given as an example. The rest of the chapter describes idioms and provides references to other published works containing idioms. This may seem to make the text incomplete, but the authors have wisely left the documentation of idioms to other well known authors.

Notice that the names of the individual patterns have not been given in this review. A summary of each of the patterns would not sufficiently describe any of the patterns, as the literary format of a pattern is already very concise. A listing of the patterns can easily be obtained by browsing the table of contents.

The remainder of the chapters (five through eight, if you are keeping count) expound on the various issues confronting the present day patterns movement. These chapters are important reading for anyone involved in shaping the evolution of patterns for the future. This information also provides background on and insight into the current pattern work. It may serve a historical purpose in the future. The casual reader could skip this part of the book and still feel that the rest of the book was worth reading.

The first of these chapters describes pattern systems, often referred to as pattern languages. The authors further describe how to create a pattern system and break it into meaningful categories of patterns. The evolution of a pattern system is discussed, covering the discovery of new patterns, the integration of patterns into the system, and the maintenance of a pattern system. The chapter closes with a proposal for the creation of a system of software patterns and a mapping of the patterns in the book, along with the patterns in *Design Patterns,* into the categories of the proposed system. If nothing else, this chapter serves as fuel to the ongoing discussion of the organization of patterns.

The second of these chapters focuses on the integration of patterns into the current software architecture process. It discusses the various aspects of software architecture and design and the role that patterns can play. For the casual reader, this chapter is probably the most important in this section. It goes beyond the mere presentation of patterns to expound on the importance of using patterns in the software design process. It provides many insights on why patterns are important to the future of software development and are not just hype.

The third of these chapters provides some history on the patterns community. This is a short chapter and it makes interesting reading. The final chapter gives a summary of where patterns are going. This provides some perspective on the future of patterns, though much of the information presented will quickly become history. The book closes with appendices on "Notations," "Glossary," and "References." An "Index of Patterns" is included, but the book lacks a true index, which may make it difficult to find information not directly related to a pattern.

If I have anything negative to say about the book, it is that some of the language and grammar usage feels awkward to the reader. Early versions of the patterns reviewed on the World Wide Web suffered in the use of the language and grammar, but subsequent editing has fixed most of the readability problems. Some portions of the narrative text suffer some of the same stiffness and flow problems, but the importance of the content causes the reader to overlook the style issues.

Overall this text is good and I recommend it as an addition to any collection of books on patterns. It also serves as good reading for those interested in topics on software development. As stated earlier in this review, this text should be viewed as a supplement, not a replacement, for existing pattern literature.

Object Models: Strategies, Patterns, and Applications (First Edition)
Peter Coad with David North and Mark Mayfield
Prentice-Hall, Inc

Reviewed by David E. DeLano

Peter Coad is not considered mainstream in the current patterns movement, but few disagree that he is a pioneer. Peter published one of the first
articles on patterns in the September 1992 issue of *Communications of the
ACM* titled "Object-Oriented Patterns." He continues to work in the realm
of patterns, as evidenced by the fact that the second edition of this book has
just been published. Peter distances himself from other patterns "researchers"
in the preface of the book. He points out the differences that he has with
other pattern works, but they are largely semantic differences in practice. His
view of patterns is that they are templates for use in designing software.

The book takes the reader through five applications, introducing strategies for resolving the problems encountered in designing the applications.
Patterns are added along the way as a method for implementing the strategies. A final application chapter goes through each of the applications
again, to overview the process a designer goes through in deciding what
strategies to use and which patterns to apply. In all, 148 strategies and 31
patterns are introduced. The remainder of the book is a handbook of the
strategies and patterns and a set of supporting appendices.

The strength of this book is the evidence that the strategies and patterns
presented are from real world experience. Peter and his coworkers found
themselves solving the same problems repeatedly, client after client. They
eventually captured these patterns to make their lives easier and to reduce
the amount of time it took to develop each individual client's application.

The weaknesses of this book are the choppy writing style and the over-
abundance of similar looking data. It takes time to adjust to the writing
style, which can be a detriment to new readers. After becoming familiar
with the style, you can appreciate the succinct nature of the writing. Little
space is wasted on useless rhetoric. The patterns and strategies look too
similar in their presentation, and it takes a while before the reader can comfortably distinguish them. Don't expect to read and understand this book with
one reading.

While the book claims to present applications that occur in a wide range
of industries, the patterns and strategies are more oriented to storing and
manipulating data. This is great if you are developing a custom database.

If you are developing an embedded real-time system, it will take more effort to discern any immediately useful patterns.

It should be noted that the book comes with a floppy that contains an automated tool, called Playground(tm). This tool is not a full-blown CASE tool, but it supports the diagramming notation used in the book and can be used for documenting a design.

Advanced C++ Programming Styles and Idioms
James O. Coplien
Addison-Wesley Publishing Company, 1994

Reviewed by Bill Haney

"Coplien's book is good because it is unique. It has a creative approach to the language and it distinguishes itself from other books in the field. Its creativity is one of the primary reasons I recommend it above other books on C++."[1] *Advanced C++ Programming Styles and Idioms* remains on the JOOP Top Ten List[2] in 1996 and probably will for years to come. In our dynamic field, this is quite a testimony for a book first published in 1992.

What can I add to all that's been written about this now classic text? Perhaps a different perspective and a look from the patterns viewpoint.

Advanced C++ is clearly a landmark effort; however, it is truly an advanced book and shouldn't be your first C++ book. It probably will not be your second, either. I had the privilege of attending one of Cope's patterns classes and he advised that for someone learning C++, Tom Cargill's book *C++ Programming Style*[4] should be read ahead of his, especially the chapters on Symbolics.[3] I followed his advice and, as you might expect, found it to be extremely beneficial. Neither of these books is for beginners, so you'll probably have been through more than one C++ textbook before coming to these. That certainly is the recommendation.

Cope's book could be considered two or more books in one, for one price! Chapters 1–7 cover the C++ language and object-oriented design at the level of normal practice. "Normal" if you are an advanced C++ developer. This is the stuff you want to know if you aspire to be an advanced C++ developer. The remaining chapters cover symbolic programming, Smalltalk-like, and System issues. Detailed appendices give several items ranging from a discussion of object copying to specific code listing examples for Symbolic Shapes. Perhaps the breadth of coverage in this book is one of its strongest attributes; another must be its depth.

To paraphrase a popular country song, "Cope was Patterns when Patterns wasn't cool." Supporting my paraphrase I offer the links between the Handle/Body idiom and the GOF Bridge[5] pattern. Also, the GOF acknowledge the overlap with Cope's book.[6]

I'm not going to debate, at least not here, what's a pattern and what's an idiom. I counted 31 unique idioms indexed by Cope. You can do your own count since some idioms have multiple references. There definitely is a significant number of idioms presented in the book. This is a wealth of information, hence my statement on breadth. The multiple references to idioms such as handle/body and envelope/letter seem to attest to the book's depth. In addition, a thoughtful and useful "when to use idiom" section in the index contains 26 entries. I especially like both the index and the detailed entries for the follow-up times I ask myself "What did he say about that?"

Is the book perfect? Most reviews give at least some constructive feedback. Given the "cookbook" nature of most patterns formats, and the years since *Advanced C++* was published, I suppose expectations have risen on formats and presentations. If a new edition were published, I'd like to see "Names" of the idioms above the "When to use." Also, a summary, such as Chapter 10 in the cited Tom Cargill book, could be a useful addition to the Appendices.

Advanced C++ Programming Styles and Idioms is an uncontested great book. Any professional in the C++ or patterns arena would find it a useful part of his or her personal library. Most probably have already. In the context of patterns, the book seems to have been ahead of its time. Both fundamental patterns and foundational idioms can and should be gleaned from this book. I've given you my perspective and noted the relationship to the instantly classic GOF patterns book, so I have at least accomplished my goals. I highly recommend this book to all C++, Patterns, and Object-Oriented developers.

1. *Journal of Object-Oriented Programming,* September 1996, p34,
   "Sorting thru the plethora: The 'unofficial' JOOP book awards"
   by Stephen Bilow.
2. ibid.
3. *C++ Programming Style* by Tom Cargill, Addison-Wesley Publishing
   Company, Reading Massachusetts, 1992, ISBN 0-201-56365-7.
4. Personal Communication with Jim Coplien, July 1995.
5. *Design Patterns* by Erich Gamma, Richard Helm, Ralph Johnson,
   and John Vlissides, Addison-Wesley Publishing Company, Reading

Massachusetts, 1992, ISBN 0-201-63361-2, pp. 153–156. (# 1 on the
JOOP 1996 Top Ten. See.[1])
6. ibid., p357.

Software Patterns: A White Paper
James O. Coplien
SIGS Publications, 1996

Reviewed by Linda Rising

This book is the place to start for anyone who wants to know what patterns
are all about. Written by Jim Coplien (Cope), a member of the Hillside
Group, it is the source of a lot of essential information about patterns and
the patterns movement.

The table of contents lists the following:

- What is a pattern?
- What are pattern languages?
- Pattern Domains
- Classifying Patterns
- Pattern Pragmatics
- Generativity
- The Pattern Value System
- History
- References

One strong message comes through all of Cope's writing—studiously avoid
hype. I say studiously because, as a patterns fan myself, I know that it's
easy to get carried away with premature enthusiasm. Cope reminds us that
patterns are "just documentation" and that:

> Their success depends on people, and particularly on the most human
> aspects of software development and its culture. This white paper accen-
> tuates that perspective: we want to accentuate the value of people in
> design, and to diminish hype.

Well put.

Cope's book was added to JOOP's Top Ten OO Books and was also
named The Best Personal Experience with Object Technology and The
Best Book of 1996.

In his article on the JOOP book awards,[1] Steve Bilow said:

> Jim is absolutely, blatantly, articulate. He will probably be embarrassed about this but that is just too bad. Jim Coplien is surely among the brightest practicing software technologists. His *Software Patterns* is a manifesto in the direct lineage of the cognoscenti throughout the 20th century. He is writing from pure passion for the discipline of patterns. He does not want us to agree with him; just to clearly understand his position. No junk, no hype, just clarity. . . . Coplien's book will go a long way toward directing the future of patterns development. . . .

If you pick up this book and begin to read you'll be carried away by the power of his talent and his intelligent approach. This is a book to have and enjoy.

1. Bilow, Steven. "Sorting through the plethora: The "unofficial" JOOP book awards," *JOOP,* September 1996, pp. 33–67.

Pattern Languages of Program Design
Edited by James O. Coplien and Douglas C. Schmidt
Addison-Wesley, 1995

Reviewed by DeLoy Bitner

The First Annual Conference of Pattern Languages of Programs (PLoP) was held near Monticello, Illinois in August of 1994. This book contains a carefully edited collection of papers presented at that conference. PLoPD1, as we shall call it here, is a varied collection of documents that provide some new insights into many aspects of the world of programming. Topics touched upon include frameworks, architecture, process, design patterns, events, and object usage. A wide range of issues, all written in some "pattern form" suitable to the author and his/her topic, are dealt with.

In many ways, PLoPD1 is a milestone publication: it begins the process of documenting and collecting patterns that are relevant to the business of creating software. Some apply to high-level aspects of frameworks or architectures; others are relevant to detailed coding idioms. Still others demonstrate insight, in true Dilbertian fashion, of the processes and interactions that occur within organizations developing software. The collection of patterns is far from universally applicable; certain patterns are language or domain specific.

At the same time that the variety of essays within PLoPD1 is one of its major strengths, it is also one of its weaknesses. The collection is worthwhile, but is still fragmented; it is unlikely any single developer will find use for every pattern. In addition, despite being heavily edited, there is a lack of consistency with the style and tone of each chapter that some will find distracting. Without question, however, virtually everyone can relate to at least some of the patterns within this book.

It is not uncommon to see references to PLoPD1 in articles on patterns. After *Design Patterns*,[1] this has been one of the more important books in the patterns movement. The PLoP conference has become a primary influence as patterns move toward mainstream technology.

Chapter 13 contains, what was considered at the time, a controversial set of patterns, "A Generative Development-Process Pattern Language" by Jim Coplien. Many powerful, almost obvious insights are documented here and clear guidelines are provided for establishing a world-class software development house. That is, if people are willing to listen. Many people will consider this chapter, alone, worth the price of admission. These are patterns of process and organization, something very different from software design patterns.

There are many other chapters of similar magnitude, each an important contribution in its own right. Significant insights by significant players in the industry abound, and each is worth at least a quick perusal, to see if it applies to your situation.

Even as the body of formal patterns documents expands, *Pattern Languages of Program Design* will remain a significant part of the library of pattern literature.

1. Gamma, E., R. Helm, R. Johnson, and J. Vlissides, *Design Patterns: Elements of Reusable Object-Oriented Software,* Addison-Wesley, 1994.

Design Patterns: Elements of Reusable Object-Oriented Software
Erich Gamma, Richard Helm, Ralph Johnson, and John Vlissides
Addison-Wesley Publishing Company, 1994

Reviewed by DeLoy Bitner

As much as any other single book or publication, *Design Patterns* has been instrumental in propelling the patterns movement into mainstream software engineering and, particularly, that of object-oriented software engineering. Gamma, Helm, Johnson, and Vlissides, affectionately known as the "Gang of Four" (GOF), have brought together in this volume a distillation of expertise from many object-oriented projects covering many years. The book is compelling reading for anyone involved in the development of object-oriented systems. Experts in the industry find in *Design Patterns* a reference book of best practices, giving name and form to techniques they already use. To the neophyte OO designer, *Design Patterns* presents many critical concepts in a very palatable fashion. It provides "instant" expertise to effectively solve a wide range of problems that will be encountered during an OO software project.

Design Patterns is divided into three basic parts: an introduction and case study, a catalog of the 23 design patterns, and the conclusion, glossary, etc. The introduction addresses the great question, "What is a pattern?" and summarizes the pattern catalog. Issues regarding the technique for documenting and using design patterns are also addressed. A consistent format is used to document each of the design patterns, and subtleties of that format are addressed. Each pattern is documented both with text and using an OMT-based notation. These pictures help to understand relationships among the contributing classes and provide a means to recognize the design pattern when integrated into a design.

The case study discusses the design of a document editor and demonstrates practical examples of how design patterns can be applied to a real-world design, showing tradeoffs that must be made with almost any design. It provides insight into applying design patterns and, when read first, provides a preview of many of the design patterns from the Design Pattern Catalog. A minor issue with this is that, after reading the case study and then reading the Catalog, one encounters a serious case of deja vu, and you wonder where you saw a pattern before. Despite this, it seems most useful to read the book cover to cover when beginning your exploration of patterns, and then using the Catalog as a reference during future design.

The heart of the book is the Design Pattern Catalog, which lists 23 design patterns in three different categories: creational, structural, and behavioral. Creational patterns are concerned with creating objects, structural patterns deal with composition of classes or objects, and behavioral patterns characterize the way objects interact and distribute responsibility. The names of the design patterns are of critical importance. Names are used to succinctly convey the purpose of the patterns and to provide a mnemonic aid to remember them. Names are handles that, once assigned and published, stick with the pattern forever. The names used in *Design Patterns* evolved somewhat as the book was written, but are now forever cast in the vocabulary of OO designers. They seem appropriate and intuitive.

For this discussion, it really won't help to summarize the patterns and what they mean. Such a summary does not become useful until the patterns have been learned and understood. Conveniently, the authors have provided a one sentence summary of each design pattern on the inside front cover of the book, making it easy to recall a particular pattern after a quick perusal of the list. For reference, here is a list of the pattern names to give an idea of their scope and encourage further study:

Creational: Abstract Factory, Builder, Factory Method, Prototype, Singleton.

Structural: Adapter, Bridge, Composite, Decorator, Facade, Flyweight, Proxy.

Behavioral: Chain of Responsibility, Command, Interpreter, Iterator, Mediator, Memento, Observer, State, Strategy, Template Method, Visitor.

The *Design Patterns* summary provides some historical perspective on patterns and how the book came to be. While not germane to a given application of a design pattern, the history is interesting and provides some roots to the burgeoning pattern movement. The Gang Of Four are pioneers in this trek toward better and more reusable software systems. Their perspective provides insight and direction. *Design Patterns* can be given credit for providing the catalyst to the integration of patterns as a mainstream technology in our industry. It is safe to say at this point that *Design Patterns* has reached the status of "classic."

The bottom line is this: get the book, read it, and use it until it's worn out.

Data Model Patterns: Convention of Thought
David C. Hay
Dorset House Publishing, 1996

Reviewed by Roger Tomas

In this book, author David Hay presents a number of data model patterns for modeling businesses. Hay claims that the underlying structures and processes of most businesses are similar and that it is possible to model them in a similar manner. Furthermore, these similarities can be captured in a set of patterns that serve as a starting point for anyone assigned the task of modeling a business. The book presents patterns for modeling fundamental aspects of businesses including employees, organizational structures, assets, raw materials, products, manufacturing processes, resource usage, work orders, contracts, accounting, etc.

Applying the patterns in Hay's book, an analyst modeling a business gains a head start because the fundamental aspects of the business have already been modeled. The analyst need only address issues unique to the business being modeled. This primarily means adding additional elements to the model beyond what is provided by the patterns, but it also means modifying the patterns. While Hay acknowledges the patterns may need to be modified for different businesses, the modifications should be minimal because the patterns have been sufficiently generalized. Throughout the book, each pattern is introduced in a simple form and then evolved through several levels of generalization. These generalizations are driven off two key criteria: applicability to different businesses and robustness.

An important point made by Hay is that the set of patterns presented in the book is really a tool kit of individual data model components. Readers should not assume they will use all of the patterns presented in the book. Instead, they should consider the patterns as individual pieces of a model they can mix and match together as needed to build the desired model.

Direct application of the patterns presented in the book can result in significant time savings to anyone tasked with business modeling. Even if the patterns are not directly applied, simply understanding the patterns can provide valuable ideas on how to make a model robust. The book provides a vocabulary that allows analysts to better discuss a model's problem domain and solution. Another extremely valuable aspect of the book is the discussion of why and how each of the patterns are generalized. Understanding why and how to generalize models allows analysts to better optimize models on their own. In effect, Hay's generalizations and their accompanying discussions provide the reader practice in optimizing data models. This is also valuable to anyone contemplating creating patterns of their own.

Designing Object-Oriented C++ Applications Using the Booch Method
Robert C. Martin
Prentice Hall, Inc.

Reviewed by Bill Haney

Robert Martin has written a valuable resource for learning OO Design and Analysis. His book is practical and thorough. He uses a case study method of teaching by example. Some familiarity with patterns in C++, especially Iterator, is required. A strong C++ knowledge is required for the implementations in the case studies. Martin says, "This book presents the fundamental concepts of object-oriented design and shows how to apply those concepts using C++." He achieves this purpose!

He gives complete examples of analysis and design from requirements through code. Some of his analysis includes false starts and emphasizes the iterative nature of design. Martin provides full code listings for several designs. This has the advantage of letting each student/practitioner read and review design details at the proper level for individual comprehension. A system of metrics is provided for judging the relative merit of one design versus another.

Chapter 1 describes the steps in object-oriented analysis and design (OOA/D). Later chapters illustrate the procedure with ever more detailed examples.

Advanced C++ techniques are used in a practical way. Some examples are Coplien's [Cope 92] envelope/letter idiom, template containers, and namespaces. Pattern usage, in addition to Iterator, includes Surrogate (Proxy), Bridge, and Abstract Factory [GOF 95]. An appendix gives a useful tutorial/review of multi-processing.

A quote from Robert Martin illustrates his practical approach to design and the challenges designers face

> One wayward thought, deep in the bowels of design, caused a major restructuring of the analysis of the project. This is typical of nearly all analysis and design efforts. . . . these very upheavals cause the greatest improvements in our designs.

I highly recommend this book to all who would practice the art of OOA/D.

[Cope 92] J.O. Coplien, *Advanced C++ Programming Styles and Idioms,* Reading, MA: Addison-Wesley, 1992.

[GOF 95] E. Gamma, R. Helm, R. Johnson, J. Vlissides, *Design Patterns: Elements of Reusable Object-Oriented Software,* Reading, MA: Addison-Wesley, 1995.

Dynamics of Software Development
Jim McCarthy
Microsoft Press, 1995

Reviewed by Linda Rising

This is a captivating, easy-to-read book about one of the most intriguing organizations in the world. Regardless of our feelings for Bill Gates or Windows '95, those of us connected to the world of software development are fascinated by that company in the Pacific Northwest. We wonder, "How do they do what they do?"

This book won't answer all your questions about Microsoft but it tells a lot about their development process. The format for that telling is very close to patterns. The book is a collection of 53 guidelines for successful software development. There is sufficient text and pictures (Jim's brother produced the art work) to extract patterns; in fact, I've done just that for the most famous guideline in the book, "Don't Flip the Bozo Bit." see http://www.agcs.com/bozobit.html.

McCarthy's work has some commonality with that of Christopher Alexander. While Alexander talks about the quality without a name, McCarthy digresses on the topic of esthetics. The quality without a name, according to Alexander, is tied to those moments when we feel most alive. McCarthy describes the "esthetic experience" as one that wakes people, alerts their senses. He neatly contrasts this with anesthetics, which put people to sleep. I believe Alexander and McCarthy are describing the same thing, and McCarthy and the patterns community are trying to help us incorporate that concept into our software.

Some of my favorite guidelines from this book: "Be like the doctors"— they're highly trained professionals who always begin treatment with caveats and warnings of side-effects and they still get paid! "After a slip, hit the next milestone, no matter what," and "The world changes: so should you." I enjoyed this book, especially since Jim McCarthy made a trip to AG Communication Systems shortly after I had finished it, so I had the chance to tell him about patterns!

Taming C++ Pattern Classes and Persistence for Large Projects
Jiri Soukup
Addison-Wesley Publishing Company, 1994

Reviewed by Paul Bramble

Jiri Soukup's book contains information that serious students of patterns should consider. He contends that large object-oriented systems are so complex that designers and programmers need to use special techniques when creating them. Soukup describes significant problems inherent in developing large object-oriented software systems. These problems affect object-oriented systems as they grow in size, and include increased message passing complexity due to the magnitude of inter-class dependencies, and loss of design clarity due to the magnitude of classes and objects. His solutions to these problems include patterns, frameworks, and reusable class libraries.

Soukup champions the use of patterns. He believes patterns provide order in a system by controlling the interactions between individual objects. The book includes a brief history of patterns and framework evolution, as well as a short, concise, though slightly dated, description of frameworks. He believes that commonly used patterns can reside in a library, and that some properly designed libraries approach framework status. He describes some techniques for developing reusable object-oriented libraries using patterns, templates, and code generators. In addition to the use of patterns, Soukup describes techniques for developing reusable object-oriented libraries, namely data structures, templates, and code generation.

It is significant that this book discusses problems inherent to patterns and possible solutions to these problems, something not found in other pattern books. While patterns help clarify and organize complexity in a system, they tend to introduce more classes into a system to support this organization. These extra classes can significantly increase the amount of message passing and inter-object dependency in a system, making testing, rework, and system provability very difficult. Moreover, Soukup makes a strong case that complex designs tend to hide patterns from developers who assume responsibility for a system in the later stages of the life cycle. His controversial solution advocates separate pattern classes that control the access to each pattern in the system. These pattern classes provide layering, which tends to encapsulate the various components of the system and reduce the number of dependencies between classes. Pattern objects also serve to document patterns, forcing future maintainers/developers to recognize each pattern in the system. This proposed solution has sparked much heated debate.

Even if one disagrees with Soukup's recommendations, this book is valuable for analysts and designers using patterns to design large object-oriented systems. His discussion of the advantages and drawbacks to patterns is excellent and very pertinent.

Pitfalls of Object-Oriented Development
Bruce Webster
M & T Books, 1995

Reviewed by Linda Rising

I started reading this book, as I have many books, on an airplane. It was a long flight, from Munich to JFK, so I had plenty of time to enjoy this wonderful collection of pitfalls. A pitfall is not a pattern but there is a "pitfall form," defined by the author, that begins with a statement of the pitfall, followed by a few paragraphs that describe the context or situation, then in close order are given: Symptoms, Consequences, Detection, Extraction, and finally, Prevention. Those of us in the patterns community are prime targets for this kind of information. We see similarities between pitfalls and patterns, especially when the information is presented in this orderly fashion.

This book contains a brief introduction to object-oriented development (which you will probably skip) and then launches into: Conceptual Pitfalls, Political Pitfalls, Management Pitfalls, Analysis and Design Pitfalls, Environment Pitfalls, Language and Tool Pitfalls, Implementation Pitfalls, Class and Object Pitfalls, Coding Pitfalls, Quality Assurance Pitfalls, and finally, Reuse Pitfalls. Yes, folks, he's got 'em all!

As I happened on each pitfall, I would usually let out an involuntary guffaw or cheer, something like, "Right!" or "Oh, yeah!" and then proceed to scribble a couple of notes capturing the essence of a section. Finally, my companion (we occupied the two seats on the outside row of a 767) commented that he was also in the software business and couldn't help noticing the book title and wanted to know more. Well, there went my reading time, but we had an interesting series of discussions beginning with OO software development and moving on to differences between Europeans and Americans in the areas of dining, working, and so on. As a result, I had to wait until a week or so later to actually finish the book, but I certainly did finish it. Now I have several pages of notes capturing thought-provoking hints, tips, and quotes. Here are a few of my favorites. You'll see that most of them have much broader application than OO, much broader application than software!

"... you are always better off underpromising and overdelivering than the other way around." p. 49

". . . if you knowingly oversell, telling yourself that you can manage things down the road, you will almost certainly be wrong. Resist that temptation. It will always get you into trouble, and your own integrity will be diminished. It's just not worth it." p. 59

". . . [there] is a suspicion on the part of upper management that engineers are more interested in doing something 'cool' or 'elegant' than in doing something profitable. What upper management may not understand is that elegance—architecture and code that are concise, yet clear and comprehensive, tending toward orthogonality—always pays off. Always. . . . Ironically, when the engineering staff is able to rapidly deliver the features requested by upper management, it is often because of a previous investment in elegance; likewise, when features take a long time to implement or bugs take a long time to fix, it's often because of architectural gaps and past short-cuts." pp. 64–65

". . . create a cult of learning. . . . the best people thrive in an environment such as this. . . ." p. 35

"It was Benjamin Franklin, in *Poor Richard's Almanac,* who said, 'Experience keeps a dear [expensive] school, but fools will learn in no other.' More fools we, then, who for twenty-five years have had the time, opportunity, and experience to learn how best to conduct software development in general, and object-oriented development in particular, yet persist in making the same errors time and again." p. 238

"A lot of what has been learned about software engineering during the past thirty years has been in vain, because no one takes the time to read about it. The idea here is to help you avoid errors that have been made before; it's interesting (and perhaps significant) that the oldest books are in many ways the most relevant and timeless. " p. 241

Maybe patterns will help?

APPENDIX B:
WEB SITES

I've collected all the web sites in one place. Most of these were mentioned throughout the book. The easiest approach is to start with the AG Communications Patterns Home Page and find links to all of them—http://www.agcs.com/patterns/index.html—enjoy! There's an overwhelming amount of information on the web about patterns—about anything really! So, this list will provide some good places to start, based on your own interests.

Sites devoted to general patterns information:

WWW Patterns Home Page:
http://st-www.cs.uiuc.edu/users/patterns/patterns.html
The first place to start gathering information about patterns. The site is
located at the University of Illinois.

Wiki Wiki Web:
http://c2.com/cgi-bin/wiki
A writeable site where patterns folks gather to get feedback on patterns
and share ideas on pattern topics.

Sites with specific patterns information:

HTML Pattern Language
http://www.anamorph.com/docs/patterns/default.html

Patterns for Concurrent Programming in Java
http://g.oswego.edu/dl/pats/aopintro.html

Patterns for Business Transaction processing
http://c2.com/cgi-bin/wiki?TransactionsAndAccounts

Sites of pattern notables:

Doug Lea's Home Page and Patterns FAQs
http://gee.cs.oswego.edu/dl/
Doug Lea maintains a Patterns FAQs (frequently asked questions). He
is the creator of patterns for avionics systems and the author of a book
on concurrent programming in Java.

Aamod Sane's Home page
http://choices.cs.uiuc.edu/sane/patterns.html
Aamod Sane is at the University of Illinois. His research interests are
software architectures and design patterns for distributed systems.

Doug Schmidt's Home Page
http://www.cs.wustl.edu/~schmidt/
Doug Schmidt's home page has extensive references on patterns for
distributed systems.

Jim Coplien's Home Page
http://www.bell-labs.com/user/cope
Jim Coplien (Cope) is a recognized leader in the patterns community
and the author of *Advanced C++ Programming Styles and Idioms.*

Jim Coplien's Process Patterns
http://www.bell-labs.com/user/cope/Patterns/Process/index.html
The source of 42 patterns on team structure and process.

Risk Management Patterns
http://members.aol.com/acockburn/riskcata/risktoc.html
Alistair Cockburn has lots of good information on risk management
and other organizational issues.

Frameworks Sites:

A framework is a collection of patterns that has been implemented. The
powerful advantages of code reuse can only be obtained with frameworks.

Frameworks at the University of Illinois
http://st-www.cs.uiuc.edu/users/johnson/frameworks.html

Frameworks at the University of Kariskrona
http://www.ide.hk-r.se/frameworks

IBM Sharable Frameworks
http://www.softmall.com/sf/index.html

Miscellaneous Patterns Links:

AntiPatterns
http://c2.com/cgi-bin/wiki?AntiPatterns
An antipattern presents a solution that sounds good but doesn't work!

Phoenix Patterns Group
http://www.radsoft.com/patterns
The Phoenix Patterns Group meets monthly to discuss patterns topics.

ObjectCurrents
http://www.sigs.com/objectcurrents
This is a free on-line journal sponsored by SIGS Publishing.

INDEX